HUMAN-CENTERED SOFTWARE ENGINEERING – INTEGRATING USABILITY IN THE SOFTWARE DEVELOPMENT LIFECYCLE

HUMAN-COMPUTER INTERACTION SERIES

VOLUME 8

Editors-in-Chief

John Karat, *IBM Thomas Watson Research Center (USA)*
Jean Vanderdonckt, *Université Catholique de Louvain (Belgium)*

Human-Centered Software Engineering – Integrating Usability in the Software Development Lifecycle

Edited by

Ahmed Seffah
Concordia University, Montreal,
Quebec, Canada

Jan Gulliksen
Uppsala University, Sweden

and

Michel C. Desmarais
Ecole Polytechnique de Montreal,
Quebec, Canada

 Springer

A C.I.P. Catalogue record for this book is available from the Library of Congress

ISBN-10 1-4020-4027-X (HB)
ISBN-13 978-1-4020-4027-6 (HB)
ISBN-10 1-4020-4113-6 (e-book)
ISBN-13 978-1-4020-4113-6 (e-book)

Published by Springer,
P.O. Box 17, 3300 AA Dordrecht, The Netherlands.

www.springeronline.com

Printed on acid-free paper

Printed in the Netherlands.

Contents

List of Figures

List of Tables

Human-Centered Software Engineering:
Bridging HCI, Usability and Software Engineering

From its beginning in the 1980's, the field of human-computer interaction (HCI) has been defined as a multidisciplinary arena. By this I mean that there has been an explicit recognition that distinct skills and perspectives are required to make the whole effort of designing usable computer systems work well. Thus people with backgrounds in Computer Science (CS) and Software Engineering (SE) joined with people with backgrounds in various behavioral science disciplines (e.g., cognitive and social psychology, anthropology) in an effort where all perspectives were seen as essential to creating usable systems. But while the field of HCI brings individuals with many background disciplines together to discuss a common goal - the development of useful, usable, satisfying systems - the form of the collaboration remains unclear. Are we striving to coordinate the varied activities in system development, or are we seeking a richer collaborative framework? In coordination, Usability and SE skills can remain quite distinct and while the activities of each group might be critical to the success of a project, we need only insure that critical results are provided at appropriate points in the development cycle. Communication by one group to the other during an activity might be seen as only minimally necessary. In collaboration, there is a sense that each group can learn something about its own methods and processes through a close partnership with the other. Communication during the process of gathering information from target users of a system by usability professionals would not be seen as something that gets in the way of the essential work of software engineering professionals. Knowing how software engineers will turn the requirements into a functioning system would not be seen as an unnecessary detail to HCI staff.

The distinction between cooperation and collaboration is subtle but important to understanding what the form of the bridge between HCI, Usability and Software Engineering should be and what tools might be used to form the bridge. In the case where coordination is seen as sufficient, a "human-centered software engineering aware" project planning tool - something that was aware of best-practice methods in the different fields - might be all that we need to connect the fields. For coordination, the different disciplines need to be only generally aware of the methods of the other groups. Deep knowledge about SE by Usability researchers or staff might be intellectually satisfying for some, but in general it would be unnecessary and not seen as worth the cost of additional training. If collaboration is required or seen as beneficial beyond its costs, we might need to jointly explore how to better communicate the methods and practice in one specialty to the other and not just the results needed by one group to carry out their own part of the development process.

I raise this point because I am not sure we in the HCI field know whether we are looking for a bridge that facilitates cooperation between distinct communities or one that facilitates mixing of cultures. The researcher in me favors the notion that mixing the knowledge and approaches of behavioral and technical specialists is beneficial because it will lead to broader, improved perspectives by all. Building a bridge here would mean working closely with software engineers as partners in discovering how to design and develop our systems. However, the practitioner in me is aware that development of large complex systems can require resources that might be more efficient if they are specialized and coordinated. Building a bridge here would mean providing the knowledge of what part of the task is mine and what part is someone else's. What I actually believe is that most of the researchers in HCI would like to think that collaboration and thus joint exploration of how to approach system development is necessary, but that most real world system development proceeds on the assumption that coordination of specific tasks is what is required. Researchers like to think that interesting and wonderful things can emerge from the chaos of mixing perspectives. Practical development calls for more structure and predictability in processes.

I believe that progress can be made in building both bridges for cooperation and bridges for collaboration. Specialists in usability can work on developing and documenting methods for best practice in informing system design from an understanding of the needs of people and organizations. Specialists in software engineering can work on developing and documenting best practice in developing quality software systems - in all that that entails - from requirements. We can recognize that there are differences between HCI and SE and go about the necessary task of focusing on what is necessary for one community to know about the other. This is a practical approach that acknowledges that a very broad range of skills are necessary and that individuals are not likely to be able to possess them all. It is also a statement that some dialogue between disciplines is important to the broader field. At a minimum each discipline needs to be able to distinguish what is important for development of skills within its area from what is important knowledge for others to have about its processes. I contend that currently Usability and SE communities focus primarily on their own disciplines and have not had as much to say on the issues that arise out of multidisciplinarity. Certainly these professionals know that they do not exist in a vacuum - they understand that they make fairly specific contributions to the design of a wide range of systems. There is nothing wrong with having a focus on the core of one's discipline. However, there is also considerable value in looking beyond that discipline - beyond User Centered Design (UCD) or SE to look for ways to improve a process which involves many skills and perspectives. Beyond the dialog necessary for cooperation, I also see value in efforts aimed at the more difficult task of collaborating to improve the overall activity in which both Usability and SE play a role.

I think that bridging behavioral approaches and SE approaches to the development of usable systems has been a constant issue within HCI. I was focused on this in my own research in the early 90's through a series of workshops devoted to slightly different views of the problem. In 1990, I conducted a workshop at the ACM Special Interest Group on Computer-Human Interaction with the a general theme of bringing behavioral science and computer science focused individuals together to talk about methods that each thought were important to designing usable systems. The book that emerged in 1991 from this workshop (Taking software design seriously: Practical techniques for human-computer interaction design, Academic Press), represented the sort of result one might expect at the time. UCD and SE researchers and practitioners described what they did, and hoped that description of the methods of each field would inform and benefit the other. While this was and is certainly useful - particularly when there are multiple specific skills that are recognized as contributing to an activity - it takes more than just describing one specialty's activity to the other specialty to make for a productive dialogue. In addition, in 1989 and again in 1993, I was a part of workshops organized at IBM TJ Watson Research in which a specific effort was made to bring the HCI and Object-Oriented software development communities together to explore common threads in the use of scenarios as a unifying representation for bridging Usability and SE. It became clear in these workshops and the contributions that went into the books that resulted that the SE and Usability communities had very different notions of what constituted "success" or "quality" in design and development. Specifically, "meeting requirements" had a much more specific sense for SE than it did for Usability work. I view the emergence of Usability Engineering, with a focus on more specific identification and measurement of usability objectives, and the development of scenario based techniques as positive outcomes of these early dialogues, and examples of bridges that are emerging between the communities.

In this book assembled by Seffah, Gulliksen and Desmarais, the editors and contributors have provided much more than an unconnected of chapters that are vaguely about the same thing: integrating HCI and Software Engineering (SE). They represent the efforts of people who are making a real effort to "advance the dialogue" between two groups. What I find in this volume is evidence that HCI and SE specialists have listened each others works, have formulated questions to help understand the role it plays in the shared mission of developing usable systems, and have used that understanding to propose new ways of moving forward.

I believe that the reader will find that this book provides an exciting glimpse into a world in which the pains of mulidisciplinarity "pay off" though new insights and methods for developing the technology that will impact all of our lives.

JOHN KARAT

Research Staff Member IBM T.J. Watson Research Center
Past Chair IFIP Technical Committee on Human-Computer Interaction (TC13)

Dedicated to our beloved ones,

Pour la cheminée de Papa !
Anna, Fanny, Johanna and Jonas,
Béatrice, Laurence, and Linda.

Contributing Authors

Robin James Adams is pursuing a Master's degree part-time while working as a Research Associate with Drs. Bonnie John and Len Bass on their Usability and Software Architecture (U&SA) project. In the recent past, he graduated from Virginia Tech with a degree in Computer Science, then went to Orca Computer, Inc. to architect and implement the Evaluation Environment, Orca's flagship web application.

James D. Arthur is an Associate Professor in the Department of Computer Science at Virginia Tech. He is a member of the Department's Software Engineering Research Group that is focused on Distributed Software Engineering issues. His research interests include Software Engineering (Requirements Engineering, Verification and Validation, and Methods and Methodologies supporting the Assessment of Software Quality and IV & V Effectiveness), Parallel Computation, and User Support Environments.

John M. Artim is a consultant working for Expert Support, Inc. in Mountain View, California. John has been a practitioner since 1988 when he started work at the IBM Santa Teresa Usability Group. His practice includes software specification and use case authoring, user interface design, business process and software development process analysis, technical documentation, joint designer-user-customer specification review, and teaching and mentoring.

Len Bass is a Senior Member of the Technical Staff at the Software Engineering Institute (SEI) and participates in the High Dependability Computing Program. He has written two award winning books in software architecture as well as several other books and numerous papers in a wide variety of areas of computer science and software engineering. He is currently working on techniques for the methodical design of software architectures and to understand how to support usability through software architecture. He has been involved in the development of numerous different production or research software systems ranging from operating systems to database management systems to automotive systems.

Lisa Battle is a senior designer at Lockheed Martin. She has consulted on user interface usability and designed software applications and web sites for a variety of government and commercial clients. Her career began with the design of information resources, and progressed to electronic performance support systems and then to user interface design. In her current position at Lockheed Martin, she leads user-centered design for web-based applications at the Social Security Administration, as well as contributing to standards definition, integration of user-centered methods into project lifecycles, and mentoring project teams in user-centered methods. She holds a master's degree in cognitive psychology/human factors from George Mason University. She is a member of the Usability Professionals' Association (UPA) and the Association for Computing Machinery (ACM-CHI).

Stefan Blomkvist is a Ph.D. student in Human-Computer Interaction from Uppsala University, Sweden. He is also a usability designer and systems developer at the company Profdoc AB and has more than six years of experience of developing IT-systems, mainly for healthcare organizations. His research interests are in Usability and User Centered Design and its integration with Software Engineering, as well as Information visualization.

Inger Boivie is a PhD student at the Department of Information Technology, Uppsala University, Sweden. Inger is presently at the last stages of her PhD studies. She has co-authored and published papers in international journals and conferences on usability issues and users' needs in practical software development. Before becoming a PhD student, Inger worked for more than 10 years as an IT consultant, with usability and users' needs in software

John M. Carroll is Edward Frymoyer Chair Professor of Information Sciences and Technology at the Pennsylvania State University. His research interests include methods and theory in human-computer interaction, particularly as applied to networking tools for collaborative learning and problem solving, and the design of interactive information systems. He has written or edited 14 books, including Making Use (MIT Press, 2000) and HCI Models, Theories, and Frameworks (Morgan-Kaufmann, 2003). He serves on 9 editorial boards for journals, handbooks, and series; he is a member of the US National Research Council's Committee on Human Factors and Editor-in-Chief of the ACM Transactions on Computer-Human Interactions. He received the Rigo Award and the CHI Lifetime Achievement Award from ACM, the Silver Core Award from IFIP, the Alfred N. Goldsmith Award from IEEE, and is an ACM and IEEE Fellow.

Jim A. Carter is a Professor of Computer Science and Director of the Usability Engineering Research (USER) Lab at the University of Saskatchewan, in Saskatoon, Canada. He is a Canadian technical expert involved in the development of various international standards in the fields of Ergonomics (ISO TC 159) and User Interfaces (ISO/IEC JTC 1 / SC 35).

Åsa Cajander is a Ph.D. student in Human-Computer Interaction from Uppsala University, Sweden. Her research interests include Usability and User Centered Design with a special focus on occupational health. She has also several years of industrial expertise as a IT consultant.

Lester Cowley is a Senior Lecturer in the Department of Computer Science and Information Systems at the Nelson Mandela Metropolitan University (NMMU) in Port Elizabeth, South Africa and Vice-head of the NMMU Centre of Excellence in Distributed Multimedia Applications. His research interests include UI design patterns and their use in user-centred system design, multimedia computing and E-learning.

Michel C. Desmarais is an Assistant Professor of Computer Engineering at École Polytechnique de Montréal, Canada, since 2002. Before that position, he lead the HCI group at the Computer Research Institute of Montreal for ten years before managing software engineering teams in a private software company for four years. Besides user-centered engineering, his research interest are in Artificial Intelligence and User modeling.

Xavier Ferre is an Assistant Professor of Software Engineering with the Computing School at the Universidad Politecnica de Madrid in Spain since 1999. He has been a Visiting PhD Student at CERN (European Laboratory for Particle Physics) in Switzerland, and at the HCIL (Human Computer Interaction Laboratory) at the University of Maryland (USA). He is a member of the ACM and its SIGCHI group. His primary research interest is the integration of Usability into Software Engineering development practices.

David Fourney is a graduate student completing a Master's of Science degree in Computer Science at the University of Saskatchewan, Saskatoon, Canada. He is a Canadian technical expert involved in the development of various international standards in the fields of Ergonomics (ISO TC 159 / SC 4) and User Interfaces (ISO/IEC JTC 1 / SC 35). A Researcher with the Usability Engineering Research (USER) Lab of the Department of Computer Science, his primary research interest is in Universal Usability.

Bengt Göransson is a senior usability expert, Usability Designer, at the IT-consultancy Guide Redina in Sweden. He is the leading architect behind their UCSD profile, and has co-authored a number of books and scientific papers on how to make usability and user-centered systems design applicable in practice. Bengt has a PhD in HCI from Uppsala University, Sweden.

Jan Gulliksen is a professor in human computer interaction from Uppsala university. He has a master in engineering physics and a PhD in Systems analysis. Jan is the chairman of IFIP WG 13.2 on "Methodologies for User Centered Systems Design" and a member of ISO standardization on Software Ergonomics and human computer dialogues and human centered design processes for interactive systems. Jan runs a research group on Usability and User centered systems design that does applied research in cooperation with several industries and public authorities.

H. Rex Hartson is a Professor Emeritus of Computer Science at Virginia Tech, where he has been a faculty member since 1975. In 1979, he founded a pioneering HCI program at Virginia Tech. His research interests include usability engineering, usability development methods and support tools, and integration of usability engineering and software engineering development processes.

Steven R. Haynes is Assistant Professor of Information Sciences and Technology at The Pennsylvania State University. His research interests include design rationale, design evaluation, human-computer interaction with complex systems, and explanation. He has worked at Apple Computer, Adobe Systems, and several start-up software companies in the United States and Europe as a programmer, designer, analyst, and application development project manager.

Bill Jerome is a Research Programmer/Project Director at Carnegie Mellon University working for the Open Learning Initiative. Having obtained a B.S. in computer science and then a Masters in HCI from CMU, he currently is focused on using both skills to produce software infrastructures and evaluate their use for putting full courses online. Research interests have also included user community development via online tools in online gaming environments and the interaction of software engineers and usability experts in the non-academic world.

Bonnie John is a professor at Carnegie Mellon University's Human-Computer Interaction Institute and director of the Master of Human-Computer Interaction Program. She teaches courses in HCI design and evaluation methods. She was hounoured the National Science Foundation Young Investigator Award in 1994 and she is the authors of many influencial papers in the domains of usability, HCI techniques and cognitive modeling. She also work on bridging the gap between HCI and software engineering, specifically including usability concerns in software architecture design.

Timo Jokela is an acting professor in the Department of Information Processing Science at Oulu University, Finland, since 1999. In his earlier carrieer he has worked e.g. at Nokia Mobile Phones where he was setting up and pioneering usability engineering activities. His research interests are processes, methods and organizational issues of user-centered design.

Natalia Juristo is a Full Professor of Software Engineering with the Computing School at the Universidad Politecnica de Madrid in Spain since 1997. She has been the Director of the UPM MSc in Software Engineering for ten years. She has been fellow of the European Centre for Nuclear Research (CERN) in Switzerland and staff of the European Space Agency (ESA) in Italy. During 1992 she was resident affiliate of the Software Engineering Institute at CMU (Pittsburgh, USA). She has been program chair for SEKE in 1997 and 2005 and for ISESE in 2004, and general chair in 2001 for SEKE and for SNPD in 2002. Prof. Juristo has been key speaker for CSEET03. She has been guest editor of special issues in several journals. Dr. Juristo has been member of several editorial boards, including IEEE Software. She is senior member of IEEE CS. Her main research interests are Empirical Software Engineering, Usability and Software Architectures, and Software Testing.

Rick Kazman is a Senior Member of the Technical Staff at the Software Engineering Institute of Carnegie Mellon University and Associate Professor at the University of Hawaii. His primary research interests are software architecture, design and analysis tools, software visualization, and software engineering economics. He also has interests in human-computer interaction and information retrieval. He is the author of over 70 papers, and co-author of several books, including "Software Architecture in Practice", and "Evaluating Software Architectures: Methods and Case Studies". Kazman received a B.A. and M.Math from the University of Waterloo, a M.A. from York University, and a Ph.D. from Carnegie Mellon University.

Sari Kujala is a researcher in Software Business and Engineering Institute, at the Helsinki University of Technology, Finland. She has degrees in Psychology and Cognitive Science, including a Ph.D. in Computer Science. Her research interests are in User-Centered Design and Requirements Engineering.

Jun Liu is a Master's of Science candidate in the Human Computer Interaction (HCI) Lab of the Department of Computer Science at the University of Saskatchewan, in Saskatoon, Canada. His research interests are in Computer Supported Cooperative Work (CSCW), Usability Engineering and Tangible User Interfaces (TUI).

Eduard Metzker is a researcher and consultant at the software technology devision of the DaimlerChrysler Research Center, Ulm, Germany. He received a M.Sc. and a Ph.D. in Computer Science from the University of Ulm. He is doing research in requirements engineering and usability engineering processes and tools for Mercedes Benz Car Group and Mercedes Benz Commercial Vehicle Group. His research interests lie in requirements engineering for automotive software systems as well as in the intersection of the fields of software engineering process improvement and usability engineering.

Ana M. Moreno is an Associate Professor with the Computing School at the Universidad Politecnica de Madrid in Spain since 2001. She is Director of the UPM MSc in Software Engineering since 2001. She has been visiting scholar at the Vrije Universiteit (The Netherlands) and visiting professor at the University of Colorado at Colorado Springs (USA). She was program chair for NLDB'01 and SNPD'02 and general chair for CSEET03. She has published papers in relevant journals like IEEE Software, Data & Knowledge Engineering or the Journal of Systems and Software. In 2001 she has published a book titled "Basics on Software Engineering Experimentation". Her main research interests are Empirical Software Engineering, and Usability and Software Architectures.

Manuel A. Pérez-Quiñones is an Assistant Professor of Computer Science at Virginia Tech. He is the lead of the research group on Multi-Platform User Interfaces, and a member of the Center for Human-Computer Interaction at Virginia Tech. He has taught at the University of Puerto Rico-Mayaguez, the US Naval Academy, and as a research scientist at the US Naval Research Laboratory in Washington DC. He has many years of experience doing software development for personal computers and web applications. His research interests are in Human-Computer Interaction, Multi-Platform User Interfaces, and Cultural Effects on Usability Engineering Methods.

Jenny Öhman Persson is working with the Swedish State Audit Institution. She has a PhD in Human Computer Interaction from Uppsala university. Her research dealt with basic values in software development and organizational change.

Pardha S. Pyla is a PhD candidate in the Department of Computer Science and a member of the Center for Human-Computer Interaction at Virginia Tech. His research interests include Usability Engineering, Software Engineering, Human-Computer Interaction, and Computer Science Education.

Dave Roberts is a Senior Designer working in IBM's Ease of Use Strategy and Design group in Warwick, UK. Dave has been with IBM since 1974. He has worked in many areas of computer development and support, including hardware design, systems support and the design of OS/2 Presentation Manager. Since 1986 he has worked on user interface architecture topics including all versions of Common User Access. He was a principal architect of the 1992 version of CUA. Since 1992, Dave has worked with Tony Temple on the ease-of-use of new technologies, and the creation of methods and guidelines for the development of user interfaces. Dave is also working as a consultant on ease-of-use for several IBM clients.

Mary Beth Rosson is Professor of Information Sciences and Technology at Pennsylvania State University. Her research interests include scenario-based design and evaluation, the use of network technology to support collaboration, especially in learning contexts, and the psychological issues associated with use of high-level programming languages and tools. She is co-author of Usability Engineering: Scenario-Based Development of Human-Computer Interaction (Morgan Kaufmann, 2002), author of Instructor's Guide to Object-Oriented Analysis and Design with Application (Benjamin Cummings, 1994), as well as numerous articles, book chapters, and tutorials. Dr. Rosson is active in both ACM SIGCHI and ACM SIGPLAN, serving in numerous technical program as well as conference organization roles for the CHI and OOPSLA annual conferences.

Kevin Schneider is an Associate Professor of Computer Science at the University of Saskatchewan, Saskatoon, Canada. His primary research interests include: software architecture, software transformation, reengineering, domain specific languages, and human computer interaction. From 1995 to 2000 he was president and chief executive officer of Legasys Corporation, a software technology company specializing in legacy software system analysis and renovation. Professor Schneider received his B.Sc. in Computational Science from the University of Saskatchewan in 1980, and his M.Sc. and Ph.D. in Computing and Information Science from Queen's University in 1990 and 2000, respectively. Dr. Schneider is a member of the Association of Computing Machinery (ACM), IEEE Computer Society, and the IFIP Working Group 2.7/13.4 (User Interface Engineering).

Ahmed Seffah is an associate professor in the department of computer science and software engineering. Since 2000, he is the Concordia research chair on human-centered software engineering, a term he coined. His research interested are at the intersection of human-computer interaction, psychology and software engineering, with an emphasis on usability and quality in use metrics and measurement, human experiences modeling as well as patterns as a vehicle for capturing and incorporating empirically valid best human-centric users and developers experiences into software engineering processes. He is the co-founder of the Usability and Empirical Studies Lab which provides an advanced facility to support research and development in the field of human-centered software. Dr. Seffah is the vice chair of the IFIP working group on user-centered systems design methodologies and the co-chair of the first Working conference on Human-Centered Software Engineering.

Alistair Sutcliffe is a full Professor of Systems Engineering, and Director of the Centre for HCI Design, in the School of Informatics, University of Manchester, UK. His research spans software engineering, human computer interaction and cognitive science. He is a leading authority on multimedia user interfaces, has authored 6 books and 200+ publications.

Janet Wesson is Professor and Interim Head of Department of the Department of Computer Science and Information Systems at the Nelson Mandela Metropolitan University (NMMU) in Port Elizabeth, South Africa. Janet is also the Head of the NMMU Centre of Excellence in Distributed Multimedia Applications. Janet completed her

PhD at the University of Port Elizabeth in 1997 with a title "An Investigation into Design Methodologies for Usability". Her current research areas include user interface (UI) design patterns, information visualization, mobile computing and user-centred design. She is South Africa's national representative on IFIP TC.13 (Human-Computer Interaction), vice-chair of TC.13, secretary of WG13.2 (User-centred Design) and vice-chair of CHI-SA (the South African chapter of ACM SIGCHI).

I Introductory Chapter

1 Introductory Chapter

1 AN INTRODUCTION TO HUMAN-CENTERED SOFTWARE ENGINEERING:

INTEGRATING USABILITY IN THE DEVELOPMENT PROCESS

Ahmed Seffah*, Jan Gulliksen**,
and Michel C. Desmarais*** with inputs from the book contributors

*Human-Centered Software Engineering Group, Concordia University, Canada
**Uppsala University, Sweden
***École Polytechnique de Montréal, Canada

Abstract

This book aims at bridging the gap between the field of software engineering (SE) and Human Computer Interaction (HCI), and addresses the concerns of integrating usability and user centered systems design into the development process. This can be done by defining techniques, tools and practices that can fit into the entire software engineering lifecycle as well as by defining ways of addressing the knowledge and skills needed, and the attitudes and basic values that a user centered development methodology requires. This introductory chapter highlights the major challenges and obstacles in integrating usability and user-centered design techniques in the software engineering lifecycle. The discussion is centered on the following key issues:

- When and how to involve users and user interface design specialists in the design and development process

3

A. Seffah (eds.), Human-Centered Software Engineering – Integrating Usability
in the Development Process, 3–14.
© 2005 Springer. Printed in the Netherlands.

- Practical experiences of using usability engineering techniques and artefacts in the analysis, design and evaluation processes

- Organizational obstacles to user-centered design

- Role of the UCD facilitator and usability professionals in the development processes and teams

- Communication problems that occur when usability experts with varied skills and expertise communicate with software and computer scientists

The chapter also provides some basic definitions especially about usability, its measurement and its place in the mainstream development lifecycle. Most of the integration problems briefly discussed in this chapter are detailed in other chapters.

1.1 INTRODUCTION

Usability tests and user-centered design techniques are now recognized as important milestones in the development of interactive applications including Graphical User Interface (GUI) oriented applications, e-commerce web sites, mobile services and eventually wearable technology. However, the problems suffered by many application development projects suggest that this recognition has yet to be reflected into Software Engineering methods.

Several studies have shown that 80% of total maintenance costs are related to user's problems with the system and not technical bugs (Boehm, 1991). Among them, 64% are usability problems (Landauer, 1995). A survey of over 8000 projects undertaken by 350 US companies revealed that one third of the projects were never completed and one half succeeded only partially, that is, with partial functionalities, major cost overruns, and significant delays (Standish Group, 1995). Executive managers identified the major source of such failures from poor requirements (about half of the responses) — more specifically, the lack of user involvement (13%), requirements incompleteness (12%), changing requirements (11%), unrealistic expectations (6%), and unclear objectives (5%). For a more detailed discussion of cost-justifying usability efforts as a whole, independent of specific UE methods, consult for example Mayhew, 1999, Landauer, 1995, Karat, 1997, and Donahue, 2001,.

These problems are mainly due to the fact that in developing highly interactive software with a significant user interface, most software engineering methodologies do not propose any mechanisms for: (1) explicitly and empirically identifying and specifying user needs and usability requirements, and (2) testing and validating requirements with end-users before, during, and after the development. As a consequence, the developed systems generally meet all functional requirements, and yet are difficult to use with effectiveness, efficiency and satisfaction. The lack of adequate methodologies explains a large part of the frequently observed phenomenon whereby large numbers of change requests to modify are made after its deployment.

Human-centered design (HCD) philosophy and related usability engineering (UE) methods provide powerful solutions to such problems (Norman and Draper, 1986; Vredenburg, 2003; Mayhew, 1999). However, widespread software engineering methods, such as RUP (Rational Unified Process) or the more recent agile development approaches, still lack explicit integration of HCI/UE methods and processes (Kazman et al., 2003; Seffah and Metzker, 2004).

Today, even if software development teams recognize its appropriateness and powerfulness, usability remains the province of visionaries, isolated departments, enlightened software practitioners and large organizations, rather than the everyday practice of the typical software developer. Knowledge and theory is still scarce about how to efficiently and smoothly incorporate UE methods into established software development processes. While standards such as ISO 13407 (Human-Centered Design Processes for Interactive Systems) provide a detailed description of the major UCD activities as well as strategies to assess an organization's capability to adopt HCD practices, they lack guidance on how to effectively integrate usability in a specific development team, project or context. Often, it remains unclear to software and UE professionals if, and why, certain UE tools and methods are better suited than others in a certain development context.

Moreover, HCD has been historically presented as the opposite, and sometimes as a replacement, to the system-driven philosophy generally used in software engineering (Norman and Draper, 1986). The reality is that UE and software engineering techniques each have their own strengths and weaknesses and their objectives overlap in some areas but differ in others. UE methods should be a core part of every software development activity, yet despite their well-documented paybacks, they remain to be widely adopted. We argue that an integrated framework that incorporates design, development and evaluation principles from both fields will bring more effective use of UE within software development.

However, the empirical evidence required can be extracted indirectly by deploying UE methods in practice and studying their adoption by practitioners. In industrial software development projects, data on the perceived quality of UE techniques can help in understanding how to integrate UE on a case by case basis.

1.2 MAJOR OBSTACLES FOR EFFECTIVE INTEGRATION

Taking into account usability in the software development lifecycle is not an easy endeavor. The path is littered with major fallacies, myths and obstacles that have hampered efforts to bridge HCI and SE concerns together in an integrative perspective. Here, we summarize some of the major obstacles; an exhaustive discussion of the obstacles can be found in Seffah and Metzker, 2004.

1.2.1   The Meaning of Usability

Usability means different things to different people. For many, it simply means "ease-of-use" or "user friendly", a term introduced in the early days of HCI. It is the expression we still find in many project requirements definitions, standing alone among other non-functional requirements, as though this term encompasses all there is to know about the field. The IEEE Std.610.12-1990 standard reflects this definition: "The ease with which a user can learn to operate, prepare inputs for, and interpret outputs of a system or component"

HCI specialists have borrowed concepts grounded in psychology and cognition to define usability as a set of attributes such as user performance (task completion and execution time, error rate), satisfaction and learnability. The following definition illustrates this view: "The capability of the software product to be understood, learned, used and attractive to the user, when used under specified conditions" (ISO/IEC 9126-1, 2000)

A more recent view of usability refers to it as software quality with respect to the context of use, which is a fundamental element in usability studies (Bevan, 1999; Maguire, 2001a):"The extent to which a product can be used by specified users to achieve specified goals with effectiveness, efficiency and satisfaction in a specified context of use" (ISO 9241-11, 1998).

As software engineering teachers, we are often surprised at how few students understand usability beyond the basic ease-of-use concept, and how students have little idea of how to decompose or measure it. As consultants in software engineering projects, we are also surprised at how usability is viewed as a "window dressing" discipline with a focus on style guides as the ultimate usability reference for the project.

1.2.2   The People Gap

UE specialists, who are often psychologists, are sometimes regarded as mere nuisances who get in the way of those who, in the end, will really deliver the product, the software engineers. User interface development is seldom allocated sufficient time in the crucial early phases of the development schedule even if the user interface code is often more than half of the whole code for a project and takes a comparable amount of development effort (Myers and Rosson, 1992).

This "people gap" is exacerbated by the fact that the two groups do not share the same culture. They do not share the same perspective and they do not understand the respective constraints under which each group has to operate. It has been our experience that when the UE specialist is also a strong programmer and analyst, UE methods are systematically much better accepted by the software engineers and integrated in the development process.

Furthermore, software engineers need to understand and master usability engineering in their own languages and cultural contexts. Usability specialists often do not understand why and how technical choices and constraints influence a product's design.

Seffah, 2003, describes a list of 14 HCI design skills that are needed by developers in order for them to do a good job of designing interfaces. The paper recommends establishing several "usability advocates" within the company. The paper also proposes offering a 3-day user interface design workshop in which the project team works with end-users to design part of their project. The workshop is also an opportunity for both groups to learn HCI design methods. Another way for the usability professional to educate technology-driven professionals in user-centered approaches would be to provide them with a comprehensive step-by-step framework that lays out the entire process. This is an effective way for software organizations and engineers to learn from usability engineering and at the same time to improve collaboration between usability engineering and software engineering.

1.2.3   The Responsibilities Gap

The role of user interface is often perceived as that of decorating a thin component sitting on top of the software, with the software being the "real" system. Software engineers build the software and all its functionality, and once the bulk of the work is done, the usability people make the interface layer user-friendly. The usability people, on the other side, view their role as designing the interface first; it is only later on, once all the functionality is defined and validated, that the software engineers implement the back-end to support this design, under constant revision by usability inspectors.

These views of each other's role are of course in direct opposition and often result in frustrations within one group for not being given sufficient influence on the final product.

One view is that if usability engineering is an engineering discipline, it has to share some basic values with engineering. Usability specialists have to think and work like engineers (Mayhew, 1999). Although this view may not be shared by all, it is worth considering as it addresses this important gap.

1.2.4   The Modularity Fallacy

Traditional interactive system architectures such as MVC and PAC decompose the system into subsystems that are relatively independent, thereby allowing the design work to be partitioned between the user interface and underlying functionalities. Such architectures extend the independence assumption to usability, approaching the design of the user interface as a sub-system that can be designed and tested independently from the underlying functionality. This Cartesian dichotomy can be dangerous, as functionalities buried in the application's logic can sometimes affect the usability of the system.

In the field of interactive systems engineering, architectures of the 1980s and 1990s such as MVC and PAC are based on the principle of separating the functionality from the user interface. The functionality is what the software actually does and what information it processes. The user interface defines how this functionality is presented to end-users and how the users interact with it. The underlying assumption is that usability, the ultimate quality factor, is primarily a property of the user interface. Therefore separating the user interface from the application's logic makes it easy to modify, adapt or customize the interface after user testing. Unfortunately, this assumption does not ensure the usability of the system as a whole.

We now realize that system features can have an impact on the usability of the system, even if they are logically independent from the user interface and not necessarily visible to the user. Bass observed that even if the presentation of a system is well designed, the usability of a system can be greatly compromised if the underlying architecture and designs do not have the proper provisions for user concerns (Bass and John, 2001b). We propose that software architecture should define not only the technical interactions needed to develop and implement a product, but also interactions with the users.

At the core of this vision is that invisible components can affect usability. By invisible components, we mean any software entity or architectural attribute that does not have visible cues on the presentation layer. They can be an operation, data, or a structural attribute of the software. Examples of such phenomena are commonplace in database modeling. Queries that were not anticipated by the modeler, or that turn out to be more frequent than expected, can take forever to complete because the logical data model (or even the physical data model) is inappropriate. Client-server and distributed computer architectures are also particularly prone to usability problems stemming from their "invisible" components.

Designers of distributed applications with Web interfaces are often faced with these concerns: They must carefully weigh what part of the application logic will reside on the client side and what part will be on the server side in order to achieve an appropriate level of usability. User feedback information, such as application status and error messages, must be carefully designed and exchanged between the client and server part of the application, anticipating response time of each component, error conditions and exception handling, and the variability of the computing environment. Sometimes, the Web user interface becomes crippled by the constraints imposed by these invisible components because the appropriate style of interactions is too difficult to implement.

Like other authors Bass and John, 2001b; Folmer et al., 2003, we argue that both software developers implementing the systems features and usability engineers in charge of designing the user interfaces should be aware of the importance of this intimate relationship between features and the user interfaces. This relationship can inform architecture design for usability. With the help of patterns, this relationship can help integrate usability concerns in software engineering.

1.2.5 Dispensability of UE

Some software managers feel that their project cannot afford to spend so much time on usability. They worry that the UE iterations will never end, due to HCI people trying to get everything perfect. There are two answers to this. First of all, there should be measurable usability objectives set as part of the project plan. And secondly, these managers should consider the longer-term effect of quality work on the self-esteem (and hence productivity) of their developers. When deciding on how user interface development is going to be integrated into the wider development process, managers should keep in mind the "Hawthorne Effect". DeMarco and Lister state this as: "people perform better when they're trying something new" – because of this, they recommend that each project should vary the techniques used just for the sake of variety (DeMarco and Lister, 1999).

1.2.6 Shortage of Training and UE Expertise

Another barrier to the wider practice of UE methods is that their techniques are still relatively unknown and difficult to master, making them inaccessible to small and medium-sized software development teams and individual developers. While software developers may have high-level familiarity with such basic concepts as requirements analysis and usability testing, few understand the complete process well enough to incorporate it into the larger software development lifecycle. Furthermore, although some software engineering standards adhere to goals similar to those promoted in ISO standard 13407, in practice the standards often seem very different. This is because they are formulated using different terminology, notations and languages. An example of this would be the IEEE standards on software quality and the ISO collection on quality in use (see IEEE-1061 Standard on Software Quality Metric Methodology and ISO/IEC-9126 Standard on Quality Characteristics and Guidelines for their Use).

1.2.7 Organizational Shift

The organizational learning approach asserts that the integration of UE into software engineering lifecycles is not primarily a problem of a lack of UE methods: The organization's natural inertia is the obstacle and the solution must be also understood as a problem of organizational learning and software process improvement.

In organizational terms, UE must be understood not merely as a process improvement to SE, but as a paradigm shift. In conditions of paradigm shift, those who follow the old paradigm tend to reject new paradigms, even when the new paradigm is heavily supported by scientific evidence (Kühn, 1962). Kühn was relatively cynical about paradigm shift, concluding that followers of the old paradigm never convert, and that a successful paradigm shift requires replacing them with followers of the new paradigm. Contemporary management approaches often take the more humanistic position that organizations and individuals can change (for example, Senge, 1999). The truth likely lies somewhere between these two extremes: Organizations and individuals can change, but change is hard and requires openness and intent.

1.2.8 Empirical Evidence

The existence of a credible body of evidence concerning the actual value of specific UE and UCD methods is often believed to be a prerequisite for organizational learning and process improvement in UE. Unfortunately several surveys on information system methodology research indicate that, in most cases, empirical studies of the effects and acceptance of proposed techniques is largely missing (Glass, 1995; Zelkowitz and Wallace, 1998; Basili et al., 1999).

There is a reason for this lack of empirical evidence. To empirically evaluate the value of a specific UE method using classical scientific techniques, it would be necessary to compare the same project repeated under conditions employing UE techniques versus not employing UE techniques, while controlling for skill, motivation, SE approach and other possible differences between the two project teams. This challenging experiment would need to be repeated many times with different project teams, different software engineering frameworks and on different projects in order for the results to achieve statistical validity.

1.3 THE SERIES OF WORKSHOPS ON HCI/SE INTEGRATION

This book originates in good part from several workshops that have been organized over the last decade with the explicit focus of attacking the problem of cross-pollinating between the fields of HCI and SE (Artim et al., 1998; Seffah and Hayne, 1999; Gulliksen et al., 1998; Gulliksen et al., 2001; Gulliksen and Boivie,

2001; Harning and Vanderdonckt, 2003; Kazman et al., 2003; John et al., 2004a) The starting point of all these workshops was the two workshops organized by Artim et al at CHI'97 and CHI'98 conferences on Object-Oriented Models in User Interface Design and on incorporating Task Analysis Into Commercial And Industrial Object-Oriented Systems Development (Artim et al., 1998).

The conclusions of these investigations brought to light some of the major integration issues, which applied in particular to object-oriented methodologies, including:

1. Mediating and improving the communication line between users, usability experts and developers (Kujala et al., 2001a; Antunes et al., 2001).

2. Extending software engineering artefacts for UI specification and conceptualization, such as annotating use cases with task descriptions (Constantine and Lockwood, 1999; Rosson, 1999; Dayton et al., 1996),

3. Enhancing object-oriented software engineering notations and models (Nunes and e Cunha, 2000; Artim and van Harmelen, 1998; Kruchten, 1999; da Silva and Paton, 2001).

4. Extending requirements engineering methods for collecting information about users and usability. Examples are field observations and interviews, scenario, task models and use cases modeling techniques and personae (Cooper and Reimann, 2000) as a way to understand and model end-users.

5. Developing new processes for interactive systems design such as (Nielsen, 1999; Mayhew, 1999; Roberts, 1998), as well as approaches complementing existing use cases-driven methodologies. (Constantine and Lockwood, 1999; Kruchten, 1999).

6. Representing design artefacts including prototypes using different formalisms that convey the same information about an object but in different forms and terms which are more suitable to developers or usability experts

7. Conveying UCD attitudes, not just tools and methods, to support UCD activities. UCD must be escalated to management level by means of, for instance, business cases. One way is to create a demand for usability guarantees on the consumer/user side.

1.4   WHY HUMAN CENTERED SOFTWARE ENGINEERING?

As defined by Pressman, 2005a, Software engineering is "a well-established discipline that encompasses the process associated with software development, the methods used to analyze, design and test computer software, the management techniques associated with the control and monitoring of software projects and the tools used to support process, methods, and techniques."

By adding that SE should be human-centered, we want to emphasize that there is a need for a shift of focus in systems development towards putting the goals, needs, and wishes of the users in the first room.

By "humans" we do not only mean the ultimate end-users of the system but also the secondary users of the system. For example, while a particular physician might be the ultimate end-user of a system, there are several other users: the patients that are affected by their doctor's use of technology and the professionals involved in the development of the technology. All of these users need tools:

■   to be able to capture and assemble requirements;

■   to be able to use their imagination, skills and innovative abilities in designing new and well-functioning solutions to meet these requirements;

■   to be able to construct technology that enables these designs;

■   to be able to test and improve the systems; and finally

■   to deploy, maintain, and eventually de-install the system.

We are not saying that one of these groups have preference above the others, but that all of these need tools that can enable them to interact efficiently to produce the desired outcome.

1.4.1   Requirements on Human-Centered Software Engineering

We need to acknowledge the needs of these different stakeholders in our attempts to bridge the gap between HCI and SE.

1. *From the user side.* Users are valuable and often underused resources in the software development process. Users are the only ones who actually have the potential of explaining how they interact with the system and how they use the system as a support to achieve their other tasks. But on the other hand, we know that users may have difficulties expressing their ways of interacting, since a lot of the interaction is tacit knowledge (Polanyi, 1966). This has been emphasized in the book in which the concept of User-centered systems design was coined in Donald Norman's theory of action (Norman and Draper, 1986). Therefore we need to apply methods to observe and analyze the users to be able to get some evidence to help deducting these requirements. But on the other hand, active involvement of the users can improve the user's ability to develop their understanding of the potential of the technology and also helping them to see how their tasks could develop and change due to the impact of the new technology. Several studies show great benefits in involving the users actively in the design process (Greenbaum and Kyng, 1991; Göransson and Gulliksen, 2003).

2. *From the developer side.* Developers have for a long time been suffering from the limitations in existing tools to turn requirements into designs that will work under the limitations that existing technology provides. Most developers that we have seen have, contrary to what many others report, been very happy to get more help in the process of making design decisions. The saying that such tools

that help the developers do better design would take the fun out of software development is a myth. Developers want to do a good job, they want to produce a system with the highest possible level of usability. But developers also work under restrictions: restrictions in time and budget, and restrictions imposed by the limitations of the technology and the methods used. Therefore it is natural that developers can express some hesitation towards too much of their time being consumed by cooperation with the users.

3. *From the usability professional's side.* Usability professionals are interesting to study in this process since they often get the responsibility of vouching for the usability of the system in the project. In many cases they face the risk of becoming surrogate users (Boivie et al., 2003; Gulliksen et al., 2003a).

1.5   AUDIENCE

Since the purpose of this book is to bridge the gap between two communities, Human-Computer Interaction (HCI) and Software Engineering (SE), it is written for both software developers and usability experts as well as educators. The frameworks described in this book can support any person interested in the general problem of promoting user-centered design in the software development community. These frameworks can be useful for usability and software practitioners and researchers who are interested in the development of methodologies and standards, who have researched or developed specific user-centered design techniques or who have worked with software development methodologies. They also offer insights, for software development organizations, in how to integrate user-centered design techniques and tools with software engineering courses and tutorials. Software engineering students and educators can use them to extend and improve their skills, and to learn techniques for communicating with usability "guru" and supporters.

1.6   A QUICK TOUR OF THE BOOK

The book is divided into 5 parts. This introductory chapter highlights some the fundamental challenges in integrating usability in the software engineering lifecycle. It also summarizes the major contributions of this book.

Part 2 discusses **"Principles, Myths and Challenges"**. It comprises four chapters that all together give a solid and deep analysis of the multiple integration faces. In Chapter 2, Gulliksen and others propose a definition of UCSD – user-centered systems design. We have identified 12 key principles for the adoption of a user-centered development process, principles that are based on existing theory, as well as research in and experiences from a large number of software development projects. Seffah, Desmarais and Metzker review in Chapter 3 some of the most relevant frameworks. It assesses their strengths and weaknesses as well as how far the objective of integrating HCI methods and principles within different software engineering methods has been reached. Finally, it draws conclusions about research directions towards the development of a generic framework that can: (1) facilitate the integration of usability engineering methods in software development practices and, (2) foster the cross-pollination of the HCI and software engineering disciplines. Kazman and Jerome from

Carnegie Mellon and the University of Hawaii, provide a supplement of the state of the research that lies at the conjunction of HCI and Software Engineering. They also present the results of a survey that examines how HCI practitioners and software engineers interact in industry. The survey shows a substantial lack of mutual understanding among software engineers and HCI specialists, and the results from research do not appear to be strongly influencing this interaction. The chapter by Sutcliffe reviews different conceptions of scenarios, artefacts, theories and models with contributions they make to the design process in SE and HCI. It explores the potential for constructive contrasts between scenarios as concrete, grounded examples and generalized, abstract models in an integrated view of systems development that encompasses both HCI and SE.

Part 3 is dedicated to **Requirements, scenarios, and use-cases.** Adams, Bass and John introduced in Chapter 6, the concept of architecturally sensitive usability scenarios as an important usability concerns that require early consideration in software design so that architectural support can render them easy and cost-effective to implement. They also report an experience of applying this type of scenario to the design of MERBoard, a wall-sized interactive system developed by NASA to assist Mars Rover science teams with collaborative data analysis. In Chapter 7, Kujala justifies the need to bridge the gap between informal user need descriptions and formal user requirements. She details how user-centered requirements analysis can be effectively integrated to use case-driven requirements engineering. She proposes a three-stage approach to gather user needs directly from users using semi-structured, small-scale field studies. The results are then summarized in user need tables to ease their utilization and their linking to use case descriptions. The user need tables are transformed into use case descriptions. Timo Jokela, in Chapter 8, suggests a teamwork method for determining usability requirements based on the definition of usability in ISO 9241-11. A usability specialist facilitates a software development team in determining usability requirements in a set of workshop sessions. The concrete outcome of the workshops is a set of measurable usability requirements (in the form of a usability requirements table) that informs design drivers for the later phases of software design. Another outcome of the workshops is of educational and motivational nature. In Chapter 9, Carter et al. propose the Putting Usability First (**PUF**)UML methodology of Usability Engineering as an approach to solving the limitations of Unified Modeling Language (UML). PUF identifies and specifies usability and context related information that are transformed into UML diagrams.

Part 4 provides a deeper analysis and comparison of the **UCD, Unified and Agile Processes**. In Chapter 10, Ferre et al. propose to characterize selected usability techniques and activities using SE terminology and concepts, according to what kind of activity they belong to and at what development stage their application contributes most to the usability of the final software product. Software developers may then manage usability activities and techniques, include them in their software process, and understand in which activities usability and SE techniques have to be merged to achieve concurrent objectives. The proposed framework is aimed at software development organizations with a defined iterative development process that are looking to enhance their process with usability aspects. Dave Roberts from IBM, in Chapter 11 introduces one of the most comprehensive UCD methods, IBM User Engineering. This method provides a process that guides teams though a complex project. It uses CASE tools to help to manage information. It includes abstraction paths that help the team to understand the whole problem before they divide it. IBM User Engineering helps the development team to build the solution; providing many heuristics to guide progress. Pardha S. Pyla, M.A. Perez-Quinones, James D. Arthur, and R. Hartson present in their chapter another methodology to bridge HCI and SE called Ripple. It is a database-centered, event-triggered, shared design representation framework that provides a development infrastructure within which the usability engineering and software engineering life cycles co-exist in cooperative and complementary roles. Compared to IBM User Engineering, Ripple does not merge HCI and SE processes into a single life cycle; rather it coordinates each life cycle's activities, timing, scope, and goals using a shared design representation and management for the two life cycles. Ripple incorporates techniques to accommodate communication about design insights and change.

The last part of this book, entitled **UCD Knowledge and UI design Patterns**, explores avenues related to integration, management, and use of multidisciplinary system design knowledge. First, Steven R. Haynes, John M. Carroll, and Mary Beth Rosson from the *School of Information Sciences and Technology, The Pennsylvania State University*, outline the need for repositories and other points of exchange for system design knowledge, and conceptual catalysts to support value-added integration of the results from multidisciplinary design research and practice. In Chapter 15, Lisa Battle, from Lockheed Martin, presents four process-sensitive patterns that illustrate best practices for integrating user-centered design with the software development lifecycle. Process patterns describe a proven, successful approach or series of actions (Coplien, 1995; Ambler, 1998), and are based on the idea of design patterns originally introduced in architecture by Christopher Alexander (Alexander et al., 1977). In Chapter 16, John Artim describes a formal and recursive UI design pattern description supporting UI design work subsequent to use-case-based specification. The multipart representation described in this chapter balances the need to define task elements supported by the pattern, the design elements comprising the pattern's prototypical solution, as well as the elements needed to map from the pattern to a specific domain of use. Chapter 17 written by Janet Wesson et al. shows how, in the context of an e-commerce Website development, patterns can help to bridge requirement and design.

Acknowledgements

We thank all the reviewers of this book that are listed in the beginning of this book. Our thanks also to the individual authors of each chapter as well as those authors whose chapter we could not fit into this book. We received 27 submissions and accepted 14. All chapters were peer reviewed by at least two reviewers.

II Principles, Myths and Challenges

2 KEY PRINCIPLES FOR USER-CENTRED SYSTEMS DESIGN

Jan Gulliksen, Bengt Göransson, Inger Boivie,
Jenny Persson, Stefan Blomkvist, Åsa Cajander

Uppsala University,
Department of Information Technology, Human-Computer Interaction,
PO Box 337, SE-751 05 Uppsala, Sweden;
e-mail: Jan.Gulliksen@hci.uu.se

*Note: This chapter is reproduced from Gulliksen et al., 2003b,
with permission from Taylor & Francis*

Abstract

The concept of user-centered systems design (UCSD) has no agreed upon definition. Consequently, there is a great variety in the ways it is applied, which may lead to poor quality and poor usability in the resulting systems, as well as misconceptions about the effectiveness of UCSD. The purpose of this chapter is to propose a definition of UCSD. We have identified 12 key principles for the adoption of a user-centered development process, principles that are based on existing theory, as well as research in and experiences from a large number of software development projects. The initial set of principles were applied and evaluated in a case study and modified accordingly. These principles can be used to communicate the nature of UCSD, evaluate a develop-

*A. Seffah (eds.), Human-Centered Software Engineering – Integrating Usability
in the Development Process*, 17–36.

ment process or develop systems development processes that support a user-centered approach. We also suggest activity lists and some tools for applying UCSD.

2.1   PURPOSE AND JUSTIFICATION

This chapter describes the results of our current research on UCSD and our experiences of applying UCSD in software development projects. Our purpose has been to compile knowledge and experiences of UCSD, in order to give the concept a more precise meaning and to increase its power. The main point in our chapter is that applying UCSD requires a profound shift of attitudes in systems development, and our main goal is to promote that attitude shift.

2.2   BACKGROUND

Our main concern has been the lack of an agreed upon definition of UCSD, turning it into a concept with no real meaning. UCSD was originally coined by Norman and Draper, 1986. They emphasized the importance of having a good understanding of the users (but without necessarily involving them actively in the process):

> '*But user-centered design emphasizes that the purpose of the system is to serve the user, not to use a specific technology, not to be an elegant piece of programming. The needs of the users should dominate the design of the interface, and the needs of the interface should dominate the design of the rest of the system.*' *(Norman and Draper, 1986)*

Several other definitions and understandings have been proposed over the years. The lack of a shared understanding of the meaning of UCSD (or User-Centered Design, UCD) has actually been pointed out as a quality in its own right by Karat:

> '*For me, UCD is an iterative process whose goal is the development of usable systems, achieved through involvement of potential users of a system in system design.*' *(Karat et al., 1996)* '*I suggest we consider UCD an adequate label under which to continue to gather our knowledge of how to develop usable systems. It captures a commitment the usability community supports—that you must involve users in system design—while leaving fairly open how this is accomplished.*' *(Karat, 1997)*

The consequence of such general and non-specific definitions of user-centered design is that it, in practice, becomes a concept with no real meaning. We have therefore identified a set of key principles[1] for UCSD.

The principles summarize our research results and experiences from software development projects in a large number of organizations and projects. They are based on principles specified elsewhere (Gould et al., 1997; ISO/IEC, 1999), and on our experiences made from trying to apply UCSD in systems development projects using processes such as the Rational Unified Process (Kruchten, 1998). Our principles also take into account the Scandinavian tradition of extensive user involvement in the development process (Greenbaum and Kyng, 1991) in some communities known as par-

---

[1] A principle is a commonly accepted fundamental rule or law that can be used to define other principles.

ticipatory design. Other well-known approaches such as contextual design (Beyer and Holtzblatt, 1998), goal-directed design (Cooper, 1999), usability engineering (Nielsen, 1993; Mayhew, 1999) have also contributed to the result.

Below we describe one of the projects that had particular impact on the principles in that it was conducted with the explicit goal to capture critical success factors for UCSD.

2.3   THE PROJECT

The pilot project was an in-house development project within the Swedish National Tax Board with the purpose to develop a new computerized case-handling tool for administrators working with national registration. We were able to follow the project from the very start. In the first project meeting we emphasized the importance of following a UCSD approach and introduced our set of principles to the project team.

These principles were specific for the organization and had been identified in an earlier research effort (Gulliksen and Göransson, 2001). They were:

- The *work practices of the users* control the development. Early focus on users and tasks. The designer must understand the users, their cognitive behavior, attitudes and the characteristics of their work tasks. Appropriate allocation of function between the user and the system is also important to prevent unnecessary control;

- *Active user participation throughout the project*, in analysis, design, development and evaluation. This requires a careful user selection process emphasizing the skills of typical users, including both:

  - *work domain experts* (continuously through the development project);

  - and *actual end-users* (for interviews and observations as well as evaluation of design results).

- *Early prototyping* to evaluate and develop design solutions and to gradually build a shared understanding of the needs of the users as well as their future work practices;

- *Continuous iteration of design solutions.* A cyclic process of design, evaluation and redesign should be repeated as often as necessary. The evaluation process should include empirical measurement in which tests are conducted where users perform real tasks on prototypes. The users' reactions and attitudes should be observed and analyzed;

- *Multidisciplinary design teams.* Mainly achieved by including a usability designer (Göransson and Sandbäck, 1999) in the process;

- *Integrated design.* The system, the work practices, on-line help, training, organization, etc. should be developed in parallel.

The project decided to act in accordance with the above principles.

2.3.1   Research Methods

We used an action research approach in the project, i.e. our aim was to introduce changes in the development process as regards user involvement and usability issues, and to observe and record the outcomes of these changes. Our activities included introducing a set of UCSD principles as described above, and facilitating the project team's commitment to these principles. We also facilitated collaborative prototyping activities with users.

To observe the outcomes of the activities and actions, we used qualitative data collection methods as described below.

- Observations of the work of the development team, for instance, by continuously participating in the project meetings of the software development team

- Observations of the current work practices (mainly paper-based) of the administrators working with national registration

- Semi-structured interviews based on open-ended questions with software developers and user representatives about their attitudes to and experiences with working with users and usability

- Semi-structured interviews based on open-ended questions with users about their work

- Continuous discussions with members of the software development team and representatives for the current work practices to check possible discrepancies in our interpretation of the observed activities and actions

Meanwhile, we continued working with the principles. As a result of intermediate findings in the pilot project and findings in other, parallel, research efforts we modified the set of principles to cover the twelve key principles described in this chapter. The applicability of these principles was then assessed in a number of workshops with researchers and practitioners.

2.3.2   Results

As a result of the introductory meeting, the project group decided to apply UCSD as defined by the initial set of principles.

We could not influence the choice and customization of the development process – the organization had recently shifted to using the Rational Unified Process (RUP) (Kruchten, 1998). We were, however, able to introduce additional activities to complement the process as needed, e.g. activities for performing a thorough user and task analysis, for developing design solutions iteratively and in cooperation with the users, and for including a usability designer throughout the project.

One of the more successful events was a collaborative prototyping activity in which the users could develop their vision of the future system and work situation, integrating a future system and future work practices (Figure 2.1).

These collaborative prototyping sessions were facilitated by a usability designer in cooperation with a researcher. The users brought sketches illustrating their own view

Figure 2.1   Collaborative prototyping in which the usability designer facilitates the users' production of mock-ups

of the future system as a basis for a negotiation on the most appropriate design of the system.

Low-level prototyping tools were used since the users regarded them as the most flexible tool for their purpose (Figure 2.2).

Prior to the collaborative design sessions the usability designer had conducted a user analysis and created personas. According to Calde et al., 2002, user models, or personas, are fictional, detailed archetypical characters that represent distinct groupings of behaviors, goals and motivations observed and identified during the research phase. Cooper, 1999, describes personas as a tool for communication and design within the group of designers, software developers, managers, customers and other stakeholders. The purpose is not to give a precise description or a complete theoretical model of a user. Instead, it is aiming at a simple, but good enough description of the user to make it possible to design the system. (Figure 2.3).

From the software engineering side they had been performing use case modeling to specify the detailed requirements on the system. A use case specifies the sequence of actions, including alternatives of the sequence, that the system can perform, interacting with actors of the system (Jacobson et al., 1999). Use case modeling is today one of the most widely used software engineering techniques to specify user requirements. Unified Modeling Language (UML) is one of the most common formal notations to describe use cases (Fowler and Scott, 1997). Rational Unified Process (RUP) (Kruchten, 1998) builds heavily upon these techniques.

According to the users, the personas gave a much more concrete picture of typical users than what came out of the use case modeling sessions running in parallel with the collaborative prototyping activities.

Figure 2.2   Low-fidelity prototyping tools were used as these were the most convenient for visualizing the future use situation without limiting the design space

Halfway through the project all participants were very satisfied with the activities so far and the results achieved. The project was committed on all levels to UCSD. The principles communicated the essentials of UCSD very well.

From then on, however, there was a gradual increase of problems and obstacles to the user-centered approach. Despite efforts from our side and from the project, the problems were never really resolved. Some of them were outside the control of the project.

The major problems in the project are briefly described below. The problems reflect why the initial principles were not sufficient and therefore each of the problems is related to the subsequent definition and 12 key principles of User Centered Systems Design. The outcome of the project can be compared with the consolidated list of twelve key principles, and each problem in the project map well against one or more of the principles.

- **No lifecycle perspective on UCSD.** The developers focused on short-term goals, such as, producing models and specifications prescribed by RUP. The long-term goals and needs of the users regarding their future work situation were ignored or forgotten. Moreover, towards the end of the project, meeting the project goals and deadlines became much more important than achieving some sort of minimum level of usability. We believe, that had the project decided to give the usability activities higher priority than, for example, to develop absolutely all the functionality the end result could have been a lot better, without any of the missing functionality causing any big problems in the long run. We emphasize the importance of a lifecycle perspective in our definition of

Gudrun

Personal background

Professional background

Work settings

Colleagues and contacts

Miscellaneous

Figure 2.3 Personas were used to describe typical users. In this example, the persona 'Gudrun' is described based on personal background, the work setting, colleagues and contacts

UCSD in the next chapter as well as in a number of the principles, for instance, the user involvement principle and the usability champion principle. The lack of lifecycle perspective also indicates that there was no real commitment to UCSD in the project which points to an attitude problem.

- **Usability designers were ignored.** Despite the skilful and experienced work that the usability designers performed, their results and their opinions were ignored in the later phases of the project. The usability champion principle points out that the usability champion/designer[2] should have the mandate to decide on usability matters. The project ignoring the input of the usability designer clearly indicates that this was not the case[2].

- **Use case mania.** When the project started, the organization did not have enough experience with use case modeling. The modeling went out of hand and the results could not be used efficiently in the development process. The project got literally bogged down in use cases, but did not really know what to do with them. The use case mania indicates that there was a problem with user focus in the project. Despite the confusion regarding the use of the use cases, producing them became more important than understanding the users' real needs.

- **Poor understanding of the design documentation.** The design was documented in UML and the users were invited to evaluate it. The users had severe difficulties predicting their future use situation based on the UML notation. One of the users said that after having worked with use case modeling, the collaborative prototyping was like 'coming out of a long dark tunnel'. The design representation principle emphasizes the importance of using representations that are easy to understand for all the stakeholders, in particular as regards the future work/use situation. UML is clearly not suitable in that respect.

- **Major changes in the project.** Halfway through the project a strategic decision was made within the organization, against our advice, to change the technical platform and continue the development in a web-based environment. The decision was crucial in that it made it very difficult to meet the usability requirements. Insufficient experience with and expertise in the new technology as well as the page metaphor in html created problems. The decision was made with little or no attention to usability matters. This indicates that there was a problem with the attitudes to UCSD and usability within the organization and a problem with user focus.

- **Problems establishing a user centered attitude.** Single individuals in a project can make a crucial difference when it comes to UCSD. We noticed, for instance, problems with resolving conflicts between personal goals and business goals within the project, on an individual level. Again, this indicates that there was a problem with attitudes and user focus in the organization. It also indicates

---

[2]To us the usability designer is a role that has a clear position in the development project (see for instance Göransson and Sandbäck, 1999). Usability champion has more of a mentor status and is not a role that somebody can shoulder. To be able to act as a usability champion you must have extensive knowledge and experience of the work in practice and also an ability to act as a mentor.

problems with the professional attitude described in the principle on multidisciplinary design.

This case describes how a project with explicit intentions to apply UCSD, nevertheless ran into several problems and obstacles that made it very difficult to pursue the UCSD approach. Our conclusion is that one needs to be very specific about what it takes from the process to comply with UCSD to prevent problems such as the ones described in the pilot study.

Based on the results of the project, we concluded that the principles listed in Gould et al., 1997, and ISO 13407 are not sufficient to maintain a UCSD approach in a project or in an organization. We therefore modified our initial set of principles to clearly indicate that it takes much more to work in a user-centered fashion. We have also run a number of workshops with researchers and practitioners to discuss and confirm the principles. The resulting set is listed below together with a definition of UCSD.

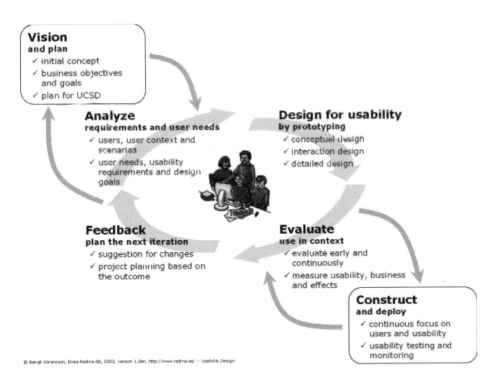

Figure 2.4   User-centered system design (UCSD) is a process focusing on usability throughout the entire development process and further throughout the system life cycle

2.4 DEFINITION AND KEY PRINCIPLES

User-centered system design (UCSD) is a process focusing on usability[3] throughout the entire development process and further throughout the system life cycle (Figure 2.4). It is based on the following key principles:

- **User focus – the goals of the activity, the work domain or context of use, the users' goals, tasks and needs should early guide the development** (Gould et al., 1997; ISO/IEC, 1999). All members of a project must understand the goals of the activity, the context of use, who the users are, their situation, goals and tasks, why and how they perform their tasks, how they communicate, co-operate and interact, etc. This helps in creating and maintaining a focus on the users' needs instead of a technical focus. Activities, such as identifying user profiles, contextual inquiries and task analysis, must be a natural part of the development process. Make sure that all project members have met real or potential users, for instance, by visiting the workplace. Descriptions of typical users, tasks and scenarios could be put up on the walls of the project room/area to maintain a user focus.

- **Active user involvement – representative users should actively participate, early and continuously throughout the entire development process and throughout the system lifecycle** (Gould et al., 1997; ISO/IEC, 1999; Nielsen, 1993). The users should be directly involved, both in the development project and in related activities, such as, organizational development and designing new work practices (Greenbaum and Kyng, 1991). The users must be representative of the intended user groups. Plans for involving users should be specified from the very start of the project. Identify appropriate phases for user participation and specify where, when and how users should participate[4]. Emphasize the importance of meeting the users in context, for instance, at their workplace.

- **Evolutionary systems development – the systems development should be both iterative and incremental** (Gould et al., 1997; Boehm, 1988). It is impossible to know exactly what to build from the outset. Hence, UCSD requires an approach which allows continuous iterations with users and incremental deliveries. This, so that design solutions can be evaluated by the users before they are made permanent. An iteration should contain a proper analysis of the users' needs and the context of use, a design phase, a documented evaluation with concrete suggestions for modifications and a redesign in accordance with the results of the evaluation. These activities do not have to be formal. An iteration could be as short as half an hour, as long as it contains all three steps. Incremental

---

[3]Usability is defined as 'the extent to which a product can be used by specified users to achieve specified goals with effectiveness, efficiency and satisfaction, in a specified context of use' (ISO/IEC, 1998), Please note that this definition includes the concept of utility or usefulness, often seen as separate from usability.
[4]Please note that involving users on a full-time basis in a project quickly turns them into domain experts rather than representative users. It is therefore important to involve user representatives on a temporary basis as well.

development means that, based on an overall picture of the system under development (SUD), priorities are set and the system is divided into parts that can be delivered for real use. Each increment is iterated as described above. Evaluations of the increments in real use should influence the design of the subsequent increments. Let the software grow into the final product.

■ **Simple design representations – the design must be represented in such ways that it can be easily understood by users and all other stakeholders** (Kyng, 1995). Use design representations and terminology that are easily understood by all users and stakeholders so that they can fully appreciate the consequences of the design on their future use situation. Use, for instance, prototypes (sketches and mock-ups) and simulations. Abstract notations, such as use cases, UML diagrams or requirements specifications are not sufficient to give the users and stakeholders a concrete understanding of the future use situation (Bödker, 1998; Mathiassen and Munk-Madsen, 1986). The representations must also be usable and effective. The goal is that all parties involved share an understanding of what is being built.

■ **Prototyping – early and continuously, prototypes should be used to visualize and evaluate ideas and design solutions in cooperation with the end users** (Gould et al., 1997; Nielsen, 1993). Use multiple paper sketches, mock-ups and prototypes to support the creative process, elicit requirements and visualize ideas and solutions. The prototypes should be designed and evaluated with real users in context (contextual prototyping). It is essential to start with low-fidelity materials, for instance, quick sketches, before implementing anything in code. Start with the conceptual design on a high level and do not move on to detail too quickly. If possible produce several prototypes in parallel, since this helps the designers in maintaining an openness and creative attitude to what is being built. Far too often the design space is unnecessarily limited by only sticking with the first set of designs produced.

■ **Evaluate use in context – baselined usability goals and design criteria should control the development** (Gould et al., 1997; Nielsen, 1993). Critical usability goals should be specified and the design should be based on specific design criteria. Evaluate the design against the goals and criteria in cooperation with the users, in context. Early in the development project, one should observe and analyze the users' reactions to paper sketches and mock-ups. Later in the project, users should perform real tasks with simulations or prototypes. Their behavior, reactions, opinions and ideas should be observed, recorded and analyzed. Specify goals for aspects that are crucial for the usability and that cover critical activities as well as the overall use situation.

■ **Explicit and conscious design activities – the development process should contain dedicated design activities** (Cooper, 1999). The user interface design and the interaction design are of undisputed importance for the success of the system. Remember that to the users the user interface is the system. The design of the SUD as regards the user interaction and usability should be the result of dedicated and conscious design activities. The construction of the SUD should adhere to that design. Far too often, the UI and interaction design 'happens' as a result of somebody doing a bit of coding or modeling rather than being the result of professional interaction design as a structured and prioritized activity.

■ **A professional attitude – the development process should be performed by effective multidisciplinary teams** (ISO/IEC, 1999). Different aspects and parts of the system design and development process require different sets of skills and expertise. The analysis, design and development work should be performed by empowered multidisciplinary teams of, for instance, system architects, programmers, usability designers, interaction designers and users. A professional attitude is required and so are tools that facilitate the cooperation and efficiency of the team.

■ **Usability champion – usability experts should be involved early and continuously throughout the development lifecycle** (Kapor, 1990). There should be an experienced usability expert (usability designer) or possibly a usability group on the development team. The usability designer should be devoted to the project as an 'engine' for the UCSD process from the beginning of the project and throughout the development process and system lifecycle (Buur and Bödker, 2000). The usability designer must be given the authority to decide on matters affecting the usability of the system and the future use situation.

■ **Holistic design – all aspects that influence the future use situation should be developed in parallel** (Gould et al., 1997). Software does not exist in isolation from other parts of, for instance, a work situation. When developing software for the support of work activities, the work organization, work practices, roles, etc, must be modified. All aspects should be developed in parallel. This includes work/task practices and work/task organization, user interface and interaction; on-line help; manuals; user training, work environment, health and safety aspects, etc. Other parts of the context of use such as: hardware, and social and physical environments, must also be considered in the integrated design process. One person or team should have the overall responsibility for the integration of all aspects.

■ **Processes customization – the UCSD process must be specified, adapted and/or implemented locally in each organization.** Usability cannot be achieved without a user-centered process. There is, however, no one-size-fits-all process. Thus the actual contents of the UCSD process, the methods used, the order of activities, etc, must be customized and adapted to the particular organization and project based on their particular needs. A UCSD process can be based on a commercial or in-house software development process, where activities are added, removed or modified. Existing methods and techniques may well be re-used, if they comply with the key principles.

■ **A user-centered attitude should always be established.** UCSD requires a user-centered attitude throughout the project team, the development organization and the client organization. All people involved in the project must be aware of and committed to the importance of usability and user involvement, but the degree of knowledge may differ depending on role and project phase (Boivie et al., 2003). The key principles defined in this chapter can serve as a common ground.

The above 12 principles facilitate the development, communication and assessment of user-centered design processes for creating usable interactive systems, covering analysis, design, evaluation, construction and implementation. Several benefits come with applying the principles, such as their help in maintaining the focus on the users and the usability throughout the entire development process. The UCSD poster is reprinted in Appendix 1.

We fully appreciate that it will be more or less impossible to implement all the principles in one strategic shift. Adopting them gradually is probably more feasible and practicable. It is, however, important to comply with the principles to as high a degree as possible at any point in time.

2.5   TOOLS FOR APPLYING UCSD

The principles are, necessarily, general and rather abstract in nature, and cannot be applied as is in practice. We are therefore currently working on activity lists, with potential tools and techniques, for each principle. These lists will provide support for applying the principles and help in understanding and assessing them.

2.5.1   Activity List

The purpose of the activity list that accompanies each principle is to elaborate on what it takes to apply a principle. The activity list suggests activities of a general nature alongside appropriate methods, tools and techniques. The principles are general but the activity lists should be developed specifically to fit each organization.

2.5.2   Complying with the Activity Lists

The lists suggest activities and it is important to evaluate the applicability of each activity within the current project. If one chooses not to perform a particular activity, it is important to make clear why, and that all parties involved agree with the decision. The activity list serves as both a To-do list and a checklist, where each item can be 'ticked off'. There are three options for each activity:

- No = we decided to not perform this activity. We gave rationales for this decision and had a general agreement on the motives.

- Yes = we performed this activity, in full or to the extent that the project team and management, found appropriate.

- N/A = we found that this activity was not applicable. The rationales for this were clearly stated and agreed on. We have conducted other actives to compensate for this.

Below is a draft activity list for the principle User focus:

2.5.3   *Activity List, Tools and Methods for the Principle; User Focus*

- Vision, purpose goal and constraints of the target activity analyzed and understood by all project members.

  - Tools and methods: Goals analysis, Focus groups

- Identification, description and prioritization of all user groups.

  - Tools and methods: User analysis, personas

- Visualization and characteristics of target user groups made available to everyone in the project.

  - Tools and methods: Decorate a project room with artefacts, etc. that illustrate the users' work situation, environment and characteristics.

- Potential limitations and restrictions in the users' capabilities (for instance vision impairments or language problems) are clear to everyone in the project.

- The development team has focused on the needs of target user groups.

- The users have expressed their impressions of current system and expectations on future system.

  - Tools and methods: Users asked about good things and bad things in their current work situation, Think-out loud.

- Users observed as they were performing their tasks in context.

  - Tools and methods: Analysis of information utilization, Context-of-use analysis, Field studies, Contextual inquiry.

- Use situation documented

  - Tools and methods: Video and still camera, scenarios, personas

- Tasks analyzed.

  - Tools and methods: Task analysis

- Copies of artefacts (forms, documents archives, notebooks, etc.) used by the users collected.

2.6   APPLICATION

In the pilot project described above, an initial set of principles was used to define a UCSD process. The consolidated list of principles was subsequently used to identify mismatches between the development process and a UCSD approach. The definition and principles for UCSD can, however, be used for a number of purposes as listed below::

- *Explanation model* – to analyze and communicate why organizations, projects or processes did not meet their goals as regards usability

- *Process development* – for defining a UCSD process

- *Process/Organization customization* – to customize or adapt an organization, project or development process to UCSD, for instance, a commercial development process, such as Rational Unified Process- - RUP (Kruchten, 1998). Even though RUP prevents rather than promotes UCSD, it may be modified to integrate some of its features (Gulliksen and Göransson, 2001).

- *Process/Organization assessment* – to assess the user-centeredness of an organization, project or process. Using the principles to identify mismatches, problems may be identified in time to do something about them, which increases the chances of producing a usable piece of software.

- *Knowledge transfer* – to teach and transfer knowledge about UCSD and to communicate the basic philosophy of UCSD,

- *Procurement support* –support for procurers as a basis for specifying requirements on the design process as such

- *In client-contractor relations*– the client can demand that the contractor work in accordance with the definition and key principles for UCSD. At present, usability is often taken for granted. Clients do not understand that it takes systematic work according to a UCSD philosophy to achieve usability.

Our definition and key principles originate from our experiences and research in contract and in-house development of bespoke software for work situations. We nevertheless see a potential for applying them in other types of development projects. Regardless of the project and the organization, the principles must always be adapted to the context.

2.7   AGILE APPROACHES AND UCSD

Recently, agile approaches to software development have gained a lot of attention. The rationale behind the agile perspective is to shift the overall focus of software development to a more agile or 'lightweight' perspective. This shift can be seen as a contrast to more formal commercial processes. Agile is not a single, well-defined process; instead, it is a generic name for several different processes or methods, sharing a set of core ideas, values and principles of software development. The principles are defined in the Agile Manifesto (Agile Alliance, 2001). The most well known of the agile processes is probably eXtreme Programming, XP.

What is interesting about agile methods is that they are addressing some of the problems of the development process that we found in our research project. For instance, the project focused on short-term goals such as producing models and other artefacts while loosing the overall goal of delivering a usable system. Other problems include use-case mania and poor understanding of the design documentation. Agile processes emphasize the pragmatic use of light, but sufficient rules of project behavior and the use of human and communication oriented principles (Cockburn, 2002). Hence, people are more important than processes and tools. Working software is more important than comprehensive documents and model building, Models and artefacts are only means of communication; consequently prototyping and simple design representations are preferred. Agile developers argues that projects should be communication centric, which implies that effective human communication with project members and users are important, e.g. face-to-face is the ideal way of communicate within a project and with users. Usually, there is a direct collaboration with users and customers – preferably, users and developers should sit in the same room during development.

The problems with the agile approach, is that the different processes have not paid much attention to usability and UCSD. The main focus of agile methods is on delivering working software. This is of course excellent, as usable software also must be delivered and be working. But to get there, the development is focused on making coding effective and there is a risk that usability issues gets lost, as there is no explicit user-centered focus. Agile projects include some roles that are supposed to work with user interface design and user requirements, but this is in most cases not enough. The whole project must be committed to the importance of usability. Another problem is that the users involved in the development are not always end users. Sometimes they are customers or domain experts. The agile methods seldom make a difference.

Agile processes do not in itself apply to all the key principles of UCSD. But, so far we have not seen any reason why agile processes could not be customized or adapted to UCSD.

2.8   DISCUSSION/CONCLUSIONS

The reader may ask why we have defined yet another set of principles for user-centered systems design, since those existing are not used or do not work they way they were intended. Below, we discuss some of the main reasons why we believe a more precise definition of UCSD is required.

Our pilot study shows that even with an explicit commitment to user-centered design and a usability focus, usability may get lost in the software development process. Since few projects have the explicit goal to produce systems with poor usability, we believe that there are obstacles to usability and user involvement in the actual development process. Such obstacles have been described in numerous studies, for instance, Poltrock and Grudin, 1994, and Wilson et al., 1996; Wilson et al., 1997. Our main concern has therefore been to address shortcomings and obstacles in the development process that derail the focus on usability and users' needs.

User-centered design (UCD) methods have gained a great deal of attention recently. According to a recent study (Vredenburg et al., 2002) the opinion is that user-centered methods generally increase the utility and usability of computer systems. However, the degree to which organizations adopt UCD methods varies significantly. There is, according to the study, no information on whether or not it is possible to save time and resources by adopting UCD methods. Cost-benefit tradeoffs are, nevertheless, a key consideration when adopting UCD methods (see for example Donahue, 2001). This calls for close integration of UCD methods into the development process. Unfortunately, the most common approach is to perform single usability activities using informal UCD methods (Hudson, 2001). Such an add-on approach to usability increases the risk of its being cut out when deadlines get tight. We believe that usability faces the risk of becoming a sidecar problem – if somebody in the project is pointed out as having the responsibility for usability all others involved resign from their part of the responsibility. Thus, cost-benefit analysis may in certain situations be used as an argument against usability activities rather than for if they are not tightly integrated.

In a survey examining the attitude about strategic usability (Rosenbaum et al., 2000) the authors identified the following obstacles to UCD:

- Resource constraints (28.6 %)

- Resistance to UCD/usability (26.0 %)

- Lack of understanding/knowledge about what usability is (17.3 %)

- Better ways to communicate impact of work and results (13.3 %)

- Lack of trained usability/HCI engineers (6.1 %)

- Lack of early involvement (5.1 %)

- No economic need – customers not asking for usability (3.6 %)

We believe that all of these factors are related to a lack of knowledge on how to apply UCD methods and their potential benefits which provides another reason for defining and describing UCSD in more specific terms.

Many organizations pay lip service to usability and UCSD but seem at a loss as to how to achieve it. We have studied organizations that claim that they are committed to usability and UCSD but who are not willing to change their practices in developing software. The same problem applies on the individual level. There is a growing concern among software developers about the usability of the products or software they release on the users. But they often do not know what to do about it.

Yet another reason for a more precise definition of UCSD is that many organizations still do not recognize the benefits of involving users in the development process, despite the fact that active user involvement was judged to be the number one criterion on how to be successful in IT-development projects in the CHAOS-report (Standish Group, 1995). Clegg et al., 1997, for instance, report that most projects in their study had failed to involve users in a satisfactory manner. Nor did they adopt an integrated approach. The impact of new technology on work organization and job design was considered '... hugely important but largely ignored in practice' and if addressed, it was usually late in the process and because it was discovered that the new piece of technology was going to change job designs.

UCD has also been criticized on the grounds of its being ambiguous and vague. Constantine, 2002, for example, claim that UCD is a '... loose collection of human-factors techniques united under a philosophy of understanding users and involving them in design'...'Although helpful, none of these techniques can replace good design. User studies can easily confuse what users want with what they truly need. Rapid iterative prototyping can often be a sloppy substitute for thoughtful and systematic design. Most importantly, usability testing is a relatively inefficient way to find problems you can avoid through proper design.' (Constantine, 2002, p. 43). Their remedy is 'usage-centered engineering' where the emphasis is on the usage, not the users, and on model-driven development. We readily agree with the critique against UCD, but not with the remedy. Model-driven approaches rely on skilful designers/developers using abstract models of the domain to base their design on. Model-driven approaches represent a move away from user-centered design, reducing user involvement to that of the users being informants rather than co-designers. We believe, and argue in this chapter, that user participation is a key success factor for designing for usability (see also the CHAOS report, Gould et al., 1997, and ISO/IEC, 1999) and that software development needs to move towards a user-centered approach rather than away from it. Computer systems (in particular in a work context) must support not only the 'official' rules and version of the work practices but also the particularities in each situation (Sachs, 1995; Beyer and Holtzblatt, 1998; Harris and Henderson, 1999), which requires a deep understanding of the context of use. Few development teams have that understanding, and we believe that writing requirements documents or creating abstract models is simply not enough to create that kind of understanding. Only the users themselves can provide that. This view is also supported by Harris and Henderson, 1999, as they argue for computer systems that must be much more flexible to meet the evolving human organizations.

To summarize the above discussion, we believe that user-centered systems design must be defined in terms of a process where usability work and user involvement are tightly integrated with the development process. Adding the key principles, furthermore, helps in communicating the essence of UCSD where user involvement is an essential part. By providing a more precise definition of UCSD, we can also avoid problems with ambiguity and vagueness and argue against the use of approaches that are not user-centered.

Hence, the main aim of our definition and key principles is to support the development process. This can be achieved by incorporating roles, activities and artefacts for maintaining a focus on usability and users' needs throughout the entire system life-cycle. The definition and key principles may also be used when specifying a UCSD process or when customizing a commercial development process, such as Rational Unified Process – RUP (Kruchten, 1998). The key principles originate from our experiences and research in contract and in-house development of bespoke software for work situations. We nevertheless see a potential for applying them in other types of development projects.

Our research, as well as our experiences, shows that by applying the definition of and key principles for UCSD, the chances increase of identifying problems in time to do something about them. Consequently, the chances of producing usable software increase.

Finally, we would like to emphasize that what we want to achieve is not simply yet another usability method. We see UCSD as, a new paradigm requiring a profound shift of attitudes towards systems development and user involvement. The attitudes that are required for a truly user-centered approach are embodied in the key principles.

Acknowledgements

This project was performed with financial support from the National Agency for Innovation Research, the Council for Work Life and Social Science Research, and the Swedish National Tax Board. The input received from the number of seminars leading up to the principles, such as IFIP TC 13, and our industrial partners Enea Redina AB, Tieto Enator AB and Antrop AB was greatly appreciated.

Appendix 1: The UCSD Poster

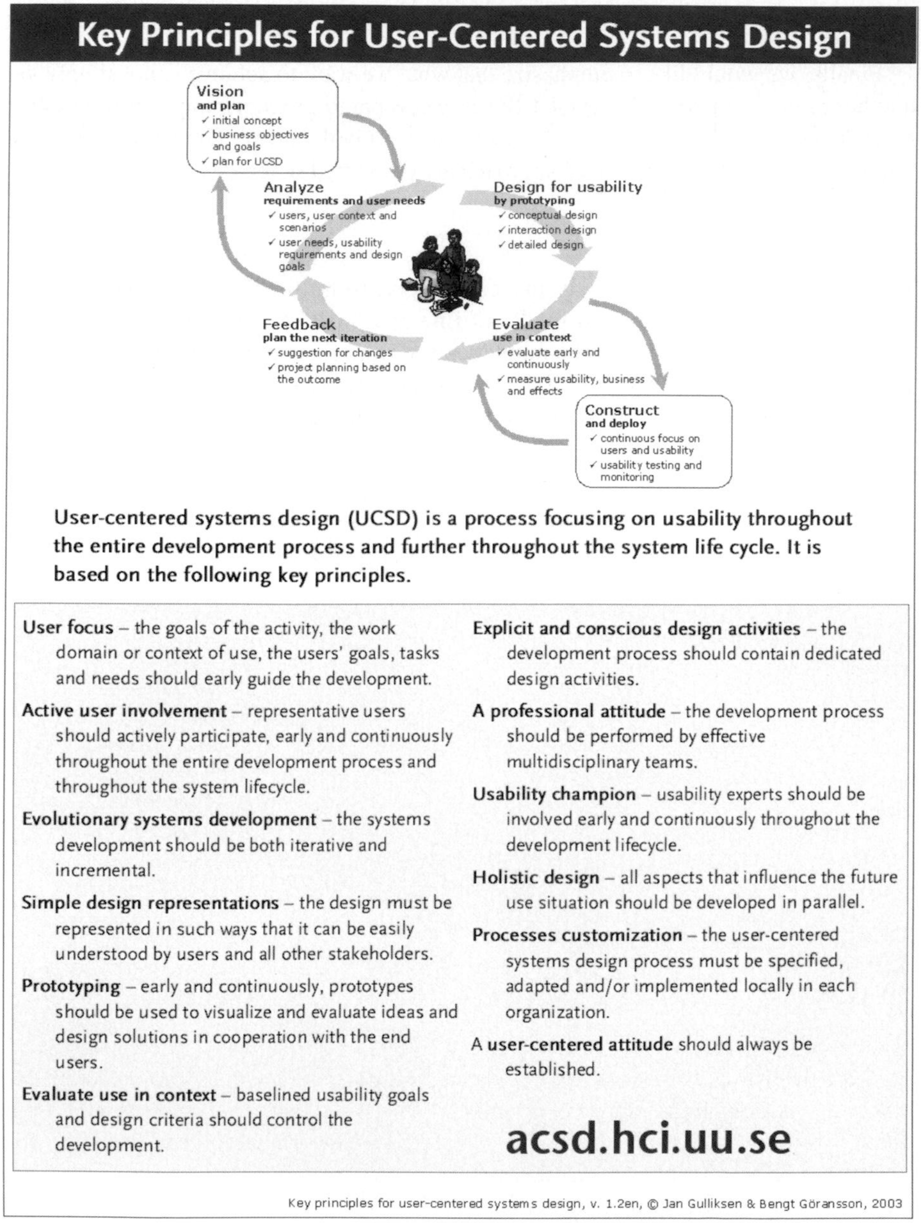

Key Principles for User-Centered Systems Design

Vision and plan
- ✓ initial concept
- ✓ business objectives and goals
- ✓ plan for UCSD

Analyze requirements and user needs
- ✓ users, user context and scenarios
- ✓ user needs, usability requirements and design goals

Design for usability by prototyping
- ✓ conceptual design
- ✓ interaction design
- ✓ detailed design

Feedback plan the next iteration
- ✓ suggestion for changes
- ✓ project planning based on the outcome

Evaluate use in context
- ✓ evaluate early and continuously
- ✓ measure usability, business and effects

Construct and deploy
- ✓ continuous focus on users and usability
- ✓ usability testing and monitoring

User-centered systems design (UCSD) is a process focusing on usability throughout the entire development process and further throughout the system life cycle. It is based on the following key principles.

User focus – the goals of the activity, the work domain or context of use, the users' goals, tasks and needs should early guide the development.

Active user involvement – representative users should actively participate, early and continuously throughout the entire development process and throughout the system lifecycle.

Evolutionary systems development – the systems development should be both iterative and incremental.

Simple design representations – the design must be represented in such ways that it can be easily understood by users and all other stakeholders.

Prototyping – early and continuously, prototypes should be used to visualize and evaluate ideas and design solutions in cooperation with the end users.

Evaluate use in context – baselined usability goals and design criteria should control the development.

Explicit and conscious design activities – the development process should contain dedicated design activities.

A professional attitude – the development process should be performed by effective multidisciplinary teams.

Usability champion – usability experts should be involved early and continuously throughout the development lifecycle.

Holistic design – all aspects that influence the future use situation should be developed in parallel.

Processes customization – the user-centered systems design process must be specified, adapted and/or implemented locally in each organization.

A **user-centered attitude** should always be established.

acsd.hci.uu.se

Key principles for user-centered systems design, v. 1.2en, © Jan Gulliksen & Bengt Göransson, 2003

Figure 2.5   UCSD poster

3 HCI, USABILITY AND SOFTWARE ENGINEERING INTEGRATION: PRESENT AND FUTURE

Ahmed Seffah*, Michel C. Desmarais**, and Eduard Metzker***

* Human-Centered Software Engineering Group Computer Science Department,
Concordia University,
** Computer Engineering Department,
École Polytechnique de Montreal, Quebec, Canada
*** Software Technology Lab, Daimler Chrysler Research and Technology Centre,
Ulm, Germany

Abstract

In the last five years, several studies and workshops have highlighted the gap between software design approaches in HCI (Human Computer Interaction) and software engineering. Although the fields are complementary, these studies emphasize that they are not well integrated with each other. Several frameworks have been proposed for integrating HCI and usability techniques into the software development lifecycle. This chapter reviews some of the most relevant frameworks. It assesses their strengths and weaknesses as well as how far the objective of integrating HCI methods and principles within different software engineering methods has been reached. Finally, it draws conclusions about research directions towards the development of a generic framework that can: (1) facilitate the integration of usability engineering methods in software

A. Seffah (eds.), Human-Centered Software Engineering – Integrating Usability
in the Development Process, 37–57.

development practices and, (2) foster the cross-pollination of the HCI and software engineering disciplines.

3.1 INTRODUCTION

It is no coincidence that the titles of some chapters in this book evoke the terms "solitudes" and "competition" to characterize the relation between the fields of HCI (Human-Computer Interaction) and SE (Software Engineering) (cf. Jerome and Kazman, chapter 4; Sutcliffe, chapter 5). This uneasy cohabitation dates back to the early days of HCI when human-centered design has been presented as the opposite, and sometimes as a replacement, to the system-driven philosophy generally used in software engineering (Norman and Draper, 1986). Although numerous HCI researchers and practitioners view User Centered Design (UCD) as a process and as a set of specific methodologies to design and develop interactive software applications, HCI is by no means considered a central topic in SE. For example, the SWEBOK, an IEEE initiative for the definition of SE knowledge and practices, defines HCI as a "related discipline", termed "software ergonomics" (Abran et al., 2004). Usability is considered one of many non functional requirements and quality attributes. No reference is made to specific UCD methods such as those found in the ISO 13407 standard, "Human-centred design processes for interactive systems" (ISO/IEC, 1999).

The reality is that UCD and software engineering techniques do have overlapping objectives of defining which methods to use in the software development process, what kind of artefacts (documents and deliverables) to use, and what quality attributes to prioritize. However, we argue that they have different perspectives on the software development process itself, as depicted in figure 3.1. The SE community focuses on the "system 1" perspective in Figure 3.1: software development is driven by specifications provided for defining the application, including the interface. The user interface has to meet the functional and usability requirements, but the requirements are tied to the system, that corresponds to the application itself. The focus is on the software application and the interface is one of many components that has to meet certain requirements.

In contrast, the proponents of UCD, and more specifically the "quality in use" approach (Bevan, 1999), focus on the "system 2" perspective: The priority is to ensure that each class of users can perform a given set of tasks with the application. The ultimate requirements are tied to what the user can perform with the application. Consequently, the software development process is driven by the need to define and validate these requirements and closely depends on the tasks defined and the users' capabilities and characteristics.

The two perspectives do not differ solely from their philosophical stance. The can have significant impacts on the how the software development process will be defined and planned, which activities will be conducted, which tools will be used, and the expertise of the team members and its leader. The impacts are particularly important with regards to the requirements management and quality control activities.

While both perspectives are valid, the SE approach is always necessary, since there necessarily is a "system 1" perspective. It either stands alone in the absence of a significant user interface component, or it is embedded in the "system 2" perspective

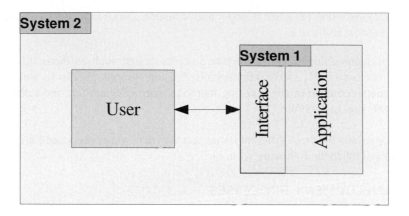

Figure 3.1   The two system perspectives

otherwise. But when the application's degree of interactivity and interface complexity is high, the "system 2" perspective, we argue, should prevail. The whole development process must then put the emphasis on defining, validating, and measuring what the use can do with the application. Thus the need to integrate UCD approaches to the SE development process.

Bringing together the SE and UCD approaches was the major goal of several workshops organized during the last decade, as well as the goal of a number of research efforts. These workshops highlighted the UCD and SE (Software Engineering gaps and the importance of addressing them (van Harmelen et al., 1997; Artim et al., 1998; Seffah and Hayne, 1999; Nunes and e Cunha, 2000; Gulliksen et al., 1998; Gulliksen et al., 2001; Harning and Vanderdonckt, 2003; Kazman et al., 2003; John et al., 2004b). The starting point of all these workshops was the two workshops organized by van Harmelen et al at CHI'97 and CHI'98 conferences on Object-Oriented Models in User Interface Design and on incorporating Task Analysis Into Commercial And Industrial Object-Oriented Systems Development (van Harmelen and Wilson, 1997; Artim et al., 1998).

As will be detailed in this chapter, the conclusions of these investigations brought to light some of the major integration issues, including:

■ Extending software engineering artefacts for user interface specification, such as annotating use cases with task descriptions (Constantine and Lockwood, 1999; Rosson, 1999; Cockburn, 1997; Dayton et al., 1996),

■ Enhancing object-oriented software engineering notations and models (Nunes and e Cunha, 2000; Artim et al., 1998; Kruchten, 1999; da Silva and Paton, 2001).

■ Possible extensions of UCD methods for requirements gathering through field observations and interviews, deriving a conceptual design model from scenario, task models and use cases (Rosson, 1999; Paternò, 2001; Benyon and Macaulay,

2002) and using personae (Cooper and Reimann, 2000) as a way to understand and model end-users.

■ New methodologies for interactive systems design such as those introduced by Nielsen (1995, 1993), Mayhew (1999), and Roberts (1998), as well as approaches complementing existing methodologies (Constantine and Lockwood, 1999; Kruchten, 1999).

We will review the these different issues and the frameworks proposed for integrating UCD and SE in the following sections.

3.2 DEVELOPMENT PROCESSES

HCI practitioners and researchers have proposed a number of development processes that take into account the particular problems encountered in the engineering of highly interactive systems. Examples of the large number of methodologies are the Star Lifecycle (Hix and Hartson, 1993), LUCID ("Logical User-Centered Interface Design" method of Smith and Dunckly, 1998), the Usability Engineering Lifecycle (Mayhew, 1999), Usage-Centered Design (Constantine, 1999), SANE Toolkit for cognitive modeling and user-centered design (Bosser et al., 1992), SEP (for user-centered requirements using scenarios) (McGraw, 1997) and IBM-OVID (Object, View, Interaction and Design) (Roberts, 1998; see also Roberts, chapter 11 in this book).

Reviewing of all these approaches would go beyond the scope of this chapter. Some of these methods, and in particular those aiming to bridge object-oriented models, scenarios, and task models are detailed in Van Harmelen (1997). In the following sections, we focus some of the main approaches, namely scenario-based approach (Carroll, 2000), contextual design (Beyer and Holtzblatt, 1998), the star lifecycle (Hix and Hartson, 1993), the usability engineering lifecycle (Mayhew, 1999), and usage-centered design (Constantine and Lockwood, 1999). We also refer the reader to Roberts' recent coverage of the OVID and IBM's approaches (see Roberts, chapter 11 in this book) and the Cognetic's corporation's LUCID framework[1].

3.2.1 Scenario-Based Design

Carroll and Rosson (Carroll, 2000; Rosson and Carroll, 2002) developed a usability engineering approach centered around different stages of scenario definition (see Figure 3.2). Scenarios are not a novel concept. They are known by both the human factors community, for conducting task analysis, and by the software engineering community, as instances of use-cases. However, the scenario-based usability engineering process places a much greater emphasis, and provides greater details on their role during the early phases of the software lifecycle.

Scenarios are used for clarifying usability requirements and for driving the iterative design process. Scenarios describe an existing or envisioned system from the perspective of one or more real or realistic users. They are used to capture the goals,

---

[1]See http://www.cognetics.com/lucid/index.html.

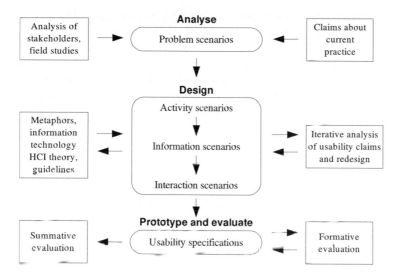

Figure 3.2 Carroll and Rosson's scenario-based framework (adapted from Carroll and Rosson, 2002)

intentions, and reactions of the user. Carroll attributes several merits to scenarios, in particular improving the communication between users, designers and stakeholders. As previously mentioned, communication with different groups involved in the design process is one of the major integration obstacles for UCD methods. Because scenarios are formulated in plain natural language, they have the advantage of being understood both by users and designers. This enables all project participants to share in the design process and discuss potential solutions.

Claims are the second core concept of scenario-based design (see section 3.4.4). Claims are developed in parallel to scenarios. The core elements that are addressed in a scenario are listed with their potential advantages and drawbacks. This clarifies which effects each element has on the usability of the system. If the drawbacks of an element outweigh the advantages, it is usually discarded.

3.2.2 Contextual Design

Contextual design, developed by Beyer and Holtzblatt (Beyer, 1998), stresses the behavioral aspects of the system design process. In their view, almost all of the system design process is driven by these aspects. Software requirements engineering, as a subsequent phase, is viewed as a response to the systems design process. In other words, the complete system design process should be an input to the software requirements engineering process. The key activities of contextual design are: Observe and interview the customer, construct and consolidate work models, redesign work models, and design the system.

Beyer and Holtzblatt (Beyer, 1998) emphasize that "the ability to see, manipulate, and design a process for delivering systems is a fundamental skill when it comes to establishing their techniques in software development processes". However, they have provided only very generic recommendations for adapting and tailoring the overall approach to different project configurations. They recommend for example 'to recognize which parts are critical and which are less necessary in each case', 'what works for a two-person team won't work for a fifteen person team', 'what works to design a strategy for a new market venture won't work for the next iteration of a 10-year old system', 'tailor things you pick up to your problem, team and organization' and finally 'what you do with it is up to you' (Beyer, 1998).

3.2.3   Star Lifecycle

The star lifecycle proposed by Hix and Hartson (1993), focuses on usability evaluation as the hub process activity. Placed around this central task are the following activities: (1) system, task, functionality, user analysis, requirements and usability specifications, (2) design, design representation and rapid prototyping, (3) software production and deployment. The results of each activity are subjected to an evaluation before moving on to the next process activity. It is possible to start with almost any development activity. The bi-directional links between the central usability evaluation task and all other process activities cause the graphical representation of the model to assume a star shape.

One of the drawbacks of this approach is outlined by Hix and Hartson (1993). Project managers tend to have problems with the highly iterative nature of the model. They find it difficult to decide when a specific iteration is completed, thus complicating the management of resources and limiting their ability to control the overall progress of the development process. An obvious solution to this problem is to establish control mechanisms such as quantitative usability goals that serve as stopping rules.

Hix and Hartson give some basic advice on tailoring the overall approach to a specific development context. They suggest a top down approach if the development team has some experience with and prior knowledge of the target system structure. Otherwise they favour a more experimental bottom-up approach. They suggest that the overall approach should be configured to accommodate the size of the project, the number of people involved, and the management style. They explicitly emphasize the necessity to view usability engineering as a process, but they agree that the design phase is one of the least understood development activities. They provide special methods and notations to support the process. For example, the user action notation (UAN) specifies user interaction in a way that is easily readable and yet unambiguous for implementing the actual interface. Usability specification tables are employed for defining and tracing quantitative usability goals.

3.2.4   Usability Engineering Lifecycle

Proposed by Deborah Mayhew, the usability engineering lifecycle is an attempt to redesign the complete software development process around usability engineering knowledge, methods, and activities (Mayhew, 1999). This process starts with a structured requirements analysis concerning usability issues. The data gathered from the requirements analysis is used to define explicit, measurable usability goals for the proposed system. The usability engineering lifecycle accomplishes the defined usability goals via an iteration of usability engineering methods such as conceptual model design, user interface mock-ups, prototyping and usability testing. The iterative process terminates if the usability goals have been met or the resources allocated for the task have been consumed.

As outlined by Mayhew (1999), the usability engineering lifecycle has been successfully applied in various projects. However, some general drawbacks were discovered by Mayhew during these case studies. One key concern is that redesigning the overall development process around usability issues often poses a problem to the organizational culture of software engineering organizations. The well-established development processes of an organization cannot easily be turned into human-centered processes during a single project. Furthermore, development teams often have insufficient knowledge to perform the UCD activities, which hampers the establishment of UCD activities in the engineering processes. Precisely how the UCD activities proposed in the usability engineering lifecycle should be integrated smoothly into engineering processes practiced by software development organizations was declared by Mayhew to be an open research issue.

Mayhew names several success factors for practicing UCD. First, all project team members should carry out UCD process steps. Mayhew stresses the importance of ultimately formalizing UCD within a development organization and methodology. Project team participation is necessary and having a design guru on board is not enough.

3.2.5   Usage-Centered Design

Usage-centered design, developed by Constantine and Lockwood (1999), is based on a process model called the activity model for usage-centered design (see figure 3.3). The activity model describes a concurrent UCD process that starts with the activities of collaborative requirements modeling, task modeling, and domain modeling in order to elicit basic requirements of the planned software system. The requirements analysis phase is followed by the design activities of interface content modeling and implementation modeling. These activities are continuously repeated until the system passes the usability inspections carried out after each iteration. The design and test activities are paralleled by help system and documentation development and standards definition for the proposed system. This general framework of activities is supplemented by special methods like essential use case models or user role maps.

Constantine and Lockwood provide many case studies where usage centered design was successfully applied, yet they encountered many of the same organizational obstacles as Mayhew (Mayhew, 1999) when integrating their UCD approach into the software engineering processes in practice. They propose that 'new practices, processes, and tools have to be introduced into the organization and then spread beyond the point of introduction'. A straightforward solution to these problems is the establishment of training courses for all participants of UCD activities offered by external consultants. However, this solution is regarded as time consuming and cost intensive in the long run. Also, it tends to have only a temporary effect and thus does not promote organizational learning in UCD design methods. Constantine and Lockwood conclude that it is necessary to build up an internal body of knowledge concerning

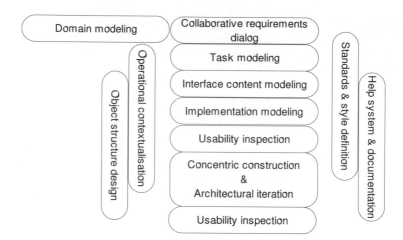

Figure 3.3   Constantine and Lockwood's usage-centered design (adapted from Constantine and Lockwood, 1999)

UCD methods, best practices and tools, in a way that is tailored to the needs of the development organization.

3.2.6   ISO Standards 13407

This review of process oriented integration of UCD and SE would be incomplete without mentioning the ISO 13407 standard (ISO/IEC, 1999). This standard defines the characteristics of what a user-centered development project must hold. It does not define a user-centered process by itself, only its characteristics. Neither is it meant to be a replacement, but instead it is intended to suggest a number of complementary means of addressing usability engineering issues.

A total of 36 activities are identified for the "human-centered design" framework (Maguire, 2001). They are classified into five categories that represent different phases of the development lifecycle: (1) planning, (2) context of use analysis, (3) requirements analysis (4) design, and (5) evaluation. Example of such activities for each respective phases are *usability planning and scoping*, *task analysis*, *scenarios of use*, *paper prototyping*, and *participatory evaluation*. ISO 13407 can also be used in conjunction with ISO TR 18529 for assessing the development process according to the "usability maturity model" (Earthy et al, 2001).

3.2.7   The Status UCD and SE Processes in Reality

The UCD processes we briefly surveyed provide frameworks for planning the software development processes and activities. How widespread they are used, and how deeply they affect the software development and management processes remains an open question.

Jerome and Kazman's chapter in this book (4) suggest that their penetration in the real world of software engineering is relatively low. Roberts (chapter 11) and Vredenburg

(2003) point out the importance of UCD and the OVID methodology at IBM, but there is no quantitative figures to assess the impact in reality. There are compelling accounts that some UCD processes are adopted and that they drive the whole development process. Some examples can be found in Rosson and Carroll's (2002) or in Landauer's book (1995). However, such examples do not constitute evidence of a trend itself. Our own experience is that the application of UCD processes remain an exception in general.

Our own assessment is that what is likely a mainstream practice is the adoption of some HCI practices, such as usability testing. Such fundamental UCD activities are probably widespread in many projects and corporations, but the whole software development process does not necessarily qualify as a UCD process.

While this section covered processes and activities, we now turn to another approach of integrating UCD and SE that relies on artefacts and documents.

3.3 ARTEFACTS

Besides activities, artefacts—the intermediate and final deliverables of software development project—are the elements that characterize an SE methodology. A number of researchers have attempted to identify artefacts that can help bridge UCD and SE approaches and techniques. They have looked for similarities and complementarity that could help merging typical UCD and SE approaches. We will focus on artefacts around scenarios (Carroll, 2000, Benyon, 2002), use cases (Cockburn, 1997; Seffah, 1999; Constantine, 1999), object-oriented notations such as UML (Paterno, 2001; Krutchen, 1999; da Silva, 2001; Markopoulos, 2000) and task models (Artim, 1998; Dayton, 1996; Rosson, 1999).

These investigations demonstrate that in use case-driven software development, human-centered design processes in general and task analysis approaches in particular are highly compatible. This may be considered as a starting point for cross-pollinating functional and user requirements engineering techniques and tools. For example, user centered requirement artefacts such as task and user models can substantially improve certain basic weaknesses of the functional requirements approach. One weakness addressed by the user-centered approach is in identifying the context of use.

3.3.1 Scenarios as a Vehicle for Bridging Object Oriented Analysis and Design

As an artefact for capturing user requirements, scenarios have been promoted both in HCI (Carroll, 2000) and software engineering (Jarke, 1999). However the concept of scenarios has not been consistently defined. Jarke (1999) proposed to clarify the purpose and manner of using scenarios in the modeling process, since scenarios can be used in very different manners. Jarke points out that scenarios are used in software engineering as intermediate design artefacts while Carroll argued that scenarios could be used as a driving force in the entire design process.

Rosson (1999) suggests enhancing the object-oriented analysis and designing approach with a scenario-based approach. Once scenarios are completed, she proposes first extracting elements that are potential computational objects, and then organizing them as a network of collaborating objects. The next step is to focus on a specific object and try to assign functionality to it. This object-by-object analysis is supported by the Point-Of-View Browser that maintains user-relative descriptions of each object. The communication approach is middle-out, since it iteratively elaborates a set of user tasks (described in user interaction scenarios) in two directions: toward networks of collaborating computational objects on the one hand, and toward detailed user interaction episodes on the other. This is the opposite of prototyping tools such as Visual Basic, which are outside in, because the focus is on screen design.

Such an approach guarantees a good object model as well as satisfying the need to take into account the user's point of view. It also addresses our main concern: The incorporation of the user's needs in the software development process. However, in this technique the user interface design relies only on the user's description of their tasks and usability claims. Rosson already determined that this would cause mismatches with the user's view, which she says to be minor compared to the need of structure in the task model (needed for evocativeness). She defines an intermediate philosophy. The aim is not the user and their needs, or a good structure of the software; the aim is to have a good midpoint construct that helps establish a good interface as well as a good program structure. This solution did not seem to develop in the industry market, perhaps because it is too different from the methods currently in use.

Similar to Rosson's work, Jarke (1999) also proposed to clarify the purpose and manner in which to use scenarios in the modeling process. He defines scenarios as constructs that describe a possible set of events that might reasonably take place; they offer "middle-ground abstraction between models and reality". Scenarios are typically used in four approaches:

- Capture a sequence of work activities

- View a sequence of representations or interfaces

- View the purpose of users in the use of the software

- View the lifecycle of the product.

One of the major weaknesses of scenarios as an integration artefact is the fact that informal representations of scenarios, generally statements in natural language, are often insufficient for overcoming the difficulty of communication between users, developers, usability expert and stakeholders with differing backgrounds. Scenarios in natural languages suffer from ambiguity and imprecision. Formal representations of scenarios provide a solution to the ambiguity problem and facilitate formal proof and analysis of properties of requirements. However these formal specifications are often difficult to understand and develop for newcomers to this area. A trade-off is needed between the precision of formal representations and the ease of communication of scenarios in the context of accomplishing a task. Designers and users need to able to develop and reason about scenario descriptions throughout the development lifecycle in a variety of media, purposes, and views, either to discuss existing options or to stimulate imagination.

3.3.2 Bridging Task Analysis and Object-Oriented Models

In model-based task analysis as practiced in HCI, the objective is normally to achieve a generic and thus abstract model of the user tasks, typically in a hierarchical form of goals, sub-goals and methods for achieving the hierarchy of goals. In object-oriented development, use cases are often employed in gathering functional requirements. Can task analysis models be improved by use case techniques? Can use cases be improved by the incorporation or consideration of formal task models? Are there ways of integrating the two approaches? Such questions have been widely discussed (Dayton, 1996, Artim, 1998; Seffah and Hayne, 1999; Forbrig, 1999; Engelberg, 2001).

Cockburn (1997), for one, recognizes that use-cases are not well defined and many different uses coexist, with differences in purpose, content, plurality and structure. He proposes to structure them with respect to goals or tasks. Although this approach may appear unusual as a structure for requirements, it follows a natural hierarchical organization typical of task analysis techniques (Dayton, 1996). The goals are structured as a tree containing "Summary goals" as high-level goals, and "User goals" as atomic goals (e.g. performing summary goal A involves performing user goal A1 then A2).

3.3.3 Extending UML Notation for User Interface Modeling

Several research investigations have been conducted with a view to improving the unified modeling language (UML) for user interfaces and interactive systems engineering. Nunes and Cunha (2000) proposed the Whitewater Interactive System Development with Objects Models (WISDOM), as a lightweight software engineering methodology that uses UML to support Human-Computer interaction techniques. WISDOM is evolutionary in the sense that the project evolves incrementally through an iterative process. A novel aspect of this work is the addition of extensions to UML to accommodate task analysis. The modelling constructs have to accommodate:

- A description of users and their relevant characteristics

- A description of user behavior/intentions in performing the envisioned or supported task

- A specification of the abstract and concrete user interface.

WISDOM applies many changes and additions to UML to support this: change of class stereotype boundary, control and entity; add of task, interaction space, class stereotype, add-ons of the associations communicate, subscribe, refine task, navigate, contains, etc. But concerns arise about the frequent communication misadventures between HCI and Software Engineering specialists, as well as the tendency to misinterpret constructs such as use-cases, caused by different cultures having a different understanding of a versatile language like UML.

In the same vein as this work, Markopoulos (2000) and da Silva (2001) also proposed extensions to UML for interactive systems. In contrast, a task is represented as classes in WISDOM and by activities in the UMLi framework proposed by (da Silva, 2001). Mori, Paterno et al (2002) also suggested an extension of their task modeling notation, CTT (Concurrent Task Tree).

The above research shows that UML suffers from a lack of support for UI modeling. For example, class diagrams are not entirely suitable for modeling interaction, which is a major component in HCI. The IBM-OVID methodology is an attempt to provide an iterative process for developing an object-oriented model by refining and transforming a task model (Roberts, 1998).

3.3.4   Augmenting Use Cases for User Interface Prototyping

Artim (1998), Constantine and Lockwood (1999), and Kruchten (1999) all tried to augment use cases to support interface design and prototyping. This integration is based on the synchronization of the problem specification and the solution specification; these two specifications are updated at each iteration through an assessment of impact of the changes in the models.

Theoretically, having a consistent use cases model that provides simple views for any actor and automatically includes the user's concerns should be enough to enable the software engineers to keep track of the user's needs during their design process. However, as Artim and the participants in his workshop (Artim, 1998) pointed out, the culture of software engineering does not include collaborating with the user in the process of building a better system. These sociological forces within development teams severely limit the user's impact in the development of the system, thus providing a system that fits to user interface specifications, rather than optimizing the fit to the user's needs. Thus, even though the development method directly determines the product being created, it is not the only factor.

Constantine and Lockwood (1999) try to harness the potential of use-cases with the goal of replacing task models and scenarios, which are generally proposed as a starting point for UI prototyping. They structure their method into five kinds of artefacts, organizing the three center ones by a map, so we respectively have the following:

- Maps:

    - User Role Map structuring the user roles (which hold the user information),

    - Navigation Map structuring the content models (which hold the interface views),

    - Use Case Map structuring the use cases (which hold the task descriptions),

- Domain Model, which holds glossary, data and class models,

- Operational Model, which holds environmental and contextual factors.

These maps and models can be developed or enhanced concurrently, which departs from more traditional (albeit iterative) sequential approaches. In the attempt to completely specify the design methodology, they define the notion of essential use-cases. These essential use-cases aim to enhance usability by focusing on intention rather than interaction, and simplification rather than elaboration. The use-cases provide an inventory of user intentions and system responsibilities, focusing only on information considered essential and hiding unneeded information; this approach helps use-cases adapt to eventual technological or environmental changes. Constantine gives a structure to essential use-cases, at the same time defining the syntax of the narratives. He also acknowledges the limitations of essential use-cases in the domain of software engineering; for this reason he advocates the use of essential use-cases only in the core process, where usability characteristics are essential.

Krutchen (1999) proposes to add a new artefact to the Rational Unified Process: the use-case storyboard. This artefact provides a high-level view of dynamic window relationships such as window navigation paths and other navigation paths between objects in the user interface. Use-case storyboards have to be written at analysis time, at the same time as the use-cases. They include many useful constructs such as:

1. Flows of events, also called storyboards. These are textual user-centered descriptions of interactions.

2. Class Diagrams. These are classes that participate in the use-cases.

3. Interaction Diagrams. These describe the collaboration between objects.

4. Usability Requirements. These are textual version of usability requirements.

5. References to the User-Interface Prototype. This is a text description of the user-interface prototype.

6. Trace dependency. This is a type of map of the use cases.

Krutchen (1999) also proposed guidelines on how to use this new construct. He recommends that a human factors expert should write these documents, because traditional software engineers will not design or use this artefact correctly, not being used to its philosophy. A big concern about this new technique comes from its practice of specifying the interface and the interactions at the beginning, rather that deriving them from the UI design, thus "putting the cart before the horse" and limiting the possibilities of the interface (Constantine, 1999). This also illustrates that use-cases can adapt to usability engineering, but there is no assurance that designers will use them adequately.

3.4 DESIGN KNOWLEDGE

In addition to efforts made by the UCD and SE communities to bridge the technical aspects of their methods, communication factors are also important. Like others (Sutcliffe, 2000; Henninger, 2000), we strongly argue that methods and tools for capturing and disseminating HCI and usability design knowledge and best practices can facilitate the integration and cross-pollination of the HCI and software engineering disciplines.

HCI has a long tradition of devising ways to capture knowledge so as to guide the design and evaluation of interactive systems. Prominent examples are guidelines (Vanderdonckt, 1999), interaction patterns (Erickson, 2000; Tidwell, 1998) and claims (Sutcliffe, 2000). Here, we summarize these methods and discuss how they can be extended to support effective integration.

3.4.1   Guidelines

Vanderdonckt, (1999) defines a guideline as "a design and/or evaluation principle to be observed in order to get and/or guarantee the usability of a user interface for a given interactive task to be carried out by a given user population in a given context". A prominent example of a guideline collection is Smith and Mosier's set of 944 general-purpose guidelines (Smith, 1986).

A detailed analysis of the validation, completeness and consistency of existing guideline collections has shown that there are a number of problems with guidelines (Vanderdonckt, 1999). Guidelines are often too simplistic or too abstract, they can be difficult to interpret and select, they can be conflicting and they often have authority issues concerning their validity. One of the reasons for these problems is that most guidelines suggest a context-independent validity framework but in fact, their applicability depends on a specific context.

The general utility of detailed design guidelines for augmenting development processes has also been questioned. We argue that the massive context information that is necessary to describe the context of use of a guideline together with the problem of conflicting guidelines makes guidelines virtually useless for developers who are not experts in usability. Hartson and Hix (1993) noted that applying guidelines to specific situations requires a higher level of expert knowledge and experience than most interaction designers have.

Although guidelines remain an important tool for teaching user interface design, their utility to professionals is questioned and, until we find better means to help people apply them in specific context, they cannot be considered a successful avenue for the integration of HCI practices and SE.

3.4.2   Style Guides

A style guide is a document that contains descriptions of the usage and style of particular interaction components such as menus, dialogue boxes and messages. Commercial style guides such Apple "Human Interface Guidelines" (Apple, 1987), the Microsoft Windows Interface Style Guide (Microsoft, 1995), or the Java Look and Feel style guide from Sun Microsystems (Sun Microsystems, 1999) are often associated with a commercially available toolkit. They can act as a basis for customized style guides that are tailored for the products of an organization.

Style guides are mainly used during development and usability inspection of user interfaces to ensure consistency of user interaction designs. The development of a style guide is an important early activity for project teams. Style guides are a useful way to capture and document design decisions and to prevent constantly revisiting these decisions.

Although more specific than guidelines, style guides suffer from many of the same problems, such as conflicts, inconsistencies, and ambiguities. Furthermore style guides are limited to a very particular type of application or computing platform. Therefore, their ability to disseminate established HCI and usability practices to a wide audience is limited.

3.4.3   HCI and Usability Design Patterns

The limitations of guidelines and style guides motivated some researchers to introduce interaction patterns, also called HCI patterns (Erickson, 2000, Tidwell, 1998). An HCI pattern is described in terms of a problem, a context and a solution. The solution is assumed to be a proven one to a stated and well-known problem. Many groups have devoted themselves to the development of patterns and patterns languages for user interface design and usability. Among the heterogeneous collections of patterns, Common Ground, Experiences and Amsterdam play a major role in this field (Tidwell, 1998).

Patterns provide more useful and specific information than guidelines, by explicitly stating the context and the problem and by providing a design rationale for the solution. Patterns contain more complex design knowledge and often several guidelines are integrated in one pattern. Patterns focus on "do this" only and therefore are constructive and less abstract.

In contrast, guidelines are usually expressed in a positive or negative form; do or don't do this. Therefore guidelines are useful for evaluation purposes. They can easily be transformed into questions for evaluating a UI.

Erickson (2000) proposed to use pattern languages as a descriptive device, a lingua franca for creating a common ground among people who lack a shared discipline or theoretical framework. In contrast, both Alexander (1977) (the father of patterns) and the software pattern community tend to use patterns more prescriptively. The software pattern community focuses on using patterns to capture accepted practice and to support generalization; Alexander's central concern is using patterns to achieve the ineffable "quality without a name," which characterizes great buildings and houses. HCI design patterns are generalizations of specific design knowledge that can increase quality of design.

Certain issues remain to be addressed in patterns and current HCI patterns languages. To begin with, there are no standards for the documentation of patterns. The Human-Computer Interaction community has no uniformly accepted pattern form. Furthermore, when patterns are documented (usually in narrative text), there are no tools to formally validate them. There should be formal reasoning and methodology behind the creation of patterns, and in turn, pattern languages. A language in computer science has syntax and semantics. None of the current pattern languages follow this principle; rather they tend to resort to narrative text formats as illustrated in the Experiences example. Finally, the interrelationships described in the patterns are static and not context-oriented. This is a major drawback since the conditions underlying the use of a pattern are related to its context of use.

3.4.4   Claims

Another approach to capturing HCI design knowledge is claims (Sutcliffe, 2000). Claims are psychologically motivated design rationales that express the advantages and disadvantages of a design as a usability issue, thereby encouraging designers to reason about trade-offs rather than accepting a single guideline or principle. Claims provide situated advice because they come bundled with scenarios of use and artefacts that illustrate applications of the claim. The validity of claims has a strong grounding in theory. This is also a weakness of claims, because each claim is situated in a specific context provided by the artefact and usage scenario. This limits the scope of any one claim to similar artefacts.

3.5   ORGANISATIONAL APPROACHES

We now turn to organisational approaches to filling the current gap between UCD and SE.

3.5.1   Evidence Based Usability Engineering

Evidence-based Usability Engineering (EBUE) is an approach that addresses the problem of the integration, adoption, and improvement of UCD methods at the organizational level (Metzker, 2003). It acknowledges that a team and an organization in general has to adopt new techniques in a progressive manner, first by recognizing and assessing the strengths of certain approaches and then by a process of selecting and refining these techniques. EBUE is art of an integrative framework - a UCD meta-model - to support measurement-based integration of usability concerns in any software engineering process.

EBUE discards the philosophy of a static, one-size-fits-all UCD process model. Instead, it proposes using a configurable pool of UCD methods. Examples of UCD methods considered for the UCD method pool are heuristic evaluations, card sorting, cognitive walkthroughs and user role maps.

Based on the characteristics of the project at hand, specific methods are selected from the UCD method pool. The selected methods form a UCD process kit, which is tailored to the characteristics of the project at hand. During the course of a project, qualitative feedback such as comments on and extensions of UCD methods is gathered from the project team and used to improve the method pool. This could be done in post-mortem sessions, which are already successfully used in software development projects to reflect on software processes (Birk, 2002). Additionally, quantitative feedback on the utility and usability of UCD methods from the perspective of the project team should be collected in the form of quick assessments. The results of such assessments are a measure of the quality of UCD methods as perceived by project team members.

The quantitative feedback is accumulated and integrated across project boundaries and used to extract relationships between UCD methods, project characteristics and the perceived utility of UCD methods. These relationships can be exploited in future projects as a body of evidence to choose optimal UCD method configurations for defined project characteristics. Figure 3.4 provides an overview of the UCD meta-process as suggested by EBUE.

The first cross-organizational studies on the acceptance of the EBUE framework by practitioners show a high level of acceptance of the approach and a good compatibility with current industrial software development practices (Metzker, 2003).

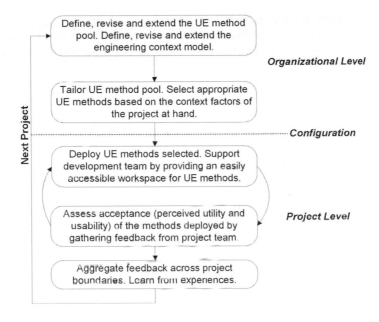

Figure 3.4   Meta-Model for institutionalizing UCD methods

In our view, adoption-centric approaches such as EBUE have a high potential impact on current software development practice, helping to overcome the lag between usability engineering research and practice.

3.5.2   Concurrent Evolution of Interface and Software Components

There is a compelling need to define a more flexible and efficient software development process that can support concurrency in the design process and requirement process. If software architecture and UI design are interdependent, as Bass and his colleagues have demonstrated (Bass and John, 2003), how should the software development process be organized? Although a better understanding of these interdependencies is emerging, it is not yet clear how to represent and coordinate them in the software development process.

3.5.3   Concurrent Processes and Cultures

Throughout most of the previous sections, we have assumed that a software engineering approach is already established in a software development team, and that the task is to determine where user-centered design techniques could be incorporated. Although this is correct in many cases, the inverse can also occur. A development process may be dominated by HCI concerns and we may fail to integrate a software engineering method into it. For example, Web site design and development is often driven by an information content management paradigm or one of graphical interface design. However, Web sites are evolving toward providing advanced features such as electronic payment and intranet services. In this context, we are moving away from a paradigm of online brochure to one where Web sites are Internet-based transactional services. Web designers have to consider new design issues such as software maintenance, quality management, security, etc.

Web development is not the sole example. To some extent, the computer gaming industry is another domain where software development is driven by non-traditional methods. In this industry, the entertainment perspective is the dominant paradigm. Role playing and user experience are often at the core of the game development cycle. Although game producers do have software engineering processes in place, it is quite common to find the production department struggling with the problem of interfacing the creative team with the developers, or struggling to implement a rigorous software quality process in a culture that thrives on creativity.

It remains an integration challenge to determine how to merge traditional software engineering techniques into a culture and a process dominated by methods inspired from other fields such as content publishing, entertainment and HCI driven approaches.

3.5.4 Supporting Continuous Improvement

The integration of HCI and SE will obviously not yield a one-size-fits-all solution. A better understanding will be required of the appropriateness of solutions to contexts. What are the factors that should be involved in adapting or improving an integration framework in a given context? This question needs to be addressed in the following four dimensions:

1. Activity, including synchronization between activities;

2. Actor, including team organizations and communication schemes;

3. Artefact, including the formats and structure of the artefacts;

4. Tool, including the use of tools to facilitate the communication.

In developing any integration framework, three types of improvements can be supported in the software development lifecycle:

Elementary improvements are modifications that affect only one element of the SDL (software development lifecycle). For example we can change a very specific artefact, and thereby indirectly change the way to perform the corresponding activity. A typical example is what Krutchen called use-case storyboards. Another elementary improvement can be the addition of usability inspection in certain activities.

Complementary improvements consist in adding new elements in the SDL. For example, we can propose a framework for using usability research methods (usability walkthrough, user testing) in the SDL. This approach complements the existing SDL and does not force a change in the structure.

Structural improvements affect the communication process or the structure of the SDL. They add a set of activities in the SDL that can change the sequence of activities. Constantine uses an outside-in communication scheme in his usage-centered design.

Nunes adopts a loose communication scheme that is only constrained by the need to support the dual model (analysis model, interaction model).

3.5.5   Agile Methods and UCD

Agile methods are gaining significant acceptance, or at least visibility, in the software engineering field, and they are also gaining adepts in industry and even in some engineering schools. The Agile approach emerged as a response to highly organized and documentation intensive processes such as RUP(©), the Rational Unified Process that is widely in use nowadays, and other proprietary processes. The claim made by the agile community is that heavy documentation and processes create latency, inefficiency, and a tendency for the development team to adhere to inappropriate requirements instead of responding to changes in their definitions. Because user requirements are particularly prone to changes as the users uncover new needs and correct their initial requirements as the software application unfolds, this claim appears to address an important issue in HCI.

Moreover, the Agile movement also emphasizes the importance of human factors in the development process as expressed by two of their four core values: (1) individuals and interactions over processes and tools, and (2) customer collaboration over contract negotiations (see http://www.agilemanifesto.org). Here, again, the agile movement appears to lean towards a user-centered approach.

In spite of these principles that suggest the approach is user-oriented, agile processes have come under criticism from the UCD community, such as this quote from Constantine (2001):

> Informants in the agile process community have confirmed what numerous colleagues and clients have reported to me. XP and the other light methods are light on the user side of software. They seem to be at their best in applications that are not GUI-intensive. As Alistair Cockburn expressed it in email to me, this "is not a weak point, it is an absence." User-interface design and usability are largely overlooked by the agile processes. With the possible exception of DSDM [(http://dsdm.org)] and FDD http://www.featuredrivendevelopment.com/, users and user interfaces are all but ignored.

Amongst the most important shortcomings addressed to agile methods, the lack of distinction between the client and the user is probably the most critical. Because clients are often represented by people from marketing or from management, user needs are often misunderstood. Moreover, Agile methods do not provide guidance on how to validate user requirements. There is no reference to principles such as those found in ISO 13407 or Maguire (Maguire, 2001b) and, thus, the resulting application could still miss important user requirements. This problem is particularly important in software designed for teamwork where social interactions and business processes are difficult to anticipate; the problem is also common in software with a high degree of novelty.

However, recent efforts are addressing the shortcomings in agile methodologies by integrating UCD principles. Patton (2002), for one, reports a successful experience in integrating the interaction design approach in an agile approach already in place. But more research is required to arrive at a comprehensive integration of agile approaches and UCD.

3.6 CONCLUSION

In this chapter, we highlighted some of the obstacles to integrating HCI and usability concerns in mainstream software development. We surveyed many of the approaches proposed for filling in the current gaps between HCI, usability and software engineering. The fundamental questions addressed in this chapter are:

1. How can the software engineering lifecycle be re-designed so that end users and usability engineers can participate actively?

2. Which usability artefacts are relevant and what are their added values and relationships to software engineering artefacts?

3. What are the usability techniques and activities for gathering and specifying these relevant usability artefacts?

4. How can these usability artefacts, techniques and activities be presented to software engineers, as well as integrated in the software development lifecycle in general? What types of notations and tool support are required?

The frameworks summarized in this chapter provide partial answers to these questions. Although the answers are not complete, they are useful for usability and software specialists who are interested in the development of methodologies and standards, who have researched or developed specific user-centered design techniques or who have worked with software development methodologies. They offer insights in how to integrate user-centered best practices and user experiences with software engineering methodologies.

Patterns and use cases are useful artefacts for bridging gaps between HCI and SE. Boundary objects serve each discipline in its own work and also act as a communication tool to coordinate work across disciplines. For example, a designer uses patterns to explore design ideas in the space of presentation and navigation; a usability expert uses them to perform an early usability test; a software engineer uses them as part of the specification of the interface code. The patterns perform different functions for each discipline, yet provide common ground for sharing knowledge.

However, we have not covered all aspects of integration. In particular, the cultural gaps between the SE and HCI is an important aspect that is not addressed here. We refer the reader to the chapters in this book by Jerome and Kazman (chapter 4), Sutcliffe (chapter 5), and also Blomkvist (chapter 12). We could also have raised the issue of academic and professional training, which are key factors to cultural and interdisciplinary team integration. It is our own teaching experience that some software engineering students are enlightened by sunddenly discovering the importance of human factors in designing interactive software. Yet, most of them will have very little training in HCI. The same could be said about software project managers who are often the ones responsible for implementing the development process, defining and staffing the activities, etc. Our knowledge of software management processes indicates that it suffers a lack of awareness of the need to integrate UCD and SE practices. All these issues would deserve to be covered.

Finally, we believe a forum is required for promoting and improving HCI and usability engineering techniques and software engineering approaches in the two communities. An example of this type of forum would be to combine the IEEE-ICSE and ACM-SIGCHI conferences for one year where avenues for:

- Sharing ideas about potential and innovative ways to cross-pollinate the two disciplines

- Disseminating successful and unsuccessful experiences in how to integrate usability into the software engineering lifecycle, in different sizes of organization

- Building a tighter fit between HCI and software engineering practices and research.

Acknowledgements

The authors would like to express their sincere thanks to all of the participants in the workshops that they organized over the last five years. Thanks also to the National Science and Engineering Research Council of Canada and Daimler Chrysler, Software Technology Centre, for their financial support. We are also grateful to Fran cois Aubin for sharing with us figure 3.1's perspective.

4 SURVEYING THE SOLITUDES: AN INVESTIGATION INTO THE RELATIONSHIPS BETWEEN HUMAN COMPUTER INTERACTION AND SOFTWARE ENGINEERING IN PRACTICE

Bill Jerome, Rick Kazman

Human Computer Interaction Institute, Carnegie Mellon University; ITM Department, University of Hawaii and Software Engineering Institute, Carnegie Mellon University

Abstract

In this chapter, we analyze the state of software engineering and Human-Computer Interaction research and practice. In particular we are interested in the overlaps and interfaces between these two influential fields. We begin with an analysis of the state of the research that lies at the conjunction of these two areas, and then present the results of a survey that examines how HCI practitioners and software engineers interact in industry. The main findings of the survey are disturbing: there is a substantial lack of mutual understanding among software engineers and HCI specialists, and the results from research do not appear to be strongly influencing this interaction. Furthermore, there appear to be important differences in how software engineers and HCI practitioners view their interaction in the software engineering life cycle. The final, and perhaps most serious, finding of this chapter is that software engineers and HCI

A. Seffah (eds.), Human-Centered Software Engineering – Integrating Usability
in the Development Process, 59–70.

practitioners tend to interact and communicate with each other late in the software life cycle; too late to fix the most fundamental usability problems.

4.1 INTRODUCTION

Almost half of the software in systems being developed today and thirty-seven to fifty percent of efforts throughout the software life cycle are related to the system's user interface (Myers and Rosson, 1992). For this reason the issues, methods and practices from the field of human-computer interaction (HCI) affect the overall process of software engineering (SE) tremendously. Given the enormous efforts that go in to implementing the user interface portion of a system, one would naturally assume that software engineers (typically in charge of the overall system development) would need to work closely with and interact early and often with HCI experts. One would be wrong in this assumption.

Despite the strong need amongst development organizations to practice and apply effective HCI methods and integrate these smoothly into the overall product development life cycle, it is evident that there still exist major gaps between suggested practice, primarily coming from academic communities, and how software is actually developed in industry. And, not surprisingly, there are major gaps of communication between HCI and SE groups within software development organizations.

More specifically, the application of HCI methods continues to be an afterthought in the development of software despite many suggested practices of tightly intertwining HCI methods with software development processes. There is an apparent lack of overlap between current formally defined SE processes and HCI methods. Software engineers' and HCI practitioners' misconceptions about each others' fields further exacerbate the problems created by misalignments between SE processes and HCI methods. To ensure that software is developed efficiently while guaranteeing optimal usability, it is important to minimize problems resulting from these points of misalignment.

This chapter identifies a number of problematic issues in the relationship between the fields of SE and HCI through discussion of the current state of the intersection between the two respective fields. Discussion of these issues is broken into two sections: the first section consists of a background overview of the current state of the research at the intersection of the SE and HCI fields. The second section discusses SE and HCI in practice by examining how SE and HCI professionals interact in practice, in addition to assessing their respective knowledge of each others' fields. Data in the second section is drawn from the results of a survey that we administered to 96 SE and HCI professionals — 63 HCI practitioners and 33 software engineers.

We will begin by looking at the state of the research in both fields (obviously at a high level of granularity) to try to gain an appreciation for the level of mutual understanding and cooperation that is possible when trying to combine these two fields.

4.2 THE STATE OF THE RESEARCH

While HCI, as a distinct field of study, is not as old as SE, the processes and tools for the design and development of interactive systems have steadily expanded and matured. The final goal of this evolution is a true engineering discipline (Shaw, 1990) for achieving system usability. HCI methods focus on developing systems that support users to accomplish their tasks effectively, efficiently, and with high satisfaction (Hefley et al., 1994), and to do this within the project's budget and schedule constraints. This is consistent with being, or attempting to be, an engineering discipline. How does this then relate to software engineering?

To understand and gauge the amount of mutual understanding between the SE and HCI fields, we begin by examining the research trends in both fields, concentrating on the intersection between the fields.

Historically, the most obvious ties between SE and HCI manifested themselves through software design patterns and architectures for interactive systems, such as the Model View Control (MVC) paradigm originally applied to GUI development in SmallTalk (Krasner and Pope, 1988), and the Presentation Abstraction Control (PAC) pattern (Coutaz, 1987). Other advancements in formally defined software architectures continue to influence user interface development in both SE and HCI (Jambon et al., 2001).

In the evolution of HCI establishing itself as a distinct discipline within computer science, a number of methods have developed that have focused more on product development—contextual inquiry and design, for example—as opposed to pure R&D such as hardware interaction. Such methods focus on the processes used to develop artefacts that directly address end user concerns (Whiteside et al., 1988). More recent literature (1998 though 2002) including publications of the International Conference on Software Engineering (ICSE) workshops on SE-HCI tends to show HCI embracing methods for designing software akin to product design methods typically used in human factors. Semi-formal Human-Centered Design (HCD) methods, for example, attempt to gather software requirements data through forms of ethnographic interviewing and observation before SE processes begin (Metzker and Offergeld, 2001) and throughout the software development phases. Traditional HCD methods have been modified for HCI to cope with organizational obstacles typically found in industrial software development organizations. For example, maintaining a degree of emotive sensitivity towards users needs is addressed through participatory design and in designing for cultural aspects. Formerly only associated with HCI, these semi-formal methods of design appear to be becoming increasingly relevant in research relating to both SE and HCI (Makarainen et al., 2001).

GOMS modeling (Gray et al., 1993) has proven to be a powerful example of HCI adopting structured methods as a way of performing task analysis. While not an adoption of SE processes, it is a clear illustration of HCI methods approaching stricter, more scientific basis. These models have proven their value via empirical methodologies, further legitimizing the formal nature of HCI as a field.

Formal, empirical methods used in gathering requirements and specifications for developing user interfaces include the MAD (Scapin and Pierret-Goldbreich, 1990) and the User Action Notation (UAN) (Hix and Hartson, 1993); or Hierarchical Task Analysis (HTA) (Paternò, 2001) and GOMS (Gray et al., 1993), used for formal task-based evaluation and modeling. Such methods continue to be commonly referenced in current HCI research, although this does not imply widespread use outside of the research community. In fact, there are a growing number of attempts to use (and extend) the UML as a tool to help link these existing formal HCI methods with more broadly accepted SE practices. Already frequently used in object-oriented software development, the UML is a widely embraced standard. The UML provides a lingua franca through which it is conceptually possible to link SE development practice to HCI practice (Paternò, 2001). This is done through object models derived from task analysis and modeling (Artim et al., 1998).

However, attempts to find a means to directly link SE processes to HCI methods extend beyond the UML. HCD methods have been integrated into the software development process by applying the framework of the Usability Maturity Model (UMM) (Earthy, 1999; Metzker and Offergeld, 2001). This reference model has a number of HCD activities from different human-centered design approaches. The UMM is based in part on the Capability Maturity Model (CMM) from the Software Engineering Institute (Paulk et al., 1993). The CMM defines five maturity levels for software processes and describes the processes that are typically in place in organizations at each maturity level. The CMM offers specific guidance about how to appropriately conduct software development by prioritizing improvement activities. Similarly, the UMM enables usability professionals to maintain an efficient process by using usability data to determine which HCI methods should be used during which stage of software development. The UMM makes a concerted attempt to create a model that mimics the CMM. The CMM benefits both HCI practitioners and software engineers by offering a means by which both groups can work in parallel on the CMM and the UMM respectively since their process models are similar to each other. These parallel activities can benefit both groups by allowing and managing process overlaps in SE and in the application of HCI methods. The similarities between the CMM and the UMM potentially make it possible for both sides to understand and interact with each other more easily.

Computer supported collaborative work (CSCW) has recently developed as a bridge between SE and HCI. The HCI approach towards CSCW has begun to necessitate a SE influence because of the complicated architectures required for CSCW systems (Dewan, 1996; Prakash et al., 1999). Systems such as desktop sharing, application sharing, shared virtual worlds, and remote file management all require complicated software architectures, bringing SE to bear on the subject (Dourish, 1999).

There are a number of other topics being heavily researched that necessitate a strong bridge between SE and HCI: toolkit development, new input/output devices, user interface plasticity, ubiquitous computing, wearable computers, and mobile computing. These areas are relatively new to computing research in general; both the SE and HCI camps are involved more or less from the inception of this research and so overlap in work being done is not surprising here. These topics continue to be major research areas for SE and HCI.

This has been a high level view of the state of the research that bridges HCI and SE. Any such overview must necessarily be brief and high level. The point is not to present an exhaustive overview of all research at the intersection of SE and HCI, but to point out the major themes in the research, as a guide to investigating how it has been affecting practice (or not). Such research is commonly 3-10 years ahead of practice. While it is important and necessary for researchers to lead, in an engineering discipline we must also look long and hard at the current state of the practice. This is important for two reasons:

1. understanding the state of the practice helps us gauge how effective and influential past research has been on changing the way that software professionals develop their products. There is no point leading where no-one is willing to follow, and

2. this feedback can guide and focus the research community in our future efforts. Understanding the state of the practice points out areas that are in immediate and pressing need of assistance.

This need to examine software development practices leads to the second major portion of this chapter. In this portion we take a close look at software development practices and attitudes within software development organizations, from the dual perspectives of software engineers and HCI practitioners.

4.3   THE STATE OF THE PRACTICE

In an effort to assess the current state of SE and HCI knowledge and practices in industry, we electronically distributed a pair of surveys to groups of software professionals from both of the disciplines. The survey was distributed in two forms to the two different audiences; one survey was aimed at software engineers, and one was aimed at HCI practitioners.

The surveys attempted to gauge each individual's knowledge of their own field as well as the field with which he or she was not directly involved. In one survey we asked software engineers about their knowledge of HCI, and in the other we asked HCI practitioners about their knowledge of SE. 96 software professionals completed the survey in total (63 HCI practitioners and 33 software engineers), which was delivered via a web site. We solicited involvement in the survey via electronic mailing lists to the SE and HCI practitioner communities such as the British HCI Group, various SIGCHI chapters, the International Software Engineering Research Network (ISERN) mailing list, as well as Carnegie Mellon's HCI and SE alumni mailing lists. Participation was voluntary and unpaid.

Each survey consisted of twenty questions, eighteen of which contained a multiple choice component. Most questions were single-select options, although some allowed respondents to select multiple responses. Fifteen of the questions contained at least one open text field for free responses related to the question, such as places to specify details when selecting "Other" as an answer to a question. Respondents were asked to identify their field of work and were asked about their general knowledge of HCI or SE principles. Software engineers were asked primarily about HCI principles and vice-versa in an effort to gauge the level of familiarity the respondent had with the field that they are not primarily involved in practicing. Following these questions, respondents were asked how their organizations involved software engineers and HCI specialists on projects (if at all) via a series of questions regarding product life cycles and the frequency of interactions with the other group.

What we found from the surveys was disturbing: the application and adoption of methods and processes from SE and HCI research has not yet trickled down into industry. Not only has the research not reached industry, but the collaboration between software engineers and HCI practitioners has not yet grown as it has in the respective research areas. The two fields are still relative islands. The usability engineering life cycle and the software engineering life cycle are not aligned—sometimes they even use different names for the same activities. And the two groups of practitioners even have differing perceptions regarding how often they communicate.

4.4   KNOWLEDGE OF SE AND HCI

An overwhelming majority of these professionals learn about each other's field not through taking courses or through reading published material, but rather through personal contact with other professionals.

12 of the 54 HCI practitioners answered they didn't keep up with SE at all. In fact, only 13 of the 63 practitioners claim to have a degree in HCI or a related field, and only 5 others claimed to have taken classes in HCI methods. Thus, the vast majority of our HCI practitioners are self-taught. The HCI practitioners' knowledge of software engineering follows much the same pattern: 35 of 62 respondents claim that their knowledge stems from interactions with software professionals, 5 have a degree in software engineering, and 6 have taken classes in the field.[1]

Similarly 18 of 26 software engineers who answered the question said they learned about HCI entirely through informal processes. A mere 6 had a degree in software engineering and a further 2 claimed to have taken classes in the field. Their knowledge of HCI was also relatively informally grounded: 10 of 31 claimed that they learned about HCI through interaction with HCI professionals (who, as we have seen from the previous discussion are themselves seldom formally trained in the field), only 3 software engineers, fewer than 10%, reported having taken a class in HCI, and the remainder learned from books and "other". Furthermore, our sampling, if anything, should have been biased in favor of academics, and practitioners who have had academic training (since we used several academic mailing lists, e.g. alumni lists, in our dissemination of the survey). Given this potential bias these results seem even more troubling.

We also asked our two groups of survey respondents "What methods or channels of communication do you use to keep abreast of research developments in [the other field]?" The results were, from our perspective, not encouraging. 33% of software engineers (8 of 24 relied on ad hoc means, to keep up with HCI: "Personal communication with field specialists". A full 38% (9 of 24 replied "none"; they did not keep up at all with HCI. The HCI practitioners answered similarly, saying that they kept abreast of developments in SE primarily through personal communications (28 of 54 or 52%) or "none" (12 of 54 or 22%). Only a small minority of practitioners in both groups read journals or mailing lists, or attended conferences.

---

[1] Note that we have made no attempt to analyze these numbers for statistical significance. This is because the sample populations were not controlled for; for example, we did not draw track whether the SEs and HCI practitioners came from a single corporation or, more likely, from a wide variety of corporations. Hence we do not feel that any statistical inferences made from such a diverse population would be interesting. We have therefore chosen to simply present summarizations of the data as we received it, and leave it to the reader to determine whether they agree with the conclusions that we draw from the available evidence.

4.5 WORKING TOGETHER IN THE WORKPLACE

However, the majority of our survey respondents reported a distinct separation between the roles of software engineers and HCI practitioners. The literature in both SE and HCI strongly advises that professionals from both fields work closely together in the design and implementation of software. Yet, according to our survey results, most professionals *do not* closely collaborate with other professionals outside of their area.

For example, we have evidence that key software design decisions that affect the user interface are made by software engineers without consulting HCI practitioners (13 of 19, or 68% indicated that this was the case). An even greater percentage, 91% (52 of 57), of HCI practitioners believed that software engineers were making crucial design decisions without consulting the HCI practitioners. Why did they do such things? Several of our respondents claimed that time constraints often prevent software engineers from waiting for HCI data to be collected—and that HCI data could potentially affect the underlying software architecture. One respondent said that the reason some HCI recommendations were not implemented was that ". . . they were an issue of time to implement, not ability to implement." There are two implications that arise from the responses to this question: 1) there is a large disconnect in the perceptions of software engineers and HCI practitioners regarding their shared development process; and 2) a substantial number of user interface design decisions are made primarily by software engineers, and these decisions are made without the benefit of usability data.

There is also a large difference of opinion regarding how internal testing of the usability of software is conducted. 50% of software engineers (14 of 28) answered that "Quality assurance handles usability". A further 10 of 28 answered that software engineers conduct the usability testing, and 4 of 28 responded that "other departments suggest usability changes". This is in stark contrast to the HCI practitioners who responded overwhelmingly that *they* conduct the usability testing (48 of 53, or 91%). The remaining 9% is split between "quality assurance" (2 or 53 respondents) and "outsourced quality assurance" (3 of 53 respondents). Software engineers did not rate even a single mention by the HCI practitioners as internal usability testers. There two views of the world are obviously irreconcilable.

These results are particularly significant, and troubling, in relation to the software engineers who took part in our survey. Almost half claimed that they are directly responsible for applying and practicing HCI methods at their organizations. Thus, a majority of the organizations whose members participated in our study expect their software engineers to perform the dual duties of both software engineer and HCI expert.

4.6 SOFTWARE PROCESS INTERACTIONS

Another difference of opinion lies in the two groups' beliefs about how often they interact. HCI practitioners have the perception that they have frequent contact and correspondence with software engineers. Software engineers, on the other hand, are more likely to believe they have little or no contact with HCI practitioners. 40% of HCI practitioners (24 of 60) say that this contact happens "very frequently" and another

43% (26 of 60) of them said "occasionally" when asked how often they correspond with software engineers. Thus the vast majority of HCI practitioners thought that they had at least occasional contact with their SE colleagues. When we turn to the software engineers, we once again see a different view of the world. Their responses were split down the middle: 20% (4 of 20) felt that they "correspond with each other in the software development process" "very frequently", with 30% (6 of 20) saying that this happens "occasionally". On the other hand another 20% (4 of 20) said that this happens "rarely", and a full 30% (6 of 20) said that it "never" happens. One possible explanation is found in this HCI practitioner's comment: "I think there is more reluctance for Software Engineers to adopt HCI processes than for HCI people to 'fit in' with Software Engineers."

As the research trends presented in the first portion of this chapter suggest, a shared software development process is crucial for efficient and productive interaction between software engineers and HCI practitioners. Such a process provides for common names for things, common techniques, checkpoints and measures for success.

The received wisdom is that the earlier a problem can be eliminated in the software process, the less costly that problem will be. So we would expect, or at least hope, that software engineers and HCI practitioners correspond with each other often, particularly in the early phases of the software life cycle. Just the opposite is, unfortunately, the case. 29% of software engineers (6 of 21) said they corresponded with HCI practitioners during the coding phase of software development. 33% of software engineers said they corresponded with HCI practitioners after software development had been completed (during the testing or release phases) and 24% (5 of 21) indicate that they have no correspondence at all with their HCI "colleagues". Only 1 software engineer responding to this survey claimed to correspond with HCI practitioners in the gathering and writing of software specifications.

The HCI practitioners reported slightly different numbers, but these were similarly bleak in their implication. 78% (47 of 60) indicated that they corresponded with the software engineers during the testing or release phases of the software—i.e. far too late to fix usability problems economically and with minimal user impact. A mere 3% (2 of 60) claimed that they worked with software engineers during the specification phase of the project. This is consistent with the numbers reported by the software engineers.

To add further evidence to this result, we also questioned both groups about when HCI methods are used in the software development process. The vast majority of HCI specialists (43 of 61 or 70%) indicated that these methods were used when the software was "already in production", and a mere 8% (5 of 61) said that these methods were used at the requirements stage. One practitioner spoke of the result of this problem, saying "In extreme cases, products sometimes need to be re-architected to improve consistency or usability." Similarly, one response included the comment "we work closely with the product team to influence the design decisions. There are also cases we cannot change most of the UI because we get involved late in the product development cycle." The pattern of the software engineers was similar, but not as pronounced. 30% of the responses (6 of 20) indicated that the software engineers believe that HCI methods are used when the software is in development and 25% (5 of 20) claim that this occurs when the software is in production. In contrast, just 20% (4 of 20) believed that such methods were used at the requirements phase. The magnitudes of the discrepancies were different among the software engineers and the HCI practitioners, but the results are still demoralizing: HCI methods are being used far too late in the life cycle to be truly cost and time efficient. One software engineer noting this situation stated "HCI and design occur simultaneously to reduce development time. Sometimes this requires later re-design." Another pragmatic response talks about a "web interface in which the architecture of the design is often mixed with the User Interface. Not that it is right, but it happens."

4.7   IMPLICATIONS OF THE PROCESS ISSUES

When you consider the last few results, it becomes clear that there is little collaboration happening between software engineers and HCI practitioners in industry. Furthermore, what little collaboration there is, is occurring too late in the life cycle to be effective.

A lack of collaboration between software engineers and HCI practitioners, coupled with different perceptions about how and when collaboration occurs, suggests that HCI practitioners are less involved in the design of software than they think. In fact, few practicing HCI professionals are aware when changes occur in the software processes that are used by their organization. The same is true with regards to software engineers' knowledge of when new HCI methods are adopted at their organizations. Only about 40% of survey respondents could name an exact type of process or method, outside of their own field, that was being adopted at their organization. 52% of HCI respondents could not even give a time frame as to approximately when such processes or methods were adopted.

Software engineers and HCI practitioners are not keeping informed about changes being made in each other's development processes. This could explain why software engineers are often forced to make decisions that impact the user interface without HCI practitioners having the opportunity to perform a full analysis. One HCI practitioner, in a comment field, said "The constraints are not on the part of the HCI, but of the SE methods; in general SE methods do not take the user into account much, or if they do, when the testing is done mostly programmers and the designer team run the walkthroughs, which in some cases leaves out most of the target audience who have different expectations than programmers and designers." A software engineer signaled agreement in the statement that "Many times the current architecture or toolkit doesn't allow us to do what we intend, and we are blocked by architecture redesign. For instance, we would like to use a single-field control for entering dates with a spin button and masked controls, but our toolkit doesn't provide one, and we need to work on the toolkit so that it does." One HCI practitioner said "Designers have to work around the architectural decisions of the SW Engineers" while another respondent, commenting on compromises between SE and HCI professionals said "None. [Software engineering] always wins."

4.8   USE OF HCI METHODS

One section of the survey aimed at the HCI practitioners enquired about their use of HCI methods and tools. 27% (46 of 173) of the tools utilized were cognitive walk-throughs; 24% (41 of 173) utilized were rapid interface prototyping; another 27% (47 of 173) were think aloud protocols; and a slightly lower 19% (33 of 173) was made up by ethnographic interviewing. The unexpected result from the survey was the lack of adoption of heuristic evaluation (HE) (Nielsen, 1993). A mere 3% (6 of 173) of the tools used by those surveys was given to HE. Given that HE is one of the least expensive methods that can be used to evaluate software usability (heuristic evaluations can be quickly performed by individuals—even those involved directly with the implementation of software—by going through a checklist of about ten usability heuristics) this was surprising. HE may not be the most reliable of available methods, but it

Software engineers also do not use heuristic evaluation as a means to evaluate the usability of the software they develop; not a single software engineer reported doing so. The software engineers reported relying primarily on rapid interface prototyping (33% or 14 of 43). 12% of the responses (5 of 43) indicated that software engineers use no HCI methods and a further 3 of 43 didn't know what HCI methods their organization used.

Surprisingly, both HCI practitioners and software engineers regularly use the HCI "think aloud" method to evaluate the usability of their organizations' software (approximately 27% of methods used in both cases). The think aloud method requires an independent third party to be used for testing software and is often more expensive and time consuming than many other techniques (such as heuristic evaluations).

When asked about the usability tools, methods, and languages that HCI practitioners used in their organizations, computer-based mockups and paper prototypes were the primary responses—88% of the respondents used one of these to do rapid prototyping for usability. Of these tools, about 34% (53 of 158) of them were paper mockups of an interface, 11% were Flash, 15% were Visual Basic, and 28% were HTML to prototype their interfaces.

4.9   CONCLUSIONS/RECOMMENDATIONS

There is a strong strain of research in the areas of HCI and SE that reflects a cross breeding of ideas between the two fields and a genuine concern to work on shared problems, and to produce shared methods, processes, notations and tools. This cross breeding of ideas is much more pervasive throughout today's SE and HCI literature than it was even five years ago. The publications of five years ago that involved the interaction of these fields were limited to specialist conferences and workshops, such as the International Conference on Software Engineering's Software Engineering/HCI workshop in 1992 or the tri-ennial EHCI (Engineering for Human Computer Interaction) conferences. This interaction was not important enough to be discussed outside such these relatively rarified forums, or perhaps in the occasional software engineering or HCI textbook. Today there is a small but noticeable change in this trend. For example, the inclusion of usability considerations into the UML and the creation of maturity models for usability indicate a growing awareness of the need for the fields of software engineering and human-computer interaction to interact.

Yet despite these growing trends in research that are steering organizations towards the use of an amalgamation of SE and HCI activities, most industry professionals have yet to follow suggestions from the academic and industrial research communities. For the most part, software engineers and HCI practitioners continue to work separately— they are relative solitudes. While collaboration between the two groups does occur (as it must, since products do eventually get produced and these products frequently have a user interface), the collaboration does not happen frequently enough or early enough in the software development life cycle. Infrequent contact leads to misperceptions about what is happening in the software development process. We have certainly seen such misperceptions and miscommunications as indicated by the responses to our pair of surveys.

HCI methods should be used to design usable software from the ground up. HCI methods should not be applied as patches to software after major development has already occurred; nevertheless that is exactly what is continuing to occur in industry today. To ensure successful system development it is necessary to increase emphasis on defining appropriate HCI processes and to integrate such processes with existing system and software development processes. We, as a community, need to be advocates for both education and industry, to ensure that this happens.

4.10 FUTURE RESEARCH

Our surveys have provided an initial glimpse into the divide between SE and HCI in practice, although a more thorough inspection should yield more insight into the causes of the problem and hopefully allow us to make further recommendations.

In particular, we are currently pursuing the application of a modified form of our survey within a single organization. This will allow us to claim with more confidence that the data that we collect reflects true divisions among the HCI and SE groups, and is not an artefact of a self-selection bias or some other obfuscating factor. Going further in this direction, collecting this information among people who are working under the same conditions, most specifically on the same projects, would allow for more direct comparisons among the responses.

Finally, we hope to be able to perform this sort of research at a broad selection of institutions, where the surveys could be augmented by interviews and data about software life cycles and communications among software engineers and HCI practitioners.

Acknowledgements

The authors wish to thank Bonnie John for putting us together to work on this project. We would also like to thank Len Bass for his help in providing us with some early guidance in our research. We extend a thanks to those individuals and groups that distributed information about our surveys to their memberships. Finally we must thank the members of IFIP WG 2.7/13.4 who provided the initial motivation for this research as well as defining the original set of background research topics that lie at the intersection of SE and HCI.

Notes

1. The full text of the surveys can be found at: `http://www.billjerome.com/seihci/new/index.php`.

2. Note that not all questions were answered by all survey participants. This question, for example, was only answered by 26 of the 33 SE survey respondents.

5 CONVERGENCE OR COMPETITION BETWEEN SOFTWARE ENGINEERING AND HUMAN COMPUTER INTERACTION

Allistair G. Sutcliffe

Centre for HCI Design, School of Informatics, University of Manchester

Abstract

HCI and SE share design as a common concern but have different roots in theory, processes for design and views on design representations. Models are essential for engineering approaches to design, assumed in SE and HCI. Both disciplines also use scenarios and artefacts. Models inevitably have limitations in their comprehensibility even with informal notations, but formal models have become embedded in SE. Scenarios have received much attention as an effective means of user-designer communication; in SE, they are seen as a starting point for generating models, while in HCI scenarios are used as prostheses for design inspiration. The chapter reviews different conceptions of scenarios, artefacts, theories and models with contributions they make to the design process in SE and HCI. It explores the potential for constructive contrasts between scenarios as concrete, grounded examples and generalised, abstract models in an integrated view of systems development that encompasses both HCI and SE.

A. Seffah (eds.), Human-Centered Software Engineering – Integrating Usability
in the Development Process, 71–84.

5.1 INTRODUCTION

Software Engineering (SE) and Human Computer Interaction (HCI) are both concerned with design. They both aim to design software systems although with different emphases. One only has to inspect text books in each discipline (e.g. Dix et al., 1998, for HCI; Sommerville, 2002, for SE) to see that the two disciplines "tread on each other's turf". For instance, formal models of interaction and software (CSP) appear in Dix et al., 1998, while Sommerville, 2002, has a chapter on the user interface and system context. This overlap can be viewed either as competition between the disciplines or convergence towards a synthesised design discipline. While I suspect a true synthesis is unlikely because of social rather than intellectual reasons, in this chapter I will examine the competitive advantage that both SE and HCI may lay claim to. I will examine two perspectives, the design approach adopted by each discipline and the theoretical underpinning of the design process. If readers are curious about why I do not expect a synthesis to emerge the explanation lies in the sociology of academia. Disciplines tend to have self-perpetuating mechanisms since they form communities that mutually support individual survival via peer review; HCI and SE occupy separate ecological niches with little incentive to merge so long as they fulfil the career ambitions of their members.

To return to my prime theme, the design process can be characterised along a dimension from more or less engineering-oriented, i.e. formal and model-based, to informal exploratory design. SE has tended to take a model-based approach to design either as informal graphical models, exemplified by the Unified Modelling Language, or as more formal models. However, more lightweight model-based approaches have been advocated for some time in RAD methods (DSDM, 1995), and this trend has been augmented by the appearance of agile methods and extreme programming. Similarly, HCI has had a model-based tradition of design driven by task analysis, although this has never been as influential as conceptual modelling in SE. Both HCI and SE communities have been influenced more recently by use of scenarios, examples and use cases in the design process. Underlying these developments is a tension between model-driven and example-driven approaches to design, which this chapter sets out to examine. Models, scenarios, and artefacts (prototypes) are shared by both disciplines but they are interpreted from different viewpoints with different design agendas. I will examine how the role of knowledge in HCI or SE, from the designer's perspective, influences the roles that boundary objects, shared by both disciplines, play.

Theory is a vexed topic for both disciplines, which tend to be regarded by their parent subject, computer science, as more peripheral to theoretic, process-oriented subjects (EPSRC, 2002). The theoretical core of computer science, e.g. algorithmic complexity and computability, hardly seems relevant. Both SE and HCI have sought theoretical underpinning for design. I will review the progress made in developing theory within the disciplines as well as connecting theories drawn from other subjects to the design process.

The rest of this chapter is structured as follows. First, contributions of models, scenarios and artefacts to the design process are examined, then their role in HCI and SE. How HCI and SE view these design representations is followed by a review of

Table 5.1 Contributions of software engineering to theory, methods and tools

Contribution	Examples	Validation approaches
Theory	Formal Models, CSP, CCS Jackson, Problem frames?	Formal reasoning, peer citation
Design process: methods	SSADM, RUP-UML, OO methods, RAD and Agile methods, Requirement methods:Volere, VORD, ScenIC, win-win, scenarios, use cases	Utility demonstration, case study, use in practice, effectiveness in practice
Product (support tools)	CASE tools, Rationale ROSE, UML model editors, DOORS, Goal modellers, Model checkers	Utility demonstration, case study, use in practice, effectiveness in practice
Analysis methods	Ethnographic studies, some surveys	Experiments, insight gained, triangulation of results

the role of theory, and the final discussion section concludes with reflections on the competitive advantage for each discipline.

5.2 DESIGN PROCESSES AND METHODS

SE has a long tradition of producing methods and effective uptake of such method in industry (see Table 5.1); however, it is debatable whether the source of SE methods has been academic research or pragmatic invention by practitioners. Structured methods such as SSADM and their object-oriented successors have evolved into the *de facto* standard RUP (Rationale Unified Process) which accompanies UML (Unified Modelling Language—Rational Software Corporation, 1999). SE also has an extensive tradition of "cut-down or lightweight" methods which have been created in reaction to the perception of structured methods as being too ponderous and cumbersome to use. Rapid Applications Development (DSDM, 1995) has been followed by agile methods, allied to the XP (extreme programming) movement in the new millennium (Beck, 2000). Process-methodological research is relatively immature in the requirements area of SE, although it has made significant process. For instance, the Inquiry Cycle (Potts et al., 1994) uses scenarios as specific contexts to test the utility and acceptability of system output. By questioning the relevance of system output for a set of stakeholders and their tasks described in a scenario, the analyst can discover obstacles to achieving system requirements. Other methods, such as Volere (Robertson and Robertson, 1999) and Viewpoint-oriented Requirements Engineering (Sommerville and Sawyer, 1997), have influenced industrial practice, as have more limited negotiation methods such as win-win (Boehm et al., 1994). Formal Methods such as VDM (Jones, 1986) have been an important contribution of SE towards creating reliable software; however, their mathematical basis has created a barrier to update, and evidence for widespread adoption in industry is difficult to find (Fenton and Neil, 1999). HCI has also shared an interest in formal specification (Thimbleby, 1990), but with similar minimal impact on industrial practice.

HCI process-design methods (see Table 5.2) have, in comparison to SE, had only modest success. Task analysis, functional allocation and task design have been the prime deliverables from HCI but their influence on mainstream software development practice has been minimal. HCI task models all contain variations on a narrow range of semantic components, e.g. actions, events, states, objects, agents, goals, attributes and relationships, although some richer models describe the role of work artefacts in ecological interface design (Vicente, 2000) and communication between agents in collaborative tasks (van Lamsweerde and Letier, 2000; Sutcliffe, 2000). However, user-centred design (ISO/IEC, 1999), which is a development approach rather than a structured method, has become influential in industrial practice, and adopted in organisations favouring prototyping styles of development. HCI has produced copious guidelines which have become incorporated in international standards, e.g. ISO 9241, ISO 14915, so it may claim to have influenced design. HCI can also can claim considerable success in evaluation and quality assurance, where a range of methods are widely practised, from quick and dirty heuristic evaluation (Nielsen, 1993) to analysis of observed user problems (Monk et al., 1993) and cognitive walkthroughs (Wharton et al., 1994).

Table 5.2 Contributions of HCI to theory, methods and tools

Contribution	Examples	Validation approaches
Theory	ACT-R, EPIC, GOMS, Norman's action model, Activity Theory, Distributed Cognition	Experiments, Computer Models, design influence, principles
Process	Task Analysis methods, User-centred design, Evaluation methods, scenarios Principles & Guidelines, ISO standards	Usability, utility, use in practice, effectiveness in practice
Product	User Interface Design Environments, UI tool kits, widgits	Usability, utility, use in practice, effectiveness in practice
Analysis	Ethnographic studies and experimental analysis of UI designs	Experiments, insight gained, triangulation of results

Scenario-based design has emerged as an important design approach from the convergence of HCI and Interaction Design (Carroll, 2000). Scenarios are arguably the starting point for all modelling and design, and contribute to several parts of the design process (see Figure 5.1). Scenarios are gathered as examples of system use during requirements analysis and form the subject matter for creating models. The process of generalisation inevitably loses detail and the analyst has to make judgements about when unusual or exceptional behaviours are omitted. Models have to omit detail which may be vital, while scenarios can gather such detail but at the price of effort in capturing and analysing a "necessary and sufficient" set of scenarios.

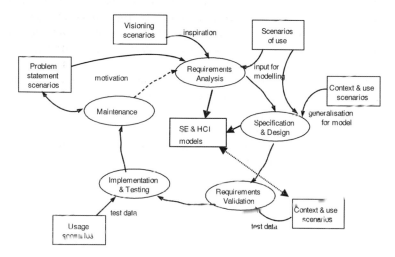

Figure 5.1   Use of scenarios and models in different phases of the HCI/SE design process

Some SE-RE methods, e.g. Inquiry Cycle (Potts et al., 1994), use scenarios as specific contexts to test the utility and acceptability of system output. By questioning the relevance of system output for a set of stakeholders and their tasks described in a scenario, the analyst can discover obstacles to achieving system requirements. Obstacle analysis has since been refined into a formal process for discovering the achievability of system goals with respect to a set of environmental states taken from scenarios (van Lamsweerde and Letier, 2000). Scenarios, therefore, can fulfil useful roles either as test data, as a stimulant to reasoning in validating system requirements, or by providing data for formal model checking.

HCI uses scenarios in a similar manner in usability evaluation, although the role of scenarios is not articulated so clearly. Carroll has proposed several different roles for scenarios in the design process including as envisionment for design exploration, requirements elicitation and validation (Carroll, 1995). Other roles are usage scenarios that illustrate problems, and initiating or visioning scenarios that stimulate design of a new artefact, and projected use scenarios that describe future use of an artefact that has been designed (Sutcliffe and Carroll, 1999). Stories, which are scenarios by another name, appear in the agile movement in SE, and are associated with use cases in object oriented development (Cockburn, 2001), so scenario-based approaches are one area of convergence between HCI and SE. There are some signs of methodological convergence in Contextual Enquiry (Beyer and Holtzblatt, 1998) which provides a structured method that addresses HCI issues and socio-technical systems design with models and processes that analyse the users' work context as well as functional requirements. In the human factors area, Ecological Interface Design (Vicente, 2000) follows a similar approach with more emphasis on design of interface metaphors and representations to match users' mental models. However, in SE incorporation of HCI design concerns into the design process has been limited to treating user interface design as a simple matter of configuring user interact components such as menus and form-filling dialogues.

HCI has also contributed methods for analysis of data collected in experiments, surveys and case studies. These methods have been borrowed from psychology. Analytic research in HCI has also adopted ethnographic approaches for requirements analysis (Vicente, 2000) and evaluation. Some case study and field research has been carried out on HCI methods and tools in practice, but these studies are infrequent. Analytic research is not common in SE, although some field studies and surveys have been carried out on perceptions of requirements problems and practices in industry (Greenspan et al., 1982; Rengell and Horst, 2001). In addition, SE has adopted ethnographic methods as part of its requirements analysis toolbox in methods, which have focused on problems in real world settings with an intent to provide insight for design rather than study of the requirements process itself.

5.3   DESIGN REPRESENTATIONS IN SE AND HCI

Both SE and HCI take a model-based systematic approach to design; furthermore, both also advocate an informal design approach using prototypes and scenarios. The interesting question is how the designers' concerns affect the role of models, scenarios and artefacts in both disciplines.

5.3.1   Scenarios

Scenarios have a host of definitions (Rolland et al., 1998), ranging from narrative descriptions of system use expressed in natural language, frequent in HCI and the interactive systems design communities, to more formal representations of event sequences in SE (Kaindl, 1995). The range of definitions mirrors how scenarios are transformed into models by a process of generalisation from specific examples. Use cases are usually considered to be models but they may be supported by narrative scenarios on which they are based. The tension between concrete detail and abstract models underlies design in both HCI and SE; however, little investigation has been directed towards understanding how scenarios and models can be profitably integrated in the design process. Scenarios are used in SE as part of the requirements engineering process to discover new requirements by testing models. Scenarios are primarily interpreted as event sequences or event pathways through a model. Model checking is carried out, in effect, by testing the possible legal or illegal states in the system given the event sequence contained in the scenario. In contrast, HCI views scenarios in many different forms, ranging from rich description of a systems context, to specific sequences of interaction or vision of future systems usage. Scenarios play a design exploration role, being used to elicit requirements and consider how requirements might be realised in design (Carroll, 2000). Scenarios have been linked with generalised design principles by claims analysis in task artefact theory (Carroll and Rosson, 1992) which argues that scenarios of use with an example of the design artefact provide the context to understand a design principle. The results of evaluations are recorded in usage scenarios that describe the problem that motivated a general design principle, called a claim, with trade-offs expressed as upsides and downsides (Carroll, 2000; Sutcliffe and Carroll, 1999).

Scenarios, examples and use cases can be used as lightweight instruments that guide thought and support reasoning in the design process (Carroll, 2000). However, a scenario, or even a set of scenarios, does not explicitly guide a designer towards a correct model of the required system. An extreme scenario might bias reasoning towards exceptional and rare events, or towards the viewpoint of an unrepresentative stakeholder. These biases are an acknowledged weakness of scenarios; however, we could trust designers as knowledgeable, responsible people who are capable of recognising such biases and dealing with them productively.

At first sight the use and format of scenarios are very different in HCI and SE; however there are several similarities, as illustrated in Figure 5.1. In HCI the representation is informal, in a variety of media (text, image and video), and use focuses on design exploration as well as evaluation, where "scenarios of use" are employed as test scripts. In contrast, SE uses more formally represented scenarios often with modelling notations, and employs them for model refinement and testing. However, there are overlaps in usage in the requirements engineering area. Informal narrative scenarios have been used as test challenges to validate requirements in ScenIC (Potts, 1999) whereby the scenario expresses an obstacle to the realisation of a requirement when implemented in a system. For example in a meeting scheduling system, allocating a two-hour meeting to a non-smoking room might be challenged by the scenario that "Ann the convenor of the meeting smokes and can't stand meetings of two hours without a break". The notation of obstacles was then taken up in the SE community more formally as a set of states which expressed constraints on system input or output, and allowed formal reasoning about how scenario-expressed states might be fulfilled or violated by a system specification in the KAOS language (van Lamsweerde and Letier, 2000). This is a good example of how scenarios as a boundary object can transform their role while crossing the boundary between HCI and SE.

5.3.2 Models

Models play a key role in both disciplines although, regrettably, there is evidence of a waning role in HCI. In HCI, modelling concerns vary from cognitively motivated models (e.g. GOMS—John and Kieras, 1995) which tend to be analytic in focus, to design models which represent goals, plans and actions of the user, i.e. task models. The transition to design and the derivation of design from such models has never been one of HCI's strong points, and has tended to be driven via functional allocation principles or underspecified mappings to dialogue and presentation design. The transformation to design illustrates the tension between the disciplines. Once functional allocation decisions have been taken, design moves into the realm of SE, and HCI specifications adopt SE notations, as illustrated in HCI text books (Dix et al., 1998). SE, in contrast, has a rich tradition of notations, which enable transformation and refinement of specifications from requirements to detailed designs. Models, therefore, form one class of boundary object between the disciplines, where HCI has adopted SE models. An open question is whether SE will adopt HCI influences to augment the space of software-oriented modelling notations with others which represent people-oriented concerns. The notations in contextual enquiry (Beyer and Hultzblatt, 1998) show where the boundary might move to, although software engineers would currently not even consider social issues in analysis, so affinity diagrams have yet to become part of the shared language.

A limitation of conceptual models is that they do not capture the richness of interaction that occurs in the real world; in contrast, scenario narratives concentrate on contextual description (Kyng, 1995). SE and HCI task models all contain variations on a narrow range of semantic components, e.g. actions, events, states, objects, agents, goals, attributes and relationships. Models in both the HCI and SE traditions may be criticised for not representing the relationships between agents, activity and organisational structures, although these concepts are described in socio-technical system design frameworks such as ORDIT (Eason et al., 1996); and in requirements modelling languages such as i* that analyses the dependencies between agents, tasks, goals and resources (Mylopoulos et al., 1999). In HCI, richer models describe the role of work artefacts in ecological interface design (Vicente, 2000) and communication between agents in collaborative tasks (van Lamsweerde, 2000; Sutcliffe, 2000).

5.3.3   Artefacts and Prototypes

Artefacts play several roles in HCI and tend to be more embedded in the design process than they are in SE. For example, artefacts in HCI can be early design conceptions manifest as storyboards, mock-ups, or Wizard of Oz simulations. Prototypes, either fully functional or lightweight concept demonstrators, are shared by both traditions. In SE, artefacts are code, or code in embedded systems as prototypes, so the focus of use tends towards testing. While HCI, too, evaluates prototypes, it also uses a wide variety of artefacts for design exploration or requirements discovery (Carroll, 2000). Indeed, in Carroll's task artefact cycle, an example of a design is integrated with a claim representing design knowledge and a scenario of use. In SE, prototypes can be involved in design exploration and testing in agile development, although the emphasis on requirements exploration is less pronounced in SE/agile development literature.

Prototypes are shared between both disciplines, although their roles tend to be different. Whereas prototypes have played a central role in user-centred design (ISO/IEC, 1999), in SE they have had a less important role. The advent of agile development has refocused attention on the prototype, although the process by which design is gained for inspecting or testing artefacts is not articulated in agile methods. The process is assumed and prototypes have played an important role in the precursors of XP and agile methods in RAD approaches, such as DSDM (Dynamic Systems Development Method). Indeed, RAD methods shared many concerns with user-centred design approaches, so iterative development and prototypes also play a shared role in both communities. The testing questions asked about them, however, differ. Also, in SE, prototype-led development has tended to be viewed with some suspicion, since prototyping could be seen as a rival for more systematic methodical development. In HCI this tension rarely exists outside safety-critical domains. One consequence is that prototypes in SE have a closer relationship to models, because models are formally verified specifications of requirements which can be validated by user inspection of prototypes. In contrast, scenarios and prototypes have a closer relationship in HCI where the prototype is validated as a realisation of a future vision of use expressed in a scenario.

5.4   VIEWPOINTS IN HCI AND SE

In this section I explore the concern in both disciplines and how these lead to different views on scenarios, models and artefacts, and additionally the semantics expressed with models.

A key difference between the disciplines is the scope of the modelled world and the aspects of the design system within it. A layers model (Figure 5.2) illustrates the point. HCI concerns itself with social, cognitive and interactive phenomena. SE, while it may acknowledge all these phenomena in complex systems, e.g. the London Ambulance Service as a much discussed exemplar of system failure, is ultimately not deeply interested in social and cognitive issues. SE's mission is the design of software, the process of construction, architecture, reliable functioning and design for utility The latter concern is shared with HCI, where fit-for-purpose is also seen as fit-for-use and ease of learning.

To unpack these layers in more depth: the *social layer* concerns how people interact with each other, with artefacts in the environment (technology-enabled or otherwise), how groups form and work together, social norms, attitudes, etc. The parent disciplines in this layer are sociology and social psychology, and HCI draws several theories from these areas, e.g. Distributed Cognition (Hutchins, 1995a), Activity Theory (Nardi, 1993) and Small Groups as Complex Systems (Arrow et al., 2000) to name but a few. Although HCI has embraced the concerns of these theories, it has not led to much influence on HCI methods or models. Indeed, the connection between theory and design at this level is articulated in terms of principles or heuristics, if it is articulated at all. The social layer may be acknowledged in SE but the phenomena are not investigated, so this is one area where the two disciplines could have a synergetic relationship, especially as ICT systems are become increasingly multiparty in Computer Mediated Communication, Computer Supported Collaborative Work, Internet, etc.

The *cognitive layer* draws on the parent discipline of psychology and represents one of HCI's central missions, how to bring knowledge of the user to bear upon the design process. Models in this layer are usually detailed models of how the cognition of problem solving, perception and memory work, and how these relate to interacting with computers (Kieras and Meyer, 1997; Anderson and Lebiere, 1998). Once again the connection between theory and design practice has been difficult, although a transfer mechanism has been proposed via bridging models, claims and other means of representing design-applicable but theory-based knowledge (Sutcliffe, 2000). The GOMS family of models presents the most successful and enduring means of linking theory and design, albeit in an evaluative mode. SE treats the user as a black box, so cognitive theory and its influence on design is not a direct concern.

The *interaction layer* is the user interface where HCI and SE meet, but their viewpoints are different. Both communities, while trying to separate the user interface from underlying functionality for architectural reasons, acknowledge that the user interface and system functionality are linked. Whereas HCI focuses on design properties of the user interface for ease of use and increasing aesthetics, affective reaction and

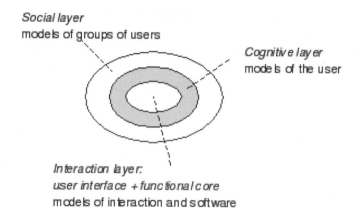

Figure 5.2   Scope of modelling in HCI and SE

attractiveness, SE focuses on how functional requirements will be delivered to the user. This difference is reflected in model and development approaches. Take Jackson's view of the interface between the real world and the design machine (Jackson, 2001). The interface determines functional requirements in terms of the properties of the world that the machine must deal with (e.g. laws of physics) and the user requirements which will be behaviours of the systems and interactive functions. The view here is one of understanding requirements as dependencies of a computer system's future behaviour and the way the real world constrains such behaviour. The HCI view of interaction, expressed in Norman's model of interaction (Norman, 1988) and others focus on the same boundary but with a different perspective on understanding how the user will interpret the possibilities for action in the world (affordances for Norman) and then understand feedback from the system's action. The interaction layer presents another interesting yet largely unexplored synergy. Interaction involves understanding not only what the user needs (functional requirements) but also how those requirements are delivered by interaction (HCI design). As many functions are interactive, i.e. the partitioning between people and machine is split, integrated modelling interaction from both an SE and HCI perspective could improve the design of decision support systems. Decision support systems are often considered to be a sub-set of information systems, yet nearly any interactive system involves helping the user decide. A combination of dependency-based SE modelling with interactive modelling may be the way forward. Integrating the cognitive and social layers is a further challenge for both communities.

5.5   THEORETICAL UNDERPINNINGS

In SE the need for theory has not been a pressing concern—see Table 5.1. Most software engineers cite formal semantics as the theoretical basis for modelling, which is a key part of the engineering approach. So the foundations of formal methods, e.g. CSP (Hoare, 1969) or CCS (Milner, 1989) underpin formal methods such as VDM (Jones, 1986), and model-checking tools, e.g. SPIN. Theories of formal semantics, if indeed they are theories rather than methods of logical representation and reasoning, generally belong to computer science as a parent discipline rather than SE. However, SE can claim to have developed and applied formal semantics in many variations, although the utility of this theoretical influence in delivering practical software solutions is still open to debate, with sceptics (Finney et al., 1999) and advocates (Hall and Chapman, 2002).

SE may also have nascent theoretical underpinnings which are beginning to emerge. In requirements engineering, understanding the dependencies between laws of the natural world, the behaviour of external agents, and the correct behaviour of software to achieve goals (or user requirements) has led to the problem-frames approach (Jackson, 2001), which is cited as a theoretical basis for requirements specification. Problem frames distinguish between indicative requirements which are imposed by the external world, domain descriptions which model them, and optative requirements which express the desired behaviour of a software system that achieves a user goal. The concept of dependency has been explored further in the i* modelling language (Mylopoulos et al., 1999; Castro and Kolp, 2002) and by formal refinement of goal system behaviours that achieve (goal) states. Barriers in the external world which may prevent goals being achieved have led to new approaches to understanding how requirements can be formally specified (van Lamsweerde, 2000; van Lamsweerde and Letier, 2000). Taken together these modelling approaches can be viewed as a proto-theory that describes and predicts how software systems should be constructed to behave correctly when faced with different types of problems or real world environments.

As well as being concerned with process, SE involves architecture of software systems. No theory has emerged in this area, although architectural frameworks have been influential, whether in the patterns movement (Gamma et al., 1995), or in systems architecture (Shaw, 1991). The relationship between software architecture and problem abstractions in the real world has emerged pragmatically via the development of application frameworks (Fayad and Johnson, 2000) and Enterprise Resource Plans (Keller and Teufel, 1998), but little research has been devoted to theories of abstraction apart from some work in requirements engineering (Sutcliffe, 2000; Jackson, 2001).

In contrast, HCI has been obsessed by the need to connect theories from cognitive and social science to the design process, as well as attempting to develop theories of interaction in its own right, see Table 5.2. A protracted effort to connect cognitive theory to design was made in the AMODEUS project (Barnard and May, 1999), which tried to connect a cognitive architecture, Interacting Cognitive Sub-systems, to design via design rationale, and programmable user models (Bellotti et al., 1995). Although this attempt at integration failed, Barnard and colleagues continued their quest with syndectic (design-oriented) modelling, arguing for a series of bridging models that could transfer influences from psychological models to models that could be directly applied to design: cognitive task models (Barnard et al., 2000). Several computational cognitive theories, notably ACT-R (Anderson and Lebiere, 1998) and EPIC (Kieras and Meyer, 1997) have been applied to HCI design, but the criticism is that these models can only deal with small-scale problems, and scaling up makes the modelling effort prohibitive (Sutcliffe, 2000).

More applicable models which have some theoretical basis have proved more successful. The GOMS (Goals Operators Methods Selection rules) family has stood the test of time (Card et al., 1983; John and Kieras, 1995) and demonstrated practical applications in evaluating interactive systems and informing design. Unfortunately GOMS also suffers from scaling problems since the granularity of modelling is at the micro level of keystrokes and mouse movements. Other pragmatic models predict the comprehensibility of menu and object names on interfaces (Blackmon et al., 2003), but these depend on considerable manual input to describe the user interface. Within HCI, models of interaction (Norman, 1988) can be regarded as proto-theoretical frameworks. Norman's model described the cycle of cognitive and physical actions a user undertakes during interaction. This model has been elaborated to account for multimedia and virtual reality user interfaces (Sutcliffe, 2003). In this elaboration a rule-based framework was proposed for each stage of Norman's model that described the sufficiency conditions for successful interaction in terms of design features supplied to the user interface and knowledge held by the user. This provides one means of bridging cognitive influences into an interaction model that can be applied to design; however, many aspects of cognitive psychology, such as emotion, have yet to be connected to design (Norman, 2004).

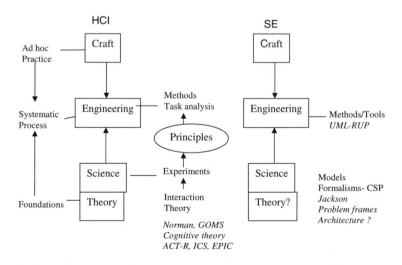

Figure 5.3   Craft, engineering and science framework for HCI and SE, adapted from Long and Dowell (1989)

HCI has been eclectic in using a wide variety of theory to inform the design process, although in most cases the connection between theory and design is not explicit. For instance, Activity Theory (Nardi, 1993) has been cited as an influence on understanding the socio-environmental context of design; however, apart from providing a framework for thought, the connection from theory to design is hard to discern. The range of theories used by HCI research from linguistics, psychology and sociology is reviewed in an edited volume of contributions (Carroll, 2003).

The position of theory in both disciplines is summarised in Figure 5.3. Both HCI and SE aim to improve the design process from craft (i.e. expertise collected by experience) to a systematic engineering approach.

In HCI, knowledge is recruited into the engineering process from experiments in psychology as well as from several theories. The connection between theory, science and design has primarily been via guidelines and principles, although some theories have been transformed into analytic techniques, e.g. GOMS (John and Kieras, 1995). HCI has also produced proto-interaction theories which can be directly applied to design, but these theories have a long way to travel before they become truly predictive theories. SE, in contrast, has few theoretical influences, although it has applied its main influence from formal semantics directly into models and tools that support the engineering process. SE has also developed proto-theory; moreover, an interesting convergence is that both HCI and SE concern interaction albeit with different viewpoints. In SE the focus is on interaction between the natural world and the software system to ensure correct behaviour, whereas HCI seeks to understand interaction between the user and the machine so design can support people more effectively.

5.6 CONCLUSIONS

In its use of theory, HCI is more mature than SE. It acknowledges that design is a multidisciplinary endeavour and applies theories from other disciplines with great gusto. The effectiveness of application may vary; nevertheless, this quest may have a competitive advantage in the long run if the connection from theory to design can be made to produce quality improvements At present, while SE has been more successful in transforming the design process from craft to engineering, the two disciplines may converge in the future as design diversifies from heavyweight methods to a spectrum of approaches. Models, scenarios and artefacts play different roles in HCI and SE. Furthermore, the roles and content of these representations are influenced by the scope of concerns ranging from the interactive, cognitive to social levels. So is there a synthesis for model-analytic and creative scenario-exploration approaches to design which can be loosely mapped to SE and HCI respectively? A partial answer is acknowledging the "horses for courses" argument. Model-analytic and creative exploratory design approaches will be necessary for safety-critical applications on the one hand, and those oriented to entertainment, education, and general commerce on the other. A more satisfactory answer is to examine the nature of methodological interventions in the design process. Methods, guidelines, principles and models are rarely used explicitly by expert designers (Guindon, 1987). Novices might use them *ab initio*, but design knowledge soon becomes internalised as the designer's skill. I argue that reusable knowledge in the form of generic models, claims and design rationale should become part of the skill-set of all system designers (Sutcliffe, 2002). Models can contribute by providing representation for reusable knowledge via documentation. Scenarios can support the design process at run time as they probe to test assumptions and stimulate creation. As scenarios have become established in both SE and HCI traditions they can form the common ground between the disciplines, and furthermore need to be integrated into development processes throughout the life cycle. Understanding the contributions models and scenarios make to design may help to integrate SE and HCI within system development.

III Requirements, Scenarios, and Use-cases

6 EXPERIENCE WITH USING GENERAL USABILITY SCENARIOS ON THE SOFTWARE ARCHITECTURE OF A COLLABORATIVE SYSTEM

Rob J. Adams, Len Bass, and Bonnie E. John

Carnegie Mellon University

Abstract

Architecturally-sensitive usability scenarios are important usability concerns that require early consideration in software design so that architectural support can render them easy and cost-effective to implement. Examples include providing the ability to cancel a command, undo commands, aggregate data, etc. This chapter reports on our experiences applying these scenarios to the design of MERBoard, a wall-sized interactive system developed by NASA to assist Mars Rover science teams with collaborative data analysis. We applied the scenarios during a major redesign of the software architecture that introduced usability as a valued quality attribute. In the process, we found that the scenarios were well-received by developers who readily understood how they related to MERBoard, that they applied to a collaborative workspace despite having been initially developed for a single-user desktop system, that they had a real impact on the architecture redesign, and that the scenario consideration process was quick and not too onerous for any of the team members.

A. Seffah (eds.), Human-Centered Software Engineering – Integrating Usability
in the Development Process, 87–112.

6.1   INTRODUCTION

The usability analyses or user test data are in; the development team is poised to respond. The software had been carefully modularized so that modifications to the UI would be fast and easy. When the usability problems are presented, someone around the table exclaims, "Oh, no, we can't change THAT!" The requested modification or feature reaches too far in to the architecture of the system to allow economically viable and timely changes to be made. Even when the functionality is right, even when the UI is separated from that functionality, architectural decisions made early in development have precluded the implementation of a system with an acceptable level of usability. The members of the design and development teams are frustrated and disappointed that despite their best efforts, despite following current best practice, they must ship a product that is far less usable than they know it could be.

Over the past five years, our research group has worked to analyze the causes of the problem described above and to develop materials to help prevent it from occurring in common practice. This chapter describes these materials and relates our experiences applying them to the NASA MERBoard software development project. First, we review the relevant prior work on bringing usability concerns to software architecture design. Next, we describe the Usability and Software Architecture (U&SA) project's approach to the problem and provide an overview of the materials we have developed. We list the questions we had about our technique prior to our intervention with the MERBoard team, describe the procedure we went through during our intervention, and then conclude with our answers to our initial questions and an overview of our current ongoing work.

6.2   USABILITY AND SOFTWARE ARCHITECTURE

Historically, software engineers viewed usability as relevant to software architecture design solely through modifiability (Bass, Clements and Kazman, 1998, p. 78). If the user interface was sufficiently separate from the main application functionality, they argued, then the interface designers could make modifications through iterative design and testing throughout the project's life cycle, thereby maximizing usability. These engineers developed "separation patterns", or generalized architecture designs that separated the user interface into components that could change independently from the core application functionality. The Java 2 Platform, Enterprise Edition (J2EE) Model-View-Controller (MVC) pattern, shown in Figure 6.1, is an example of one of these (Sun Microsystems Inc., 2003).

The separation patterns are highly successful at making "screen-deep" interface changes easy, for example, changing the size of the fonts to make them easier to read or the order of screens in a wizard to provide a more intuitive flow. Unfortunately, as our opening story illustrates, many important usability concerns are difficult to add late in the development process, even when the architecture is designed to follow one of the separation patterns. For example, often designers discover during testing that users want to cancel long-running commands. To add this functionality to a MVC-based architecture, however, requires changing the View to add a cancel button, adding a Controller that runs on a separate thread (thus possibly introducing multi-threading in a single-threaded application) to listen for the cancel request, and modifying the command itself in the Model so it can cleanly cancel its execution and roll back to its initial state. As a result, the development team frequently finds that making commands cancelable is too expensive a change to make late in the development process. The software is released without this capability, and as a result is less usable than the team knew it could have been had they considered the cancellation requirement up front.

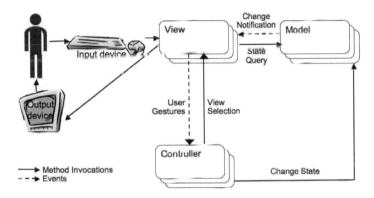

Figure 6.1   The J2EE Model-View-Controller software architectural separation pattern (Sun Microsystems Inc., 2003). Arrows represent control flow, while boxes represent the major software components. The layered boxes indicate the existence of several instances of the component type

6.3   THE USABILITY AND SOFTWARE ARCHITECTURE PROJECT

Since its inception, the Usability and Software Architecture (U&SA) project has worked to prevent the story that began this chapter. We envision a world in which routine practice brings important usability concerns to the table early enough that architectural limitations do not prevent them from getting implemented. To bring this about, we have the following goals:

1. Have usability recognized as a software quality attribute at architecture design time along with other quality attributes such as performance, maintainability, reliability, and security.

2. Understand and codify how usability impacts the architecture of software systems.

3. Improve communication between usability professionals[1] and software developers at the critical architecture design phase.

4. Provide guidance on designing architectures that support usability concerns.

For these goals to become a reality, we hypothesized that development teams required materials that clearly defined how to bring the knowledge and skills of the usability professionals and designers as well as the outputs of their design processes into the architecture design stage of the software development lifecycle. We developed the U&SA materials to satisfy this need.

6.3.1   U&SA Materials

In brief, our materials include a list of architecturally-sensitive usability scenarios, or generalized usability concerns that require difficult-to-change architectural support. Each scenario is connected to a hierarchy of usability benefits that break down *usability* into various components, such as *accelerating error-free portion of routine performance, preventing mistakes* and *supporting problem solving* which help give usability professionals a sense of what positive impacts implementing the scenario will have on the system's overall usability. The scenarios are decomposed into responsibilities of the software, which define the tasks the system must perform to properly implement the scenario as a list of requirements. For assistance with implementing the responsibilities, we provide architectural patterns that describe example implementation strategies within a particular architectural context. Finally, we describe the software engineering tactics that we employed in developing this implementation solution.

Architecturally-Sensitive Scenarios.   At the time of this writing, we have identified 27 architecturally-sensitive usability scenarios. By *architecturally-sensitive*, we mean that support for each scenario affects the functional core in a software architectural pattern based on separation of the UI, such as the J2EE-MVC. These scenarios are common to many interactive software systems and are not related to the domain functionality of any one system.

We generated scenarios by (1) reading several standard HCI textbooks and used their examples and definitions of usability to inspire scenarios (e.g. Gram and Cockton, 1996; Newman and Lamming, 1995; Nielsen, 1993; Shneiderman, 1998), (2) from our own experiences, and (3) through discussion with colleagues. Thus, the generation process was bottom-up, not theory-driven, systematic or comprehensive. However, it was sufficient to demonstrate that common usability concerns had implications for software architecture design.

The full list of scenarios can be found in table 6.1, page 96 (or see Bass and John, 2003, or Bass and John, 2001b, for the scenarios themselves). A few examples are

---

[1] In this chapter we use the term "usability professionals" to include usability specialists, human factors specialists, ethnographers, interaction designers, graphic designers and other members of the project team who are primarily concerned with user-centered issues as opposed to primarily concerned with software architecture or detailed software design and implementation.

"Supporting Undo", "Canceling Commands", and "Reusing Information" (which will be our running example). Each scenario consists of a name and a paragraph or two describing the situation in which it occurs. The scenario for "Reusing Information" is shown in Figure 6.2.

Reusing Information

A user may wish to move data from one part of a system to another. For example, an administrative assistant may need to move a large list of business contacts from a word processor to a database. Re-entering this data by hand could be tedious and/or excessively time-consuming. Users should be provided with automatic (e.g., data propagation) or manual (e.g., cut and paste) data transports between different parts of a system. When such transports are available and easy to use, the user's ability to gain insight through multiple perspectives and/or analysis techniques will be enhanced.

Figure 6.2   The "Reusing Information" general scenario description

The scenarios are intended to assist designers and usability professionals in identifying usability concerns that have architectural implications. Scenarios have a long history of applicability to user-interface design (Carroll and Rosson, 1992) and many designers and usability professionals are already familiar with them. In the spirit of Rosson & Carroll, our scenarios are "the things users characteristically want to do and need to do" (p. 183), but they are a lower level than the functionality-level of Rosson & Carroll's use scenarios, because usability issues show up at a lower level and architectural decisions must be made to support that level of use. Scenarios also appear in software development (albeit in different forms) in the Architecture Tradeoff Analysis Method^{SM} (ATAM^{SM}, Kazman et al., 2000) and in UML (Fowler, 2003b) in the form of use cases, growth, and exploratory scenarios. Our scenarios are perhaps most similar to customer stories in Extreme Programming (Beck, 2000), as they are "one thing the customer wants the system to do" (p. 179) that is testable and can be implemented in one to five weeks. Thus, we hypothesized that they would serve as an effective cross-cultural communication device.

Usability Benefits Hierarchy.   Each architecturally-sensitive usability scenario is allocated to the Usability Benefits Hierarchy, shown in Figure 6.3. The Usability Benefits Hierarchy describes the specific usability attributes of the system that implementing the scenario will enhance.   Because there was no guarantee that architecturally-sensitive usability scenarios would span previous definitions of usability, we again used a bottom-up approach, affinity diagramming (or KJ-method, Kawakita, 1982), to organize the scenarios into topics. Although it is not directly derived from other published definitions of usability, the Benefits Hierarchy covers the same general concepts of efficiency, error prevention and tolerance, and user satisfaction, as other popular usability definitions (e.g., ISO 9241-11:1998; Newman and Lamming, 1995; Nielsen, 1993; Shneiderman, 1998).   It does not cover user satisfaction in any depth, however, neglecting concepts like physical discomfort, for example (ISO 9241-11:1998). However, it includes benefits relating to reducing the impact of system errors that other usability definitions do not include.

Increases individual user effectiveness
   Expedites routine performance
      Accelerates error-free portion of routine performance
      Reduces the impact of routine user errors (slips)
   Improves non-routine performance
      Supports problem-solving
      indent Facilitates learning
   Reduces the impact of user errors caused by lack of knowledge (mistakes)
      Prevents mistakes
      Accommodates mistakes
Reduces the impact of system errors
   Prevents system errors
   Tolerates system errors
Increases user confidence and comfort

Figure 6.3   The Usability Benefits Hierarchy. For each scenario, the U&SA technique describes which specific benefits (the "leaves" of the hierarchy) apply and which do not

Increases individual effectiveness
      Expedites routine performance
         Accelerates error-free portion of routine performance
         In most cases, it is more efficient for systems to transport information from place to place than it is for users to re-enter this information by hand. Thus, systems that support information reuse accelerate routine performance.
Increases individual effectiveness
    Expedites routine performance
      Reduces impact of slips
      Automatic data transportation and/or re-entry require fewer human actions (e.g., typing, mouse movements) than re-entering data by hand. Since performing more actions introduces more opportunities for error, systems that support information reuse can prevent slips.
Increases individual effectiveness
    Improves non-routine performance
      Supports problem-solving
      When users can import and export data from one place to another easily, they may try different applications to gain additional insight while solving problems. For example, a user may export data from a traditional text-based statistics application to a data visualization application. Thus, systems that support information reuse facilitate problem-solving.

Figure 6.4   Allocation of "Reusing Information" to the Usability Benefits Hierarchy

---

Manual Reuse Responsibilities

- R1. Provide information to be reused (from Information Source)
- R2. Store information to be reused (in Information Repository)
- R3. Provide feedback on the stored information
- R4. Retrieve stored information (from Information Repository)
- R5. Receive information (into Information Sink)
- R6. Provide feedback on the retrieved information

Automatic Reuse Responsibilities

- R1. Know which data to store and retrieve from repository (e.g., via a data dictionary)
- R2. Provide information to be reused (from Information Source)
- R3. Store information to be reused (in Information Repository)
  - Retrieve stored information on request, or
  - Broadcast newly stored information
- R4. Receive information (into Information Sink)

Figure 6.5   Responsibilities for reusing information

For each scenario, the U&SA technique describes which specific benefits (the "leaves" of the hierarchy) apply and which do not. Figure 6.4 contains the allocation of the "Reusing Information" scenario to the Benefits Hierarchy. For each benefit allocation, we include a short justification for why the benefit applies to this scenario.

Responsibilities. [2]

Each scenario package includes a list of system responsibilities that can serve as a specification to developers, detailing what the system must do.[3] Like any specification, the responsibilities are intended to describe the functions of the system without dictating a particular implementation. The responsibilities for "Reusing Information" are divided into two sections: manual reuse (i.e., copy&paste) and automatic reuse (data propagation). These responsibilities are shown in Figure 6.5.

Architectural Patterns.   To provide more guidance to software developers, we have included a sample architectural pattern in each U&SA scenario package that fulfills the implementation-independent responsibilities. These patterns are similar to

---

[2] *Responsibility* is a term from object-oriented design that means "an obligation to perform a task or know information" (Wirfs-Brock & Mckean, 2003, p. 3).

[3] At the time of the intervention with the NASA development team, only 6 scenarios out of 27 included this list of responsibilities. Work continues to fill these in for every scenario.

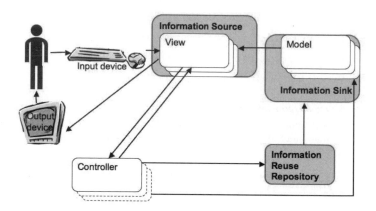

Figure 6.6   Sample architectural pattern for Reusing Information Manually

software patterns (Gamma et al., 1995) insofar as they describe generalized solutions that could be realized in a wide variety of systems, but most are at a level of abstraction similar to software architecture patterns (Buschmann et al., 1996).

Because the architectural patterns that support usability are always situated within an overarching architecture (usually a separation-based architecture discussed above), our examples must be given with respect to some overarching architecture. We have chosen to situate our examples within the J2EE Model-View-Controller architecture because that pattern is very popular in modern system development (Figure 6.6). However, the concepts illustrated in each example can be applied to other overarching architectures.

Note that the pattern defines generic, high-level components and the interactions between them. Each responsibility, listed in the previous section, is allocated to a particular component, as described in Figure 6.7.

Allocation of Responsibilities for Reusing Information Manually

View

- Accept copy/paste commands from the user (R1)
- Send data to the Controller (R1)
- Provide feedback about the copied data. (R3)
- Provide feedback about the pasted data. (R6)

Controller

- Send data to the Information Reuse Repository (R1)
- Send information about the copy operation to the View. (R3)

Model

- Receive data from the Information Reuse Repository (R5)

Information Reuse Repository (which is a Model)

- Receives data to be reused, e.g., from the Controller in response to a copy request (R2)
- Stores information to be reused (R2)
- Accepts commands to retrieve stored information, e.g., paste to the Model (R4)
- Dispense information to be reused to requesting Models. (R4)
- Provide information to the View for user feedback about the repository contents. (R3)

Figure 6.7   Allocation of Responsibilities for Reusing Information Manually. This figure describes the mappings between the Reusing Information Manually responsibilities and the components shown in the sample architectural pattern in Figure 6.6

Architectural Tactics		Increases individual effectiveness						Reduces impact of system errors		Increases confidence and comfort
		Expedites routine performance		Improves non-routine performance		Reduces impact of mistakes				
Usability Benefits →		Accelerates error-free portion	Reduces impact of slips	Supports problem-solving	Facilitates learning	Prevents mistakes	Accommodates mistakes	Tolerates system errors	Prevents system errors	
Localize Modifications	Hide information	4, 13, 14, 15, 20, 23		4, 13, 20	4, 13, 20	4, 13, 20	9, 14		23	
	Separate data from the view of that data	12, 13, 24, 25	12	12, 13, 22, 24, 25, 26	12, 13, 24	12, 13, 22, 24	12			12
	Separate data from commands	1, 24, 25	5, 17	5, 17, 24, 25, 26	5, 17, 24	1, 5, 17, 24	1, 5, 17			17
	Separate authoring from execution	1, 2	2			1, 2	1, 2			
Maintain multiple copies	Data	16								
	Commands	2	2	22		2, 22	2			
Use an intermediary	Data	7, 11, 14	11	7, 11			14			
	Function	6, 14, 20, 27	27	6, 20	20	20, 27	14			27
Recording		2, 7	2, 3, 21	3, 7, 21		2	2, 3, 21	3, 8		
Preemptive scheduling policy		15, 18, 19	3, 5, 17, 18	3, 5, 10, 17	5, 10, 17	5, 17, 19	3, 5, 17	3		17, 18
Support system initiative	Task model	18, 19	5, 17, 18	5, 10, 17	5, 10, 17	5, 17, 19	5, 17			17, 18
	User model	12, 18	5, 12, 17, 18	5, 10, 12, 17, 22	5, 10, 12, 17	5, 12, 17, 22	5, 12, 17			12, 17, 18
	System model	4, 6, 19, 23	3, 5, 17	3, 4, 5, 6, 17	4, 5, 17	4, 5, 17, 19	3, 5, 17	3	6, 23	17

Table 6.1

Key to scenarios (left page)

1 Aggregating data	14 Modifying interfaces
2 Aggregating commands	15 Supporting multiple activity
3 Canceling commands	16 Navigating within a single view
4 Using applications concurrently	17 Observing system state
5 Checking for correctness	18 Working at the user's pace
6 Maintaining device independence	19 Predicting task duration
7 Evaluating the system	20 Supporting comprehensive searching
8 Recovering from failure	21 Supporting Undo
9 Retrieving forgotten passwords	22 Working in an unfamiliar context
10 Providing good help	23 Verifying resources
11 Reusing information	24 Operating consistently across views
12 Supporting international use	25 Making views accessible
13 Leveraging human knowledge	26 Supporting visualization

Table 6.1. The Benefits / Tactics Matrix (see page left). The usability benefits are listed across the top of the table, the architectural tactics are listed down the side. The numbers in the cells refer to the specific scenario packages that give the column's benefit and employ the row's tactic. An additional scenario, Supporting Personalization, was added after this matrix was created

Software Tactics. The last part of a U&SA scenario package includes a list of the architectural tactics employed by the sample architectural pattern to implement the scenario. These architectural tactics, design decisions that influence quality attributes like usability or performance, were developed to codify best-practice solution techniques for common software design problems (Bass et al., 2003). The software tactics hierarchy for usability appears in Figure 6.8.

In the case of *Reusing Information Manually*, the sample architectural pattern uses the *data intermediary* tactic to implement the information reuse repository component. Most of the architecture examples for the other usability scenarios employ multiple tactics to implement a solution.

Benefits / Tactics Matrix. In addition to our list of scenario packages, we developed a tool to help apply the U&SA materials to a development effort: the Benefits / Tactics Matrix, shown in Figure 6.1.

When a project team wishes to determine which scenarios are important for their system, they first assess which usability benefits are critical for fulfilling their usability goals. Then they read down the column of each benefit and find the scenarios they must consider during the architecture design phase.

After the development team has determined that their architecture design includes support for all the usability scenarios they have deemed critical, or if an architecture is already in place, the team may use the matrix to identify additional scenarios that may be easy to support. They enter the Benefits / Tactics Matrix through the software

---

Software Architecture Tactics Hierarchy

    Localize modifications
        Hide information
        Separate data from commands
        Separate data from the view of that data
        Separate authoring from execution
    Maintain multiple copies
        Data
        Commands
    Use an intermediary
        Data
        Function
    Recording
    Preemptive scheduling policy
    Support system initiative
        Task model
        User model
        System model

Figure 6.8   Software Architecture Tactics Hierarchy. For each scenario, we list the tactics used in our sample solution pattern

engineering tactics they have already employed and read across the rows to identify which scenarios may be easy for them to support with their existing design. Even though these scenarios are not critical, the team may wish to consider implementing them if the architecture they have chosen will support them without much additional effort.

6.4   PRIOR USE OF U&SA MATERIALS

The U&SA materials described above had been developed and disseminated over the course of more than five years. Since we began work on this project in 1999, we have run several industry-focused tutorials on applying our materials (Bass et al., 2004; John et al., 2004c; John et al., 2004a), presented our work at usability and software engineering conferences,[4] and published information on the U&SA materials in Software Engineering Institute technical reports and software engineering magazines. We have also applied the information in the scenario packages informally in a few architecture design reviews. For example, we used a few of the scenarios as part of the ATAM^{SM} on a large commercial information system (Bass and John, 2003). However, the full set of scenarios had never been explicitly applied to a real-world software system undergoing a major architectural redesign. Therefore, although our materials appear useful, we still needed to subject them to the test of real-world use.

---

[4]For a full list of references, see http://www.uandsa.org

6.5   QUESTIONS FOR A REAL-WORLD CASE

We set out to test our materials by using them as the main discussion points for an architectural review of a real-world software project with significant architectural design problems and an emphasis on usability. Although we recognized that no single case could give us definite, generalizable answers to all our questions, we hoped to get feedback, suggestions, and new ideas that would help us refine our materials in preparation for more rigorous empirical studies. We set out with three specific questions, detailed below.

> *Would a real-world software development team accept the U&SA materials as the main discussion point of an architecture design meeting?*

Traditionally, development teams have not considered usability as a software quality attribute at the architecture design phase. Usability issues are introduced much later in the life cycle through user testing and design iteration and earlier in the life cycle through ethnography, contextual inquiry, and other field techniques. Our experience has been that usability professionals are frequently not invited to architecture design meetings, and when they are, they feel they have little to contribute because they have no training in software architecture design or its implications for producing usable systems. We created the U&SA materials to a framework within which usability professionals could contribute to a software architecture design meeting.

We had successfully introduced our scenarios for enhancing usability as a quality attribute alongside more traditional architectural quality attributes such as performance, security, and reliability during broad architectural reviews. However, as of mid-2002, usability had never been the main topic of discussion in a large-scale, real-world architecture design meeting. We were interested in discovering whether a development team confronting a larger software architecture design effort would accept usability as an architectural quality attribute and whether both the developers and usability professionals on the team would be able to use our scenarios to participate in a discussion about the system's proposed architectural design.

> *Would usability scenarios generated by considering single-user-at-a-desktop apply to a real-world design problem that may involve other domains (such as collaborative workspaces, web-based environments, etc)?*

The U&SA scenarios were initially developed through literature investigations and examinations of usability problems in common desktop applications and operating system interfaces. Most of these "single-user-at-a-desktop" applications followed the classic WIMP paradigm, executed on a single machine only, and did not support multiple-user collaboration. Single-user-at-a-desktop does not cover all possible environments that have potential software architecture and usability issues, however. Modern systems are designed to support domains with requirements that span a wide variety of paradigms, including collaborative computer-supported cooperative work environments, real-time embedded systems, ubiquitous computing, and so on. We hoped to discover how many of our scenarios would apply in these other environments, which are different in many respects from the one we had in mind while developing the scenarios. Although no single case can cover all these environments, applying our materials to a system in any environment off the desktop is a step toward answering this question.

Would our architecture design suggestions contribute to a real design project?

Ultimately, the U&SA materials are designed to improve architectural decisions made early in the life cycle with respect to their support for usability. Thus, the purpose of the scenarios is to generate design suggestions for software architectures which, when followed, help to prevent the "We can't change *THAT!*" problem described in the introduction. In applying our materials to a real-world development project, we wanted to discover whether the scenarios could, in fact, suggest design changes to the proposed architecture of a real software system so we could learn whether our materials were effective at all. We also hoped to discover whether real development teams would find these suggestions compelling enough to change their architecture design.

With these questions in mind we began to collaborate with the development team of the MERBoard project, a software development project at NASA Ames Research Center that is a participant in the High Dependability Computing Program[5]. As a participant in the HDCP, the MERBoard development team agreed to allow intervention by software engineering researchers for the purpose of testing new methods and tools.

6.6   THE MERBOARD PROJECT

The MERBoard Project is a software development effort by NASA Ames Research Center[6] to create a collaborative tool to support the engineers and scientists on the Mars Exploration Rovers (MER) mission.[7]

Two robotic probes landed on Mars in January 2004. The MER mission's scientific goals include searching for and characterizing a wide range of rocks and soils that hold clues to past water activity on Mars. The MER collects soil samples and other geological data from the Martian surface and transmits this information to NASA scientists back on Earth for analysis. Each MER is solar powered; during the Martian day, it collects data based on instructions sent to it from Earth. When night comes, it transmits this data back to Earth and goes into a low-power, low-activity mode until the sun rises in the morning. During the Martian night, scientists back on Earth must analyze the data received from the MER to determine what instructions to send to the robot in the morning. For instance, if the data indicate that there is a high probability that an old water channel might lie to the left, scientists must send orders to the MER to investigate that area in the morning. The scientists must be able to analyze the data and make decisions under strict deadlines, so that the MER does not sit idle.

To facilitate communication, the scientists work in a collocated, "war-room" style environment. Their initial technology support consisted of desktop and laptop com-

---

[5]For information about the HDCP, see http://www.cebase.org/HDCP/frames.html?/HDCP/aboutus.htm
[6]For information about MERBoard, see http://ic.arc.nasa.gov/story.php?sid=104
[7]For information about the MER mission, see http://marsrovers.jpl.nasa.gov/home/index.html.

Figure 6.9   A photograph of the MERBoard's whiteboard screen (MERBoard User's Guide, NASA Ames Research Center, September 10, 2003, by permission)

puters running a variety of software applications, projection screens, and paper flip charts to facilitate group thinking and discussion. The MERBoard Project introduced new technology to support collaborative activities like annotating images and strategic planning with storage, retrieval and sharing capabilities (Tollinger et al., 2004).

The MERBoard is a wall-sized collaborative workspace intended to facilitate shoulder-to-shoulder collaboration (Figure 6.9). The physical hardware consists of a large touch-sensitive plasma display. The software consists of four major components: a web browser for on-the-fly internet research, a collaborative whiteboard for creating and annotating visualizations of data, a remote login (VNC) client for connecting the MERBoard to the scientists' desktop and laptop computers, and MERSpace, a shared document repository for saved MERBoard sessions.

Usability had always been a key goal for the MERBoard project; their slogan was that the final system had to be to be "Palm Pilot simple". The MERBoards are intended to enhance the productivity of the scientists, who have a wide variance in their comfort with new technology, are too busy to spend much time becoming familiar with the tool before the mission, and have tight deadlines during the mission. Thus, the system must be both easy to learn and efficient to use, two key aspects of usability.

6.6.1   MERBoard Project Timeline

The MERBoard team has operated in several phases with defined deliverables (Figure 6.10). For the first phase, beginning in Fall 2001, the MERBoard project team

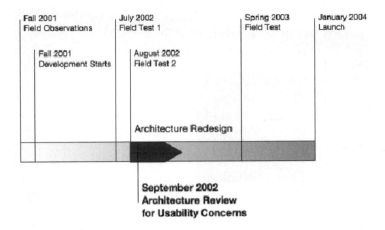

Figure 6.10 The MERBoard development timeline. We applied the U&SA materials during the architecture redesign phase at the September 2002 architecture review for usability concerns and follow-on teleconferences

conducted ethnographic field studies and user research to determine the real needs of the engineers and scientists. They then began development on a working prototype that could be user tested in the 2002 summer field tests with other MER technology. After those field tests were completed, the team took the issues identified in the user tests and began a ground-up rewrite effort, this time with an emphasis on sound architectural design for extensibility, performance, and reliability. They began with an architecture redesign meeting to set their goals for the January 2004 landing of this MER mission and for the 2009 MER mission as well.

Our intervention began at the September 2004 architecture review meeting and continued through teleconferences with a MERBoard developer.

6.7   U&SA'S APPLICATION TO MERBOARD

Since MERBoard had articulated usability as a primary goal of their system from the beginning, we proposed that it be considered as an architectural quality attribute along with their other stated attributes of extendibility, performance, and reliability. Since classic architecture design and analysis techniques do not address usability as a quality attribute, we offered to help the MERBoard team apply our U&SA materials to their proposed architecture redesign.

Our intervention took place over the course of four meetings: a face-to-face meeting where the lead architect walked through an overview of the proposed architecture redesign, a face-to-face meeting to introduce the MERBoard team to the U&SA materials and prioritize their usability goals, a teleconference with the front-end developer to review his understanding of the U&SA scenario packages, and a second teleconference with the front-end developer to review his application of the scenario packages to the details of his proposed architecture design.

6.7.1   Face-to-face Meetings: Architecture Overview and U&SA Materials

The first meeting was an architecture overview for the MERBoard project team. It took place in the MERBoard project lab and involved the entire MERBoard project team, including the project manager, the usability professionals (including an ethnographer, several cognitive modelers, HCI specialists, and a graphic designer), the lead architect and several software developers. The second and third authors were primarily observers at this architecture overview, although we were invited to ask clarifying questions. The lead architect of the MERBoard system presented the proposed architecture redesign and discussed technical concerns such as what library to use to handle gesture input, how to structure the components to support future extensibility, etc. The project manager and software developers asked questions; the second author asked a few clarifying questions; the usability professionals were generally silent listeners. The meeting took approximately four hours.

There was then a break for dinner and the majority of the MERBoard team returned to hear us describe the U&SA materials and to prioritize the scenarios for the MER-Board release (one designer had a previous commitment and could not return). We gave a short overview of the U&SA motivation and approach, and then presented our list of scenarios that form the core of our scenario packages. We led the team through a review of their architectural requirements by going over each of our twenty-seven scenarios in turn. For each scenario, the team decided whether:

- The scenario applied to the current, January 2004 target (i.e., it must be supported by the redesigned architecture and implemented in the current release).

- The scenario applied, but they did not anticipate needing it until the distant 2009 release (i.e., it was safe to delay).

- The scenario did not apply to MERBoard.

In this meeting everyone, including the usability professionals, contributed to the discussion. Unlike the previous architecture overview, the entire team debated the needs of their users and what impact this would have on their architectural requirements.

By the end of the meeting, the design and development team had found that 25 of the 27 scenarios were applicable to MERBoard. Seventeen of these scenarios were considered essential for the January 2004 release and were targeted for the next field trial. Eight were determined less critical and were postponed for the longer-term release.

Since 93% our scenarios were judged applicable by the development team, we conclude that they were highly relevant to MERBoard, a real-world project with a significant architecture design challenge. Moreover, the team accepted our scenarios as a means of discussing usability as a software quality attribute that applied to their system's architecture. Even more encouraging was the nature of the discussion our technique fostered in the team; the usability experts and software experts had common ground on which to discuss critical design decisions at a sufficiently early stage for changes to be made.

6.7.2   Teleconference to Review U&SA Materials

At the initial face-to-face meetings, the MERBoard management determined that most of the relevant U&SA scenarios applied to the design of the front-end of MERBoard, as opposed to the back-end (or server-side). Therefore, we arranged follow-up discussions with the front-end architect and developer (hereafter, FED). It was arranged that these discussions would be via teleconference because the authors and the MERboard team were separated by 3000 miles and travel budget for both groups was limited. We provided FED with a copy of our technical report on the U&SA scenarios (Bass and John, 2001b) as well as the notes packet to our 2002 CHI tutorial on applying the U&SA technique (John et al., 2004a). FED read these materials during a four-day period that spanned a weekend, while he redesigned the front-end architecture.

The following week, we had a teleconference with FED to get his reaction to the scenario packages and our technical report. There were four participants in this teleconference: FED (at NASA Ames in California), architecture expert Len Bass, usability expert Bonnie John, and research associate Rob Adams (at Carnegie Mellon University in Pittsburgh, Pennsylvania). We solicited the FED's opinions on the patterns, whether and how he felt they applied to MERBoard's architecture design, and clarified those issues about which he was uncertain. We discussed his general impressions of the U&SA materials as a whole, and then went through each scenario package in order to get his specific impressions on those that the team had decided were critical for the current release. FED described to us how he foresaw each scenario package influencing the technical decisions he was facing. The entire discussion lasted approximately one hour.

FED's reactions to the U&SA materials were primarily positive. Referring to the U&SA scenario packages as a whole (i.e. the scenarios, usability benefits, architecture patterns and software engineering tactics), he said

> "It's nice to explicitly describe it like this. I mean I managed to avoid any actual classes that actually taught architecture, this kind of design patterns, you know software engineering. So this is basically how I would write... I think I'd write [the architecture like this] anyway but it's definitely is nice to have it laid out and drawn up and written up for you. And then you can say okay this is how we're going to do it. As opposed to here's my, sort of, thoughts on the matter."

> "... it's also nice just keeping a list [of scenario packages] next to me so when I'm doing my design decision I can glance at it to make sure, you know, I haven't forgotten anything."

About the architecture patterns associated with each scenario, FED said they were "very clear" even though he did not have experience in software patterns or architecture patterns prior to using the U&SA materials. About applying them to the MERBoard front-end architecture redesign he said,

> "So, they're pretty interesting... Of the ones that tools actually used, the patterns, some patterns were somewhat useful others weren't... [some patterns] didn't really apply. And I guess some were sort of already there.., [the pattern in the U&SA documents] described something that already exists [in the MERBoard architecture]. So it's not actually wrong, it's confirmation that we're doing something right."

For example, regarding the Aggregating Command Scenario, FED judged the proposed architecture for the MERBoard's whiteboard as "very very similar to this pattern ... the grouping manager and command cluster ... have this separation described in the pattern."

Unsolicited by the researchers, FED mentioned that having a separate list of responsibilities fulfilled by the pattern was helpful (such a list was available for six patterns at the time of this intervention, in John et al., 2004a).

> "... the breakdown of responsibilities was quite nice, I felt. It wasn't critical but
> it definitely made it a lot easier to think about."

On a less positive note, when speaking about the software engineering tactics, FED was polite, as would be expected in such a discussion with researchers who developed the materials under discussion. He said they were "probably definitely helpful", but could not think of any concrete instances of how these tactics were useful to him. He thought they would be more useful if they were integrated into the description of the example architecture patterns as "key ideas" used in each pattern.

In summary, FED expressed that he was able to understand the U&SA materials and connect them to the MERBoard front-end architecture he was designing. We arranged to have an additional teleconference once he had documented his architecture design and review that design with respect to the scenarios.

6.7.3   Teleconference to Specifically apply U&SA Materials

In advance of our second teleconference (with the same participants), FED sent us a diagram of his proposed architecture design. We went through all the scenario packages that the design and development team had deemed necessary for the 2004 release and discussed how the proposed architecture supported each scenario package. The architecture expert and FED each proposed changes to the diagramed architecture in light of the considerations raised by the scenario packages, then discussed and decided on those changes. This meeting ran for approximately one hour.

General Impressions of the Application of U&SA Materials.   The discussion in this teleconference was a collaboration between FED, who was an expert on MERBoard but had no formal training in software architecture (as had been uncovered during the first teleconference), and the U&SA researchers, primarily the software architecture expert. The conversation reflects this collaboration in that 46% of the words were uttered by FED, indicating that it was not a "lecture" by the architecture expert, who uttered 44% of the words. Had it been a lecture by the architecture expert, a larger percentage of the words would have been uttered by that researcher. Nor was it a "seeded" design review where the architecture expert throws out an idea and the domain expert then dominates, or a larger percentage of the words would have been uttered by FED. Since the development team had already decided which scenarios were important to the MERBoard, the usability experts' input to this discussion was small (5% of the words), primarily asking clarifying questions in order to take notes and revise the architecture diagram. The more junior research associate primarily asked clarifying questions (5% of the words).

In the previous teleconference, FED expressed confidence in his understanding of the U&SA materials and in this teleconference he seemed readily able to apply the general scenarios to his specific architecture design problem; each scenario immediately brought to mind a specific technical challenge he was facing and he was able to use these scenarios to brainstorm potential implementation solutions. However, FED seemed less able to apply the component-level patterns we provided in the technical report to MERBoard without additional support from the U&SA team, as evidenced by the large number of changes we made during this review, described below. In one respect this shows that U&SA materials and expertise can have a influence on architecture design. On the other hand, this is evidence that the U&SA materials need to be improved for them to become a stand-alone resource for software architects in the real world.

Moving from general impressions to specific content of the teleconference, the next section details the proposed MERBoard front-end architecture and the changes we made during this teleconference.

Results of the U&SA Intervention on the MERBoard Architecture. The architecture diagram FED sent us at the beginning of the second teleconference is shown in Figure 6.11. The architecture that resulted from the discussions during that teleconference is shown in Figure 6.12. The components in Figure 6.12 and their responsibilities are as follows.

- The **GUI** contains all the user interface widgets that appear on the MERBoard and handles user input processing logic. The GUI is implemented using the Java Swing user interface toolkit.

- The **Dispatcher** receives user actions from the GUI and either handles them itself or forwards them to the appropriate component for processing.

- The **Administrator** handles all user management and personalization functions.

- The **Selector** provides a number of utilities relating to the display and manipulation of user and personalization information, thereby acting as a bridge between the user interface and the Administrator.

- The **Save / Restore Interface** takes snapshots of the MERBoard's current state and sends them to the server over the network. This allows the MERBoard to be restored in case of a system crash, minimizing data loss. It also handles manual requests for saving and restoring data.

- The **Recorder** logs usage data for later analysis by the usability professionals to identify usability breakdowns and areas that need improvement. These data are intended to feed into future collaborative systems developed by NASA.

- The **Network Interface** provides an abstraction layer for communication with the remote server component on which the MERBoard's data is saved. The remote server is not shown on the diagram.

- The **Plugins** implement specific functionality extensions to the MERBoard. The plugins developed by the MERBoard team include the whiteboard, the web browser, the VNC-based plugin for connection to a remote computer, and a specialized tool for the Long-Term Planning group called the "Sol Tree Tool".

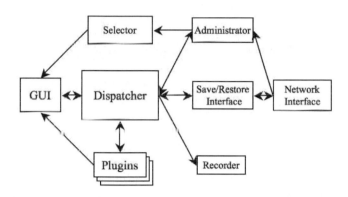

Figure 6.11   MERBoard architecture diagram proposed by FED prior to the second teleconference. The developer created this diagram after being exposed to the U&SA materials, but before consulting with U&SA researchers in detail about each scenario

Comparing Figure 6.11 and 6.12, it is easy to see that almost every component and communication line was either modified or added because of the detailed discussion of the U&SA scenarios. We audio taped the teleconference, which allowed us to identify when these changes were made in the discussion and determine what information content led to each change. Below, we examine each change by considering whether the U&SA scenario packages directly caused the change or if other aspects of this architecture walkthrough steered the design. Figure 6.12 labels each change, C1 through C6.

The first modification (C1) involved the addition of a representation of the MERBoard user to the diagram, thus giving a sense of where the user fits into the system. This constituted a simple omission on FED's part, a common occurrence when documenting complex systems from a software engineering point of view. The usability expert suggested the addition to keep the user evident in the architecture documentation. It is possible that any review of the diagram by an independent person taking a human-centered approach could have turned up this omission; no special U&SA scenario package can be credited with this addition.

The next modification (C2) involved altering the communication paths between the Plugins, the Dispatcher, and the other components. The intent of this modification was

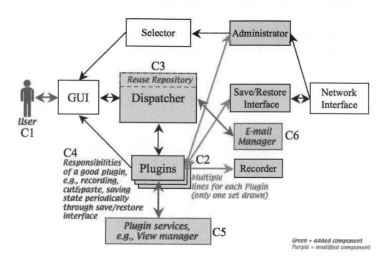

Figure 6.12   The modified MERBoard architecture diagram, developed collaboratively by the FED and U&SA researchers during the teleconference where the proposed architecture was discussed with reference to the U&SA scenarios relevant to the January 2004 release. The changes made are labeled C1 through C6 (these labels do not appear in the architecture diagram used by the developers)

to simplify the communication between the Plugin and the worker components (the Administrator, Save / Restore Interface, and Recorder) so that these potentially heavy communication channels would not all have to be routed through the Dispatcher. This change arose from a general discussion of the architecture. The architecture expert suggested this change to improve the overall conceptual integrity of the MERBoard design (a quality attribute he called "buildability"). There was no explicit reference to any U&SA scenario package.

The addition of the "Reuse Repository" in the Dispatcher (C3) addresses the need for an explicit sink for copied and pasted data (commonly known as a *clipboard*) and also speaks to the need for defined mechanisms for handling and transporting clipboard data between components. This addition arose as the result of a long discussion of U&SA's Reusing Information scenario package. The front-end developer explained his implementation of information reuse in the MERBoard and the merits of various alternatives with the architecture expert. Unlike the previous two examples, this change arose directly from the discussion of U&SA materials.

C4 is an annotation on the diagram to document the responsibilities of a "good" plugin, that is, a plugin that supports the level of usability required by the MERBoard developers and its users. Since third parties often develop the plugin components, comprehensive documentation of any architectural decision to allocate responsibilities to a plugin must be provided so that these parties realize what conditions their code is expected to handle. This annotation came from a discussion of U&SA's Supporting

Undo, Working at the User's Pace, and Observing System State scenario packages. Unlike the previous change, this change emerged from the discussion of several scenario packages rather that just one. This suggests that the combined effects of several scenario packages may produce considerations that do not arise when those scenario packages are considered singly.

The Plugin Services component (C5) was added in response to a discussion of the U&SA scenario Operating Consistently Across Views. This was the first scenario discussed to bring up the idea of having different views on the same data, therefore, it initiated a discussion of views themselves. The architecture expert connected this discussion to preliminary ideas about an object model presented at the first face-to-face meeting. He noted that there would be a lot of commonality between functions that manipulate aspects of the object model and proposed that common code inherited into the plugins would be better than making each plugin implement these common functions themselves. FED agreed and added the Plugin Services component with the View Manager as an example.

Finally, the E-mail Manager (C6) was added shortly after the Plugin Services component as the discussion of multiple views continued. The MERBoard designers had envisioned that scientists may collaborate for a while using MERBoard, then analyze data in various ways on their own laptop or desktop computers, depending on individual interests. Thus, they expected that data on the MERBoard would have to be transferred to other computers. While discussing other aspects of multiple views, FED explained that this may be done through e-mail. As soon as he mentioned using e-mail, he noticed that he had not included a component representing the e-mail manager and added it. Although the e-mail function is not specifically tied to maintaining multiple views of data (the discussion underway), its omission was discovered as a direct consequence of discussing U&SA scenarios.

In summary, many changes were made to the proposed architecture to better support the usability goals of the MERBoard team. These changes included changing communication paths, adding components, and documenting aspects of the architecture not represented by lines and boxes. The first few changes were not linked to any specific U&SA scenario and might have been made during any architecture design walkthrough that included a usability expert (not usually present in current practice) and an architecture expert. However, when we examined each scenario in turn, we made some changes that specifically supported the scenario under consideration. Some changes related to only one scenario; others to a collection of scenarios that triggered a single solution. These cases clearly show that the U&SA materials influenced the final design of the MERBoard architecture.

6.8   SUMMARY OF FINDINGS

As we've shown above, the application of our U&SA materials to MERBoard's architecture enjoyed a measure of success. Now, we revisit the questions, expressed earlier, that we hoped a real-world application would be able to answer.

Would a real-world software development team accept the U&SA materials as the main discussion point of an architecture design meeting?

We found that the entire MERBoard design and development team was not only willing to accept U&SA as the main discussion point, but actively participated in a three hour review of their system based around our scenario packages. Moreover, we found that the discussion of our scenario packages included the participation of usability professionals who were silent during the conventional architecture presentation. This is encouraging, for it provides evidence that U&SA helps to improve communication between the software development and usability communities, one of its stated goals.

> *Would usability scenarios generated by considering single-user-at-a-desktop apply to a real-world design problem that may involve other domains (such as collaborative workspaces, web-based environments, etc)?*

The MERBoard is a wall-sized collaborative workspace intended for use in a co-located, war-room style environment. It is a far cry from the single-user-at-a-desktop paradigm that we originally considered when developing the list of scenario packages, yet the MERBoard team still identified 25 of our 27 scenarios as applicable to their project; 17 of these being critical for the 2004 MER mission. Moreover, the team was able to give concrete examples of how the scenarios were realized for their users, often from their experiences performing direct observations of user behavior in the field trials.

We are encouraged to discover that so many scenarios were applicable in a CSCW application, since it implies that the scope of our technique lies beyond the single-user-at-a-desktop paradigm. Although we currently do not know how far our materials' range extends, this case provides evidence that they can be useful in at least one additional domain.

> *Would our architecture design suggestions contribute to a real design project?*

As we have shown, the proposed architecture redesign for the MERBoard was heavily influenced by the front-end developer reading the U&SA documents and participating in an architectural review with the research team. The front-end developer felt that most of the materials were clear and relevant to his design. He especially liked the list of responsibilities the software must fulfill to support a usability scenario. During the detailed review, a majority of the architecture's components were modified to take into account the issues raised by U&SA scenario packages. U&SA clearly contributed to the architecture design of MERBoard.

However, we found that the architecture design patterns were less usable for the front-end developer than we had hoped and that he seemed to think the software tactics were irrelevant to his design. We have thus changed our approach with respect to these patterns, as discussed in the next section.

6.9   ONGOING WORK

Our ongoing work was influenced in several ways by our findings from applying U&SA materials to the MERBoard architecture redesign. In particular, we have redesigned our scenario packages and we are testing the efficacy of the different components of those packages in a more controlled setting.

We have found, both through our work with MERBoard and our experience teaching the U&SA materials, that the architecture design patterns we provide (Bass and John, 2001b) as part of the scenario package are often insufficient for development purposes. Most developers find that our patterns are either not sufficiently general to be applicable to their system, or are so general that they have difficultly seeing how to apply them to their system. At the same time, both the MERBoard front-end developer and the participants in recent tutorials and classes find the architecture-independent lists of responsibilities that must be fulfilled to support a scenario extremely useful. This feedback led us to distinguish between architecture-independent responsibilities, architectural support for those responsibilities, and overarching architectural decisions related to aspects of the system other than usability. We have redesigned our scenario packages around this distinction, emphasizing responsibilities and rationale for the responsibilities (John et al., 2004c), in packages that are called *usability-supporting architectural patterns* (USAPs).

Encouraged that USAPs will be useful in software architecture design, we have collaborated with researchers on the European Union project called STATUS.[8] Some members of STATUS have also investigated the relationship between usability and software architecture (e.g., Bosch and Juristo, 2003; Folmer and Bosch, 2004; Folmer et al., 2003; Juristo et al., 2003). We expect that our combined effort will produce more USAPs than our research group could alone.

To investigate whether different pieces of the scenario packages contribute to the quality of a resulting architecture design, we are currently conducting a controlled laboratory experiment with software architects. The experiment compares three conditions: (1) only a scenario is given and the software architect is free to make architecture design changes as he or she sees fit, (2) giving both a scenario and the list of architecture-independent responsibilities to support that scenario, and (3) giving a scenario, the list of responsibilities, and a sample architecture pattern expressed in UML component and sequence diagrams. Preliminary analyses show a significant improvement in the number of responsibilities considered by software designers when using responsibilities and UML diagrams over the scenario alone, and a trend toward improvement when using the list of responsibilities alone (Golden et al., 2005). We are continuing the analysis to assess quality of the architecture design. These data provide guidance to support future development of USAPs.

Finally, we realize that this chapter provides just part of the story about the usefulness of considering usability in architecture design. This chapter stops at an informal analysis of the creation of an architecture component diagram that supports the desired usability aspects of a system. However, there are many other questions to answer in the full development process. Did support for the scenarios get implemented at all? Was the architecture as designed sufficient to support the actual implementation of the scenarios or was it changed along the way? Did the end-users of MERBoard need the usability features supported by the architecture? Did they need even more support? We are currently analyzing many aspects of the development process, the implemented

---

[8]See the STATUS website http://www.ls.fi.upm.es/status/

code, documentation, and actual user data during the MER 2004 mission to construct a more formal case study of this experience.

We also realize that a single case study cannot answer all questions regarding our materials. We are actively soliciting additional development groups wanting to explore their architecture designs from a usability viewpoint to gain more insight into the extent of U&SA materials' applicability and usefulness and to improve their design for the software architects who are our users.

Acknowledgements

The authors would like to thank the MERBoard development team for their willingness to participate in this research and for their insightful feedback on the U&SA materials. The Computational Sciences Division at NASA Ames Research Center provided support for MERBoard development and the MERBoard team's participation in our intervention. The High-Dependability Computing Program (HDCP) provided funding for the development of U&SA materials and through its testbed program provided us access to the MERBoard project for the purposes of testing the materials. Carnegie Mellon University's Software Engineering Institute (SEI) provided funding for the early development of U&SA via funding to Bonnie John as well as continuing support for the work of Len Bass.

7 LINKING USER NEEDS AND USE CASE-DRIVEN REQUIREMENTS ENGINEERING

Sari Kujala

Software Business and Engineering Institute, Helsinki University of Technology, Finland

Abstract

Requirements engineering is the first and the most critical step in software development. One of the basic questions in requirements engineering is how to find out what customers and users really need. In addition, user needs must be expressed by structured, formal user requirements. Use cases are often seen as supporting the process of capturing requirements from the user's point of view. In addition, there is increasing evidence that involving users as the main source of information in requirements engineering is a vital prerequisite in successful projects. The human-computer interaction community has developed a variety of methods for understanding the context of use and eliciting user needs directly from the users themselves. The challenge has been to bridge the gap between informal user need descriptions and formal user requirements. This chapter presents an approach that shows how user-centered requirements analysis can be effectively integrated to use case-driven requirements engineering. Firstly, user needs are gathered directly from users using semi-structured, small-scale field studies. Secondly, the results are summarized in user need tables to ease their utilization and their linking to use case descriptions. Thirdly, the user need tables are transformed into use case descriptions. The approach has been validated by several industrial cases in real development contexts.

A. Seffah (eds.), Human-Centered Software Engineering – Integrating Usability
in the Development Process, 113–125.

7.1   INTRODUCTION

Requirements engineering is the first and the most critical step in software development. One of the basic questions in requirements engineering is what is it that customers and users really need. The success of the product depends on its ability to provide the right solution for the customers and the users. The internal functioning of the system is not really of great concern to the users and customers, but they do want to perform their tasks with the system in a specific way.

Requirements engineering can also be identified as an essential activity from the usability point of view. As John Karat (Karat, 1997) writes, the acceptability of any software product is no longer seen as being dependent solely on user interface features, but on the way a system fits into its context of use. Thus, user-centered design and user interface design cannot be separated from the rest of the system development. Usability should be considered from the very beginning of the development when a "ground plan" of the system is decided.

There is increasing evidence that involving users as the main source of information in requirements engineering is a vital prerequisite in successful projects (Kujala, 2003). However, user involvement should not be viewed as being trivial. Requirements elicitation is often seen as being a difficult problem, as communication between developers and users may be poor. Developers may not even be motivated to communicate with users, as the developers do not know what it is that they should be asking. In addition, users may not know what they want and may also have difficulties in articulating their needs. One difficulty is that part of the users' knowledge has become tacit through automation (Mitchell and Chi, 1984; Wood, 1997). In well-learned tasks, much of the relevant knowledge is no longer consciously available for the individual and non-verbal skills and everyday self-evidences are difficult to articulate.

The human-computer interaction community has developed a variety of approaches and methods for involving users. User-centered design, participatory design, ethnography, and contextual design may be considered the main approaches, although the roots and methods of these approaches are closely linked and overlapping (Kujala, 2003). In addition, task analysis covers a wide range of methods in order to analyze a system function in terms of user goals and the sub-goals inherent in performing the task (Johnson, 1989; Kirwan and Ainsworth, 1993; Hackos and Redish, 1998). Much of the task analysis literature is devoted to the analysis of data, but task analysis also involves the users as informants (Jeffries, 1997).

Moreover, field studies are particularly focused on discovering tacit knowledge from users. Field studies provide a collection of techniques for studying users, their tasks, and their environments in the actual context of those environments (Wixon et al., 2002). Hackos and Redish (Hackos and Redish, 1998) describe an extensive range of field methods from observing to ethnographic interviewing. Field studies can be seen as overlapping many approaches, but the general idea is not just to ask what users want but to study their actual behavior and context of use.

Thus, field study results help to understand those tacit user needs that users cannot articulate directly. The new system is not used in a vacuum; users have needs relating to the new system depending on the context of use. For example, user needs man-

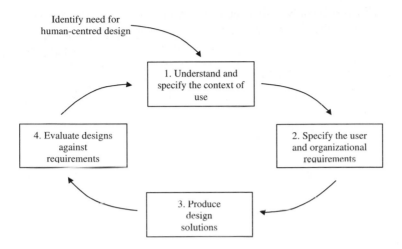

Figure 7.1 The human-centered design activities in ISO 13407 (ISO/IEC, 1999)

ifest themselves as either problems that hinder users in achieving their goals, or as opportunities to improve the likelihood of users achieving their goals.

Field studies support the first activity of human-centered design: "understand and specify the context of use" as described in the international standard ISO 13407 (ISO/IEC, 1999). Figure 7.1 shows the interdependence between human-centered design activities. According to ISO 13407, the characteristics of the users, tasks and the organizational and physical environments define the context in which the system is used; users are seen as a valuable source of this knowledge. Furthermore, user involvement and participation is seen to increase user acceptance and commitment. Understanding and specifying the context of use also helps in identifying relevant usability goals and test cases.

Understanding context of use and discovering user needs is, however, not in itself enough. Analyzing an overwhelming amount of raw data is a frequently mentioned problem of qualitative field studies; this was brought out in Kujala's (Kujala, 2003) literature review. Moreover, fieldworkers have been found to have problems with communicating results to system developers and with effecting design work (Plowman et al., 1995).

In user-centered design, a context of use description is a starting point for the user and their organizational requirements (ISO/IEC, 1999). However, the context of use description is separate from user requirements and these two documents should be linked to facilitate the information flow and the transition from activity one to activity two in Figure 7.1.

Use cases are often seen as supporting the process of capturing requirements from the user's point of view (e.g. Rumbaugh, 1994). However, in our industrial cases, use cases were often written by software engineers who had not met the users, so the use case documents were not shown to the users as Jacobson (Jacobson, 1992) recommends. The software engineers were therefore not familiar with user needs.

As their use cases described the internal functioning of the system and the technical details, they were nearly impossible for the users to understand.

On the other hand, use cases are widely accepted among developers and they provide an opportunity to transmit user needs to requirements engineering and many researchers have already presented their ideas of reconciling user-centered design (e.g. Seffah et al., 2001) or user interface design (e.g. Constantine and Lockwood, 2001) to use case-driven requirements engineering.

This book chapter presents an approach to how user-centered requirements analysis can be effectively integrated to use case-driven requirements engineering. Firstly, user needs are gathered directly from users using semi-structured, small-scale field studies. Secondly, the results are summarized in user need tables to ease their utilization and their linking to use case descriptions. Thirdly, the user need tables are transformed into use case descriptions. Finally, we describe how the approach has been validated by several industrial cases in real development contexts.

7.2 UNDERSTANDING USER NEEDS

As previously stated, field studies provide a way of understanding tacit user needs. Field study techniques go beyond gathering just verbal data by incorporating observations made in the user's environment (Wixon et al., 1990). At the same time field studies are often seen to be time consuming, providing a vast amount of unstructured data that is difficult to use in development (e.g. Bly, 1997, Hynninen et al., 1999).

In our experience gained from several industrial cases, field study methods can be very useful even when the investment is modest. The field studies need to be simple and cost-efficient enough to be practical in real-life development projects characterized by tight schedules. In our approach, efficiency is gained by combining simple basic methods and using a top-down approach to focus the study.

Field studies are new for many companies and have to be introduced for the first time. An effective strategy seems to be to use small-scale pilots to introduce simple and easy to learn field study methods (Kujala et al., 2003). In addition, guidelines, checklists, training and personal support facilitate the adoption of new methods.

A good strategy is to start with basic interviewing and observing, as described by Hackos and Redish (Hackos and Redish, 1998), Redish and Wixon (Redish and Wixon, 2003) and Wood (Wood, 1996; Wood, 1997). Interviewing may not be the best method for eliciting non-verbal, tacit information, but it is very cost-effective in understanding the high-level context of use and the users' main goals and problems. Interviewing is easy-to-learn and important information can be discovered directly and effectively from users in a short time. However, interviews should be carried out in the natural setting of the potential users and using their own task-related language. The natural setting helps the user to remember details by seeing and maybe showing and trying the tools and artefacts being discussed. In addition, observing or talking-aloud supports interviewing by providing non-verbal information (Kujala and Mäntylä, 2000b). Beyer and Holzblatt (Beyer and Holtzblatt, 1998) offer good basic principles for facilitating the interviewer-interviewee relationship.

In order to be cost-efficient field studies need to be focused. A study team sets objectives for the study and identifies the most critical themes for each study. Sometimes it may be difficult to find the critical themes if the team does not know the users' world. Wood (Wood, 1997) describes how Grand Tour questions can be used to encourage the user to verbally "show the analyst around" the physical, temporal, and conceptual space of the work domain. In this way, a high-level picture of the users' world is gained and this information can be used to guide the rest of the interview.

In addition, a top-down approach helps in identifying interviewing themes and keeping the amount of data at a manageable level (Kujala and Mäntylä, 2000b). In the top-down approach, certain details of understanding may be lost as it does not start from scratch; however it is easier to learn and an overwhelming amount of raw data is avoided. The top-down approach means that we use semi-structured interviewing in which the most important interviewing themes are predefined and used in preparing questions. The goal is to gather critical information from each topic and keep the topics in mind while observing users and their environment. A basic set of top-down interviewing topics are shown in Table 7.1. The idea is not to follow the prepared questions strictly, but to use them as a checklist and to try to understand the users' perspective.

7.3 LINKING USER NEEDS TO USER REQUIREMENTS

Understanding user needs is in itself not enough. It is impossible to meet all user needs; there are so many needs and some of them conflict with each other. User needs must be discovered, but also analyzed, prioritized, and described. Finally, informal user needs must be expressed by structured user requirements if they are to be useful to system developers.

Contextual information is often represented in a textual form, such as stories (Imaz and Benyon, 1999). In our first industrial cases, we also used written reports with figures, photographs and video recordings (Kujala and Mäntylä, 2000a; Kujala and Mäntylä, 2000b; Kujala et al., 2001b; Kujala et al., 2001a). Developers evaluated the reports, photographs and videos as useful. However, in one company, we found that it was not so easy for a technically oriented developer to use written descriptions in product development (Kujala et al., 2001a). He could not see how to use the documents in user requirements definition, even though he had written the documents himself. Thus, we realized that a slightly more formal way of representing user needs was needed, so that developers could use information in analyzing and rationally selecting a good combination of user needs for inclusion in their future systems.

We therefore developed user need tables to offer a link between context of use descriptions and structural user requirements (Kujala et al., 2001a), see Table 7.2. The technically oriented developer derived insights from a user need table which we created for him. He got enthusiastic and wanted to make such tables from all of his field study findings. His project manager assessed that he could describe 70% of the preliminary requirements of the project using the user need tables.

User need tables represent user needs as users' problems and also as possibilities, and link them to a task sequence which is an essential part of the context of use (Table 7.2).

Several kinds of user information can be summarized in the form of user problems and possibilities. Problems are obstacles that arise from users' characteristics,

Table 7.1   Interview topics

Topic	Description
Background information	Background information helps the analyst to interpret the results and classify users. Typical questions are about personal characteristics such as age, sex, profession, technical orientation, previous computer and work experience. In addition users' task related characteristics such as motivation, work role and frequency of use or geographic and social characteristics such as location, culture and social connections may be asked.
Users' goals and preferences	The goal is to understand what users want to achieve, what is important for them, and how an intended application can support their tasks and create better ways of achieving the goals.
Users' knowledge, skills and experiences	The goal is to discover what users can and cannot do, and how they employ objects and symbols in accomplishing their goals. Thus, it would be possible to utilize their existing knowledge, skills, and conceptual models in product development.
Current processes	Understanding current processes helps in identifying task hierarchies and task sequences that are natural for users, and gives timing and other benchmarks for the performance criteria of a future solution.
Context of use	It includes user characteristics, tasks, equipment, and a physical and social environment in which a product is used (ISO/IEC, 1999).
Pros and cons of current processes and tools	In redesigning the current process it is necessary to identify advantages that users are unwilling to give up. An intended system should include most of the benefits and solve the current problems.

Table 7.2   An example of a user need table

Task sequence	Problems and possibilities
Step 1: When trapped in an elevator, passenger makes an emergency alarm.	■ Problem: Passengers want to get out of the elevator as soon as possible. ■ Problem: All kinds of passengers must be able to make an alarm call (blind, foreigners etc.). ■ Problem: Sometimes passengers may make false alarms unintentionally. ■ Problem: Passengers may be in panic. ■ Problem: Passengers need instant confirmation that they have created a connection to the service center operator and that they are going to get help.
Step 2: Unoccupied service centre operator receives the emergency alarm call and asks for information.	■ Problem: Different versions and types of remote monitoring systems. ■ Problem: Passenger is the only information source. ■ Problem: Service center operator does not notice the emergency alarm call.
Step 3: Service center operator completes transmission of information to the system and sends it to the area serviceman.	■ Problem: Laborious phase for the service center operator. ■ Problem: Simultaneous calls must be differentiated. ■ Problem: Serviceman cannot see all information. ■ Problem: Inadequate information from a site system. ■ Possibility: Instructions as to how to operate the system. ■ Possibility: Possibility to open phone line from Call Center to the elevator.
Step 4: Service center operator calls the serviceman and reads the description of the failure.	■ Problem: Extra work for the service center operator.

their physical and social environment, and the overall situation. Possibilities represent users' more implicit needs, and suggest how users' tasks can be supported and improved.

In addition to a task sequence and problems and possibilities, a high priority column can also be added to the table, so that it becomes possible to attach priority information to the user need tables. It may be difficult to specify any priority order for the needs, but usually the most essential needs are often identified.

User need tables are not able to present all user needs; other representations such as user profiles and photographs can be used in parallel. However, the purpose of user need tables is to summarize several kinds of user information and to facilitate the use of this information when user requirements are defined.

7.4   WRITING USER REQUIREMENTS FROM THE USER POINT OF VIEW

User need tables form the basis of writing user requirements and in particular they help developers to write use cases from the user point of view. A use case driven approach is one way of defining user requirements. Originally Jacobson (Jacobson, 1992; Jacobson, 1995) introduced use cases as a part of object-oriented methodology. Rumbaugh (Rumbaugh, 1994) describes use cases as the possible sequences of interactions between the system and one or more actors. Thus, use cases provide a more holistic and dynamic view of user requirements than the traditional single-requirement statements alone.

Jacobson (Jacobson, 1992) employs a graphical use case model which shows the system as being bounded by a box, with each actor being represented by a person outside the box, and use cases represented as ellipses inside the box. Rumbaugh (Rumbaugh, 1994) complemented the model by proposing a written description of the use case including name, summary actors, preconditions, description, exceptions, and post conditions.

Use cases can be written in a wide variety of forms and at different levels, but we have found that the original black-box view is the most useful one from the user point of view. Thus, only the external functioning or services to the user are described. The idea is to give high level descriptions of the basic functions and not to describe user interface details. In Table 7.3, the example use case description includes some details because the system in question was a new version of an existing system and it was known that some of the details were not going to be changed.

We have found that these kinds of high-level use case descriptions have value in facilitating communication among the project team. Use case descriptions help the project team to gain a coherent view of the system. Definition work did not proceed too quickly along technical lines.

We have used Rumbaugh's (Rumbaugh, 1994) description of use cases, except that we organized the written description of the use case in steps with numbers and connected the exceptions to steps identified by numbers. We also describe the goal of the user in preconditions-part: what users are trying to accomplish and why (Constantine, 1995).

Table 7.3   An example of a use case description

Use case:	**Making An Emergency Alarm Call**
Summary:	An entrapped passenger pushes the emergency alarm button in order to get help. A service center operator receives the emergency alarm call and informs the passenger that a serviceman will come and let the passenger out of the elevator.
Actors:	Passenger and service center operator
Preconditions:	An elevator has stopped between floors and there is a passenger in the elevator. The goal of the passenger is to get out of the elevator safely and as quickly as possible.
Basic sequence:	Step 1: The passenger presses the emergency alarm button.
	Step 2: The service center operator gets a visible notification of the emergency alarm call on the screen with an optional audio signal.
	Step 3: The service center operator accepts the emergency alarm call.
	Step 4: The system opens a voice connection between the service center operator and the passenger.
	Step 5: The system indicates to both the passenger and the service center operator that the voice connection is open.
	Step 6: The system guides the service center operator as to what information to ask of the passenger.
	Step 7: The service center operator
Exceptions:	Step 1: If an entrapped passenger does not push the alarm button long enough (less than 3 seconds), the system alerts the passenger with a voice announcement.
	Step 7: If the passenger has pressed the emergency alarm button by accident, the service center operator informs the system that the emergency alarm call is false. The system resets the emergency alarm call.
Post conditions:	The entrapped passenger knows that the service center operator will contact a serviceman who will help the passenger out of the elevator safely as soon as possible.

Inventing use case steps is difficult if developers do not know the users' tasks and needs. For example, in one of our industrial cases, the use case descriptions lacked the necessary level of detail and also the user-point of view when user need information was not available (Kujala et al., 2001a). In addition, we found that gathering user feedback with use cases is not enough. Users still interpret use cases on the basis of their present way of performing the tasks. If something is missing from the use case, they assume that it will nevertheless be implemented in the product. These implicit assumptions undermine the mutual understanding between users and developers.

User need tables inform developers as to how the task should be carried out and what the basic problems to be solved are. In addition, the tasks and objects are described in the users' language. In table form the information is in an organized form and the developer can consider user problems step by step and avoid the perception of having to deal with an overwhelming amount of data.

User need tables and use case descriptions complement each other, thus it is easy to move from one to another. The difference is that a user need table describes a specific present state user situation and context of use and there can be several versions of it, whereas the use case describes the general solution to how the task is performed with the new system. The idea is not to copy the task sequence as such, but to redesign all the necessary parts in order to solve user problems or realize the opportunities. Otherwise, the task sequence familiar to users is retained merely for the sake of convenience.

7.5   EVALUATING THE APPROACH IN INDUSTRY

The approach of linking user needs to use case-driven requirements engineering was developed and evaluated in several published, and a few unpublished, industrial cases in realistic product development settings. A summary of the published studies and related research problems and data gathering methods are described in Table 7.4. The case-study research strategy and multiple sources of evidence were used, as recommended by Yin (Yin, 1994). The costs and benefits of the approach were evaluated by using documentation, participant-observations, interviews, and questionnaires.

In most of the cases the approach was piloted in companies by real developers and the role of the researchers was that of an expert or a consultant who provided information, instructions, training, and support for the practitioners. Thus, it could be seen that the approach was practical enough to be used by real developers in real product development context.

The products under development were a PDA-device, a portable communications device, elevators and escalators, an information system for building designers, and weather measurement instruments. The size of the involved companies varied from small to large.

As a result of the studies, a practical field study approach was synthesized and evaluated. The general results of the studies are summarized in Table 7.5. It was found that the approach was useful even in a short time frame with relatively low costs. The total cost of the field studies varied from 46 to 277 person hours. Developers, a usability expert, and salesmen evaluated the results of the field studies as being very

Table 7.4   The research problems and data gathering methods

Study	Name	Problem	Data gathering method
I	User involvement: A review of the benefits and challenges (Kujala, 2003)	What are the benefits and challenges of user involvement in product development?	Literature review
II	Studying users for developing usable and useful products (Kujala and Mäntylä, 2000b)	How can field studies be applied in product development?	Participant observation, interview
III	How effective are user studies? (Kujala and Mäntylä, 2000a)	What are the benefits and costs of the proposed approach to early user involvement compared to usability testing?	Documentation, experiment (replicated product design), interview
IV	Bridging the gap between user needs and user requirements (Kujala et al., 2001a)	How can user needs be represented and translated into user requirements in industrial product development cases?	Participant-observation
V	Introducing user needs gathering to product development: increasing innovation and customer satisfaction (Kujala et al., 2001b; Kujala et al., 2003)	How can the proposed approach be introduced to product development cases?	Participant-observation, questionnaire, interview

Table 7.5   The results of the studies

Study	Problem	Results
I	What are the benefits and challenges of user involvement in product development?	User involvement has clearly positive effects on system success and user satisfaction. The communication between users and developers poses challenges to product development work. Field study methods should be more cost-effective to use.
II	How can field studies be applied in product development?	A field study approach was developed. The approach was tested in one industrial case, and the results were evaluated to be useful although the resources invested were modest.
III	What are the benefits and costs of the proposed approach to early user involvement compared to usability testing?	The field study approach was evaluated to provide useful information for product development. Preliminary evidence suggested that field studies are a more effective way of improving usability of the product than iterative usability testing.
IV	How can user needs be represented and translated into user requirements in industrial product development cases?	User need tables were developed to represent user needs. It was discovered that the user needs tables help developers to bridge the gap between the user needs and user requirements when the use case approach is used.
V	How can the proposed approach be introduced to product development cases?	In introducing field studies to product development small-scale pilot studies motivated the developers. Developers and salesmen found user studies useful. Innovation and customer satisfaction were increased.

useful in interviews and questionnaires that were conducted. In addition, the field studies provided new product ideas and improvements to existing products.

Customer satisfaction seemed to increase, although it was not directly measured. In Study V, the customer evaluated the product development company as being superior compared to others after the field study. The product development company achieved direct financial benefits as the customer signed a service contract with the company.

Furthermore, user need tables were found to help developers to utilize the field study results and to write more complete and correct use cases. The developers could more easily understand user needs and write use cases from the user point of view. If user need tables were not available, the use case descriptions missed the necessary level of detail as the developers were not aware of all the steps necessary to achieve the users' goal.

Use cases helped designers to gain a coherent view of the product. Undefined missing details were identified and definition work did not proceed too quickly along

Table 7.6   The results of the comparative usability test in Study III

Product	User group	Number of users	Problems	Mean time spent (min)
Existing	Experienced	4	9	9.51
Changed	Novices	4	8	8.18

technical lines. The developers said that they could use the use cases as checklists to guide the definition work and write instructions. They also noticed that use cases could be used as test cases.

In addition to the case studies, empirical data was gathered from an experiment in Study III (Kujala and Mäntylä, 2000a). The field study approach was evaluated by redesigning the functionality of an existing product based on a field study and comparing the process and results with the baseline design process, in which the functionality was first developed. The field study included six users; the total time spent on the study was 46 person hours. The baseline design process was very iterative and rapid prototyping was used. The only direct link to users was through usability tests. An estimation of the time spent on design was not available, but a rough estimation of the resources allocated to the usability test can be derived from the fact that 33 users participated in them.

The Study III provided preliminary evidence that field studies represent a more effective way of improving the usability of the product than iterative usability testing. For example, the results of both field study process and baseline design process were evaluated in a comparative usability test. As shown in Table 7.6 four experienced users of the baseline product spent slightly more time performing the tasks than the four novices using the changed product.

Usability evaluation techniques "react" to an existing design and thus are aimed at "improving" rather than "creating" (Wixon et al., 1994). It seems to be easier to do this improving with usability testing if the user needs are properly understood at the beginning and the system is aimed in the right direction. In addition, the success of a usability test depends on how representative the test task and environment are and this information is gained from field studies. However, even if the user needs are understood their meaning needs to be interpreted and translated to a system. Thus, field studies provide essential information about user needs and use scenarios; usability testing has its own role in validating interpretations and evaluating the usability of the practical solution.

In summary, we have presented how user-centered requirements analysis can be integrated to use case-driven requirements engineeringw. The proposed approach describes step-by-step how user needs can be discovered and utilized in requirements engineering. Our case studies indicate that the approach is simple and practical enough to be used in real development contexts.

8 GUIDING DESIGNERS TO THE WORLD OF USABILITY: DETERMINING USABILITY REQUIREMENTS THROUGH TEAMWORK

Timo Jokela

Oulu University

Abstract

A teamwork method for determining usability requirements based on the definition of usability of ISO 9241-11 is proposed. A usability specialist facilitates a software development team in determining usability requirements in a set of workshop sessions. The concrete outcome of the workshops is a set of measurable usability requirements (in a form of usability requirements table) which form design drivers for the later phases of software design. Another outcome of the workshops is of educational and motivational nature. We found that the workshops are effective training of usability and make the design team committed towards user-centered design. On the other hand, systematic determination of usability requirements following the definition of usability of ISO 9241-11 was found to be a complex process, and it is challenging to fully determine the usability requirements.

A. Seffah (eds.), Human-Centered Software Engineering – Integrating Usability
in the Development Process, 127–145.
© 2005 Springer. Printed in the Netherlands.

8.1 INTRODUCTION

Usability is one of the most important quality characteristics of software intensive products. Usable systems are easy to learn, efficient to use, not error-prone, and satisfactory in use (Nielsen, 1993). Usability brings many benefits, which include "increased productivity, enhanced quality of work, improved user satisfaction, reductions in support and training costs and improved user satisfaction" (ISO/IEC, 1999).

Usability has not been defined consistently, and various definitions exist. Probably the best-know definition of usability is by Jacob Nielsen (Nielsen, 1993) usability is about learnability, efficiency, memorability, errors, and satisfaction. However, the definition of usability from ISO 9241-11 (ISO/IEC, 1998) – "the extent to which a product can be used by specified users to achieve specified goals with effectiveness, efficiency and satisfaction in a specified context of use" - is becoming the main reference of usability. In addition that it is largely recognized in recent literature, the new Common Industry Format, CIF, for usability testing (ANSI/INCITS, 2001)—supported by a number of corporations and other stakeholders - uses this standard definition as the reference of usability. In our study, we took this definition as the reference of usability.

In this chapter, we describe the KESSU URD[1] method for determining usability requirements and experiences on using the method. The method has two objectives. First, it aims to be a systematic approach for the determining usability requirements based on ISO 9241-11 definition of usability. Second, it aims to help integration of usability into software development through making project staff understand and get committed to design usability. A specific feature of the method is that it is implemented as teamwork where the designers and other project staff are the key stakeholders of the process.

Based on the definition of usability from ISO 9241-11, we consider usability requirements as *of effectiveness, efficiency and satisfaction of users achieving their goals in the defined contexts of use*. In other words, we talk about measurable requirements which are critically important to be determined as a part of development process (Good et al., 1986; Wixon and Wilson, 1997; Jokela and Pirkola, 1999; Göransson and Gulliksen, 2003; also Chapter 2 of this book). As stated in Good et al., 1986: "Without measurable usability specifications, there is no way to determine the usability needs of a product, or to measure whether or not the finished product fulfills those needs. If we cannot measure usability, we cannot have usability engineering".

Determination of usability requirements is an important factor in the process of integrating usability into the product and software design process. Usability requirements – which include the definitions of the users, users' goals, environments of use etc. – are *design drivers*. Design drivers do not provide technical solutions but guide, probably implicitly, the project team towards designing usable software. We use the KESSU UCD process model (Jokela, 2004b; Figure 8.1) – which is elaborated from the well-known process model of ISO 13407 - as generic reference for user-centered design. A specific feature in the KESSU model is that it presents usability data explicitly as design drivers. The usability requirements process covers the three first

---

[1] KESSU = name of a research project; URD = usability requirements determination

activities of the usability lifecycle (Figure 8.1): Identification of user groups; Context of use analysis; and User requirements determination.

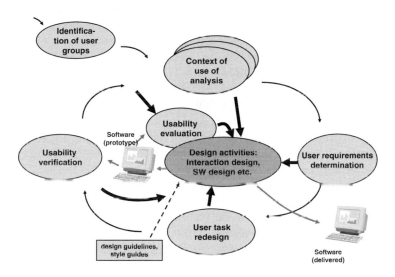

Figure 8.1   Usability activities (yellow circles) provide design drivers (the double lines) to design activities (grey circles)

Usability requirements, however, are effective design drivers only when the software designers and other members of a design team are truly committed in achieving the usability requirements. There is a risk is that usability requirements may be cast aside if time is running out in the development project (McCoy, 2002). Our basic means for achieving commitment is through active role of each member of the project team in the process of usability requirements determination. Citing the well know phrase of Stephen R. Covey, 1994: "Without involvement, there is no commitment" (Covey, 1994).

Other chapters of this book present related approaches. A user needs analysis method is proposed in by Kujala (Chapter 7 of this book) where user needs are represented as problems and possibilities in a user needs table and transformed into use case descriptions, including definition of actors, pre- and post-conditions, task sequences and exceptions. The PUF method (Chapter 9) has related elements as our method does (definition of users and tasks) but really does not address to usability requirements and mainly focuses on integration of usability to UML. Our approach provides a complementary view through describing how usability requirements in the meaning of ISO 9241-11 can be determined as teamwork.

In the next section, we briefly discuss existing methods and relate our method with them. Then we present the general features of the method, and thereafter the steps of the method. Finally, the lessons learnt and the ways how the method can be altered are discussed.

8.2 RELATED METHODS

The standard ISO 9241-11 and the evolving Common Industry Format for Usability Requirements, CIF-R, NIST, 2004, provide guidelines and examples for how to determine usability requirements following the definition of usability of ISO 9241-11. They mainly focus describing and exploring the concepts and formats related to the definition of usability: how to define measures for effectiveness, efficiency and satisfaction, and how to define context of use. Research carried out in European projects has produced guidance and templates—such as Maguire, 1998, and Thomas and Bevan, 1996—for describing users, tasks, and environments of use.

These guidelines, however, provide only limited guidelines for the *process* of determining usability requirements. For example, ISO 9241-11 states that usability measures can be specified "for overall goals (e.g. produce a letter) or for narrower goals (e.g. perform search and replace)" and "focusing ... on the most important user goals may mean ignoring many functions, but is likely to be he most practical approach". CIF-R focuses on describing the contents of usability requirements document, and does not provide guidelines for how to generate the requirements. The handbook of Maguire, 1998, provides general techniques such as stakeholder or context meetings, interviews, observations, questionnaires and task analysis. The standard ISO 13407 (ISO/IEC, 1999) identifies a process 'Specify the user and organizational requirements', including statements such as "provide measurable criteria against which the emerging design can be tested", and that the requirements should "be stated in terms that permit subsequent testing and should be confirmed or updated during the life of the project". The experience report by Bevan & et al. (Bevan and Claridge, 2002) guides: "For each chosen task and user type, estimate..." and "usability for the new system should be at least as good as for the old system".

Most of other usability engineering literature such as Nielsen, 1993, Wixon and Wilson, 1997, Beyer and Holtzblatt, 1998, Hackos and Redish, 1998, Mayhew, 1999, Rosson and Carroll, 2002b, do not explicitly use the ISO 9241-11 definition. They, however, do provide guidance for individual aspects of determining usability requirements: for identifying user groups, determining user goals and environments of use; and specifying measurable usability requirements. Some of these guidelines are rather abstract. For example, for determining user goals Nielsen presents statements such as "the users' overall goals should be studied" and "a typical outcome of a task analysis is a list of all the things users want to accomplish with the system" (Nielsen, 1993). Wixon & Wilson (Wixon and Wilson, 1997) define a six-step process for determining usability requirements but the guidance is given at rather high level of abstraction. Contextual Design, CD (Beyer and Holtzblatt, 1998) has a strong focus on understanding users' work: the three first phases of the methodology are about gathering data from users and analyzing it. CD implicitly recognizes that there are different user groups. It, however, does not provide any systematic method specifically for identifying those. It neither discusses the determination of quantitative usability goals. Altogether, we found the existing guidance quite general.

But, naturally, there exist also concrete guidelines. For example, Mayhew, 1999, has a specific step for determining 'usability goals'. She first emphasizes the importance of quantitative goals and then discusses the different types of quantitative usability goals: ease-of-use vs. ease-of-learning goals; absolute vs. relative goals; and performance vs. preference vs. satisfaction goals. She then provides a step-by-step procedure to determine quantitative usability goals: first determine qualitative goals, and then determine quantitative goals in the categories of "ease-of-learning", "ease-of-use" and "satisfaction" that are "relatively high in priority". In other words, Mayhew addresses the topic, provides guidance but not systematically driven by the ISO definition.

Further, there are only few empirical studies on the use the definition of usability if ISO 9241-11 in practical usability requirements determination. Case studies, such as Bevan and Claridge, 2002, have been contacted on how to use the definition in usability testing. However, there is a gap in research on how to use the definition systematically when determining usability requirements.

Our study complements the existing research by presenting the KESSU URD method that specifically aims for usability requirements that conform to the ISO 9241-11 definition of usability. Further, the method specifically aims to overcome the communication gaps between usability and software and other designers.

8.3 DEVELOPMENT OF KESSU URD

The development of the method stems from our experiences when carrying out *usability maturity assessments*. Usability maturity assessment is about examination of the user-centredness of a development organisation[2]. In an assessment, one may examine the extent to which development projects include user-centred activities, the extent to which UCD is part of the quality system of a company, the extent to which developers have received training on UCD, etc. The usefulness of usability maturity assessments is in the hypothesis that knowing the strengths and weaknesses in UCD provides a good basis for choosing those organizational areas where to improve the performance of UCD in the development organisation.

Probably the best-known approach for usability maturity assessment is *process assessment*, an approach that is widely used in software process improvement. There are specific models developed for process assessment of UCD processes: ISO/TR 18529 (ISO/IEC, 2000a) and ISO/PAS 18152 (ISO/IEC, 2003). These kinds of process assessment models are typically used for the examining on how user-centred activities are managed across a development organization.

In our assessments – lessons learnt of which are reported in Jokela, 2004a—we found reasonable to limit our focus on assessing the user-centredness of individual development projects (and pay less attention on management issues). Therefore, we ended up to have a simplified model of process assessment (Jokela, 2004b). A specific feature of our KESSU assessment model is that it uses the definition of usability from ISO 9241-11 as the reference of usability.

In one assessment case our finding was that the development project under assessment had included practically no UCD activities: the users of the product had not been identified, the user goals had not been determined, user tasks had not been analyzed,

---

[2]In other words, usability maturity assessment is not about evaluation the usability of the product or system.

etc. We did not find it constructive to report these kinds of 'poor' results to the project team. Instead, we organized a workshop where we started to explore together with the project team what kinds of things user-centred design had concretely meant in the context of that specific project. We brainstormed together with the project team the different kinds of user data that should have been generated: who would be the users of the product, what kinds of goals the users might have, etc.

Our experience was so positive that we used the approach also later as a kick-off of user-centred activities in other development projects. Step by step it evolved into an approach that we describe in this chapter. In total, we have had used the approach eleven times in different contexts. The applications have included mobile services, telecommunication software, and transportation and healthcare systems.

Some cases composed of several workshop sessions while other cases were carried out during one day. There was variation in the styles in which the workshops were carried out. The variation was not only due to the different time available but also due to the challenges that we met. We found that the determination of usability requirements (using the ISO 9241-11 definition as a reference) is not an easy task.

One aspect, however, remained stable throughout the cases: we used the ISO 9241-11 definition of usability as the reference. This is also probably one of our key findings: the ISO 9241-11 definition of usability was sense-making both to us - usability practitioners and researchers - and to the designers. We did not consider taking any other definition as the basis; we perceived determining usability requirements using the ISO 9241-11 definition not easy but most motivating.

8.4   GENERAL FEATURES OF KESSU URD

The KESSU URD method generally implements the principles of UCD such as user focus, iteration, and specifically multidisciplinary teamwork. On the other hand, we have typically not included end users in the requirements process, which basically violates 'user involvement', one of the basic principles of UCD (although one of the objectives of the method is that it motivates to user involvement at a later stage of development cycle).

Technically, our approach for determining usability requirements is a set of workshop sessions where usability requirements are brainstormed as teamwork. The method is a systematic process from the identification of users to the determination of usability requirements, following the definition of usability from ISO 9241-11.

At the stage of requirements determining, we do not pay attention on how to later test the designs against the requirements. As Wixon & al. (Wixon and Wilson, 1997) state: "The greatest impacts of usability engineering are related to the initial stages of goals setting. Even if you do not test at all, designing with a clearly stated usability goal is preferable".

In the workshops, the grounded knowledge that the design staff has on users – i.e. knowledge from user contacts from various situations such as customer visits, customer service, etc. – is systematically elicited and analyzed. As such, the approach resembles context of use sessions (Thomas and Bevan, 1996) and stakeholder meetings (UsabilityNet, 2003). As developments compared to these approaches, our approach has some specific features at the levels of detail: the exact steps of the workshops; the working methods used; the share of responsibilities; prioritizing of issues, etc.

The outcome of the workshop is usability requirements table which contains user group definitions, user goal definitions; measurable usability requirements, etc. (see 8.8.3).

8.4.1   The Participants and Roles

An essential feature is that all those persons who are involved in design and decision making related to the user interaction design of the product participate in the requirements process. These people include software and user interface designers but typically also the project manager, the product manager, representatives from technical documentation and customer service, etc. The workshops are facilitated by an experienced usability specialist. A workshop setting is illustrated in Figure 8.2.

Figure 8.2   A KESSU URD workshop session

There are four specific roles in the workshop sessions:

- A facilitator: a person who facilitates and guides the workshops. He or she is typically an experienced usability professional and not a member of the project team.

- A usability responsible: a person who is responsible of usability issues in the project team. He or she is the main contact with the facilitator, takes care of the note keeping during the process and of the action points between the workshop sessions.

- The decision maker: a person who is the final decision maker in different decision making situations during the processes. He or she is typically the project
manager.

- Analysts: all the other members of the workshop who contribute in the teamwork. Also the usability responsible and the decision maker are analysts (but
not the facilitator).

The participants are divided into teams of 2–4 persons. Each team works parallel. The
usability specialist and the project manager are also members of some of the teams.
The facilitator is the only person that does not belong to a team. The facilitator's role
is to follow how the teams proceed in their assignments, give feedback and hints to the
teams.

The facilitator has the responsibility of running the sessions but can also take care
of the documentation of the results together with the usability specialist. He or she
takes pictures of the notes on the wall as well as writes down the required data with a
word processor.

8.4.2   General Flow of the Process

In the first cases, we started with all-day long workshops but found it reasonable to
break them into sessions. Our experience is that people feel longer sessions too tiring,
and the risk that they do not show up in the next sessions is bigger. One session should
last approximately three hours – it should not last longer than four hours.

The number of sessions varies, depending on the resources available. In three sessions, one can systematically go through some instances of all the steps – from the
identification of user groups to determining usability requirements. Three sessions,
however, are not adequate for processing the requirements fully. On the other hand,
we have also conducted workshops of one session only.

The sessions compose of a set of break-outs for team work. Each break-out takes
5 to 30 minutes. After each break-out, the results are analyzed and agreed, and the
assignments for the next break-out sub session are given.

8.4.3   Working Techniques

Various teamwork techniques are utilized:

- Each team (of 2 to 4 persons) works as a team, discussing and producing the
outcomes that are assigned to the team.

- Depending on the phase of the process, the different teams may work on the
same subject parallel, or each team may have a different subject

- If the teams have worked on the same subject, the results are put on the wall,
and board walking (a technique that is used e.g. in Contextual Design (Beyer
and Holtzblatt, 1998) is used to combine and organize the results.

- If the teams work on different assignments, the outcomes are presented to the other teams. The other teams may comment the results. The results are commonly agreed.

- Post-it notes are used for documenting the outcomes. The outcomes are further put on the wall of the meeting room.

- Voting is used when one needs to prioritise the results. Each participant is in an equal position (except the facilitator who does not vote).

- After each step, a reality check is done: do the results appear sensible. The project manager has the final word.

The facilitator has an important role. During break-outs, he or she goes from team to another and checks whether the teams are understood the assignment correctly, and whether they are producing appropriate outcomes. This is an important task. Our experience is that "usability" means a new kind of thinking to many people, and they really need guidance and probing so that they understand what kinds of outcomes to produce.

Post-it notes are the key artefacts that the participants work with. The post-it notes on the wall are recorded with a digital camera. Simultaneously the results are documented into a usability requirements table (8.8.3), either by the facilitator or the usability expert. The requirements table - projected to a screen - is reviewed by the participants especially at the later phases of the process.

8.4.4 Summary

The key features of the workshops are summarized in Table 8.1.

Table 8.1   A KESSU URD workshop session

Every project team member participates and contributes. Actually, the outcomes of the workshop, the usability requirements, are produced by the project data (not by the usability specialists).
Various teamwork techniques are utilized to achieve the involvement and contribution of everyone.
The user data is elicited from the grounded knowledge of users that the participants have.
The role of the usability specialist is to facilitate, not to produce the data. He or she guides the process and the makes sure that the required outcomes are produced.
The project manager has the authority to make decisions.
The results are commonly agreed.
Each session lasts half a day in the maximum.

8.5 STEPS OF KESSU URD

Above, we have described the general features of the workshop sessions. In this section, we describe the steps of the method. Each step provides an outcome which is documented. One should understand that, as discussed in later sections, the process is not a mechanical one.

8.5.1 Step 1. Objectives, Scope, Organization

The facilitator first briefs the participants about the objectives and contents of the workshop. This includes a brief introduction to usability and user-centred design. Some participants may expect that one would design user interfaces in the workshop. Therefore we have found it sensible to emphasize that the purpose of the workshop is not to design user interface.

Second, one needs to make everyone agree and understand what product or system is the focus of the workshop. This is the task of the project manager. Unlike some other approaches, such as the stakeholder meeting (UsabilityNet, 2003) we do not determine the business success factors of the project at this stage. Vice versa, we find that usability related business success factors could be determined based on the results of the workshop.

Third, three or four working teams are formed. Depending on the number of the participants, the number of persons in the teams may vary (two in minimum).

8.5.2 Step 2. Identify the Users

The first 'usability' step is to determine the users of the product. Each working team identifies different users and writes down the user groups on post-it notes, one group in one note. All the notes are put on the wall, and the final set of user groups are mutually agreed on. We do not try to achieve the final truth of the 'right' set of user groups at this stage – our experience is that the following steps of the process clarify what is the appropriate set of users.

We have found it sensible to guide identifying user groups by the *job role* of the users. To keep to process manageable, we do not identify the user groups based on the experience of the users (novices, intermediate, experts etc.) nor on the cultural aspects (international users). These issues are relevant, but they can be taken into account later when usability evaluations are planned.

8.5.3 Step 3: Prioritise the Users

Next, the user groups are prioritised: which group is the most important one, which one comes next, etc. The user groups are prioritised in order to determine the working order: the most important user groups will be processed first in next phases of the process.

Voting is used to determine the priority. Each member of the workshop - except the facilitator - has an equal amount of votes (three).

8.5.4   Step 4: Identify the User Accomplishments

The next step is to brainstorm the accomplishments (goals) that the users may want to achieve with the product. Because different user groups have different accomplishments, this step needs to be done separately for each user group. We start with the most important user groups, and assign one user group for each working team. Then we ask the teams to identify the different accomplishments (goals) that users would want to gain with the product under development.

We have found this to be one of the most challenging parts of the whole process. It seems to be so much easier to think of tasks of users than the accomplishments what users should achieve. The facilitator's role at this stage is critical. The facilitator should challenge the teams and constructively not to accept too simple answers.

In our first cases, we used just brainstorming for the identification of the tasks. In some cases it worked but in other cases the teams had difficulties in identifying the variety of the different tasks that users typically have. In the latest cases, we used scenarios and personas to aid in the process of identifying user accomplishments.

A Typical Sub-step: Re-identify the Users.   We have often found necessary to go back and check whether refinements in the set of user groups are required. When determining accomplishments, one often realizes that the original set of user groups was not the right one.

8.5.5   Step 5: Prioritise Accomplishments

The next step is to prioritise the accomplishments. We have used the following criteria for guiding the prioritisation:

- Accomplishments the achievement of which is critical

- Tasks that users do frequently (to reach an accomplishment)

- Tasks that are time critical

- Tasks that are error critical

A typical sub-step: Redefine Accomplishments.   This stage, again, may lead to iteration. One is often able to refine the set of user accomplishments when the task attributes are brainstormed. For example, one may realize at there are different accomplishments related to 'testing' if one kind of testing is done frequently while another kind of testing is carried out only quite seldom.

8.5.6   Step 6: Identify Critical Accomplishments

A user-task matrix - such as proposed in Hackos and Redish, 1998 - is created. The matrix reveals whether a specific task is performed by one user group or several user groups. All the accomplishments of all the user groups are consolidated into a single table.

We ask the teams to check the priorities of the accomplishments of all the user groups, and to produce a consolidated list of most critical user accomplishments. This outcome, the priorities of all accomplishments of all user groups, is a very central result of the workshop. We now know which accomplishments by which user groups form the basis for the usability requirements of the product or software under development.

8.5.7   Step 7: Consolidate accomplishments

At this phase, we may have quite a large number of accomplishments that may be prioritised critical. While too many usability goals are impractical, one should plan how to consolidate those accomplishments into a reasonable number of usability requirements. Different approaches may be used. For example Jokela and Pirkola, 1999, used an approach where the criteria are determined with the average performance of tasks.

8.5.8   Step 8: Produce Qualitative Usability Requirements

We distribute the most important accomplishments to the working teams, and ask them to define descriptive statements about how the requirements are successfully achieved. The statements should reflect the critical attributes of the accomplishments:

- A task that is performed frequently, would probably lead to a qualitative requirement such as: "Users should be able to do the task very quickly and with little effort".

- A qualitative requirement for a task when a user configures the system: "This task is a 'one-shot' tasks and it is utmost important that the outcome of the task is correct. On the other hand, the task is not very time-critical".

8.5.9   Step 9: Produce Quantitative Requirements

The qualitative goals are transformed into quantitative ones. This is another step – in addition to the determination of user accomplishments - that is typically very challenging for the participants.

Generally, we recommend setting goals in relation to the old version of the product (or a competitive product). This is where we have often found lack of information: the members of the project team do not know about the performance of the existing product.

8.5.10   Step 10: Do the Final Reality Check

When the final set of usability requirements are produced, we take a step backwards and make a reality check. We especially remind that much of the results of this kind of work are based on the knowledge of the participants. In this case one should consider to which extent do we really know the world of user – how valid is the data that we derived?

8.5.11   Summary

The steps, with the descriptions of outcomes and comments, are summarised in Table 8.3. Our experience is that one needs three 3-hours sessions in order to go through all the steps for one user group.

Table 8.3   Key features of workshops

No	Step	Outcome	Comment
1	Workshop objectives	Definition of the scope of the workshop (what is the product)	The project manager has a critical role
2	Identification of user groups	A set of user groups; names, brief descriptions	Identified through job role
3	Prioritizing user groups	An ordered list of user groups	Based on the size or criticality of the user group
4	Identification of user accomplishments	A set of user accomplishments per user group Refinements in the set of user groups (typically more than identified in step 2)	Describe the accomplishment (not the task performance). Perceived challenging but useful. The role of the facilitator critical.
5	Prioritizing accomplishments	An ordered list of accomplishments Refinements in the set of accomplishments (typically more than identified in step 4)	Frequency, time criticality, error criticality used as guiding factors.
6	Identifying critical accomplishments	A list of critical accomplishments of all user groups	A core intermediate result
7	Consolidating requirements	Baseline for goal setting	Challenge to cope if a large number of critical accomplishments
8	Qualitative descriptions	Qualitative descriptions of achieving goals successfully	Describe successful task performance, not the accomplishment
9	Quantitative measures	Transform qualitative goals into quantitative ones.	Challenging to determine the measures. Even more challenging to determine the 'right' requirement values.
10	Final reality check	Potentially refinements in the quantitative goals.	Taking a step backwards, taking an overview of the results.

8.6   FINDINGS FROM THE CASE STUDIES

We used the method – or more precisely, the method evolved – in a set of cases. In other words, the method was not exactly similar from one case to another. Some characteristics of the method, however, were stable. The requirements process was conducted in workshops, teamwork was utilised, the definition of usability from ISO 9241-11 drove the requirements process etc.

8.6.1   On the Definition of Usability of ISO 9241-11

Generally, we found that the ISO 9241-11 definition of usability means that the determination of usability requirements is a complex task. A product typically has many different user groups. Each user group may have many different goals. The levels of different goals may be different in terms of effectiveness, efficiency, and satisfaction. We truly met a challenge in how to manage all this complexity. We used prioritising - e.g. focused on the most important user groups only. Still, we were able to carry out the process totally through only in one, not very complex case.

Another specifically challenging part of the definition relates to the identification of user goals (accomplishments) and determining measurable target levels for the usability attributes (effectiveness, efficiency, satisfaction). It was not easy for the participants to work on these issues. In the last case, we used the concept of persona (Cooper, 1999) to help in identifying users and user goals. This seemed to work clearly better than brainstorming.

On the other hand, the ISO 9241-11 definition of usability was sense-making both to us (usability practitioners and researchers) and to the participants. Determining usability requirements using the ISO 9241-11 definition was not easy but motivating. The participants gave comments such as "a new and meaningful way of thinking" and "we definitely should have done this in earlier projects". We (researchers) did not even consider giving up from using the definition.

8.6.2   On Teamwork

Overall, the participants, software designers and other members of a project team found the workshops process interesting, useful and effective training of usability. Participants reported that the process has 'opened their eyes' and the results represent a "totally new and meaningful" perspective to product requirements. In our last case (three consecutive half-day sessions), two product managers from the marketing department – typically very busy people - actively participated in all the sessions. The number of participants increased in the last session when representatives from other department of the company were invited to follow the process. The participants generally liked to do teamwork. ("I assume that we do teamwork today, too!")

On the other hand, three sessions in a row seemed to be the practical maximum. Finding time for more workshops would have been difficult. In our last case, it was agreed that the usability specialist would continue the determination work as an individual effort.

A considerable set of user data could be determined in the workshops, based on elicitation and analysis of the project team's knowledge on users. The process clearly helped the participants realize whether they do or do not have true knowledge on users.

Facilitating workshops was not a mechanical task. First, the facilitator had to continuously consider how to manage the complexity: which the issues to be worked and which ones to postpone or omit. Especially with systems with many different user groups and a large number of tasks, one has to tackle with 'space explosion' all the time (the number of items, and their combinations becomes so large). Second, the facilitator needed to guide the participants towards the 'right track' in the break-out session. Especially, the facilitator needed to guide the participants to determine user goals.

8.6.3   On Results

One limitation of the case studies was that we could not follow the process 'to the end'. In other words, we do not have any evidence on the impact of the usability requirements that were determined in the workshops on the final product. We neither have evidence on whether the apparent interest and commitment of the participants lasted throughout the project.

Anyway, some innovative design drivers were identified during the workshops. This happened especially when the teams brainstormed (measurable) target levels for efficiency for specific goals. For example, in two cases it was brainstormed and agreed (in step 8 of the process) that the achievement of specific user goals (which had been identified in step 4) actually should be automated: "Hey, actually this should happen automatically, without any user actions!"

8.7   CONCLUSIONS

Based on the findings of the case studies, we can draw the following conclusions. Overall, we conclude that the method provides some help for the integration of UCD to software development.

One obstacle of integration of usability and software engineering is that the essential contents and meaning of usability is often not understood by designers (see Chapter 3 in this book) and designers not understand what usability is "beyond the basic ease-of-use concept" (Chapter 2). We conclude that our method provides help in overcoming this problem. The workshops proved to be an effective training occasion on usability and help designer to get committed to usability. The definition of usability of ISO 9241-11 made sense to designers and other project staff such as marketing representatives. Usability requirements are a complex thing but on the other hand very logical and sense-making, helping participants understand what usability essentially is. The definition looks complex but makes sense to people after it is systematically explored.

We also find that the method helps in overcoming the people and responsibilities gaps (Chaper 2) and lack of collaboration (Chapter 9) through guiding software designers (and other projects staff) and usability professionals communicate and work together. There are no communication problems between usability specialists and designers because the designers themselves generate the usability requirements. Everyone is involved, contributes and is listened to – and thereby gets committed ("no commitment without involvement"). Designers do not need to be "forced" to do usability but they make it voluntarily because they find it sense making.

Further, the workshops seem to be a true order for user studies. We did not include users in the sessions, apart from the first one. We find, however, that this kind of setting makes a good basis for UCD activities with true user involvement. The workshops help designers to understand the need for user studies and also understand what kind of data to expect from the studies.

Finally, our approach represents a case study which is an important resource in learning UCD skills (Seffah, 2003).

On the other hand, the method also has limitations. The inherent complexity of usability makes it challenging to determine the usability requirements systematically 'to the end'. One would need many more resources than we had to complete the requirements process. The number of workshop session would be quite many, and one cannot assume that people would have time and be motivated to participate in many more sessions.

The outcomes of the workshop are typically based only partially on true user data. The quality of the outcome (i.e. the validity of usability requirements) depends on the grounded knowledge that the participants have about users. The idea behind the workshops is that the results – usability requirements - would be later refined based on true user data. However, there is a risk that the refinement work will not take place.

The process is not a matured one. Its nature is not mechanical – although systematic – especially due to the complex nature of usability. The role of the facilitator is critical. It well may be, although we do not have evidence, that (the quality of) the results depends on the personal characteristics and viewpoints of the facilitator.

8.8   DISCUSSION

A teamwork method for determining usability requirements based on the definition of usability of ISO 9241-11 is proposed. A usability specialist facilitates a software development team in determining usability requirements in a set of workshop sessions. The concrete outcome of the workshops is a set of measurable usability requirements (in a form of usability requirements table) which form design drivers for the later phases of software design. Another outcome of the workshops is of educational and motivational nature. We found that the workshops are effective training of usability and make the design team committed towards user-centered design. On the other hand, systematic determination of usability requirements following the definition of usability of ISO 9241-11 was found to be a complex process, and it is challenging to fully determine the usability requirements.

8.8.1   Limitations

An obvious limitation of the case studies is that we were not able to determine usability requirements fully, apart one relatively simple case. Therefore, we do not have data to which extent it is feasible to systematically determine usability 'to the end' in a typical case, and how to make practical use of such apparently large set of requirements.

Another clear limitation is that we could not follow-up most of the case studies. In other words, we do not have evidence on whether the interest and commitment of the participants lasted throughout the project, nor whether the usability requirements would truly have impact on the final product.

All of our cases have been product development projects – both consumer and business-to-business products. We have not had a single system development project so far. It, however, might be that the process would easier in the case of a system development project. Especially, it could be easier to understand the 'right' user groups, and the number of user groups probably would be smaller. Thereby, the process might be less complex.

8.8.2   Implications

We suggest the KESSU URD method as a useful means for determining usability requirements. If it is not feasible to assign resources for several workshops, one could make use of the method for training and motivating designers towards usability. For that purpose, even one day workshop could be enough. Anyway, the case should be real, i.e. a development project that is about to start. We suggest using a 'narrow' approach. One could start by identifying the different user groups but then start working on one (important) user group only. Further, one should continue working with the main user accomplishments only. Anyway, one should aim to go all the steps through so that at least some measurable usability requirements are determined.

The results of this study indicate that the ISO 9241-11 definition of usability a useful reference in practical usability work. There exist different definitions of usability, and there is a need for commonly agreed definition (Seffah and Metzker, 2004). We propose that the definition of ISO 9241-11[3] could be used as the 'basic' definition of usability'.

Our experiences show that it is not feasible to determine the requirements fully in workshops. Individual work is required, too. One solution could be to first run two or three workshops with the whole team, and then let the usability team to complete the work. Finally, a final workshop could be organized where the results are shared and agreed on with all the development team. It is important that there are resources are planned for the work to be carried out from the very beginning.

8.8.3   Further Research Topics

We find a true need for 'full' cases where the usability requirements could be explored 'to the end' and one could be able to follow the impact of the requirements throughout the project life-cycle. This kind of study would help in finding solutions to the management of complexity of the requirements, as well as finding effective solutions

---

[3] There are some minor problems in the definition of usability of ISO 9241-11, not discussed in this chapter.

to other challenges of the requirements process, such as determining the 'right' target levels of effectiveness, efficiency, and satisfaction.

The method could be expanded by coupling financial incentives of a development project (project bonuses that given to the project staff) with usability requirements. There is evidence (Jokela and Pirkola, 1999) that when such incentives are coupled with the achievement of usability requirements, the designers truly consider the requirements and produce highly usable design solutions.

Acknowledgements

The author would like to express sincere thanks to all the participants in the workshops: from the companies Buscom, Elbit, Nokia, Polar Electro, and TeamWARE and from the research projects KESSU and ITEA Nomadic Media. The research projects were performed with financial support from Tekes, the National Technology Agency of Finland.

Appendix

Table 8.5   Usability requirements table

Task name	Initial state	Accomplishment name	Attributes of the accomplishment	Usability requirement, qualitative description	Quantitative usability requirement (in terms of effectiveness, efficiency or satisfaction)	
					The reference level	The target level

9 TRANSFORMING USABILITY ENGINEERING REQUIREMENTS INTO SOFTWARE ENGINEERING SPECIFICATIONS: FROM PUF TO UML

Jim A. Carter, Jun Liu, Kevin Schneider, David Fourney

University of Saskatchewan, Saskatoon, Saskatchewan, Canada

Abstract

The Unified Modeling Language (**UML**) is widely used by Software Engineers as the basis of analysis and design in software development. While UML is very strong at specifying the structure and functionality of the application, it is seldom used to its potential to specify usability-related information. The Putting Usability First (**PUF**) methodology of Usability Engineering identifies and specifies usability-related information. This chapter discusses how requirements and other contextual information from the PUF methodology can be transformed into UML in order to specify the context information of the application to ensure the usability of the application.

9.1 INTRODUCTION

While the need for integrating human factors with software engineering has been recognized for over a decade (e.g., Carter, 1991; Evans, 2002), the reality has yet to

A. Seffah (eds.), Human-Centered Software Engineering – Integrating Usability
in the Development Process, 147–169.

happen to any realistic extent. Attempts to integrate human-computer interaction / usability engineering with software engineering rely on their acceptance by software engineers, who control most development projects. This is largely dependent on the impact of any proposed additions to the current software engineering practice.

This has not taken place in the process realm, where the 32 software engineering processes defined in ISO TR 15504 (ISO, 1998) failed to include any human-computer interaction processes. To meet this omission, software ergonomists developed ISO TR 18529 (ISO/IEC, 2000a) which defined 43 additional human-system life cycle processes. Considering that ISO TR 15504 expects each of these processes to be evaluated in terms of 26 generic practices, this could result in 1,950 sub-processes. In practice, developers recognize a smaller set of processes to get the job done. Clearly, there is a gap between the expectations of these process assessment standards and actual practice by developers.

The goal of integrating human factors with software engineering is to improve the resulting system. Rather than focus on processes, our approach involves integrating the documentation used to develop this resulting system.

Our starting point is a set of usability engineering requirements developed by the Putting Usability First (PUF) methodology (Carter, 1997). PUF is a user-centered approach to systems development. It identifies and structures a use model based on an interrelated set of task, user, content, tool and scenario descriptions. These descriptions provide a context of use description, as recommended by ISO 13407 (ISO/IEC, 1999) Human Centered Design Processes for Interactive Systems (ISO/IEC, 1999) that can easily be used to integrate usability concerns within other software development activities.

Our target is a set of software engineering specifications expressed by the Unified Modeling Language (UML) (Booch et al., 1999), which are currently pervasive throughout major software developments. By assisting in developing UML specifications, it is anticipated that PUF can gain greater acceptance from software engineers than previous usability engineering methodologies. Applying the PUF methodology in UML can ensure the application is developed in a context rich information environment that minimizes the occurrence of usability problems.

The transformations of usability requirements to software engineering specifications, which we identify in this chapter, allow usability engineers and software engineers to perform their own processes in their own manners while being able to better integrate their efforts.

9.2   THE PUTTING USABILITY FIRST (PUF) METHODOLOGY

Putting Usability First (PUF) is a usability engineering methodology that has evolved from previous work on Multi-Oriented Task Analysis (MOST) (Carter, 1990; Carter, 1991). It has been applied to a variety of application areas including: e-Commerce (Carter, 2002a) and educational multimedia (Carter, 2002b).

The concept behind PUF is that for a usability engineering methodology to succeed, it must be usable by developers as well as result in a usable system for end users. ISO 9241-11 Guidance on Usability defines usability as, "the extent to which a product can be used by specified users to achieve specified goals with effectiveness, efficiency and satisfaction in a specified context of use" (ISO/IEC, 1998). PUF involves a thorough consideration of usability issues in each activity of the development life cycle. Being thorough does not require following a single formalized highly prescriptive approach to usability. Rather, it recognizes all development decisions should be based on usability evaluations. These usability evaluations provide qualitative and quantitative information that can guide the development process.

Effectiveness is defined as, "the accuracy and completeness with which users achieve specified goals" (ISO, 1998). PUF structures requirements to assist developers in accurately and completely identifying specific user groups, tasks, content types, tools and scenarios that provide the context of use for the new system being developed.

Efficiency is defined as, "the resources expended in relation to the accuracy and completeness with which users achieve goals" (ISO/IEC, 1998). The PUF methodology recognizes the usefulness of a number of usability methods and allows developers the flexibility to choose those methods that are most efficient within a particular context of use. PUF provides the developers with guidance and flexibility in choosing among the usability methods identified in ISO 16982 Usability Methods Supporting Human Centered Design (ISO, 2002) to assess usability characteristics. These methods may be used to identify usability requirements (including user, task, environment, and system related characteristics) and/or to evaluate a system or a model of a system.

Satisfaction is defined as, "positive attitudes to the use of the product and freedom from discomfort in using it" (ISO/IEC, 1998). PUF enhances satisfaction for developers by supporting the integration of usability engineering and software engineering activities and specifications.

PUF recognizes that for many applications it is impractical to try and develop the perfect system all at once. Development is often spread across a series of different releases. PUF supports release-based development in its inclusion of possibilities in its analysis of the environment of current development. Iteration is crucial in allowing release-based development to respond to changing needs as well as to needs previously identified. This iteration involves ongoing cycles of analysis, design, and evaluation within each of the development activities identified in PUF.

9.2.1   Major Processes within PUF

PUF focuses on four major life cycle processes that work cooperatively towards the development of a system. These processes include: possibilities analysis, requirements analysis, design, and implementation. It is notable that testing is not considered a separate process in PUF. That is because PUF considers evaluation, which is broader than traditional testing, to be an integral part of each of these other activities. Dealing with testing in this manner ensures that it is performed when it is most effective and that it is significant in determining the usability of the resulting system.

Possibilities analysis attempts to identify and briefly describe all the main scenarios, tasks, user groups, content chunks, and tools related to the intended application system for all its potential releases. Evaluation of existing possibilities plays an important role in identifying further possibilities beyond those currently existing or obvious. Possibilities analysis starts with recording narratives of existing scenarios and moves to develop records describing each possibility. Possibilities analysis involves: identifying possibilities, identifying relationships between different types of possibilities, and identifying environmental factors influencing each possibility. Possibility records describe the current and future environment for the system being developed. Possibilities analysis is far broader and more comprehensive than initial investigations typically performed by software engineering. This comprehensiveness is essential in establishing a user-centered context of use both for usability engineers and for software engineers. While it is hoped that this work leads to a PUF requirements analysis, even this initial activity can significantly improve the usability of the resulting system.

A PUF requirements analysis expands the understanding of those possibilities that have been selected as the basis for the development of the current release. It evolves their possibility records into requirement records by adding specific usability-related information and requirements. The set of additional information and requirements is based on the particular type of possibility being analyzed. Requirements analysis in PUF focuses to a greater extent on usability requirements and to a lesser extent on technical requirements than requirements analysis typical in software engineering life cycles.

Because of the considerable overlap, it would be ideal for software engineers to make use of a PUF requirements analysis as a starting point for adding technical requirements. This can benefit software engineers by reducing the amount of work they need to do, especially in the area of gathering technical requirements. This, in turn, benefits usability engineers and end users by ensuring that usability requirements are part of future development decisions.

A PUF design focuses on new tools, scenarios and interactions that can be added to the current environment. Whereas the previous activities can easily be conducted by usability engineers apart from their software engineering colleagues, it is more likely that software engineers will be involved and often in charge of major design activities. PUF requirements need to be integrated with other software engineering requirements to ensure usability is properly considered in design.

Regardless of whether interface design is allocated to usability engineers or is included within the main design activity, PUF can provide assistance in identifying and evaluating usability issues related to this design. Design specifications recorded as or translated into PUF records combined with existing PUF records specify a use model (Rubinstein et al., 1984) that can be subject to evaluation prior to being implemented. These new records also provide an up-to-date context for the development of future releases.

Implementation is usually in the hands of software engineers. To ensure that usability engineering requirements will be considered in implementation, it is essential that these requirements be included within the formal specifications being used to construct and test the resulting system.

9.2.2   Possibility Types within PUF

The PUF methodology identifies and structures requirements based on an interrelated set of five types of possibilities: tasks, users, content, tools and scenarios, as illustrated in Figure 9.1. The combination of these records meets all the requirements of ISO 13407 (ISO/IEC, 1999) for consideration of users, goals, and the environment.

The user records in PUF specify information about the users' characteristics. The task records in PUF specify information about the users' goals. All the records and their linkage information and environmental information identify the context of the user.

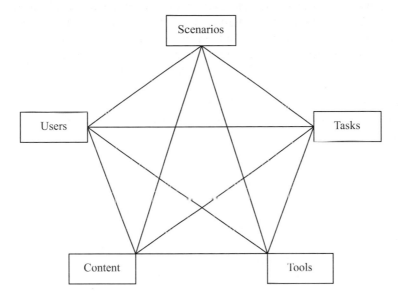

Figure 9.1   The five foci of PUF specifications

Users are not all the same and thus it is important to understand the characteristics of different user groups. Severe usability problems can occur in systems designed for a "generic" user who seldom exists. Users, while of penultimate importance, are only users if they use the system and thus are closely linked with the tasks that each of groups of users performs.

Tasks are specific accomplishments of one or more individuals in a group of users. The degree of accomplishment of a task is generally more important than the method of achieving it. Thus each of the users should be allowed to select the methods which are most usable for them. Tasks are the basis for individuals becoming users. This analysis of tasks should not be limited to only those tasks that are currently considered to be part of what an application should accomplish. The analysis of tasks should be expanded to include similar tasks and other potential tasks that may not be currently performed.

Content is the material processed by computer systems. Data can be presented in a variety of formats and can be processed to higher levels such as information and knowledge. Content serves the users accomplishing their desired tasks, and should be kept subservient to both users and tasks. Considerable usability problems can arise from structuring applications around their content rather than around how this content will be used. The content oriented "Field of Dreams" syndrome of "if you build it, they will come" (that is especially prevalent in the design of Web sites but also exists with many other applications) puts the ego of the developer ahead of the needs of the potential users.

Tools are any of the many things (computerized or non-computerized) that help a person accomplish some task (or set of tasks). Both developers and end users need and use tools. Developers use their tools to create or modify other tools (including software systems) for the end users. Different tools (or sets of tools) can be used to accomplish the same task. Tools exist at (and are designed for) various levels: from entire application systems down to individual controls within the system. Tools, like content, serve the tasks and users. Premature focusing on tools can lead to choosing tools that are "neat" to the developer but which are impractical due to various usability problems for the user.

Scenarios are specific instantiations of specific combinations of {users, tasks, content, and tools}. Each of the tasks, tools, users, and content can pose their own usability concerns. Further usability concerns arise in the specific interactions between them.

9.2.3   The PUF Record Structure

PUF uses a common format to record information and requirements for each possibility (scenario, user group, task, content, and tool), which is illustrated in Table 9.1.

The amount of information recorded about a particular possibility depends on the level of treatment that it has received in the development. As soon as a possibility is identified, the identification section of a PUF record can be filled out giving the possibility a unique name and a narrative description, and identifying the type of possibility that it is describing. A possibility analysis will add information about other related possibilities and some initial information about the environment of the possibility. A requirements analysis will add detailed specifications and requirements that are based on a variety of detailed analysis questions (Carter, 1991). Design adds additional records and modifies information in existing records.

9.3   THE UNIFIED MODELING LANGUAGE

Unified Modeling Language (UML) is a meta-language for specifying, visualizing, and constructing the artefacts of a software-intensive system (OMG, 2003). The meta-language basis of UML already has the majority of the attributes necessary to record usability engineering requirements. However, due to the distributed nature of the location of these attributes and the lack of usability engineering experience of most people utilizing UML, few usability requirements are actually recorded in most developments.

Use cases are applied to capture the intended behavior of the system being developed, without having to specify how behavior is implemented. Use cases provide a way for developers to come to a common understanding with the system's end users and domain experts. In addition, use cases serve to help validate and verify a system as it evolves during development. A use case can model the context of a system, subsystem, or class, or model the requirements of the behavior of the elements (Constantine and Lockwood, 1999). However, UML says nothing about the content of a use case.

Table 9.1   The general format of PUF possibilities records

Identification Information	
name	a unique, meaningful identifier
type	scenario/user/task/tool/content
description	clarifies meaning of name distinguishes this component from others
Linkage Information	
who	identifies related user groups
what	identifies related tasks
how	identifies related tools
with which content	identifies related content chunks
scenarios	identifies related scenarios
Environmental Information	
when	identifies current and potential temporal attributes
where	identifies current and potential physical attributes
how much	quantifies the current and potential future occurrences of the possibility
why	identifies and evaluates the justifications for possibility
Detailed Requirements	
answers to specific questions based on the possibility type	
Formal Specification	
UML translation of the above information	

9.3.1   Use Cases and Actors

Jacobson introduced the concept of a use case which has taken on an increasingly important role in software development. He recognized two levels of use cases: essential use cases and use case instances (which are also known as "scenarios"). "An essential use case describes interaction independent of implicit or explicit assumptions regarding the technology or mechanisms of implementation." (Jacobson, 1992).

Constantine and Lockwood, 1999, discussed the role of essential use cases in user interface design. Constantine, 1995, recognized the importance of the context for use cases and recommended that the developers should have the capability to represent and manipulate context as the resources for application development. He also separates the use case context into materials, tools and work areas.

Use case development is a discovery process. It is a process of finding out which information does not yet exist, and which may not yet be understood. This information is generally entered into one of the many templates available for working with UML (e.g., Cockburn, 1998). Few developers, even among those who have written numerous use cases, understand that the dynamic process for describing the use case is a process for finding new information and revising inappropriate specifications (Evans, 2002).

Malan and Bredemeyer, 1999, believed that the current use case specification is not very appropriate for documenting usability requirements. One of the shortcomings for the use case is that it uses a "non-functional" field to specify the usability requirements. Also usability requirements are not specific to use cases. A use case defines a goal-oriented set of interactions between actors and systems, both of which are documented elsewhere in UML. A use case specification needs to integrate who (actors) does what (interaction) with the system, for certain purposes (goals).

Various authors have suggested that use cases should include a greater amount of usability-related information. Lilly, 2000, stated that a good use case specification should at least answer the following questions: Who (actors), why (goals and/or context), when (the triggering events), what (normal flow) and what else (alternative and/or exceptional flow). These same questions are the basis of requirements in PUF. Cockburn, 2001, advocated that use case descriptions should include the context and all the circumstances of the primary actor's goal. Also, van Lamsweerde, 2003, discussed a model of the goal specification that contains types, taxonomic categories, attributes and linkages.

Few use case templates have the fields to document usability-related information, such as combining the context of use with the users/actors and goals. Most of them treat usability information as "non-functional requirements" that are not able to be specified or applied in UML. Thus, UML does not ensure that resulting systems are usable.

While use cases can provide a starting point for incorporating usability-related information, the current structure and practice does not go far enough to meet all the information needs identified in PUF.

UML uses actors to, "represent a coherent set of roles that users of use cases play when interacting with these use cases" (Booch et al., 1999). This purpose is equivalent to that of user groups in PUF. UML does not provide any particular guidance about what information should be recorded concerning actors. Rather UML allows developers to specify their own stereotypes to describe actors and other objects. Cockburn recognized the importance of specifying actor and stakeholder interests, but did not present a particular template for specifying properties of actors. He suggested that, "the use case's name is the primary actor's goal" (Cockburn, 1998).

Chapter 7 provides an alternate method of obtaining use case information. We have found that PUF specifications involve more elements of UML than just use cases.

9.3.2   Classes

Whereas use cases are used to document requirements, UML class diagrams are commonly used to document design. "A class is a description of a set of objects that share the same attributes, operations, relationships, and semantics. A class implements one or more interfaces." (Booch et al., 1999). Despite the goal of implementing one or more interfaces, classes do not directly document how they meet the interaction needs of actors. Rather, UML uses a set of associations between classes, use cases, and actors.

Because of their emphasis on designing software, class attributes and operations tend to be focused on technical aspects of classes. However, from a functional perspective, attributes and operations provide the closest concepts in UML to the PUF concepts of content and tools.

9.3.3   The Need to Add Usability Requirements to UML

Since current UML separates usability-related requirements from the development procedure, there is a need for some form of usability engineering, such as PUF, to supply usability-related requirements to the development. If the PUF methodology is applied ahead of the UML development, it will bridge the gap between usability requirements and functional requirements and help produce a more usable application.

9.4   APPLYING PUF IN UML

This section will consider the candidate notations in UML that can contain the PUF data and then, how each field in the PUF records can be mapped into these notations.

Figure 9.2 illustrates the high level mapping from PUF to UML. The components on the left side are from PUF and those on the right side are from UML. The layout of the PUF components has been simplified from that of Figure 9.1, to focus on the correspondence of PUF to UML components. Because scenarios are the hub of the other components in the PUF methodology, the tasks, users, content and tools serve together as the context of use for the scenarios. The layout of the UML components includes: use cases, actors, and classes. These components are linked with each other by association relationships. Use cases include both essential use cases and use case instances. Attributes and operations are subcomponents of classes that relate to PUF components. The component level mappings identified here are based on similarity of purpose. The information contained in corresponding components is often at different levels of granularity.

Tasks in PUF correspond to essential use cases and map to use cases in UML. Scenarios in PUF correspond to use case instances and also map to use cases in UML. As discussed, use case instances are sometimes also referred to as scenarios in the use case community. A scenario highlights the interaction between the user, the context, and the system.

Users in PUF map to actors in UML. Both user records and actors focus on the role of the user and relate users to other components that need to be designed to meet the needs of these users.

Contents in PUF map to attributes in UML. Content is used by PUF to describe the widest range of data types and modalities involved in an application. Attributes specify the data and information used in the application. Content information in PUF is usually more abstract than attribute information in UML.

Tools in PUF map to operations in UML. The tools in PUF exist at various abstraction levels from a complete application to individual operations. The operations in UML are focused on specific operations performed by a given object. Both tools and operations deal with how a task/use case is accomplished.

Chapter 16 describes an example of transforming use cases, which can be developed from PUF specifications, to design using design patterns.

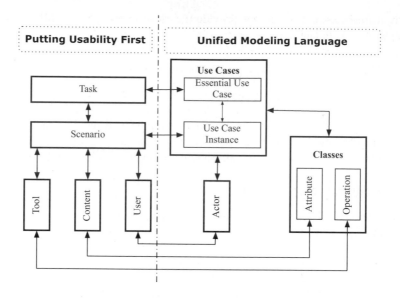

Figure 9.2   High level relationships between PUF and UML components

The following sections provide details on mapping PUF tasks/scenarios, users, content and operations to UML. Usability properties that do not directly map to a concept in UML are also discussed for each PUF component.

9.4.1   Tasks, Scenarios and Use Cases

Constantine and Lockwood's definition of essential use case indicates that, like the task record in PUF, the essential use case specifies what should be done without specifying how to do it.

An essential use case is a structured narrative, expressed in the language of the application domain and of users, comprising a simplified, generalized abstract, technology-free and implementation-independent description of one task or interaction that is complete, meaningful, and well-defined from the point of view of users in some role or roles in relation to a system and that embodies the purpose or intentions underlying the interaction (Constantine and Lockwood, 1999).

According to Rosson, 1999, scenarios, "are similar to instances of use-cases in that they capture a single thread of execution in a given usage context" . The scenario in PUF can map to use case instances. Scenarios can be more elaborate than use case instances because they narrate not only the interaction events but also the experience of the user(s) – the user's goals, expectations and reactions convey information about the system's usefulness and usability.

PUF task records map to essential use cases and PUF scenario records map to use case instances based on Cockburn's basic use case template (Cockburn, 1998) and his one-column table format of a use case (Cockburn, 2001). In UML diagrams, most of this information is not available. Table 9.2 illustrates the mapping from PUF task records to UML use case diagrams. This table shows that the identification and linkage information in PUF task records can easily be modeled in UML. This provides a good starting point for ensuring that records can be mapped successfully.

Table 9.2   Mappings from tasks and scenarios to use cases

PUF: *Task / Scenario*	UML: *Use cases*
Identification Information	
name	use case name
type: task / scenario	**use cases**
description	– via a new property
Linkage Information	
who	associated **actors**
what	(other) associated **use cases**
how	**operations** associated via **classes** and **use cases**
with which content	**attributes** associated via **classes** and **use cases**
scenarios	(other) associated **use cases**
Environment Information	
when	– via a new property
where	– via a new property
how much	– via a new property
why	– via a new property
Detailed Requirements	
task operations	– via a new property
requirements of users	– via a new property
communications	– via a new property
learning	– via a new property
error handling	– via a new property
problem details	– via a new property

Some of the detailed requirements fields in PUF task records also readily link with UML specifications. Task operations map to actions in the use cases and to operations in classes. Requirements of users map to actors.

In the Environmental Information section, the ***why***, which is used to record justification details, does not map into the current use case template. Detailed requirements in PUF task records that do not map into UML specifications include: communications, learning, error handling and problem details. These PUF fields need to be added as new properties to UML essential use case specifications.

The use case template also includes some information not provided by PUF. Use cases may specify a sequence of actions, the specified route of achieving the task, either success or failure, kinds of association and interface interactions. PUF only identifies that there are relationships among components, while UML subdivides these relationships into include and extend associations. The interface attribute describes the interaction between actors and use cases. The PUF task record only specifies the context information and does not specify the kinds of linkage and interaction.

Chapter 6 focuses on architectural design based on scenarios. PUF specifications may be able to provide additional guidance based on additional information they contain beyond scenarios.

9.4.2 Additional Usability-Related Properties for Use Cases

Although the use case and other linked UML components provide a location for some of the following information, there may be a need for additional properties to further expand upon. The following new properties should be added to UML use case diagrams, to record additional usability-related information provided by PUF:

When and Where task used. The use case may be limited by its environment, or might be used in a broader environment to achieve some greater benefits. If the use case is used in a different location, different frequency of use, and/or different distribution of peak usage, the design for the use case will be different. Designers should know how to design the use case to make it still achievable in various situations.

Why. Justification is an important predictor of potential future success. If a use case does not fit the overall development, or costs of the use case exceed either the benefits of serving it or available resources, it will be impractical to develop special tools for the use case. Developers should know the factors that will influence the feasibility and acceptability of possible designs.

Task operations. This PUF field describes operational concerns. Elaboration is needed to understand the operations of essential use cases to evaluate how well current operations work and how future operations might provide improvements. When designers start interaction design, they should know whether the interaction meets the goal of the use case, whether there are alternatives to achieve the use case, and what feedbacks the use case should provide.

Requirements of users. It is important to recognize the requirements that use cases place on actors. The developers should know how to design the interfaces or interactions for the use case to meet users' current skills and mental and physical capabilities. This information may require additional use cases or tools to help users reduce the impact of these factors.

Communications. When users interact with the application, communications take place. The task may require users to communicate with other users or tools. Developers should know how to design the current use case for different language, different frequency, different media, and different security levels in communications or whether to create some new potential use cases to better serve these communications.

Learning. To accomplish a use case, users need to learn how to interact with the application. This implies that there might be a new use case for training. Training learning through different methods, feedback, time and environments, create different learning outcomes. Developers should consider the learning needs and capabilities of the intended users. Developers should know how to design a usable learning system and be aware that different methods, feedback, time and environments could influence the users' learning results.

Error handling. Use cases should acknowledge where and when errors may occur. Developers should recognize these situations and determine how to help users avoid or handle them.

Problem details. When developers design the solution for problems, the problem details should be thoroughly known. This information will help developers develop a more effective and more efficient design solution.

9.4.3   Users and Actors

PUF identifies different user groups based on their different characteristics and interaction needs. An actor in UML identifies a role that a user can play without necessarily specifying any characteristics or interaction needs. Table 9.3 illustrates the mapping from PUF user records to UML actors based on UML specification version 1.5 (OMG, 2003) and the UML user guide (Booch et al., 1999). This table shows that most identification and linkage information in PUF user records can easily be transferred directly to UML. This provides a good starting point for ensuring that records can be mapped successfully.

Many useful fields in PUF user records are not found in current UML actor records. Without recording and using this information, there is no way of ensuring that resulting systems will meet the unique usability needs of different groups of users. A UML stereotype can be used to define these additional properties of actors for transferring user description from PUF.

Table 9.3   Mapping from users to actors

PUF: *User*	UML: *Actor*
Identification Information	
name	actor name
type: user	**actor**
description	– via a property of a stereotype
Linkage Information	
who	other associated **actors**
what	associated **essential use cases**
how	**operations** associated via **classes** and **use cases**
with which content	**attributes** associated via **classes** and **use cases**
scenarios	associated **use case instances**
Environment Information	
when	– via a property of a stereotype
where	– via a property of a stereotype
how much	– via a property of a stereotype
why	– via a property of a stereotype
Detailed Requirements	
physical characteristics	– via a property of a stereotype
mental characteristics	– via a property of a stereotype
social characteristics	– via a property of a stereotype
group characteristics	– via a property of a stereotype

The user record description field specifies the users' characteristics of membership in this group, especially focusing on how the user group is different from other related groups.

If we want to build a more usable application, we should identify all the possible contents and tools that might be used by users. Although UML does not have direct linkages from actors to operations and attributes, actors can indirectly touch the operations and attributes through linkage between use case and class responsibility. However, without more direct linkages, developers may fail to recognize situations where new tools need to be compatible with existing tools and content.

While some environmental information can be obtained by linkages to use case instances, this structure does not allow easy identification and differentiation of environmental factors that are unique to a particular user group. In user detailed requirements, PUF specifies the physical characteristics and capabilities, mental characteristics and capabilities, and social characteristics and capabilities of individuals, and characteristics of groups. This information can further help the designers to design the application according to the users' unique characteristics.

9.4.4   Additional Usability-Related Properties for Actors

The following new properties should be added as a basic structure for stereotypes for UML actors, to record additional usability-related information provided by PUF:

When and Where actors operate. Different users may operate in different environments. Each different environment, may involve different usability and accessibility challenges that need to be handled by a system for it to successfully meet the needs of that group of users.

How much. Different users may have differing levels of involvement with different use cases. High levels of involvement generally mean that users will stay familiar with the operations of systems used for the use case. Infrequent involvement may suggest the need for refresher style retraining before performing a use case or higher levels of help to assist in their performance.

Why. Justification is an important predictor of potential future success. If a user's needs do not fit the overall development, or the cost of serving the user exceeds the resources available or the benefits of such service, it will be impractical to develop special tools for the user. Developers should know the factors that will influence the feasibility and acceptability of possible designs.

Physical. There are various physical limitations and impairments the users may experience. Identifying this information, developers should consider how to design the application to fit the range of physical capabilities experienced by intended users, and whether they should design some new tools for users to reduce the impact of any physical limitations.

Mental. Users' mental characteristics influence how they typically react to a variety of interactions and interfaces. Developers should consider whether to create new tools and how to design the application to fit or change actors' mental capabilities.

Social characteristics and capabilities. Users may come from various social communities with different social backgrounds. This information is important for designers to determine how to design the interfaces and interaction sequences for users who have cultural and/or linguistic differences with each other.

Groups. Membership in a group and or acting as a representative of a group may influence a user's actions. Developers should be made aware of group membership situations that may influence the actions of a user.

9.4.5   Content and Attributes

PUF content records specify high level logical content chunks of data or information. Attributes in a class identify particular data components, generally at a detailed level. PUF content records map to high level data structures of attributes in UML. The content component in PUF may be implemented by one or more attributes in UML.

Table 9.4 illustrates the mapping from PUF content records to UML attributes based on UML specification version 1.5 (OMG, 2003) and the UML user guide (Booch et al., 1999). This table shows that most identification and linkage information in PUF user records can easily be transferred directly to UML. This provides a good starting point for ensuring that records can be mapped successfully. PUF detailed requirements are generally closer to implementation considerations and also map to UML components.

ISO 14915-3 defines content in terms of various information types that serve particular tasks and users (ISO, 2003). It classifies content type using various dimensions including: physical or conceptual content and static or dynamic content. PUF content chunks, while serving tasks and users, need not be limited to a single set of dimensions. PUF uses content descriptions to identify relevant dimensions and other attributes that may influence the use and usability of the content chunk.

UML attributes currently focus on the data contents of the attribute without considering its environment. New properties of attributes are necessary to incorporate descriptions of the content and environmental information about content chunks from PUF.

9.4.6   Additional Usability-Related Properties for Attributes

The following new properties should be added to UML descriptions of attributes, to record additional usability-related information provided by PUF:

When and Where attributes are used. Attributes may need to be handled differently in different temporal and environmental situations. For example, some situations may call for precise details while others may prefer summary data. Each different situation may involve different usability and accessibility challenges that need to be handled by a system for it to successfully work with an attribute.

How much. Attributes may be used in a system at considerably different frequencies of use. High frequencies of use generally mean that users will stay familiar with the meaning, format, and use of attributes. Infrequent use may suggest the need for higher levels of assistance in working with particular attributes.

Why. Justification is an important predictor of potential future success. If the cost of including an attribute exceeds the resources available or the benefits of such inclusion, it will be impractical to consider it for inclusion. Developers should know the factors that will influence the feasibility and acceptability of possible designs.

Although various UML components provide a location for some of the following information, there may be a need for additional properties to further expand upon:

Table 9.4   Mapping from content to attributes

PUF: *Content*	UML: *Attribute*
Identification Information	
name	attribute name
type: content	**attribute** within a **class**
description	– via a new property
Linkage Information	
who	**actors** associated via use cases, with **visibility**
what	associated **essential use cases**
how	**operations** within the **class**
with which content	other **attributes** within the class
scenarios	associated **use case instances**
Environment Information	
when	– via a new property
where	– via a new property
how much	– via a new property
why	– via a new property
Detailed Requirements	
structure	via **subclasses** also includes **multiplicity**
semantics	via **constraints**
requirements on users	**visibility**
how content handled	**operations** associated via **classes** & associated **use case instances**
when content used	**state machines** associated to **operations**
where content comes from & is used	**interaction diagrams**

Structure. Interface designers should consider where it is necessary to organize several linked attributes or whether they should create some new attributes to design more meaningful information for the users.

Semantics. The interface designer should understand the purpose of the attribute, and consider how to design the attribute to let users understand the information so that it can be used for different purposes in various use cases.

Requirements on users. There are many users who will use the attribute. The interface designer should consider where it is necessary to design the same information in different manners to be easily understood for various users with different characteristics.

How content handled. Attributes will be operated by users with various tools. Developers should know how to design a more usable attribute that can be easily handled by all of the input tools, output tools and operation tools.

When and where content is used and comes from. This concerns the environment in which the attribute is obtained and used, and what environmental factors may limit the usability of the attribute.

9.4.7   Tools and Operations

The PUF perspective on tools is that they are developed and used to serve the needs of users *and* tasks *and* contents. Tools include: physical tools, software tools, and procedural tools. An operation is a service that an instance of the class may be requested to perform. Operations are detailed software tools.

Table 9.5 illustrates the mapping from PUF tool records to UML operations based on UML specification version 1.5 (OMG, 2003) and the UML user guide (Booch et al., 1999). This table shows that most identification and linkage information in PUF user records can easily be transferred directly to UML. This provides a good starting point for ensuring that records can be mapped successfully.

PUF uses a tool record to provide an initial narrative description of the nature and operations of the tool. This description is later refined in the detailed requirements. However, it remains useful for help narratives and other more general purposes. UML operations currently focus on the internal processing of the operation without considering its environment or many of the usage-related detailed requirements identified by PUF. PUF detailed requirements of tools are critical because they relate directly with detailed requirements of tasks. This relationship is important in insuring that tools are designed to meet usability requirements identified for the tasks they serve. New properties of operations are necessary to incorporate descriptions of the operations, environmental information, and detailed requirements about tools from PUF.

Table 9.5   Mapping from tools to operations

PUF: *Tool*	UML: *Operation*
Identification Information	
name	operation name
type: tool	**operation** within a **class**
description	– via a new property
Linkage Information	
who	**actors** associated via use cases
what	associated **essential use cases**
how	other **operations** within the **class**
with which content	**attributes** within the **class**
scenarios	associated **use case instances**
Environment Information	
when	– via a new property
where	– via a new property
how much	– via a new property
why	– via a new property
Detailed Requirements	
tool operations	actions of **use cases**
requirements of users	– via a new property
communications	– via a new property
learning	– via a new property
error handling	– via a new property
problem details	– via a new property

9.4.8   Additional Usability-Related Properties for Operations

The following new properties should be added to UML descriptions of operations, to record additional usability-related information provided by PUF:

When and Where attributes are used, How much, Why. The rationale is similar to that for attributes discussed in section 9.4.6.

Requirements of users. Different tools require different skills and abilities to operate them successfully. It is important to recognize the abilities and skills that will be necessary for a given tool and then to compare them with the skills and abilities of the various proposed users.

Communications. Tools are created to communicate with users and other tools. Developers should consider the potential impact of different media and methods that might be used to communicate with users and with other linked tools. This involves recognizing the effectiveness of various current media and methods.

Learning. Developers should consider the learning needs and capabilities of the intended users. It is possible that additional tools must be built to help users learn tools being developed that serve application-related use cases.

Error handling. Tools should acknowledge what errors might occur from the user-side and tool-side. Developers should recognize these situations and determine how to help users avoid or handle them.

Problem details. This field/property is used to document known problems with this tool and tools that it is designed to replace.

9.5   IMPLEMENTING THESE ADDITIONS IN UML

As noted in Section 9.4, a number of the concepts in PUF are directly supported in UML. For example, PUF users are mapped directly to UML actors, PUF tasks are mapped to UML use cases, PUF contents are mapped to UML attributes and PUF tools are mapped to UML operations. As well, linkage information between users, tasks, content and tools are captured in UML with associations. The additional usability-related properties discussed in Section 9.4 that are not directly supported in UML include descriptions, environment information and detailed requirements. However, UML was designed to be extensible using annotations, stereotypes, constraints and tagged values. In this section we describe how UML can be used to express these additional PUF usability-related properties. We describe one approach; alternative approaches are possible given the flexibility of UML.

In our approach, each usability property that does not map directly to a UML concept is associated with a stereotype (Table 9.6). These additional stereotypes will be associated with actors, use cases, attributes, and operations either using notes or classes.

Classes with compartments for "description", "environment information" and "detailed requirements" are used to associate usability property stereotypes with users and tasks. To distinguish a class as being an actor or a user case, an actor icon or a use case oval icon is positioned in the top right corner of the class rectangle. Figure 9.3 is an example of an actor (a) and a use case (b) using this notation.

Table 9.6   Stereotypes used to identify PUF usability properties in UML

Stereotype	Use Cases	Actors	Attributes	Operations
"description"	X	X	X	X
"environment information"	X	X	X	X
"when"	X	X	X	X
"where"	X	X	X	X
"how much"	X	X	X	X
"why"	X	X	X	X
"detailed requirements"	X	X	X	X
"task operations"	X			
"requirements of users"	X			X
"communications"	X			X
"learning"	X			X
"error handling"	X			X
"problem details"	X			X
"physical characteristics"		X		
"mental characteristics"		X		
"social characteristics"		X		
"group characteristics"		X		

Stereotyped notes are used to annotate attributes and operations with usability information. The note is attached to the attribute or operation with a dependency relationship. The note will be stereotyped depending on the information that has been provided and may be structured with multiple stereotypes to reduce clutter. To further reduce clutter in the diagram, the note may be used to link to a document with the detailed information. Figure 9.4 shows examples of using stereotyped notes to express the PUF usability properties for attributes and operations.

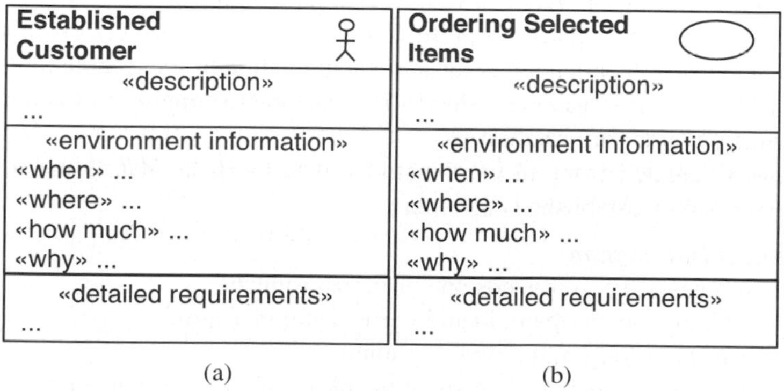

Figure 9.3   UML notation for associating PUF properties to user and task

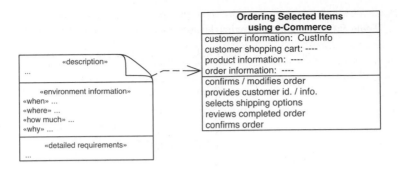

Figure 9.4   UML notation for associating PUF properties to attributes and operations

9.6   EXAMPLE TRANSFORMATIONS

This section provides examples of transformations of two PUF records from an e-Commerce application: a user record describing established customers and a task record describing placing an order for items already in a virtual shopping cart.

9.6.1   User Example

Consider the following PUF user record:

Identification Information
   Name: established customer
   Type: user
   Description: a customer who has an existing account and who has made previous purchases from this e-Commerce site.

Linkage Information
   Who: a specialization of a customer
   What: identifying items to order; selecting and deselecting items; ordering selected items; enquiring about the status of orders; returning items.
   How: the user may choose to perform tasks via telephone, via e-Commerce, in person at a physical location, or using some combination of these three tools.
   With which content: customer information, customer shopping cart contents, product information, order information.
   Scenarios: created from all combinations of tasks (from *What*) and tools (from *How*) performed by established customers.

Environment Information
   When: whenever the user needs one or more products.
   Where: at home; in an office; in an internet café; in a store.
   How much: between 1 and 6 times a month.
   Why: either to meet personal needs or the needs of some organization.

Detailed Requirements
   Physical characteristics: requires the ability to use the methods specified in the scenarios; may include disabilities that will require use of assistive technologies.

Mental characteristics: ability to make purchase decisions; may want help to understand processing options and product features.

Social characteristics: understands English language.

Group characteristics: may act as an individual or as a member of an organization; greater accountability will be expected of purchases made for an organization

Figure 9.5 shows how the user "Established Customer" fits into the inheritance structure of users involved in the e-Commerce application. As well, the stereotypes outlined in Section 9.5 are used to specify the usability properties. Common properties need only be specified once for the common ancestor.

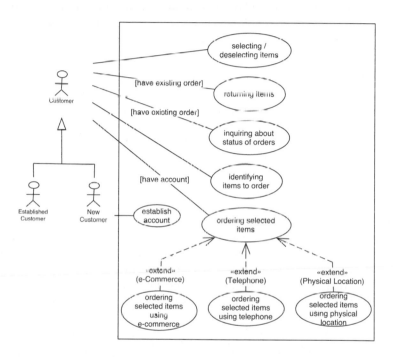

Figure 9.5   Users in the e-Commerce application

9.6.2   Task Example

Consider the following PUF task record:

Identification Information

Name: ordering selected items using e-Commerce

Type: task

Description: placing an order for items already selected and currently in the customer's virtual shopping cart.

Linkage Information

Who: customers; sales clerks

What: associated with selecting and deselecting items; enquiring about the status of orders.

How: part of an e-Commerce application.

With which content: customer information, customer shopping cart contents, product information, order information.

Scenarios: new customer ordering selected items; established customer ordering selected items; sales clerk ordering selected items.

Environment Information

When: after selecting items for shopping cart.

Where: via the internet from home; in an office; in an internet café; in a store.

How much: 2 minutes per order times 1000 customer orders per day.

Why: to allow ordering from a wide range of locations is expected to increase sales by 2000 items per day.

Detailed Requirements

Task operations: user confirms / modifies order; user provides customer identification / information; user selects shipping options; user reviews completed order; user confirms order.

Requirements of users: must have credit card; must use supported Web browser; must understand English language.

Communications: this task involves formal interactive communications between a single user and the e-Commerce system

Learning: the system must be self-descriptive and not require any training; the user may wish to access descriptive help while performing this task.

Error handling: the system should validate data at each step before proceeding and should help the user identify and make any required changes; the system should allow the user to edit all user input fields prior to confirming the order; items in an established customer's virtual shopping cart should remain until the customer deselects or orders them or until they have remained there for over one month.

Problem details: the system must be at least as usable as Amazon.com.

Figure 9.6 shows the task "Ordering Selected Items using e-Commerce" as a use case in the context of other use cases in the e-Commerce application. As well, its linkage with the actors is shown. Since "Customer" is able to "Order Selected Items" it is possible, given the generalization relationships, for an "Established Customer" to "Order Selected Items using e-Commerce".

The task may be implemented as a class as design proceeds. The class will contain attributes and operations corresponding to the content and tools of the task (Figure 9.6). Note that when a task corresponds one-to-one to a class it is possible to use additional compartments in the class to repeat the task's PUF usability properties.

9.7   CONCLUSION

Putting Usability First (PUF) methodology is a user centered approach to systems development. In this chapter we describe a mapping of PUF descriptions to a common software modeling language: the Unified Modeling Language (UML). It is hoped that expressing the PUF methodology in UML can ensure the application is developed

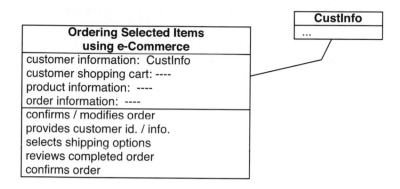

Figure 9.6 Use cases in the e-Commerce application

in a context rich information environment that minimizes the occurrence of usability problems.

We describe how many of the concepts in PUF are directly expressed in UML. We also describe how PUF usability properties can be specified using UML annotations and stereotypes. Mapping PUF to UML makes it possible to trace the usability requirements to the design specified in UML and helps bridge the gap between usability engineering and software engineering. As the design is refined during the software engineering process the usability properties can also be maintained and refined.

The transformations of usability requirements to software engineering specifications described here allow usability engineers and software engineers to integrate their efforts while performing their own processes. This correspondence between usability and software design will hopefully result in more usable software products and improve the traceability of usability requirements.

IV UCD, Unified and Agile Processes

10 WHICH, WHEN AND HOW USABILITY TECHNIQUES AND ACTIVITIES SHOULD BE INTEGRATED

Xavier Ferre, Natalia Juristo, Ana M. Moreno

Universidad Politecnica de Madrid, Spain

Abstract

Software development organizations are paying more and more attention to the usability of their software products, as increasing importance is attached to usability as a critical software quality attribute. The HCI (Human-Computer Interaction) field offers techniques aimed at producing a software product with a good usability level, but their use is often not integrated into SE (software engineering) development processes. The integration of usability techniques into SE practice is not an easy endeavor, since both fields speak different languages and deal with software development from different perspectives. This chapter presents a framework for the integration of usability techniques and activities. This framework characterizes selected usability techniques and activities using SE terminology and concepts, according to what kind of activity they belong to and at what development stage their application contributes most to the usability of the final software product. Software developers may then manage usability activities and techniques, include them in their software process, and understand in which activities usability and SE techniques have to be merged to achieve concurrent objectives. The proposed framework is aimed at software development organizations with a defined iterative development process that are looking to enhance their process with usability aspects.

A. Seffah (eds.), Human-Centered Software Engineering – Integrating Usability
in the Development Process, 173–200.

10.1   INTRODUCTION

This chapter reviews some usability and SE methods looking at how they propose to integrate usability into the overall software development process, and builds an integration framework for incorporating usability activities and techniques into a defined software development process. The importance of this framework lies in the fact that there is now little or no guidance on the integration issue from a SE perspective. Software development organizations interested in improving the usability of their software products are willing to add usability activities and techniques to improve their software process, but usability textbooks do not offer support for this concern. This is a key question bearing in mind that usability techniques and the HCI approach to development are still relatively unknown and not well integrated in SE teams (Seffah and Andreevskaia, 2003). The work presented in this chapter is aimed at software development organizations with a strong SE background that are considering incorporating usability aspects into their practices, and cannot shift to a strictly usability-led development approach. For these organizations, usability is an important concern, but not the main focus, and even if there are some usability experts on their teams, software developers are expected to apply or be acquainted with some usability techniques.

According to the ACM SIGCHI Curricula for Human Computer Interaction, HCI is "a discipline concerned with the design, evaluation and implementation of interactive computing systems for human use and with the study of major phenomena surrounding them" (ACM, 1992). It is an established field, and one of its main concerns is the usability of computer systems. Usability techniques are applied in a variety of software development projects, where attaining an acceptable usability level is a very important, if not the main, goal. These projects are mostly developed following methods peculiar to the HCI field. Where this is not the case, that is, when usability practices are applied along with SE practices, their integration is tackled on a case-by-case basis (as in Anderson et al., 2001; Radle and Young, 2001). The main obstacle to HCI-SE cooperation is that the two fields speak different languages and deal with software development from different perspectives, as detailed in chapter 5. HCI has a multidisciplinary essence, including topics related to fields like cognitive psychology, ergonomics, and sociology. On the other hand, SE is defined in the IEEE Standard Glossary of Software Engineering Terminology as "the application of a systematic, disciplined, quantifiable approach to the development, operation, and maintenance of software; that is, the application of engineering to software" (IEEE, 1990). Software engineers have traditionally focused on the internals of software, on its functionality, reliability, efficiency, and so on, and on the establishment of systematic software development practices. They have paid less attention to how the software product may better support the mental models of the user and the tasks he or she wants to perform.

In particular, the special emphasis it places on making software development systematic and disciplined has led the SE community to pay special attention to the software process. Software process refers to the development roadmap followed by an organization to produce software systems, that is, the series of activities undertaken to develop and maintain software systems. Developers follow the software process established in their organization, which is enforced due to the underlying assumption that a good process leads to a good product. Every organization may have a different software process, but some activities are common to all software processes. The software process can be described at different levels, and a feature common to different process descriptions is the description of the techniques applied in each process activity. Due to the emphasis placed on the software process in the SE community, a considerable amount of effort has gone into software process definition, evaluation, and improvement (Kawalek and Wastell, 1996; Derniame et al., 1999; Fuggetta, 2000). The goal of software process research is to improve software development practice by proposing: a) better ways of defining and modeling the development and therefore designing the developer organization processes, b) better ways of assessing the weaknesses of this organization, and c) better ways of improving this organization at the level of individual processes and the organization as a whole. Typical reasons why a software development organization may consider a defined software process valuable include: facilitating human understanding and communication, supporting process improvement, supporting process management, providing automated process guidance and providing automated execution support (Abran et al,, 2004).

It should be noted that agile methods have recently appeared in response to all the importance software development practices attach to the software process. Agile methods try to shift the focus to other issues, like individuals and their interaction, and regard the software process as an important but secondary issue in software development. The Agile Manifesto (Beck et al., 2001) sets out the main ideas behind this approach to software development. The agile philosophy is receiving a significant amount of attention in the SE field, and it looks like a promising approach from a usability point of view, as highlighted in chapter 12. Nevertheless, it is not yet considered part of the core practices of SE as defined software processes are. The SWEBOK (Software Engineering Body of Knowledge), which is a recent effort to gather what is considered commonly accepted knowledge in the SE field, does not include any reference to the agile approach in its Trial Version 1.00 (Abran et al., 2004), while defined software processes have their own chapter. Most software engineers put the accent on defining the software process in the belief that having and improving a defined process, as other production organizations do, is an approach that produces better quality software.

As they are, usability methods are hard to apply in SE, because of the conceptual differences between HCI and SE, and because overlaps with SE have not been settled. In particular, activities related to requirements engineering (an SE subfield) are tackled by both usability and SE methods. These overlapping areas are not clearly formulated from a SE viewpoint, forcing software development organizations to undertake costly research in order to plan the introduction of usability techniques and activities into such practices. The importance of the integration effort is sometimes mistakenly minimized, as a result of a perception of usability common in the SE field: it is considered to be related to just the UI (user interface). To average developers, the UI is the actual visual elements with which the user interacts and their response behavior (in visual terms), and it is therefore regarded as a graphic designer affair. Such misconceptions simplify the problem of integration in the software process modeler's mind: being a graphic designer issue, it only requires the addition of a usability activity in the process in which these issues are taken care of. In this case, there would be no or only slight overlaps. Bearing in mind usability in the software development process, however, implies including usability activities throughout the entire process, with the challenge of integrating different development cultures into the same kind of activity.

For the present decade, Dumas & Redish (Dumas and Redish, 1999) predict continued growth of interest in usability from users to CEOs. Usability is becoming an important asset for a lot of software development organizations, and they demand guidelines for integrating usability activities and techniques into their software process. This trend towards usability integration throughout software construction is illustrated by the International Organization for Standardization's (ISO) decision to include a new process, called usability process, in the standard for software processes. This change was introduced in the first amendment to ISO/IEC Standard 12207:1995, released in 2002 (ISO/IEC, 2002). The fact that an international SE standard stipulates that usability activities should be part of the software development process is an indication that usability is definitely on the SE agenda with respect to software process definition.

The goal of the work presented in this chapter is to offer a framework for introducing usability activities and techniques into any iterative software development process an organization may have in place. This framework does not define a particular software process, but sets out integration information in a way that it can be applied to a wide range of processes. The framework we propose details which kind of activities in a SE process are affected by usability techniques and when in development time each technique yields results that are most useful for the aim of raising the usability level of the final software product.

The first obstacle to the introduction of usability techniques into the software process is the difference in process terminology between HCI and SE. Therefore, for our purpose of integration, we need to extract the essence, to look at the core ideas behind the terms to find the connections between the two software development approaches. We need to identify the motivations behind each activity to find their interrelationships.

Apart from the terminology gap, HCI does not share the SE view of the software process. Some HCI authors, like Shneiderman, 1998, or Nielsen, 1993, do not structure usability efforts as activities (in the SE sense), so some usability techniques are not clearly assigned to activities in the HCI literature. The basic user-centered process (the HCI term for its process approach) is outlined in ISO Standard 13407 (ISO/IEC, 1999), but each author in the field has a particular vision of how this maps to specific activities. For effective HCI-SE cooperation, usability techniques need to be mapped to the most common activities present in user-centered processes.

The research presented in this work has been carried out as part of the STATUS project, financed by the European Commission (IST-2001-32298). The project goals include outputting methodological guidelines for integrating usability techniques into the software process, which we are presenting here. The two industrial partners in the project consortium have helped us to establish the framework's underlying premises. Pragmatically speaking, the industrial partners asked for a roadmap that could tell them which usability techniques and activities they should incorporate, and when in development time. They prefer this open solution that fits a wider range of processes to establishing the "perfect" software process integrating usability and SE practices.

The application of such a perfect process from a usability point of view would mean abandoning their current software process, which they do not wish to do.

Not all processes can be converted into proper user-centered processes by making just a few modifications. The transformation required for a process or an organizational culture based on a waterfall lifecycle approach to become user-centered would be far too drastic. This approach implies that detailed specifications are produced before any design and implementation is performed. The complexity of the human side in human-computer interaction makes it almost impossible to create a correct design at the first go. Cognitive, sociological, educational, physical and emotional issues may play an important role in any user-system interaction, and they cannot be completely predicted in advance. Therefore, the candidate for usability integration needs to be an iterative process. Of the characteristics of a user-centered process, iterativeness is the only one that is intrinsically inherent to the software process, as stated below in Section 10.7. Our framework then can help any organization with an iterative process to enhance this process with usability activities and techniques. This approach increases the practical applicability of the framework, since it does not require any specific original process as long as it is iterative. The appeal for a software development organization lies in the fact that it does not have to abandon the in-house process to adopt improvements, as it only has to modify the existing process.

The following three sections analyze how existing proposals deal with the integration problem: Section 10.2 details how integration is considered in usability methods, Section 10.3 details proposals for integrating usability techniques and activities into widely known SE methods, and Section 10.4 discusses the limitations and advantages of the proposals in the previous two sections. Section 10.5 details the mapping between usability and SE activities. Section 10.6 presents the assignment of the selected usability techniques to activities. Section 10.7 deals with the considerations on when to apply usability techniques and activities in an iterative development. The basic premises and context for the solution proposed are discussed in Section 10.8 and, finally, Section 10.9 presents the conclusions.

10.2 USABILITY METHODS APPROACH TO INTEGRATION

An organization wanting to include usability techniques and activities in the process may resort to HCI literature for help on the issue. In this section, we consider how the usability methods described in the HCI literature deal with the integration issue. We will consider just textbooks and international standards, since they are the sources more readily available to average developers with a SE background (who do not usually use conference proceedings and research journals as a source of information).

The **Star Life Cycle** by Hix & Hartson (Hix and Hartson, 1993) is a user-centered process that sets out the main usability activities. It does not prescribe a particular order for activities, but it does allocate a prominent role to usability evaluation, which is placed in the center of the star that represents the activities in the life cycle. Hix and Hartson describe the communication paths that should take place between usability activities (user interaction design) and software design. They strictly separate the development of the UI from the development of the rest of the software system, with two activities that connect them: systems analysis and testing/evaluation. The systems analysis group feeds requirements to both the problem domain design group and the user interaction design group. It is a simplistic approach to HCI-SE integration, but the authors acknowledge that "research is needed to better understand and support the real communication needs of this complex process" (Hix and Hartson, 1993).

ISO Standard 13407 (ISO/IEC, 1999) provides guidance on human-centered design activities throughout the life cycle of computer-based interactive systems. It is neither a method nor a software process, but it characterizes user-centered processes. Note that the standard authors use the term human-centered as equivalent to user-centered. We prefer the latter term, since it is more widely used in the HCI literature.

The standard reasons why a user-centered focus should be adopted in interactive systems, and it includes the characteristics of such a focus: active involvement of users and clear understanding of user and task requirements; an appropriate allocation of function between users and technology; the iteration of design solutions; and multidisciplinary design. It also describes the essential activities in a human-centered process: understand and specify the context of use; specify the user and organizational requirements; produce design solutions and evaluate designs against requirements.

The standard also establishes that the human-centered process, including the procedures for integrating the usability activities with other system development activities, e.g. analysis, design, testing, has to be planned, although this is as far as it goes on the integration issue. This requirement calls for the development of usability roadmaps that are useful for fitting usability techniques into the overall software development process.

Constantine & Lockwood (Constantine and Lockwood, 1999) propose the **Usage-Centered Design** method as a collection of coordinated activities that contribute to usability. Some HCI practitioners would not completely agree in considering usage-centered design an HCI method, but we have classed this method as such, since it is focused on the development of interactive systems for human use (and therefore fits the definition of HCI given in Section 10.1). The usage-centered design activity model includes some activities that correspond to the larger software development process (object structure design, concentric construction and architectural iteration), along with pure usability activities, like task modeling or interface content modeling. The models that Constantine and Lockwood propose are appealing to software engineers, since they are closer than other usability techniques to the kind of modeling used in SE. In particular, essential use cases, which are a cornerstone of the usage-centered approach, are a reinterpretation of the popular object-oriented technique of use cases. They can, therefore, serve the purpose of acting as a bridge between SE and HCI models. In fact, there are at least two popular SE reference books (Larman, 2002, and Cockburn, 2001), that acknowledge Constantine and Lockwood's work on essential use cases.

Constantine and Lockwood offer some advice on integrating usability and UI design into the product development cycle, acknowledging that there is no one single way of approaching this question. Therefore, they leave the issue of integration to be solved on a case-by-case basis. They state that "good strategies for integrating usability into the life cycle fit new practices and old practices together, modifying present practices to incorporate usability into analysis and design processes, while also tailoring usage-centered design to the organization and its practices" (Constantine and Lockwood, 1999). Although some techniques that are closer to SE modeling are described, Constantine and Lockwood's proposal is not formalized in process terms, and their work is more concerned with detailing the techniques than with specifying the process in terms of dependencies, products and roles.

Mayhew (Mayhew, 1999) proposes the **Usability Engineering Lifecycle** for the development of usable UIs. The process structures the activities into three phases: Requirements Analysis, Design / Test / Development, and Installation. This approach to the process follows a waterfall lifecycle mindset: an initial Analysis phase, followed by a Design / Test / Development phase, and finally an Installation phase. The Analysis stage is only returned to if not all functionality is addressed, and this is, therefore, not a truly iterative approach to software development.

Nevertheless, it is one of the more complete usability methods from the SE point of view. Although Mayhew claims that the method is aimed at the development of the UI only, the activities included in this life cycle embrace an important part of requirements-related activities (like, for example, Contextual Task Analysis). Links with the OOSE (Object-Oriented Software Engineering) method (Jacobson, 1992) and with rapid prototyping methods are identified, but Mayhew acknowledges that the integration of usability engineering with SE must be tailored and that the overlap between usability and SE activities is not completely clear. The links with OOSE and rapid prototyping are very general, and Mayhew presents UI development as an activity that is quite independent from the development of the rest of the system.

Additionally, the author surprisingly defines software engineering as "an approach to software development that involves defining application requirements, setting goals, and designing and testing in iterative cycles until goals are met" (Mayhew, 1999). Even though this is now the main trend in SE, it is not a valid definition of the discipline, since there are other development approaches that are valid from a SE viewpoint. A software engineer, taking up this work in search of help with the issue of usability integration into the software process may be put off by such misconceptions.

10.3 INTEGRATION PROPOSALS BASED ON SE METHODS

As we are trying to offer a solution for organizations that already have a process in place, this section will review integration proposals that are based on widely known SE methods. Costabile's proposal is based on the waterfall lifecycle. MUSE (Method for USability Engineering) is defined according to the characteristics of a structured method. Finally, we examine the User Experience addition to the RUP (Rational Unified Process).

Costabile (Costabile, 2001) offers a way of integrating user-centered practices into the software process to increase the usability of the software product. She condenses the user-centered approach into three main principles: analyze users and tasks, design and implement the system iteratively through prototypes of increasing complexity and evaluate design choices and prototypes with users. Costabile proposes a way of modifying the software life cycle to include usability. The basis she takes for such modifications is the waterfall lifecycle. The proposal adds two extra activities composed of pure usability activities –user and task analysis, on the one hand, and scenarios and UI specifications, on the other–, plus two intermediate activities which include the same tasks: prototyping and testing. It is possible to go back to a previous phase from any phase of the life cycle. According to the author, these backtracking paths, along with the two extra activities, emphasize the iterativeness of software development, which is necessary from a user-centered point of view.

Costabile's proposal has an important drawback in the choice of the waterfall life cycle as a "standard" software life cycle. This model goes against the user-centered aim of evaluating usability from the very beginning and iterating to a satisfactory solution. Paths that go back in the waterfall life cycle are defined for error correction, not for completely changing the approach if it proves to be wrong, since it is based on frozen requirements (Larman, 2002). Glass acknowledges that "requirements frequently changed as product development goes under way [...]. The experts knew that waterfall was an unachievable ideal" (Glass, 2003). SE literature has gradually come to accept that an iterative as opposed to a waterfall life cycle approach is the best for medium to high complexity problems when the development team does not have in-depth domain knowledge. Larman identifies the following problems with the waterfall life cycle: delayed risk mitigation, speculation and inflexibility of requirements and design, high complexity and low adaptability (Larman, 2002). Iterative development tackles most of these problems. Nevertheless, a waterfall mindset is still deeply rooted in day-to-day practice among software developers, mainly because it gives the complex activity of developing software systems an illusion of order and simplicity.

MUSE (Method for USability Engineering) (Lim and Long, 1994) is a method for designing the UI, and was one of the most well structured usability methods at the time of its publication (1994). It is divided into three phases: Information Elicitation and Analysis Phase, Design Synthesis Phase and Design Specification Phase. The method aims to ease integration with SE methods, and its integration with the JSD (Jackson System Development) method is described. The primary focus of the MUSE method is on design specification due to the identified lack of integration in this stage, whereas, according to the method creators, later stages (usability evaluation) are well covered in the existing literature.

MUSE is based on the principle of delaying design commitment, ensuring that detailed design is preceded by appropriate design analysis and conceptual definition. Comparing MUSE with the rapid prototyping approach, Lim and Long state that MUSE, as a structured method, emphasizes a design analysis and documentation phase prior to the specification of a "first-best-guess" solution. Therefore, MUSE follows a waterfall life cycle, which is an obstacle to the application of a truly iterative approach.

As MUSE is a structured method, it is presented by its authors as easy to integrate into any structured SE method. Its integration with JSD is detailed as an example of this. JSD is presented as a method that is mainly used for the development of real-time systems. Real-time systems account for a very small part of interactive systems, so the integration of MUSE with JSD is not very useful from a generic point of view. Regarding the integration of MUSE with other SE methods, its usage of techniques like structured diagrams or semantic nets makes it difficult to adapt to current SE practices, in particular to object-oriented development.

The BIUSEM project (BIUSEM, 1995) applied MUSE to three software development projects in different domains and with different SE methods to evaluate its applicability. Despite the positive outcome of the project (the application of MUSE improved the product quality, and the sharing of human factors insight with software engineers helped to elicit user-centered requirements), the project team acknowledged that "the body of published papers and the book describing MUSE are unnecessarily complicated and act as a deterrent to its wider use" (BIUSEM, 1995).

The **Unified Process** (Jacobson et al., 1999; Kroll and Kruchten, 2003) is the process that is currently receiving the greatest attention in SE, since it is sponsored by the main object-oriented methodologists: James Rumbaugh, Ivar Jacobson and Grady Booch. It advocates a truly iterative approach. It denotes the activities that the process encompasses as "disciplines" to avoid the typical identification between activity types and process stages in the waterfall life cycle. Of the processes that actually have an iterative approach, the Unified Process is the most widely used. The RUP© (Rational Unified Process) is a refinement of the Unified Process sold by IBM (previously by Rational Software Co.). The approach to usability integration presented in this section is not comparable to the above proposals in scope. It has been included, however, because of the current relevance of the Unified Process and RUP in SE.

The RUP does not consider usability directly, but it is use-case driven, and use-case modeling has some similarities with HCI task modeling. Therefore, use cases could be used as a starting point for usability integration into the software process. However, the use-case model in the Unified Process plays a secondary role as compared to system architecture. The use-case model is very important in cycle planning, but once the cycle starts, use cases are regarded as a preliminary version of elements of the internal functionality design. When design elements are labeled as use-case realizations, we are shifting use cases to the design world and, therefore, away from the user realm, losing most user-centered advantages with that shift.

The User Experience (UX) (Rational, 2002) plug-in for RUP aims to integrate the work performed in the web development domain regarding the development of the web system concept, which usually drives the whole development, into RUP. It is based on Jim Conallen's work on web modeling (Conallen, 2003), and there are big similarities between UX aims and classical HCI concerns. According to Conallen, the term User Experience "is used to describe the team and the activities of those specialists responsible for keeping the UI consistent with current paradigms and, most important, appropriate for the context into which the system is expected to run" (Conallen, 2003). Despite this promising definition, Conallen's work focuses on modeling, and he describes the artefacts for which the UX team is responsible as follows: screens and content descriptions, storyboard scenarios, and navigational paths through the screens.

Although it is an advance towards the aim of integrating usability into the software process, the UX addition to RUP does not cover the entire process and is limited to a few models. Nevertheless, it does indicate the growing interest in the web development domain for integrating usability expertise and techniques into the development process.

With regard to usability integration into object-oriented development, the **WISDOM method** (Nunes, 2001) deserves a mention, even if it is not a commonly used method. It includes an extension to UML (Unified Modeling Language) to allow user-centered models to be employed in conjunction with object-oriented models and, therefore, to facilitate usability integration in modeling efforts throughout development. The WISDOM method offers a comprehensive process for any organization interested in adopting a new process already integrating usability. The organization is then forced to adopt the process as a whole, including the underlying assumptions present in the SE part of the method. For example, the WISDOM method differentiates between an Analysis and a Design workflow, while this distinction (inherited from object-oriented methods prior to the Unified Process) is not retained in recent interpretations of the Unified Process: Kroll & Kruchten consider a single "analysis and design" discipline or workflow (Kroll and Kruchten, 2003), while Larman considers no analysis discipline and also states that the analysis model in the Unified Process is not necessary and seldom used (Larman, 2002). Nevertheless, the WISDOM method is still very interesting for software engineers, since it offers models for dealing with usability issues. Additionally, the way it deals with some process issues in a user-centered view could be mapped to processes other than the specific WISDOM method process.

10.4 SUMMARY OF INTEGRATION PROPOSALS

As presented in Section 10.2, the descriptions of the usability methods considered as to how they integrate with the overall software development process are not highly detailed. Actually, the textbooks describing these methods do not intend to detail this issue, as their main objective is to present the actual usability method. Consequently, a software engineer looking for an answer to the integration problem may find the information in these sources defined at a different level of detail than is usual in a defined SE software process. Some methods just present high-level activities, like the Star Lifecycle, the ISO Standard 13407, or the Usage-centered Design method. On the other hand, the Usability Engineering Lifecycle is more detailed, describing fine-grained activities and techniques that may be applied for each activity. But, as presented in (Mayhew, 1999), this method encompasses a not so iterative approach to software development. On top of these difficulties, the four HCI approaches considered use a terminology that is peculiar to the HCI field. Specifically, the Star and the Usability Engineering lifecycles are presented as methods for the design of highly usable UIs. As stated in Section 10.1, SE refers by UI design to just the design of the actual visual elements that form the UI and the UI response behavior in visual terms. It does not include any activity related to requirements engineering in the SE perspective. Nevertheless, both methods include standard requirements activities like task or user analysis. The terminology gap makes the task of integrating the usability methods into the overall software process especially difficult.

As for the integration proposals based on SE methods presented in Section 10.3, we have also identified some of the limitations observed in usability methods, like them not being truly iterative (in the case of Costabile's proposal and MUSE) or just addressing the design of the UI (like MUSE), and therefore confusing software engineers with regard to integration. On the other hand, the UX plug-in for RUP actually integrates some usability practices into a comprehensive process, but its main goal is to incorporate some techniques that are often used in the web development field instead of integrating usability into the process. Therefore, the UX plug-in is limited to a few usability techniques and does not cover the whole range of activities in which usability techniques may apply.

Given that the information from the HCI literature is not detailed enough for the purpose of integration and is not formulated in SE concepts and terminology, and because SE proposals do not have a proper iterative focus or cover all activities, we propose a framework that addresses these concerns in the following sections. The framework is formulated according to a truly iterative approach (expressing time constraints in the form of iterative development stages), and it covers the whole range of SE activities for mapping usability activities and techniques to all relevant kinds of activities in a software process.

10.5   MAPPING BETWEEN USABILITY AND SE ACTIVITIES

To map usability terminology to SE terminology, the activities that form part of a user-centered process must be identified. The heterogeneous landscape of methods and philosophies offered by the HCI field, like, for instance, usability engineering, usage-centered design, contextual inquiry, and participatory design, is a hurdle for this ambition. Each author attaches importance to a few techniques, and the terminology may vary from one author to another. For this reason, we have surveyed the HCI literature (Ferre et al., 2002a) to identify the most agreed upon usability activities that should be part of the software development process. We have listed these usability activities in Figure 10.1, grouped according to what type of development activity they belong to. Note that the activities are not listed in any time-related order.

There is a lot of consensus in HCI regarding analysis activities. Specification of the Context of Use is an activity whose aim is to understand and record the implications of the context of use so that they can be considered during system design. It has been named following the ISO 13407 Standard terminology (ISO/IEC, 1999), and it is divided into User and Task Analysis because some authors make a distinction between the two activities (Mayhew, 1999; Hix and Hartson, 1993; Constantine and Lockwood, 1999). Usability specifications are quantitative usability goals, which are used as a guide for ascertaining when a system has the proper usability level. They can be considered non-functional requirements.

Design activities are less well defined in the HCI literature that we consulted. The only activity cited by most authors is Prototyping. Prototypes are widely used in SE, particularly in iterative development. What HCI has to offer, however, is the particular usage of light prototyping to get more user involvement and for weighing up alternative designs. The most useful prototypes for this purpose are the less sophisticated ones, such as paper prototypes. Typical SE prototypes usually involve some degree of programming, while paper prototypes allow for faster iterations as they do not require any programming effort.

Develop the Product Concept is based on mental models (Norman, 1990; Preece et al., 1994): when the product concept is vague, ambiguous, inconsistent or obscure, there will be a divergence between the user mental model of the system and the design model that developers work with. The importance of helping the user to grow productive mental models for the usability of the system is especially stressed. Good designers always bear in mind a certain product concept, but making it explicit and highlighting its importance in the software development process will help to shape the system in a way that explicitly communicates this product concept to the user.

Interaction Design varies considerably from one author to another, but we have identified the definition of the interaction that will take place between the user and the system as a common aim in the design process. It includes designing the user-system dialogue, that is, the sequence of actions needed to operate the system, and the user-system information exchange, in detail. By interaction design we mean the design of the coordination of information exchange between the user and the system. Apart from tackling UI design (the design of the elements of the UI that will make the interaction possible), it also includes decisions that affect the internal logic of the system, to the extent that this internal logic is reflected in the user-system interaction.

Usability evaluation is the activity that is most profusely detailed in HCI literature. Usability is very difficult to strive for, due to the complex human nature. Without doing some form of evaluation, it is impossible to know whether or not the design or system fulfils the needs of the users and how well it fits the physical, social and organizational context in which it will be used (Preece et al., 1994). Usability evaluation is a core part of iterative development, in the sense that evaluation activities can produce design solutions for application in the next design cycle or, at least, more insight into the nature of the interaction problem at hand. Therefore, evaluation is not seen in HCI as a mere fail/pass test, but as a part of development. Three big families have been highlighted within the Usability Evaluation activity in Figure 10.1: Expert Evaluation, Usability Testing and Follow-Up Studies of Installed Systems.

The set of activities is based on HCI terminology, with which most software developers are not familiar. Therefore, the terms must be translated to a generally accepted SE terminology, so that developers know where to plug in the usability additions to the software process. Wherever possible, the SWEBOK (Abran et al., 2004) has been used as a basis for defining the activities in a traditional software development process. HCI terminology has been used for other activities that are new to SE and do not fit any existing activity.

The mapping of usability activities to development activities considered in this chapter is shown in Figure 10.1. Each usability activity on the left-hand side of Figure 10.1 is mapped to a development activity on the right by means of an arrow. Some activities have been added to the usual SE activities, because they do not match an existing SE activity. They are highlighted in italics (for example, Interaction Design). Only activities that are affected by usability are represented on the right, and the other activities in a software process are not included.

Regarding the analysis-related activities, note that usability activities are intertwined with standard analysis activities. Therefore, they can be directly mapped to the different types of SE analysis efforts. Following the SWEBOK definitions, we have selected the requirements activities that are likely to be enhanced by the introduction of usability techniques: Requirements Elicitation, Analysis and Negotiation; Requirements Specification; and Requirements Validation. Four activities, presented in the HCI literature as being necessary for understanding users, their context and their needs, have been highlighted within the Requirements Elicitation, Analysis, and Negotiation activity: User Analysis, Task Analysis, Develop Product Concept and Prototyping.

The activities of Develop Product Concept and Prototyping are considered differently in HCI and in SE. According to the SWEBOK, Prototyping is considered in SE as a technique that can be used in Requirements Elicitation and Validation. As for Develop the Product Concept, it is a design activity, but the kind of design that is known as invention design. According to the SWEBOK, invention design is usually performed by systems analysts with the objective of conceptualizing and specifying a system to satisfy the discovered needs and requirements, and it is not addressed in the chapter of the SWEBOK devoted to software design (Abran et al., 2004). This conceptualization activity is usually undertaken as part of requirements elicitation activities, and is fundamental for the success of requirements engineering efforts. Because of its close connection with requirements activities and because the SWEBOK considers invention design as part of the requirements analysis activity, we have considered Develop the Product Concept as part of Requirements Elicitation, Analysis and Negotiation in our framework.

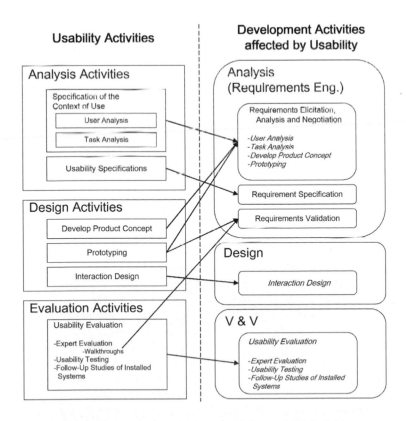

Figure 10.1   Mapping between usability and SE Activities

Usability-related design activities are quite separate from general design activities. Therefore, a new activity, called Interaction Design, has been included under the Design activities. The SWEBOK considers UI Design not as part of SE but as a related discipline. However, it also states that UI design deals with specifying the external view of the system and that it should be considered as part of requirements specification. Nevertheless, the chapter devoted to requirements in the same source (the SWEBOK) does not include UI. On the other hand, Interaction Design fits the definition provided by the IEEE Standard Glossary of Software Engineering Terminology for design: "the process of defining the architecture, components, interfaces, and other characteristics of a system or component" (IEEE, 1990). Therefore, we have considered Interaction Design as a design activity, because it is not clearly located in the SWEBOK and because it fits the general definition of design.

Regarding evaluation, a new activity, Usability Evaluation is created, since it groups usability techniques that are unconnected with other general evaluation activities. However, walkthroughs can be used during requirements validation, so they have been highlighted within Expert Evaluation (on the left of Figure 10.1) to show this link with analysis-related activities. Evaluation activities are termed V&V (Verification and Validation) in SE, so this is the label used for evaluation activities.

After having matched usability activities to their respective SE activities, we need to address the individual techniques to be employed in each activity.

10.6 ASSIGNMENT OF USABILITY TECHNIQUES TO ACTIVITIES

For developers to be able to apply usability techniques, they need to know in which activities they are applied. The previous section matched the activities in the HCI literature to their respective SE activities.

Note that the integration framework presented in this chapter is aimed at software development organizations that do not have a big usability department (if they have one at all!) and, therefore, need usability concerns to be shared with the developers throughout development. Nevertheless, for organizations where usability expertise is widely available, communication problems inside multidisciplinary teams are an important concern, and the proposed framework would also be of interest in such cases.

Bearing in mind that, in our approach, the usability techniques could be applied by non-experts in usability, we have made a selection where there was more than one usability technique with the same objective available and have included usability techniques that are less alien to a SE mindset in our framework. From more than 80 techniques described in the HCI literature (Ferre et al., 2002a), the resulting set of techniques has been reduced to just 36 techniques. They appear in the column furthest to the right in Table 10.1, which is explained in the next paragraph.

We have used the definition of each usability technique in the literature as regards its application in a particular activity to allocate usability techniques to activities, and this definition has again been compared with the definition of activities in the SWEBOK. Table 10.1 shows the classification of usability techniques according to activities. The techniques are grouped according to the activities in a generic software development process that are listed in the central column.

10.7   WHEN TO APPLY USABILITY ACTIVITIES AND TECHNIQUES

We examined the HCI literature to identify what characteristics a software development process should have for it to be considered user-centered. Shneiderman, 1998, Nielsen, 1993, ISO/IEC, 1999, Hix and Hartson, 1993, Constantine and Lockwood, 1999, Preece et al., 1994, all agree on considering iterative development as a must for a user-centered development process. The other two characteristics that are mentioned by several sources are: active user involvement and a proper understanding of user and task requirements. These two conditions can be met by introducing usability techniques that can help software developers to integrate users into the design process and to enhance requirements activities with specific usability aspects. On the other hand, the first condition (that is, iterativeness) is an intrinsic characteristic of a software process, and needs to be stated as a requirement for an existing development process to be a candidate for the introduction of usability techniques and activities.

The usability practices described in the literature are deeply rooted in this process characteristic and, for the application of usability techniques, there are indications on when in development time each technique yields the most useful results for improving the usability of the final product. These indications on the best time to apply usability techniques have to be transmitted to developers. Hence, it is not enough just to assign usability techniques to development activities, extra guidance also needs to be provided on what usability techniques are to be applied exactly when in development time. Consequently, the activities and their techniques need to be interrelated with development stages. For this purpose, we will now present a generic description for the stages of any process based on iterative development and then actually interrelate activities / techniques and stages.

Table 10.1: Allocation of usability techniques to activities

HCI Activities	Activities in Software Process	Usability Techniques
Analysis - Specification of the Context of Use - User Analysis	Analysis	Ethnographic Observation (Preece et al., 1994)
	Requirements Elicitation, Analysis and Negotiation	Contextual Inquiry (Beyer and Holtzblatt, 1998)
		Structured User Role Model (Constantine and Lockwood, 1999)
		Operational Modeling (Constantine and Lockwood, 1999)
		JEM (Joint Essential Modeling) (Constantine and Lockwood, 1999)
Analysis - Spec. Context of Use - Task Analysis		Essential Use Cases (Constantine and Lockwood, 1999)
Design - Develop Product Concept		Affinity Diagrams (Beyer and Holtzblatt, 1998)
		Visual Brainstorming (Preece et al., 1994)
		Competitive Analysis (Nielsen, 1993)
		Scenarios (Carroll, 1997)
Design - Prototyping		Prototypes (paper and chauffeured (Constantine and Lockwood, 1999); and wizard of Oz (Preece et al., 1994)
Analysis - Usability Specifications	Requirement Specification	Usability Specifications (Hix and Hartson, 1993)
Usability Evaluation - Expert Evaluation	Requirements Validation	Cognitive Walkthrough (Lewis and Wharton, 1997)
		Pluralistic Walkthrough (Bias, 1994)

Continued on next page

Table 10.1: Allocation of usability techniques to activities

HCI Activities	Activities in Software Process	Usability Techniques
Analysis - Spec. Context of Use - Task Analysis	Design	Detailed Use Cases (Constantine and Lockwood, 1999)
Design - Interaction Design	Interaction Design	Screen Pictures (Hix and Hartson, 1993)
		Card Sorting (Robertson, 2001)
		Menu-selection Trees (Shneiderman, 1998)
		Navigational Paths (Conallen, 2003)
		Product Style Guide (Mayhew, 1999)
		Impact Analysis (Hix and Hartson, 1993)
		Help Design by Use Cases (Constantine and Lockwood, 1999)
Evaluation - Expert Evaluation	Usability Evaluation / V & V	Heuristic Evaluation (Nielsen, 1993)
		Usability Inspections (Nielsen and Mack, 1994)
		Cognitive Walkthrough (Lewis and Wharton, 1997)
		Pluralistic Walkthrough (Bias, 1994)
Evaluation - Usability Testing		Thinking aloud (Nielsen, 1993)
		Performance Measurement (Dumas and Redish, 1999)
		Laboratory Usability Testing (Dumas and Redish, 1999)
		Post-Test Feedback / User Questionnaires (Mayhew 1999)
Evaluation - Follow-up Studies of Installed Systems		Questionnaires / Surveys (Mayhew, 1999)

Continued on next page

Table 10.1: Allocation of usability techniques to activities

HCI Activities	Activities in Software Process	Usability Techniques
		Structured and Flexible Interviews (Preece et al., 1994)
		Direct Observation (Hix and Hartson, 1993)
		Video / Audio recording (Hix and Hartson, 1993)
		Focus Groups (Mayhew, 1999)
		Logging Actual Use (Shneiderman, 1998)
		Online User Feedback Facilities (Shneiderman, 1998)

10.7.1   Stages in an Iterative Development Process

Different times or stages can be defined in an iterative process, where one and the same activity may be more or less important or have a different meaning. For instance, most requirements discovery and refinement is usually undertaken during the early iterations (Larman, 2004). These early iterations are packed in a stage: Elaboration. A stage comprises a sequence of iterations in development with similar basic objectives.

Even though each iterative process has its particular approach and terminology in terms of development stages, they usually follow a similar pattern in this respect. This pattern is represented in Figure 10.2. Each stage is represented by a cloud, because it is not a development phase as in the waterfall life cycle, but a set of iterations organized according to the moment in time represented by the x-axis.

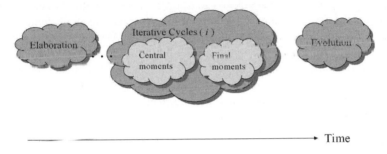

Figure 10.2   Stages in an iterative software development process

An explanation of the stages in an iterative development follows:

- **Elaboration cycles**: This stage represents the early efforts in the software development process, where the problem is delimited and the basic information is gathered for later development in the iterative cycles.

- **Iterative cycles** (i): These are the iterations found in any iterative approach. For usability techniques to be applied in the cycles, a distinction will be made between two moments:

    - **Central moments**: The main part of each cycle.
    - **Final moments**: The last part of each cycle, where certain activities are performed, typically V&V activities.

- **Evolution cycles**: These iterations represent the cycles that are undertaken after the system has been installed and is operational at the customer's site.

Any organization wanting to apply the proposed framework will have to translate these generic stages to the ones they have in place, using their specific terminology. Even if our representation of development stages is a common one in iterative processes, not all iterative development approaches will necessarily match our stage representation. For example, some projects may not have an elaboration stage, in which case the techniques to be applied in this stage would be applied in the iterative cycles instead, since this is the next stage in our representation.

10.7.2   Time Constraints for Usability Technique Application

Apart from the activity of which they are part, the description of usability techniques in the HCI literature includes indications on the moments in development time when they are to be applied. This section details this information, organized according to the stages in a generic iterative process presented in the previous section. For a comprehensive study of the time constraints for usability technique application, (see Ferre et al., 2002b).

The **Elaboration** stage corresponds to the initial cycles where the needs are identified and the general system outline is established. A general aim is for the products of this stage to be quite stable, even though they are open to changes in the iterative development cycles.

The following techniques are clearly to be applied at elaboration time, because they are good for the first examination of the problem for handling an ill-defined solution: Ethnographic Observation, Contextual Inquiry, Affinity Diagrams, Scenarios, Visual Brainstorming, and Paper and Chauffeured Prototypes.

Competitive Analysis can be applied later on, but it can help at elaboration time because it is good for coming up with design ideas on the product concept.

Analyzing the user and his or her environment, and the basic dialogue between the system and the user is a prerequisite for any development that intends to cater for the user and the usability of the resulting product. For this reason, the following techniques should be applied at elaboration time, even though they may be applied later for completing the models produced:

- Essential Use Cases

- Structured User Role Model

- Operational Modeling

- JEM (Joint Essential Modeling)

- Cognitive and Pluralistic Walkthrough: Walkthroughs evaluate an interaction dialogue. So, as soon as these dialogues are defined in the essential use cases, walkthroughs can be applied as an evaluation technique.

- Heuristic Evaluation: Low fidelity prototypes and early designs of the UI may be evaluated heuristically.

The specifications document should include Usability Specifications. So, this technique will be applied at elaboration time if such a document is created at this stage, but it can be completed as development advances.

Techniques related to UI design can be applied at the Elaboration stage, because the UI is the part of the implementation that the user can understand better. Its design may be undertaken at the early stages of development in order to get feedback from the user. Thus, even though these techniques will carry more weight in the iterative cycles, they are also present at the Elaboration stage. These techniques are Detailed Use Cases, Screen Pictures, Card Sorting, and Menu-Selection Trees. Only Navigational Paths has a predominant role at the Elaboration stage, since it is good for describing the high-level view of the navigation.

Iterative cycles may include the application of techniques which require a greater effort than the techniques detailed above, like Product Style Guide or certain prototyping techniques that demand some implementation, such as Wizard of Oz Prototypes. Both techniques might fit in well in Elaboration cycles, but they are predominantly to be applied in iterative cycles in order to avoid bulky elaboration cycles.

Some already mentioned UI design techniques carry more weight during iterative cycles, but they are fit for both stages (Elaboration and Iterative Cycles): Detailed Use Cases, Screen Pictures, Card Sorting, and Menu-Selection Trees.

Impact Analysis may be employed at the beginning of any cycle in either the iterative or evolution cycles.

Some techniques are adequate for application at the end of a development cycle, that is, in the **final moments**. They are the ones proposed in the literature for usability evaluation purposes:

- Heuristic Evaluation

- Usability Inspections: Consistency, conformance and collaborative usability inspections.

- Thinking Aloud: Constructive interaction, retrospective testing, critical incident taking, and coaching method.

- Performance Measurement

- Laboratory Usability Testing

- Post-Test Feedback / User Questionnaires

The **Evolution** stage groups the activities performed after the system has reached initial operational capability in the customer organization. The usability techniques to be applied at this time are techniques to evaluate the usability of an installed system. They are as follows:

- Questionnaires / Surveys (they may be used in previous stages as well)

- Structured and Flexible Interviews

- Direct Observation

- Video / Audio Recording (it can be used in previous stages as well)

- Focus Groups

- Logging Actual Use: Time-stamped keypresses and interaction logging.

- Online User Feedback Facilities: Online or telephone consultants, online suggestion box or trouble reporting, online bulletin board or newsgroup, user newsletters and conferences.

When the development project involves replacing a system that is already in operation, all of these techniques can also be used as data gathering techniques in the Elaboration stage of the project.

10.7.3   Mapping of Usability Activities / Usability Techniques / Development Stages

The description of the techniques to be applied at each stage in the previous section is summarized in Table 10.2. Techniques highlighted in bold face within a stage carry more weight in this stage, that is, this is the stage in which they are best suited, even though they can be applied at other stages.

Figure 10.3 shows another way of looking at the relationship between cycles and activities. It is a distribution of work across the different activity types, related to the time in the development process when each effort is performed. Each horizontal line represents an activity type, and the height of the red line indicates the amount of work of this kind to be done at that particular development stage. For example, requirements elicitation, analysis and negotiation activities are mostly performed in Elaboration cycles (with more emphasis on the early stages), while some elicitation and analysis activities are performed at the beginning of the central moments within the Iterative Cycles, and a small amount of work may be done in Evolution cycles. Slopes in different lines denote some precedence between the different activity types, like, for example, between the different requirements activities within Iterative cycles: first, there is some elicitation, analysis and negotiation followed by specification and then validation. Note that the amount of work on each activity represented in Figure 10.3 is approximate, it should not be taken literally.

Table 10.2: Usability techniques to be applied at each stage and their significance

Activities		Stages			
		Elaboration Stage (cycles 1 to i)	Iterative Cycles (cycles 1 to j)		Evolution Stage (cycles 1 to k)
			central moments	final moments	
Reqs. Eng.	Requirements Elicitation, Analysis and Negotiation	- **Ethnographic Observation** - **Contextual Inquiry** - **Affinity Diagrams** - **Visual Brainstorming** - **Competitive Analysis** - **Scenarios** - Essential Use Cases - **Paper and Chauffeured Prototypes** - Wizard of Oz Prototypes - **Structured User Role Model** - **Operational Modeling** - JEM (Joint Essential Modeling)	- Competitive Analysis - Essential Use Cases - Structured User Role Model - Operational Modeling - JEM (Joint Essential Modeling) - **Wizard of Oz Prototypes**		- Competitive Analysis
	Requirement Specification	- Usability Specifications	- Usability Specifications		- Usability Specifications
	Requirements Validation	- Cognitive Walkthrough - Pluralistic Walkthrough	- Cognitive Walkthrough - Pluralistic Walkthrough		- Pluralistic Walkthrough
					Continued on next page

Table 10.2: Usability techniques to be applied at each stage and their significance

Activities		Elaboration Stage (cycles 1 to i)	Stages		Evolution Stage (cycles 1 to k)
			Iterative Cycles (cycles 1 to j)		
			central moments	final moments	
Design	Interaction Design	- Detailed Use Cases - Screen Pictures - Card Sorting - Menu-selection Trees - **Navigational Paths**	- Product Style Guide - Help Design by Use Cases - Impact Analysis - Detailed Use Cases - Screen Pictures - Card Sorting - Menu-selection Trees - Navigational Paths		- Impact Analysis

Continued on next page

Table 10.2: Usability techniques to be applied at each stage and their significance

Activities		Stages		
		Elaboration Stage (cycles 1 to i)	Iterative Cycles (cycles 1 to j)	Evolution Stage (cycles 1 to k)
			central moment	final moments	
V & V	Usability Evaluation	- Cognitive Walkthrough - Pluralistic Walkthrough - Heuristic Evaluation - Usability Inspections		- Cognitive Walkthrough - Pluralistic Walkthrough - Heuristic Evaluation - **Usability Inspections** - **Thinking aloud** - **Performance Measurement** - **Laboratory Usability Testing** - **Post-Test Feedback / User Questionnaires** - Video/audio recording	- Pluralistic Walkthrough - Thinking aloud - Performance Measurement - Laboratory Usability Testing - Post-Test Feedback / User Questionnaires - Questionnaires / Surveys - **Structured and Flexible Interviews** - **Direct Observation** - **Video/audio recording** - **Focus Groups** - **Logging Actual Use** - **Online User Feedback Facilities**

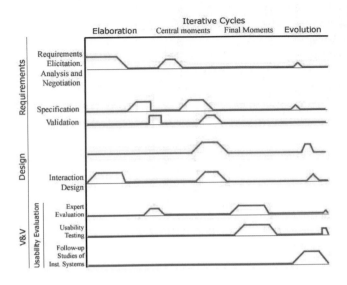

Figure 10.3   Amount of work on each activity type at the different development stages

10.8   DISCUSSION

HCI and SE take different but complementary views of software development. SE as a discipline is pervasive in software development organizations all over the world. Its concepts are the ones with which the majority of developers are familiar, and this is especially true of senior management at software development organizations. HCI, on the other hand, has been traditionally considered as a specialist field, and its view of development is not as present in software development organizations as the SE perspective. The approach taken in this chapter for usability integration into the software process tackles the integration issue from a SE point of view.

Our framework targets organizations that are considering introducing usability into their practices, but not at any cost. They want to keep the software process they have in place, because it is a valuable asset, although they aim to continuously improve this process (by adding usability activities and techniques, for example). For organizations looking for a more radical shift towards a user-centered approach with an even higher degree of user participation in design efforts, the principles enumerated in chapter 2 may apply. The proposed framework can be valuable to organizations where such principles are in conflict with organizational objectives and concerns, like limited availability of representative users or geographically distributed teams. Another alternative approach to be considered is presented in chapter 13 for organizations wanting to keep two separate processes (the usability process and the SE process), so that software development needs do not take over usability concerns. Our framework may be valuable to organizations that have not identified the need to place usability in such a prominent place in development, that is, organizations that consider usability an important quality attribute but not to the extent of considering it as valuable as all the other quality attributes together.

For the purpose of integrating usability into the process, the user needs to be placed at the center of the whole development effort. The framework includes several techniques (mainly from the Usage-Centered Design method—Constantine and Lockwood, 1999) for modeling the user and his/her tasks and the interaction between users and the software system. If the development team considers the user as the final measure of software development project success, it has already taken a big step towards the adoption of a user-centered perspective in development, and models may support this objective. Other techniques in the framework favor a higher degree of user participation, facilitating communication in multidisciplinary teams. The application of some techniques calls for a reformulation of activities that were already in place before the usability integration, but the biggest part of the development process does not usually need to be profoundly altered.

The proposed framework serves the purpose of identifying which usability activities and techniques may be useful for an organization to enrich its software process, and where they have to be incorporated in the process. But some additional issues, like how to modify existing practices in order to incorporate the new ones, must be resolved for an effective integration. The work by Gulliksen and Göransson, 2001, complements the information expressed in the framework by providing a recipe for action for evaluating a process for its user-centeredness and modifying it where necessary.

Knowing where to plug usability techniques and activities into the existing software development process is a necessary starting point, but it does not automatically make software engineers capable of applying these techniques and activities and adopting a user-centered focus in development. 'Caring about usability' is a change to the philosophy and viewpoint with which developers are accustomed. The framework for usability integration presented in this chapter needs to be supplemented by good training for developers. For the industrial partners of the STATUS project to apply the framework in practice, their developers needed to take a 24-hour course on usability principles and techniques. The course was designed to raise their usability awareness, clearing up common misconceptions about the issue. Chapter 8 presents some practices that may be helpful for educational purposes and to get buy-in between developers for the user-centered approach.

10.9 CONCLUSIONS

In this chapter we presented a framework that may allow a more successful introduction of usability techniques and activities into the software process. Usability activities and techniques from the HCI field have been positioned in the framework with regard to standard SE activities. Time constraints for the application of usability techniques and activities with respect to the stages in a generic iterative process have been detailed as well. The resulting framework targets software development organizations that have already decided to incorporate usability activities and techniques into their current development practices. The only prerequisite for its application is that the software development process currently in place must be based on iterative development. This is necessary, because iterative development is one of the essential principles of the user-centered approach. This requirement is not especially restrictive from a SE point of view, because it is in line with the current trends in SE.

The proposal does not have to be adopted as an all-or-nothing issue. It aims to provide a framework that allows decisions to be made on the inclusion of particular usability techniques and activities in any iterative software development process. It responds to the demands of software practitioners who are asking for pragmatic approaches instead of theoretical constructs that remain on the shelves unused.

Feedback from the industrial partners of the STATUS project has contributed to refinement of the present proposal, but, as changing as software development practice is, it is open to further refinement and specification as software development evolves and, hopefully, incorporates more and more usability aspects. In particular, information may be added to the framework on the products of each usability technique and their possible integration with SE models and documentation.

Acknowledgements

We would like to thank the partners in the STATUS project for their input and their cooperation, and we would like to acknowledge the support of the European Union under grant STATUS (IST-2001-32298).

We would also like to thank the anonymous reviewers of the chapter and the editors of the book for the thorough job they have done, and for the valuable insights their comments have provided.

11 COPING WITH COMPLEXITY

Dave Roberts

IBM

Abstract

IBM User Engineering provides a process that guides teams though a complex project. It uses CASE tools to help to manage information. It includes abstraction paths that help the team to understand the whole problem before they divide it. User Engineering then leads the team to the solution; providing many heuristics to guide progress.

This chapter provides an overview of User Engineering. It describes the key artefacts and the processes that relate them. The chapter focuses on the parts of User Engineering that relate to software engineering. It shows how the UE process leads the team through the research and design needed to create a compelling user interface. It describes how the artefacts of design are assembled within a CASE tool and used to provide an unambiguous specification for the software engineering processes that are interlinked with User Engineering.

11.1 INTRODUCTION

User Engineering (IBM 2004) is a method developed by IBM over the last 15 years. The first outline of the approach was published as part of "Common User Access" (CUA) in the early 1990s (IBM 1992). A UML based version was published later that decade under the name OVID (Roberts et al, 1998). User Engineering is both user and stakeholder centred. It is driven from the goals and values of each of the user and stakeholder groups. The process includes continuous validation with both stakeholders and users.

A. Seffah (eds.), Human-Centered Software Engineering – Integrating Usability
in the Development Process, 201–217.

User Engineering is designed for teams. It is based on a structured set of phases (See Section 11.1.2). It uses the notions of *UE Activities* and *Work Products*, each allocated to various team members. Team members have designated UE roles (Table 11.1). Specified roles lead the *UE Activities* to produce *Work Products*. The *Work Products* form the main means of ensuring team communication. Further details of the *UE Roles, Activities* and *Work Products* are available from the IBM web site (IBM 2004).

Table 11.1 User engineering roles

Role	Goal
User eXperience Leadership Overall responsibility for superior user satisfaction	**Satisfy Project Goals** Maximum value delivered to users and stakeholders
Market Planning Core information on business opportunity	**Business Driven Offering** Comprehensive definition of business and market expectations
User eXperience Research All required information about users	**Complete User Requirements** Comprehensive understanding of users' domain
User eXperience Design Model, structure and flow of the user interface	**Leadership** Design Leadership and productive user experience
Visual & Industrial Design Overall appearance, form-factor, layout and style	**Physical Appeal** Physical and emotional experience represents the brand
User eXperience Evaluation User studies to continually assess design progress	**Cost Effective Evaluations** Objective design evaluations

UE also suggests the use of CASE tools to hold all the *Work Products* for the project. The recommended tools are from the Rational family. However, these could be substituted with any others that are capable of creating and managing UML diagrams and connecting them with related artefacts.

The central core for any UE project is a UML model, the *Designers' Model*, which links both the user's views of the system and the implementers' understanding of the solution. These areas of the model are connected to give traceability from the problem to the solution. Each *Work Product* is either created within the *Designers' Model* or is associated with some other element of that model.

11.1.1 Pragmatic Usage

Although User Engineering can, at first inspection, appear to be a very prescriptive approach, it is not. UE provides a framework which allows teams to select the *UE Activities* that they need. One of the first *Work Products* that emerge from the Business Opportunity phase is the draft version of the User Engineering Plan. This describes, in outline, the *UE Activities* and *Work Products* that will be used for this project.

This pragmatic approach also extends to the tools that are used to facilitate the process. UE is based on the use of a UML enabled CASE tool. However, other solutions can be adopted if they are more appropriate to the situation. For example, when the stakeholders (customers) already have a preferred method for distributing information. However, User Engineering relies on a subset of UML to provide a language to portray the design in an unambiguous form. When UML is not used it increases the risk that information will be degraded during the process.

11.1.2   Overview of Phases

User Engineering consists of a set of phases. These phases each end with a checkpoint that controls the start of the next phase.

1. **Business Opportunity** - Identifies a marketplace opportunity and relates it to business goals.

2. **Understanding Users** - Establishes user requirements in accordance with the business and market requirements.

3. **Initial Design** - Used to establish the conceptual design.

4. **Development** - Establishes the detailed design.

5. **Deployment** - Used to verify the implementation in the users' domain.

6. **Life Cycle** - Captures relevant user experience feedback that can be used as input for subsequent projects.

Although this series of phases may appear similar to a traditional waterfall approach to development, this is not the intention. The phases are designed to ensure that the project does not proceed until prior work has been validated, or at least the status is well known. The whole process is iterative and it is possible that a finding in a later stage might return a project to an earlier phase.

The first four phases of UE are described in more detail later in this chapter.

11.1.3   Tools

User Engineering suggests that as much information as possible is held in Computer Aided Software Engineering (CASE) tools. These tools have developed over many years to hold information for software engineering teams. The tools typically have a number of characteristics that allow the team to work effectively with the project.

1. Provide for the ownership of the information by the appropriate team member.

2. Provide facilities to create versions of a project with different elements included in each version.

3. Allow the team to document and follow the relationships between various elements.

4. Check the validity of the information against a variety of heuristics.

5. Create prototypes of new information based on the existing information.

Teams can use the facilities provided within the tools to cope with the complexity of the project. Large projects can be divided into smaller, manageable units.

UML (Unified Modeling Language) is commonly used in software engineering to describe the design of software projects. The use of UML in other areas is growing. Some use is being made of UML for business process modeling (Cesare 2003). User Engineering promotes the use of UML for all user related (HCI) information. Using UML avoids the reliance of the interpretation, and misinterpretation, of natural language as design medium. The cross-disciplinary use of UML as the *lingua franca* of the team is one of the keys to coherent transfer of knowledge.

User Engineering suggests ways in which UML can be used to describe all the elements of the project. This includes elements that are not normally modelled in this way such as stakeholders and their goals. At the same time, User Engineering recognises the need to convey design in other ways.

Many users and stakeholders are not able to understand a design when it is expressed as UML. So the design team acts as a gatekeeper to the model. The team will create artefacts that portray the design to those who need to understand some part of it to give feedback. This might be in the form of a prototype that is used when communicating or testing with users. It could be in the form of a Persona when sharing role descriptions with a stakeholder.

11.2   THE DESIGNERS' MODEL

One premiss of User Engineering is that even in a complex situation a complicated system must not be delivered to the users. At the heart of the design phases is a conceptual model which is called the *Designers' Model*. The *Designers' Model* is a description of the system that will be constructed. It can be considered as the mental image that the most astute user (should such a user exist) would develop of the system. Elements of this model are shared by all users. However, as each user's experience of the system will be unique then many users will not adopt the entire model of the system.

Overall, the process of obtaining a good solution can be envision on a two dimensional space (Figure 11.1). From left to right the space represents the transition from a problem to a solution. From bottom to top the space represents the change from the concrete to the abstract.

At the bottom left, the existing problem is concrete. At the bottom right, the solution will be concrete at the end of the deployment. A development process moves a project from the problem to a solution. Different methods take different paths between problem and solution. During most development processes a series of models, with varying degrees of abstraction are built. User Engineering focuses on a *Designers' Model* with a relatively high degree of abstraction.

The system is implemented as a series of perspectives on the *Designers' Model*. Each perspective is designed for use by one or more of the user roles. Because all the perspectives are based on a single conceptual model the roles have a known amount

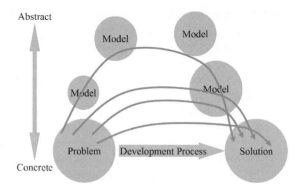

Figure 11.1   Modeling and the design space

of shared knowledge. This shared knowledge, or common ground, allows each of the users to communicate about the system.

11.2.1   Related Models

User Engineering also recognises two other models: the User's Model and the Implementers' Model. These two models are related to the *Designers' Model* and the finished product as shown in Figure 11.2.

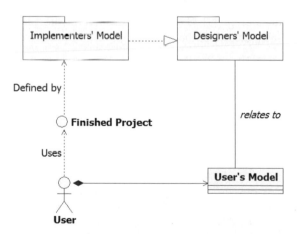

Figure 11.2   The relationship between the User Engineering models

User's Model.   A User's Model only exists in the mind of each of the users. It is formed by each user as they experience the product. They may see advertising or training material related to the product and this will begin the formation of the user's model. They may interact with the product and continue the development of the model. But each of these experiences is unique to each user. In UE the researchers try to discover what models will be formed. They contact users by whatever means they have available (survey, focus group, field study, workshop. . .) to gather information. They record this information during the Understanding Users phase. The information then forms the basis of the design.

The designers create, within the *Designers' Model*, a collection of model fragments that represents their best understanding of the aggregate user's model for each of the recognised user roles. These model fragments are described as objects and views. During the objects and views will be validated. In a typical validation study a sample of users will be presented with materials that are derived from the *Designers' Model*. Users might be asked to work with or discuss these materials, or to perform typical tasks to confirm that the model is a reasonable representation of the users internal model.

11.2.2   Implementers' Model

The Implementers' Model is the basis for the construction of the product. It will include elements such as software that has to be created, software components that are used and hardware that is used. In UE the Implementers' Model should be constructed within the same CASE tool as the *Designers' Model*.

Implementers take the *Designers' Model* as a specification for elements of the implementers model. This is described in more detail later in this chapter (Section 11.3.4).

11.3   USER ENGINEERING MODELING

A UML model, the *Designers' Model*, is at the core of the User Engineering process. This model integrates all of the information that the project team has gathered or created.

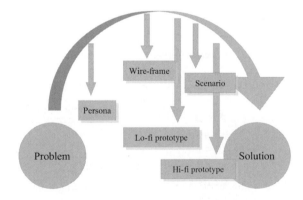

Figure 11.3   Examples of artefacts created to provide concrete descriptions of abstract elements

The model is an abstract expression of both the problem and the solution. For many stakeholders and most users the model will not be easy to understand. The project team acts as a gateway to the model. They interpret the model for the stakeholders and users as they need to. They also take information from the stakeholders and users and feed it into the model.

Throughout the project there will be abstract descriptions of an element and then one or more concrete descriptions of the same element (Figure 11.3). For example, during a field study a task analysis may be conducted. A report of the study will be created in some form. In the CASE tool an activity diagram will be created for the designers to use. The report of the study will be attached to the activity diagram so that full details of the study are available when required. Further, the activity diagram will be connected to the actor that represents the user role that was studied.

As a further example, in the *Understanding Users* phase the *user roles* provide and abstract description of the users and the corresponding personas (Cooper 1999) provide a more concrete description. The personas would be attached to the user role within the CASE tool. Similarly, the solution model from *Initial Design* is an abstract form; this is made concrete as a low fidelity prototype.[1]

User Engineering defines a number of UML stereotypes. The stereotypes identify the role of the elements of the *Designers' Model*. For example, the stereotype *<<ougoal>>*[2] is used to identify a user goal and the stereotype *<<osgoal>>* identifies a stakeholder goal. Further details of the stereotypes are given in the sections below.

11.3.1   Business Opportunity

The Business Opportunity phase provides the key goals for the project. These are the stakeholder's goals that will measure the final outcome of the project. They are not expressed in terms of the implementation that is to be created, but rather in terms of what the project will achieve for the business. For example, a goal at this stage might be that the new sales method will increase sales by 10%. The first phase also provides an outline of the market into which a project will be launched: the competing solutions; the intended audience.

As with many other UE elements models are created using the *stereotype* feature of UML. To represent the stakeholders an *actor* is created with the stereotype <<osrole>>. Attributes of the actor and the associated documentation are used to record the details. Goals are modeled as classes with the stereotype <<osgoal>>. Attributes record details of the goal. In particular the attributes record the measures that will be used to check if the project meets these goals. Relationships are added between the stakeholder and the goals to indicate which stakeholders are interested in which goals. Other relationships are added to show how the goals are connected to one-another. Figure 11.4 shows a fragment of a stakeholder/goal diagram connections that could be shown. Table 11.2 lists the model elements and how they are used.

During this phase an outline view of the users of the project will be documented. This information is recorded as actors with the stereotype of <<ourole>>. These

---

[1] Those familiar with object oriented concepts might consider this as a class/instance pairing. For example, a role is a class and a persona is an instance of that class.
[2] *<<ougoal>>* can be read as OVID User Goal.

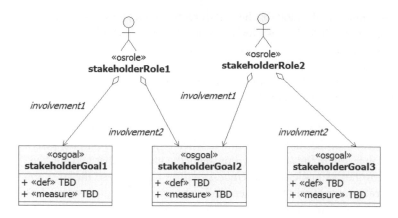

Figure 11.4   Fragment of a stakeholder-goal diagram

will be refined during the next phase. Further detail of this is included in the next section.

Table 11.2   Elements modeled during Business Opportunity phase

Element	Description	Model
Stakeholder	Someone who has an interest in the outcome of the project.	Actor <<osrole>>
Stakeholder Goal	Some state that one or more stakeholders wish the project to achieve.	Class <<osgoal>> Attributes defined measures of the goal.
User Role (draft)	Someone who will use the result of the project in some way.	Actor <<ourole>>

Other information gathered or created during the business opportunity is not modeled in UML. Work products such as the draft of the User Engineering Plan will be documented in the most appropriate format for the team. This might be as a document created by a word processor or as a plan within a project planning tool. Further description of these work products is not included as they do not have a direct relationship with the user engineering models or the software engineering process.

11.3.2   Understanding Users

The business opportunity phase produces clear documentation of the stakeholders and their goals for the project. But this information only provides an outline of the detail that will be needed for the project. In the *Understanding Users* phase the process continues with a variety of research activities that discover the missing information which is added to the Designer's Model. The phase seeks to document, in detail, the roles of all the users with all the significant attributes and relationships between them.

It will describe the relationships between the users and the stakeholders. It may also refine the descriptions of the stakeholders.

The *UE Activities* also document the current tasks that the users undertake to achieve goals that are related to the project. These two collections of information are the main input to the project. Table 11.3 lists the elements that are added to the *Designers' Model* during this phase.

Table 11.3   Elements modeled during Understanding Users phase

Element	Description	Model
User Role	Someone who will use the result of the project in some way.	Actor <<ourole>> Attributes define characteristics of the users in detail.
User Goal	Some state that one or more users wish the project to achieve.	Class <<ougoal>> Attributes defined measures of the goal.
User Task	A description of something a user **currently** does to achieve one or more user goals.	Class <<outask>> Activity diagrams or other attached documents are used to describe the task.
Use Case	A description of something the project will include to allow a user to achieve a goal.	Use Case
Proposed Task (draft)	An ideal process for completing one of the tasks that some of the users need to perform.	An Activity diagram. Swimlanes represent users and system.

The techniques chosen for each activity will depend on the project type. For example, for a small, known audience the *UE Activities* might include more contextual research or collaborative design. For a widely distributed audience such as 'the buying public' the research might tend towards mass market techniques. Whichever technique is employed, the ultimate aim is to provide a roles and goals model as an abstraction that will lead to the use-case model for the system.

During this phase current or competing products are examined. Models are created as an abstraction of these environments. As shown in Figure 11.5, this starts with refinement of the user roles and recording of the current task processes. This information is abstracted to a goal model and design begins by documenting the use-cases that will be implemented.

Capturing Users' Current Tasks.   The UML Activity diagrams are used to describe the way users go about doing their tasks today. The diagrams allow the researchers to capture procedures in detail. Studies are made of any competing solutions; whether they are competing products or existing methods. The information forms a baseline for performance comparisons. The models also allow the researchers to investigate the 'pain points' in any existing solutions: the place where current solutions fail.

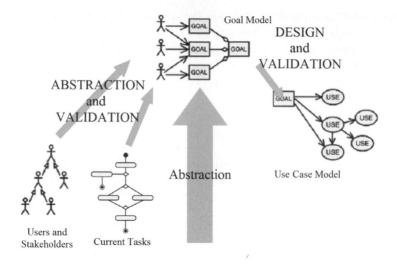

Figure 11.5   Modeling in the Understanding Users Phase

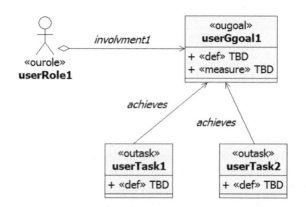

Figure 11.6   A fragment of a user-task model

As well as providing information to feed the abstraction process (see Defining the Goals) the detailed task information has several uses later in UE. It collects the names and descriptions of the objects that the users are dealing with. This will be of use during Initial Design. Further, the information is used in comparison to the final task description. This provides essential information to feed the creation of training programmes.

Defining the Goals.   A third model created during the Understanding Users is often called the 'roles and goals' model. It contains the Users and Stakeholders model and adds the goals of both the users and the stakeholders. Many of the stakeholder goals may have been expressed as 'requirements'. The user's goals are discovered as the desired outcomes of the tasks. Any new goals that are not related to existing tasks are added to these. All of the goals, for both stakeholder and users, are described with completion criteria. These are measures of what has to be achieved to claim that a goal has been reached. They are also measures of related requirements such as how long it should take to reach a goal.

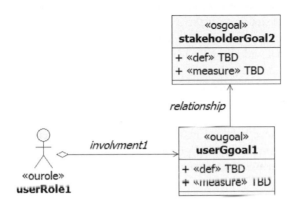

Figure 11.7   A fragment of a user-goal diagram

The goals are each connected with the roles that hold that goal (Figure 11.7). They are also connected to the other goals, where any relationship can be established. The key to this stage is to keep asking 'Why?' For each user goal there must be a higher goal that provides the reason for that goal being important. System related goals are noted, but these might be ignored later, the new system may not need to satisfy prior system goals. Ultimately, each of the user's goals will connect to a stakeholder goal.

Research activities are used to validate the goals with both stakeholders and users; ensuring that the final version of each goal and their relationships are correct. The research should also provide detail of the frequency with which each goal is reached. This later information, along with the number of user roles related to the goal, give a measure of the importance of a goal in the formation of the objects in the *Designers' Model*.

Figure 11.8   A fragment of a goal-use case diagram

Each goal should have a number of measures. Each measure is a statement of some condition that must be satisfied in order to achieve that goal. The measures are prescriptions for how the goal might be measured during the development process. The measures may be direct or indirect. For example, a cash issuing machine design might have a goal about delivering cash. Delivering the right amount of cash is a direct measure of the goal; doing this within 15 seconds is an indirect measure[3]. In cases where it is difficult to assign measures to a goal then the goal can be decomposed, to a collection of sub-goals, until useful measures can be determined.

Define User Experience Use Cases.   Having modelled users, goals and current tasks, the next step is to make a statement of which goals the new project will satisfy. User experience use cases are added to the model. Each case describes a well defined function that will allow the user to reach one or more goals (Figure 11.8).

The first step in defining the use cases is to review all the goals. The process starts with the most important goals; those that need to be reached most frequently or by most users. The use cases are named with verb phrases that describe the process that will be used to reach the goal. These may coincide with current tasks. The designers must judge the balance between matching current tasks (which may reduce training costs) or differing from current tasks (potentially increasing training costs but reducing operating costs). The use case names and descriptions can be validated by a variety of user research activities.

11.3.3   Initial Design

In the Initial Design phase a collection of models are created that describe the user's experience with the new system. Starting with the use cases that meet the most important goals the first step is to create a collection of user objects. At the same time as the objects are defined, the tasks in which they are used and the views that the users will need are also defined. Table 11.4 lists the elements that are added to the *Designers' Model* during this phase.

Throughout the phase the artefacts are validated with users. This often involves a translation of the UML models in to forms that can be readily understood by the users. The phase continues until the validation activities show that a successful outcome is likely.

Figure 11.9 shows the modeling during this phase. The goal and use-case model is used as the main source of information. A cycle of modeling begins that includes user objects, new task models, views, object and view states and detailed task flows. This process continues until validation indicates that the design will meet the goals.

Designers' Object Model.   The *Designers' Model* contains a UML class model that defines the objects that the users will find in the system. The objects[4] represent the concepts that the users will internalise to form their User's Model.

These objects must be well defined with short, meaningful names and clear descriptions. Using heuristics to guide the process, the most important objects form the core of the model. The objects are described by classes with attributes showing the infor-

---

[3]Indirect measures are sometimes called 'non-functional requirements' or 'usability requirements' in some development methods.
[4]The objects do not represent the interactive elements the users will meet. User Engineering represents the interactive elements as *views* which are described later.

Table 11.4 Elements modeled during Initial Design phase

Element	Description	Model
Object	An object that some users are expected to include in their internal model of the system	Class <<ouo>> Attributes define characteristics of the object in detail.
View	Some state that one or more users wish the project to achieve.	Class <<oav>> Attributes defined attributes of the related object that are visible.
Proposed Task	An ideal process for completing one of the tasks that some of the users need to perform.	An Activity diagram or a Sequence diagram. Swimlanes/lifelines represent users and views.
Object or View states	A description of the way an object or a view changes during usage.	A Harel diagram and a state transition table.

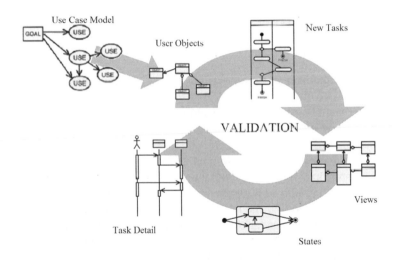

Figure 11.9 Modeling during Initial Design

mation that users will understand about those objects. Connections are made between the classes to describe the relationships that the users will know.

Candidate objects are obtained from the goal and task descriptions. A candidate object, from the problem, will not be included in the solution until a new task design proves the need for that object. When the object is included, the name and description of the object and its attributes are all written in the terms that the user will be exposed to (Figure 11.10). The language must match both the user's capabilities (such as reading age) and the domain jargon (the user's domain, not the technology domain). The

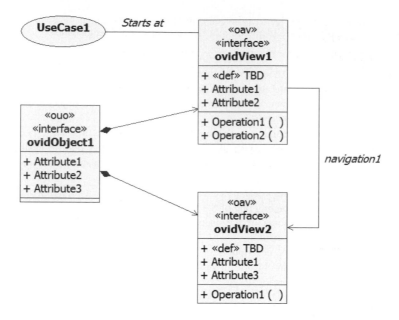

Figure 11.10   A fragment of an object-view diagram

names and descriptions must be validated with the users; typically using a low fidelity prototype.

The object model is a key asset in teaching users what they should know about the system.

New Task Model.   Outline task models for the new system are created, using activity diagrams, in a similar way to the models that describe the current tasks. The new task models normally use two swim-lanes to describe the breakdown between user and system elements of the tasks. This is the designer's chance to remove the pain points found in current tasks. The activities must all be described in terms of processes that operate on the objects in the class model. Operations are added to the objects to support their roles in each task.

Abstract Views.   Utilizing the designers' object model and task model, the abstract views define the selection of attributes of each object that are required to support a given task (Figure 11.10).

During early iterations the easiest process is to create a new view for each of the objects that are needed in any task. Views are needed at any point in a task where control passes between the swim lanes of the activity diagrams.

Operations are added to each view to describe each of the functions that can be initiated from that view. Connections are made between views to show the navigation paths for the system. (Navigation paths all carry the implicit action of 'navigate this path'; these are not added as operations.) During the development phase, the designers will choose whether the paths will be implemented as a change of page/window or as an embedding of the subsequent information.

As the design process iterates the views are consolidated so that a minimum number can be provided. This reuse of views helps both the development team (they have less to create) and the user (they have less to understand).

Detailed Task Flows.   Detailed task flows are developed using either activity diagrams or sequence diagrams. These diagrams elaborate the new task models with details of which of the views are used at which stages of the task. Creating these diagrams allows for validation of the navigation paths and the operations of each of the views.

In the refined task diagrams the users are only shown to interact with the views, not the objects. The views then have connections to the objects to obtain and change data or to initiate operations.

Object and View States.   Object states are modelled to describe the way in which objects change as a consequence of users interaction with the object (through views). The states are mainly a transcription of each of the detailed task flows, from the perspective of a single object. As well as using the state charts in UML (which use the Harel notation) the states are transcribed to a state/action table. This allows the designers to inspect all of the potential state/action cases without clutter in the diagram.

In some cases there is a need to develop state models for a view as well as for the object that it represents. This might be used when delays in the connection between a view and the related object are introduced because of system or user needs. The state models are developed in the same way as those for objects.

11.3.4   Development

In User Engineering development begins with a validated *Designers' Model*. During the development phase, each element of the *Designers' Model* is translated into an appropriate, concrete form ready for deployment.

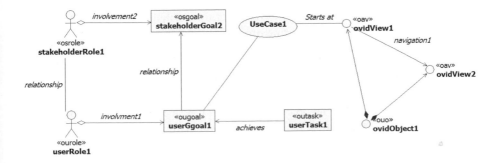

Figure 11.11   Traceability within the Designers' Model

For each of the element types there will be a related series of recipes[5] that might be applied. Each of these might be applied by some automatic system: some form of generator. They could also be applied manually by a team of skilled people such as programmers or graphic designers. Whichever element, recipe or process is concerned; the general activity is the same.

Development will also include a variety of validation activities. Tests are conducted without users, to ensure that these concrete elements are faithful to their abstract specifications. Tests are conducted with users to ensure that all the agreed measures (of goals) are met.

Activities.   The *Designers' Model* includes one or more activity diagrams for each of the use cases. These diagrams show the flow from the user's perspective. The diagrams have several uses during the Development Phase. Each diagram can be:

1. the basis of a test case;

2. the basis of a user test;

3. the outline of training material, either online or offline;

4. an outline for an element of the help system.

Writers and/or trainers are presented with a well specified outline of a user's activities. This can be readily converted into the forms required for their work. Further, when the information is presented in a CASE tool, they can trace the activities to the related goals and the measures of those goals. From a combination of the goals and the role descriptions they can understand the context of use. They can also see the equivalent activity diagrams for the prior ways of working. This allows them to consider the learning needs of a user who is migrating from one solution to another.

Where testing is concerned, the same access to a full context for each task allows for a complete specification of a test. The goals include the success criteria that must be measured. The roles include the information that is needed when screening users who will participate in tests and trials.

Objects.   The *Designers' Model* contains a description of all the objects that the users need. Each object has full descriptions of the attributes and the user triggered operations. For objects with interesting life cycles, there is a state model showing how the operations change the objects. The activity diagrams explain when and where each object is used. This complete description allows a user object to be implemented as a business object within the project. The biggest benefit comes from the use of a CASE tool.

As the specification for the objects is held in a CASE tool the process of converting from abstract to concrete is facilitated. Software engineering artefacts are linked

---

[5]Depending on the environment these recipes may be called: patterns, recipes, heuristics, standards or guidelines.

directly to their counterparts in the *Designers' Model*. When changes are implied by tests during development, the impact can be traced back to earlier decisions. Hence, the delivered version of the system is less likely to become disconnected from the specification.

Views.   In a similar way to objects, the views that have been defined during the initial design have a full specification: attributes, user actions, links to other views, state models and activity diagrams to provide context. Further, the user's characteristics and their goals are available. This combination provides a clear starting point for the development of the web pages, dialogs or physical artefacts that instantiate a view.

Where a project requires interaction in different contexts, such as pervasive interfaces that might appear both on a PC and via a telephone, further view specifications can be created. For example, an abstract view might imply too much content to fit on the screen of a mobile phone. Further *view* classes can be added to the model that show how it is to be broken down into appropriate sections. Conversely, groups of abstract views might be combined when there is a larger screen available to the user. These decisions are all captured by refinement of the *Designers' Model*.

Standard patterns of views can be used to fit the implementation to the user's needs. These may be incorporated at the abstract level: such as a pattern of view classes implementing a wizard; or at a lower level; a group of attributes is mapped to a defined set of controls (widgets). Different patterns might be implemented for different users or for different delivery devices.

11.4   CONTINUED DEVELOPMENT

This chapter has outlined the processes and tools that are used by IBM's User Engineering. The principal benefit is comes from a well defined process based on information in cross-disciplinary notation held in a store with well controlled access. There are further benefits to be gained from the capability of many CASE tools to provide

Proof of concept projects such as the one presented at the TUPIS workshop (Azevedo et al, 2000) demonstrate how information in the *Designers' Model* can be transformed into implementation elements. The project took an object-view model and generated a simple user interface. Similar code-generation processes can be applied to reduce the manual effort in applying the recipes needed to a UML model. This brings the major benefit of reducing the gap between the specification and the implementation because the cost of keeping these in step is reduced.

User Engineering also allows organisations to improve the transfer of information between projects. If an organisation adopts UE for a number of projects there is significant potential for transferring information between them in a more tractable form. This sharing can occur at many levels: from sharing role descriptions to sharing view implementations.

User Engineering continues to evolve as it is used in different contexts. For example, the early ideas came from the examination of IBM's internal development processes, but it is now being applied directly to customer problems; this brings new insights into the flexibility required.

12 TOWARDS A MODEL FOR BRIDGING AGILE DEVELOPMENT AND USER-CENTERED DESIGN

Stefan Blomkvist

Dept. of Information Technology/Human-Computer Interaction
Uppsala University
PO Box 337, SE-751 05 Uppsala, Sweden

Abstract

As a reaction to the complexity and rigor of commercial software development processes, "agile" software development methods have gained increasing attention. Agile methods prioritize delivering working software over producing extensive models and documentation. Agile processes focus on the people involved and the required interaction instead of on processes and tools. Furthermore, it emphasizes that responding to the changes that invariably take place over the course of a project is more important than strictly adhering to a contract or plan. From the perspective of usability and user-centered design, however, agile methods do not inherently provide the required support to the development process. This being said, the agile philosophy does not prevent focusing on usability during the design process: in fact, the agile and user-centered approaches have the potential to work very well together. This chapter intends to describe the core principles of agile development and investigate to what extent usability-enhancing activities can be supported within the agile approaches. As a conclusion, it will outline a model for integrating agile development and user-centered design.

A. Seffah (eds.), Human-Centered Software Engineering – Integrating Usability
in the Development Process, 219–244.

12.1   INTRODUCTION

Developing interactive software is all about people: not only about the people that will use the software, but also about those who develop it. Most developers of interactive software deliver some sort of enhanced support for end-users, and as such, their knowledge about the users and the use situation is crucial to the outcome of the process. Although there are numerous methods and techniques to capture information about the users and tasks, it is the attitude and basic values of those who develop the software that will inevitably make a difference in the results.

For some time now, one of the main ways of introducing usability and user-centered design into systems development is to focus on the processes by which the systems are designed and developed. The importance of this was stressed in 1991 by Liam Bannon (Bannon, 1991):

> "... more attention needs to be paid to the process of design, to working with users in all stages of design, to see the iterative nature of design, and the changing conception of what one is designing as a result of the process itself. This is in contrast to a view of design that proceeds from a set of fixed requirements without iteration, and without involvement of the users."

More recently, it has been recognized that processes alone cannot guarantee usable systems. Göransson, 2004, argues that systems that fit well into the workplace are ultimately the product of some kind of user-centered development process and a user-centered focus during development. This means that the real users and their needs, goals, context of use, abilities and limitations should be guiding development, instead of development being driven by technology. Persson, 2003, opines that development processes are mainly controlled by time and money, and that there is an increasing trend to rely on whatever models and methods are currently in vogue. This approach reflects the organization's basic values, as well as a lack of awareness regarding the consequences of various strategic decisions.

Agile approaches to software development (Agile Alliance, 2001; Cockburn, 2002; Ambler, 2002; Highsmith, 2002; Fowler, 2003a), such as *Extreme Programming, XP* (Beck, 2000), have recently received increasing attention. They place less emphasis on the process and its deliverables, and center instead on the people involved and their cooperation in order to produce results more quickly with reduced risk of failure or delays. The driving force behind the agile perspective is to impart more agile or 'light-weight' qualities on software development.

One issue related to the various agile processes is that they do not sufficiently address usability and user-centered design (or UCD) concerns (Constantine and Lockwood, 2002; Hudson, 2003; Armitage, 2004; Jokela and Abrahamsson, 2004). The main focus of agile processes is how to organize the required tasks to reach the overall goal of delivering working software. Delivering working software is obviously a mandatory condition for any *usable* system. However, agile development focuses on making coding more efficient, and usability issues can potentially fall to the wayside since an explicit user-centered focus is lacking.

The overall focus of the agile approach is somewhat different from that of UCD. Agile values and practices are concerned primarily with project management and team organization in combination with detailed coding tactics. UCD, on the other hand, focuses more on methods for usability design and evaluation. The two disciplines do not target the same systems development issues. Nonetheless, both perspectives deal essentially with the development of IT systems, therefore it is possible to compare the approaches, at least to a certain extent. Furthermore, this similitude raises the question of to what extent agile approaches are user-centered. Is it possible to integrate user-centered values and practices in agile processes? Can the two disciplines cross-pollinate each other with new ideas and practices? User-centered processes could benefit from becoming more agile and paying closer attention to internal project issues. In UCD, the people using the software are the focus (as they should be), but the approach is less concerned with the individuals working on the project. Agile values deal considerably with these issues, for example, team communication, individuals' skills, overtime work and the developers' responsibilities. These issues can be viewed as a parallel to the discussions about user participation and empowerment that were broached in the Scandinavian Tradition and Participatory Design (Ehn 1989).

This article is a first step towards bridging the gap between agile software engineering and UCD. As our perspective is spawned from the precepts of UCD, it is natural to discuss the *user-centeredness* of the agile approach. This will be done by analyzing the user-centered design qualities in the agile software development approach. Another topic we will cover is how to integrate the two perspectives – if at all possible.

A challenge inherent to this evaluation is that neither the agile approach nor user-centered design is comprised of a single, clearly-defined process. Agile is an *umbrella term* for a number of different processes that share a set of core ideas on software development, as described concisely in the *Agile Manifesto* (Agile Alliance, 2001). The best-known agile process is *Extreme Programming, XP* (Beck, 2000). User-centered design is in a similar position. There is no agreed-upon definition of user-centered design, however; Gulliksen et al. (2003b, also Chapter 2 of this volume) propose a definition whereby where UCD is characterized by a set of 12 key principles.

It is beyond the scope of this article to compare specific agile processes with their UCD counterparts. A first step is to analyze the essence of the agile and UCD approaches. Consequently, we will base the following discussion on the most primary material on agile: writings/publications by Cockburn and Fowler, as well as the *Agile Manifesto*. Though the discussion will be general, some concrete examples from *Extreme Programming* will be given, owing to its unique position in the agile community. The main source on UCD is the key principles provided in Gulliksen *et al.* (Chapter 2 of this volume).

12.2 SOFTWARE DEVELOPMENT RISKS – REASONS FOR THE AGILE APPROACH

The software engineering community has long been searching for a "silver bullet" to solve the typical problems that are ubiquitous in systems development. Although if we now realize that there is no such panacea, methods and processes have long been regarded as one of the primary strategies to tackle these problems. Over the years, various proposals for the ultimate process have come upon the scene– only to later fade away.

The traditional approach to software development is to focus on extensive planning and structured processes in order to mold development into an efficient and predictable activity (Boehm, 2002). According to the proponents of the latest trend in software engineering, agile development, this approach is not the best strategy to employ for successful software projects. Instead, agile developers call for a shift in the overall focus to a more agile or 'light-weight' perspective. Below, we will summarize four of the major problems in traditional software development that agile approaches attempt to address.

12.2.1 Changeability

Systems development is variously affected by a number of external and internal changes. These changes are either caused by new or evolving conditions during development, or stem from the fact that not all requirements could be clarified early on in the development process. Such new or changing conditions may involve anything from volatile technical or business conditions to updates in work tasks and organization. Introducing new or modified features after freezing the requirements specification is difficult, time consuming and expensive. According to Boehm's Life Cycle Cost Differential theory (Highsmith and Cockburn, 2001, p.120), the costs related to reacting to changes increase as the project develops. The problem is classical; for example, Brooks, 1987, identified the *changeability* of software as one of the major software engineering difficulties. In addition, today's development projects must contend with a higher degree and speed of change that was introduced during the Internet era in the mid-nineties.

According to the CHAOS report (Standish Group, 1995), as many as 83% of all projects fail in one way or another, e.g. cancellation, increased costs and delays. Incomplete and changing requirements are among the most important problems for impaired and/or challenged projects.

Generally speaking, changeability can be handled in two ways. One alternative is to authorize few or no modifications once the requirements specification has been established. The drawback is that the system may be inadequate or outdated before it has been launched. Another approach is to allow changes in the requirements specification. However, this will introduce the risk of changes that are difficult to cope with in the development process, leading to delays and budget overrun, or even cancelled projects. Since the latter scenario is far too common, many projects strive to freeze the requirements at different junctures in the development process.

12.2.2 Software's Complex and Intangible Nature

The waterfall model and similar traditional processes assume that we can predict the complete set of requirements on a new system beforehand, if only we try hard enough (Highsmith and Cockburn, 2001, p.120). The argument against exhaustive, pre-prepared specifications is that systems consisting of software, people, organizations and hardware are often enormously complex, and consequently it is exceedingly difficult to predict all requirements.

In reality, requirements are pervasive, dynamic and rarely well-defined. And even if possible, traditional requirements analysis tends to be time-consuming. The difficulty is also related to software's intangible nature. In Brooks' list of software engineering difficulties (Brooks, 1987), he refers to this characteristic as the *invisibility* of software. The requirements stipulated by users are not always easy to specify since a lot of the users' knowledge is tacit. The problems in software engineering are often considered *wicked problems* lacking an unambiguous solution (Poppendieck, 2002). Consequently, systems are difficult to entirely specify in advance. Fowler, 2003a, describes the problem as follows:

> *Estimation of requirements and cost is hard for many reasons. Part of it is that software development is a design activity, and thus hard to plan and cost. Part of it is that the basic materials keep changing rapidly. Part of it is that so much depends on which individual people are involved, and individuals are hard to predict and quantify.*

Another argument against specifying requirements in advance is that even if it were possible to capture a complete set of requirements early on in the project, they will probably change as the project develops. Half a year after the project starts, the requirements will most likely have changed.

12.2.3   Heavy Processes and Lack of Feedback

According to the agile approach, the true problem is the inability within the traditional software development methods to handle changes without causing delays and increasing costs, and not the changes themselves as such. Prohibiting or restricting changes leads to rigid systems that age quickly and are poorly adapted to the users' current needs. Changes are inevitable, according to the agile proponents, and must therefore be permitted and treated carefully throughout the system lifecycle (Highsmith and Cockburn, 2001, p.120). In addition to the above arguments, there exists the business argument that we must be able to deliver product development according to customers' demands.

But why are traditional methods so ineffective at managing change? According to Boehm, 2002, traditional methods can be characterized as plan-driven because they focus on extensive planning and structured processes to make development into an efficient and predictable activity. According to the agile proponents, however, this approach does not work well in a world characterized by rapid changes.

> *Engineering methods tend to try to plan out a large part of the software process in great detail for a long span of time; this works well until things change. So their nature is to resist change.*

> (Fowler, 2003a)

Since specifying requirements is such a problematic process in a changing world, other mechanisms are needed to specify a system, such as requirements that grow over time through feedback from the development work. Traditional development processes tend to have lengthy feedback cycles. Extended periods of time are dedicated to planning, documentation of requirements, and modeling. A considerable amount of development time will elapse before the software reaches a state in which it can be exposed to the users. Feedback from users on what is being developed is thus far too slow in coming. At the worst, feedback will not arrive until the project is completed and the system has been delivered. It is only then, that the crucial discovery is made that the requirements specification was erroneous and that the system does not match the user's task.

12.2.4 Process Focus

The problems inherent to software engineering were discovered long ago (Brooks, 1987), but many of them still remain. The findings from the Standish Group (Standish Group, 1995), reporting that an average 83% of all projects fail in one way or another, are an indicator thereof. Methods and processes have always been important in managing the problems, mainly processes that are disciplined, engineering oriented, predictable and repeatable. There is a belief that such processes can solve all problems. This has led to an increasing focus on the process per se, and following a process has come to be recognized as one of the key success factors. Fowler, 2003a, criticizes the heavy focus on processes:

> *Methodologies impose a disciplined process upon software development with the aim of making software development more predictable and more efficient. They do this by developing a detailed process with a strong emphasis on planning inspired by other engineering disciplines. The most frequent criticism of these methodologies is that they are bureaucratic. There's so much stuff to do to follow the methodology that the whole pace of development slows down.*

Modeling is an essential part of today's software development. But according to Cockburn, 2002, thinking of software development as model building leads to an inappropriate focus, since the interesting parts of what we want to express are not captured in models. Models are useful in many ways, but cannot serve as an overall metaphor. Fundamentally speaking, software development is not model building. A model is a medium of communication, and is sufficient as soon as it permits others to move on with their work.

Software development processes are not truly repeatable. Furthermore, software development has much more to do with individual skill and adaptability than strictly following plans and process descriptions. Predictable processes require components that behave in predictable ways. However, people are not quite as predictable and display significant differences from one to the next. Too often, the problem is that methodology has been opposed to the notion that people are the first-order factor in project success (Fowler, 2003a).

12.3 CHARACTERISTICS OF AGILE DEVELOPMENT

> *"For many people the appeal of these agile methodologies is their reaction to the bureaucracy of the monumental methodologies. These new methods attempt a useful compromise between no process and too much process, providing just enough process to gain a reasonable payoff."*

(Fowler 2003a)

Various solutions to the problems inherent to software engineering have been proposed over the years. One current trend that started in the 1990s is based on the idea of developing software using a more "light-weight" or agile approach. This trend can be seen as a response to more traditional software processes. Not all concepts in the light-weight processes were completely new; they had been practiced in a number of projects for some years already (Abrahamsson et al., 2003). For example, pair programming was a well-established practice prior to XP (Constantine and Lockwood, 2002). The ideas originated primarily from practical development projects, and not from theoretical studies. These new methods gradually evolved into a number of different software development processes, including *Extreme Programming* (Beck, 2000), SCRUM, DSDM, Crystal and Lean Development (Abrahamsson et al., 2003; Highsmith, 2002). XP is in a unique position, in that it has attracted the most attention and is better known than "agile" overall.

An important step was taken in 2001. A group of leading software methodologists gathered in Snowbird, Utah, USA, to discuss light-weight development practices (Cockburn, 2002; Fowler, 2002). Those assembled included Kent Beck, Alistair Cockburn, Ward Cunningham, Jim Highsmith and Ken Schwaber. To support their ideas on light-weight software development, the group agreed to describe the lowest common denominator, in the form of four core values and twelve other principles expounded in greater detail. They did not ultimately succeed in agreeing on a more detailed level – detailed project tactics. They did, however, conclude that this was in fact advantageous in order to foster the development of competing software processes. For the same reason, they agreed not to create a "unified light methodology." These values and principles constitute the *Agile Manifesto* (Agile Alliance, 2001), in which the term "agile," instead of light-weight was adopted.

Consequently, agile is not a distinct, well-defined process. Instead, it is a generic term and common ground for several different processes or methods, each sharing a set of software development core ideas, values and principles. In order to describe the gist of agile development without describing each and every agile process, a natural place to begin would be the content of the *Agile Manifesto*.

The four key values of agile software development (Agile Alliance, 2001) are described below. According to the agile founders, these values are not antithetical to other approaches to software development. Each of the following values should be interpreted thus: "while there is value in the items on the right, we give preference to the items on the left."

1. *Individuals and Interactions* over processes and tools.
   It is people, not processes and tools, who develop software. Therefore, each individual's skills and interpersonal communication are crucial – dialoging face-to-face is the most effective way to communicate (Cockburn, 2002). Pair programming, for example, is a result of this.

2. *Working Software* over comprehensive documentation.
   Requirements, documents, models and other intermediate products are only pertinent as means of communication during development. Although they can be highly practical, they should only be worked on as long as they serve a purpose in delivering working and useful software (Cockburn, 2002).

3. ***Customer Collaboration*** *over contracted negotiation.*
This value describes the relationship between the people who want the system, and those who are building it. Successful projects involve systematic and frequent customer feedback. Instead of depending solely upon contracts, the customers work in close collaboration with the development team – if at all possible, customers and developers should work in the same room during the project.

4. ***Responding to Change*** *over following a plan.*
Plans are useful in software development, and each of the agile methods includes planning activities. The agile approach advocates planning for and adapting to changes, as opposed to prescribing strict conformity to a plan in every situation (Cockburn, 2002). This is necessary because the prerequisites for most systems will evolve during development. Moreover, the initial requirements will be influenced by the fact that communication between people is always more or less incomplete.

Agile developers do not deny the value of engineering- or model-based methods of software engineering. However, they do believe that the answers to successful software development have much more to do with craft, community, pride and learning. The essence of agile is the pragmatic utilization of light, but sufficient, rules of project behavior and the use of human- and communication-oriented rules (Cockburn, 2002). Agile developers embrace individual skills, communication, swift adaptation to change and delivering working, useful software. They are trying to strike a balance between a pragmatic, soft approach and a non-rigorous, sufficient use of engineering methods.

The agile values are described in greater detail by the twelve principles below (Agile Alliance, 2001):

1. The highest priority is to satisfy the customer through the early and continuous delivery of valuable software.

2. Welcome changing requirements, even late in development. Agile processes harness change for the customer's competitive advantage.

3. Deliver working software frequently, from every few weeks to every few months, with a preference for the shorter timescale.

4. Business people and developers must work together daily throughout the project.

5. Build the projects around motivated individuals. Give them the environment and support they need, then trust them to get the job done.

6. The most efficient and effective method of conveying information to and within a development team is a face-to-face conversation.

7. Working software is the primary measure of progress.

8. Agile processes promote sustainable development. The sponsors, developers and users should be able to maintain a constant pace indefinitely.

9. Continuous attention to technical excellence and good design enhances agility.

10. Simplicity — the art of maximizing the amount of work not done — is essential.

11. The best architectures, requirements and designs emerge from self-organizing teams.

12. At regular intervals, the team reflects on how to become more effective, then readjusts its behavior accordingly.

These four values and twelve principles constitute the Manifesto's definition of agile software development. However, in order to understand the essence of agile, this definition requires greater precision. Other definitions could help to achieve a broader understanding.

According to Lindvall et al., 2002, agile methods can be defined as:

- **Iterative** – Delivers a full system initially, then changes the functionality of each subsystem upon each subsequent release.

- **Incremental** – The system, as specified in the requirements, is partitioned into smaller subsystems by functionality. New functionality is added upon each new release.

- **Self-Organizing** – The team has the autonomy to organize itself in order to best complete the work items.

- **Emergent** – Technology and requirements are "allowed" to emerge through the product development cycle.

Boehm and Turner, 2003, characterize agile methods by four main categories: application, management, technical and personnel (Table 12.1).

12.3.1   Extreme Programming

As *Extreme Programming* has a unique position in the agile community, a concise description of XP should interest those who are unfamiliar with it. Because there are also some examples from the XP process in the subsequent parts of this chapter, a cursory understanding of it and some related key concepts would be beneficial.

Constantine and Lockwood, 2002, gives the following brief description of XP:

> *"The rules of the agility game are relatively simple. Work in short release cycles. Do only what is needed without embellishment. Don't waste time in analysis or design, just start cutting code. Describe the problem simply in terms of small, distinct pieces, then implement these pieces in successive iterations. Develop a reliable system by building and testing in increments with immediate feedback. Start with something small and simple that works, then elaborate on successive iterations. Maintain tight communication with clients and among programmers. Test every piece in itself and regression test continuously."*

A *user story* is a short textual description of something that the customer wants the system to do. User stories are a very high-level requirement, and should as such be

Table 12.1   Boehm and Turner, 2003, characterization of agile methods

Characteristic	Description as Pertaining to Agile
Application	
Primary Goals	Rapid value, responding to change
Size	Smaller teams and projects
Environment	Turbulent, high change, project focused
Management	
Customer Relations	Dedicated on-site customers, focused on prioritized increments
Planning and Control	Internalized plans, qualitative control
Communications	Tacit interpersonal knowledge
Technical	
Requirements	Prioritized informal stories and test cases, undergoing unforeseeable change(s)
Development	Simple design, short increments, refactoring is assumed to be inexpensive
Tests	Executable test cases define requirements, testing
Personnel	
Customers	Dedicated, collocated, collaborative, representative, authorized, committed, knowledgeable performers
Developers	At least 30% highly skilled; no developers with below-average skills (this is a rough approximation based on values from Boehm and Turner's model of developer skills)
Culture	Comfort and empowerment via many degrees of freedom (thriving on chaos)

testable (Beck, 2000). They are usually written by customers/users on index cards. A story is first written in succinct terms, along with its name and purpose. It is a driver for the rest of the development effort and is elaborated if needed during the project. Stories are divided into tasks that are in turn implemented in code. Automated functional tests are later run to verify that the story is wholly and accurately reflected by the code's behavior. Functional or acceptance tests are written in cooperation with customers.

Refactoring is the method of changing a piece of software in such a way that it does not alter the external behavior of the code, yet improves its internal structure in areas such as simplicity, flexibility, understandability or performance (*ibid*). In XP, the activity of programming is regarded as a *technical design* process (not to be confused with user interface design), where a particular feature is implemented in the system. Once the feature has been implemented and the code verified by tests, the code must be improved through refactoring. Ideally, refactoring should not change the implemented feature's external behavior. This is measured by running a series of prewritten automatic test cases. If the test cases are still running, the external behavior is unchanged.

Testing is an essential activity in XP, and it is preferably automated in order to fast-track development. An automated test case runs without human intervention and checks that the code calculates the excepted values (Beck, 2000, p.177). There are several categories of tests, each serving a different purpose. Unit tests are used to verify code units. Functional or acceptance tests are specified by the users/customers and are used to verify a user story in its entirety.

12.4 USER-CENTERED DESIGN

User-Centered Design (UCD) is a way to consciously work towards producing systems that are highly usable and meet the expectations and needs of their real users. Unfortunately, UCD has become a buzzword in software development, denoting some vague sort of quality, but for most people meaning an approach to development that involves iterative design and user involvement (e.g. ISO/IEC, 1999, or Gould et al., 1997). The problem with such a vague definition of the concept is that more or less anyone can state that their product follows the tenets of user-centered design – without having to make any commitments about what to do or even knowing what it actually means. This confusion was epitomized by John Karat in a proposal whereby *any* approach focusing on producing usable systems, iterative design and user involvement can be considered as UCD (Karat et al., 1996). The consequence of this can be a process that in itself involves little or no *active* user participation, as is manifest in the following quotation:

> *"A user-centered design process is one that sets users or data generated by users as the criteria by which a design is evaluated or as the generative source of design ideas."*
>
> Dennis Wixon, cited in Karat et al., 1996

To resolve these issues, Gulliksen *et al.* (Chapter 2 of this volume,) have defined user-centered systems design as:

> *"... a process focusing on usability throughout the entire development process and further throughout the system lifecycle. It is based on the following key principles":*

- *User Focus* – The goals of the activity, the work domain or context of use, the users' goals, tasks and needs should all guide the development from the very beginning.

- *Active User Involvement* – Representative users should actively participate, early on and continually, throughout the entire development process and system lifecycle.

- *Evolutionary Systems Development* – The systems development should be both iterative and incremental.

- *Simple Design Representations* – The design must be represented such that it can be easily understood by users and all other stakeholders.

- *Prototyping* – Early on and continuously throughout, prototypes should be used to visualize and evaluate ideas and design solutions in cooperation with the end users.

- *Evaluate Use in Context* – Base-lined usability goals and design criteria should control the development. Evaluate the design against the goals and criteria in cooperation with the users, in context.

- *Explicit and Conscious Design Activities* – The development process should contain dedicated design activities.

- *A Professional Attitude* – The development process should be performed by effective multidisciplinary teams. A professional attitude is required, as are the tools that facilitate the team's cooperation and efficiency.

- *Usability Champion* – Usability experts should be involved early on and continually throughout the development lifecycle.

- *Holistic Design* – All aspects that influence the future use situation should be developed in parallel.

- *Process Customization* – The UCD process must be specified, adapted and/or implemented locally in each organization.

- *A User-Centered Attitude should always be established.*

To be equally clear about their understanding of the usability concept, Gulliksen et al., 2003b (also Chapter 2 in this volume) refer to ISO 9241-11's definition of usability, given below:

> "... *the extent to which a product can be used by specified users to achieve specified goals, with effectiveness, efficiency and satisfaction in a specified context of use.*" *(ISO/IEC, 1998)*

The purpose of such a definition is to provide further guidance to stakeholders who wish to orient their process towards focusing on users and usability. This chapter will, in its discussion of the agile approaches, adhere to this perspective of what user-centered design is or should be.

There exist several user-centered processes that are more or less complete and with varying interpretations of UCD, such as Contextual Design (Beyer and Holtzblatt, 1998) and the Usability Engineering Lifecycle (Mayhew, 1999). Two other UCD-related processes are Goal-Directed Design (Cooper, 1999) and Usage-Centered Design (Constantine and Lockwood, 2002). The latter process emphasizes models and 'usage.'

12.5   USER-CENTERED DESIGN QUALITIES IN AGILE DEVELOPMENT

Is there support for a user-centered design approach in agile software development, or do agile methods prevent focusing on usability and the users' needs? This question highlights a potential problem with the various agile processes: they are not explicitly concerned with users, usability and user-centered design. Nevertheless, there may be other aspects in agile processes that implicitly support UCD or facilitate integration with user-centered methods. It is therefore necessary to examine to what degree the user-centered approach is either promoted or hindered by agile values, principles and practices.

As stated in the Introduction, this analysis is based on the set of twelve key principles of user-centered design that was presented in Chapter 2. We have compared each principle with the values and practices prescribed in agile development and analyzed to what extent the principle is either supported or prevented. The results are summarized and discussed below. The agile view is mainly based on writings by Cockburn, Fowler and Beck, as well as the *Agile Manifesto*. Until now, only a few articles concerning the issue of agile software development and UCD have been produced, namely Constantine and Lockwood, 2002, Hudson, 2003, Kane, 2003, Armitage, 2004, and Jokela and Abrahamsson, 2004. These articles are also included in the following discussion.

12.5.1   Project Organization and the Roles of Usability People

In many respects, the agile approach is concerned with strategies for effective teamwork, project management and organization culture. In contrast, UCD is less concerned with these issues, even though these issues are targeted by the UCD principles of professional attitude, usability champion and process customization. The agile values regarding 'individuals and interactions' and 'customer collaboration' have many implications in this area. For example, the following values are also considered important in UCD:

- Communication between people is essential, *i.e.* face-to-face conversations are preferred.

- Build projects around motivated and skilled individuals; trust them and give them the support and the environment they need.

- Cooperation and responsibilities for business people and developers is vital.

- Promote sustainable development. The people involved should be able to maintain a constant pace without burning out (e.g. in XP projects, people should normally work no more than 40 hours a week and should have fun at work in order to perform at their best).

- The project should be organized into small, effective, multi-disciplinary teams, where collaboration and communications are present on all levels. Self-organizing teams yield the best results.

- The team should reflect on how to become more effective and fine-tune its behavior at regular intervals, if needed.

A direct result of valuing people, skills and teamwork is empowering the various roles in a project to make decisions and take responsibility for their area of profession. For example, programmers are the best placed to decide on technical matters, business people should be responsible for business matters, etc. Analogous with this thinking, projects should have skilled usability experts with the authority to rule on matters affecting usability during the system life cycle. In practice, however, many agile processes have a narrow view on what competencies are needed in a system development project. The roles of programmers, business people and customers are usually filled, but interaction designers and other usability experts are routinely overlooked. Although roles to work with use cases and user interface design/programming are defined for some projects, customers (not necessarily end users) often contribute by providing user stories, reviewing use cases and writing acceptance tests. Their input then becomes the source for the developers when designing the system's user interface. Without specialists devoted to the design and evaluation of usability, as well as related activities such as writing help systems and training material, the chances of producing usable systems are slight. This is a serious weakness affecting most agile processes. The lack of awareness is probably due to an inadequate grasp of the importance of usability. Heightened awareness of usability matters could lead to the basic values of agile promoting the UCD principle that states that the development process should be performed by empowered multidisciplinary teams, including usability champions.

12.5.2   User Participation

A key UCD principle is that users should be actively involved when designing the system. The agile approach comprises a number of values that can promote active involvement. Agile developers value people, communication and pragmatic collaboration with different stakeholders, which should include users or customers. In practice, these values emphasize the following:

- The participation of users (or customers) in the development process is the most effective way of communicating the users' needs to the developers. Users and developers should preferably be co-located in order to take part in the work.

- *Extreme Programming* captures user needs through *user stories*. Other agile processes opt for use cases instead.

- Users test software on different levels. Frequently delivering software increments makes it possible for users to evaluate the software under real conditions.

- It is ultimately people, not processes and tools, who create working software.

These practices sound promising from a UCD standpoint. However, a common stumbling block is that agile processes seldom distinguish between *customers* and *users* – all too often, they are regarded as one and the same. For this reason, the agile approach pays too little attention to the end-users and their roles in the development process. According to Armitage, 2004: *". . . the agile community rarely mentions users or user interfaces at all, which means that either they neglect the user experience or are focusing on projects with less need for sophistication in user experience."*

Customers/users participate in agile development by writing and prioritizing system features (known as *user stories* in XP) and specifying acceptance tests. Users can express what they need to a certain extent, but on their own, it is difficult for them to actually design a new system. User stories or use cases, which are often used to spec-ify user needs, fail to capture many aspects of user interaction. Hudson, 2003 (pp.2-3), summarizes a number of problems with the agile approach to user participation:

- Too little user participation

- Users are not customers

- The challenge of selecting the right users to work with (*i.e.*, distinguishing be-tween typical and atypical users)

- Users and tasks in a context

By letting the users write their user stories themselves, there is a risk that the devel-opers will transfer the responsibility of the system's usability to the users/customers (Jokela and Abrahamsson, 2004).

Even if confusion often arises between the different roles of users and customers, Beck, 2000, p.143 suggests that the best customers are those who will actually use the system. Therefore, nothing in the agile philosophy prevents the active involvement of real, typical users.

12.5.3 Simple Design Representations

The values espoused by proponents of the agile approach promote communication and simplicity. Communication between project team members is therefore essential. Simplicity emphasizes the need to minimize unnecessary work, e.g. never produce artefacts for their own sake. Models and other design representations are seen as valuable means of communication between people in a project, otherwise they are considered to be pointless activities. This is in accordance with the use of concrete and simple UCD design artefacts, such as sketches, mock-ups and paper prototypes. On the other hand, showing abstract notations such as UML diagrams to the user should be avoided. This does not imply that model-based approaches are invalid, however. Constantine and Lockwood, 2002, opines that a model-based approach is necessary for developing usable systems with agile methods. Agile modeling (Ambler, 2002; Highsmith, 2002) is another approach that emphasizes modeling, as suggested by its name. A risk inherent to modeling approaches is that the project's focus will shift towards producing models instead of producing a usable working system; a risk that agile processes strive to eliminate. One example is the use case mania reported by Gulliksen et al., 2003b, (Chapter 2 of this volume). Furthermore, models are by definition a simplification of the real world, and as such carry the risk that important information such as the context of use will be overlooked.

12.5.4 Evolutionary Systems Development

Evolutionary systems development, *i.e.*, development that is iterative and incremental, is a fundamental part of agile processes. The primary objective is to manage change in the development process, which is expressed in the fourth agile value: *Responding to change over following a plan*. Responding to change is also an essential element of user-centered design. Evolutionary design, along with prototyping, provides support for the need to respond elegantly to change, which is also in keeping with the agile values.

It is important that users be involved in the evolutionary process. In agile development, the customers/users are the main source for the system's design; in XP, for example, customers write user stories. Because working increments of software are finished and tested on a frequent basis (such as every few days or weeks), providing feedback on the usability of the end system by both users and developers is facilitated. In longer iterations (such as every few months), parts of the system are delivered and deployed at the target environment, providing the opportunity to test under real conditions. The feedback generated from the hands-on experience with the real working system (or parts thereof) benefits developers and users alike in their understanding of the system under development, user interaction and context of use.

Many agile processes rely on very short iterations that range from hours to days or even weeks. However, according to Armitage, 2004 (p.18), there is a difference between how iterative development is used in agile processes and UCD, respectively: "... while iterative design [in UCD] typically seeks to model, assess, and revise larger systems at low and high fidelities, XP builds and releases smaller systems strictly at extremely high fidelities."

Two reasons for this dissimilarity are the methods of *automated testing* and *refactoring*. Automated testing is a prerequisite for rapid development in agile processes, and involves completing tasks such as verifying refactored code. Refactoring is a method in which a piece of software is changed, preferably without altering the features' external behavior (described previously). The extent to which external behavior has been affected is measured by running a series of prewritten automatic test cases. However, doing so only verifies functions that lend themselves to automatic testing – which is rarely the case for usability measurements. This means that a refactored piece of program may have changed its appearance or interactive behavior from its initial design, which complicates maintaining a coherent usability design. Also, due to its automated nature, this type of testing is not very useful when evaluating usability. According to Constantine and Lockwood, 2002, automated user-interface testing is difficult, if not impossible, except at the most elementary level. Unfortunately, testing user interfaces is labor intensive and time consuming, as compared to automated tests.

Automated functional tests and customer acceptance tests need to be complemented by explicit usability evaluations, either separate from or integrated with the other tests. However, such evaluations can also introduce new issues, of which Kane, 2003, identifies three different scenarios:

1. Conducting usability testing at the end of the development process means there is a risk of having inadequate time and resources to respond to the usability issues raised in the testing.

2. Performing usability acceptance tests early on in the process has the potential side-effect of introducing usability defects in later iterations, since there is no regression usability capability like there is for feature validation.

3. Attempting to carry out usability tests as frequently as feature acceptance tests will drive costs to exorbitant levels.

In sum, one of the strengths of agile practices and their focus on iterative and incremental development is the possibility to test real software in real settings, such as at the users' workplaces. Tests can be carried out at different levels, from simple evaluations of paper prototypes to full-scale beta testing. However, in order to validate that the system fulfills the specified usability goals, the evaluation must be performed methodically, with real end users, and in the proper context. Real usability evaluations must be completed in addition to the usual software/acceptance tests. The acceptance test that is used in XP, for example, does not usually fulfill these conditions.

12.5.5 Big Design Up Front Versus Evolutionary Development

Another recurring debate focuses on evolutionary development versus the so-called heavy or *Big Design Up Front* (BDUF) development, where all aspects of the system's usability are tackled and resolved in an early and explicit design phase. The agile design process minimizes the big design up front and relies instead on repeated refinements to shape the user interface. Armitage (2004, pp.20-21) argues for the agile evolutionary approach in order to handle change:

> "The effort to eliminate changes to requirements has always been a losing battle [. . .] The more work that is done on a project, the more the project context changes. Agile methods seek to benefit from the intelligence of experiencing the real product's existence, and the sooner the better. Design, conversely, aims to predict what the entire product will be before it exists. Proponents of heavy upfront design, such as Alan Cooper, claim that adequate product intelligence should reside in a specification. This can be true, but in cases where technology is new or untried, requirements are volatile, the domain unfamiliar, or the complexity immense, it can be too risky to heavily invest in assumptions without adequate 'reality checks'."

However, there are also arguments against the more radical processes based upon evolutionary design:

> "The most critical shortcoming of nearly all techniques that are based on iterative expansion and refinement in small increments is the absence of any comprehensive overview of the entire architecture. For internal elements of the software, this shortcoming is not fatal, because the architecture can be refined and restructured at a later time. [..] User interfaces are a different story. [. . .] Iterative prototyping is an acceptable substitute for thorough UI design only when the problems are not too complicated. We need a more sophisticated model-driven approach."

(Constantine and Lockwood, 2002)

Although agile processes devote very little time to an explicit design phase and BDUF, there are nevertheless a few activities that also support the design of a more holistic view of the system's usability:

- Users participate to various degrees in the development, which makes it possible for them to point out many aspects of their tasks/work practices, work context, need for training, etc.

- Iterative development and responding to change. Many aspects that influence a system under development are complex or tacit, and therefore difficult to specify in advance. The depth of understanding of the users and their work will grow during development. Software that is tested or used under realistic conditions will enhance understanding even further. It is then possible to evaluate and comprehend a fuller range of aspects affecting usability, and generate feedback to the next development iteration. A process that is flexible to changes after the initial specification is advantageous.

However, without explicit and coordinated usability design activities, the agile approach is generally insufficient. There is a critical risk that many elements that are not obvious parts of the user interface (context of use, user diversity, health and safety aspects, social environments, user training) will be overlooked during development. Although certain aspects are possible to detect and address through iterative and incremental development methods, there is still a need to design and coordinate the system's usability.

A similar problem related to agile processes is the lack of methods to determine and specify usability goals that can direct the iterative development effort. Agile processes do not entail an explicit analysis of usability goals, regardless of the users' (or customers') participation in the development effort. It is also unrealistic to expect users to elaborate detailed accounts of their needs, while working more or less on their own. Usability designers are required to perform an in-depth analysis with users, and transform the information they collect into usability goals and design criteria. The techniques employed in agile processes in order to capture the users' needs, for example, user stories in XP (Beck, 2000) and use cases in Crystal (Cockburn, 2002) are too coarse to define many usability goals. For example, Jokela and Abrahamsson, 2004, reported on a study of a typical XP project, where user stories proved to be more or less functional requirements without any explicit analysis of the users' goals. These techniques failed to capture many significant aspects of the full context of use. Hudson, 2003, identified a number of these shortcomings as follows:

- Would real users do that?

- How would they know?

- Where does that information or understanding come from?

- Is the required behavior consistent?

- Does the story fit in with their work flow?

- Is it reasonable to expect that the whole story can be completed without interruption, or is greater flexibility required?

At best, the UI design is developed iteratively by skilled designers and users. At worst, the design is the fortuitous result of someone simply writing some code then refactoring it. As a general rule, agile processes leave out dedicated techniques and activities for usability design. There is rarely a specialized role in the team with the skills and responsibility to coordinate the interaction design work. The upshot is that usability design lies in the hands of the customers/users and the developers. Users are supposed to know what features they want, prioritize them, then inform the developers (e.g. by writing user stories). Users can often express what they need, but it is more challenging for them to devise solutions for how the system should support their tasks, or attempt to design the user interface itself. An even worse case arises if the real users are replaced by "customers" who will not be using the software. The real users need to participate in the design process alongside usability people.

12.5.6 Prototyping

Although there reigns a positive attitude towards prototyping in the agile community, prototypes are not a fundamental driver of design. Instead, agile processes rely heavily on iterative and incremental methods and focus on delivering working software. This is not contradictory—iterative development and prototyping work well together. Finely-incremented software can, of course, be seen as a sort of prototype, especially because it is allowed to change. However, using prototyping as a means to increase the understanding of usage and design user interfaces is not a common tradition in agile practice.

Agile processes value simplicity, which obviously applies to the use of models and prototypes in the development process. Methods that are sufficiently straightforward in order to develop and evaluate prototypes are preferred. The important aspect of prototypes (and other models), as far as agile processes are concerned, is that they are a medium of communication, and are adequate as soon as they enable developers to move on with their work (Cockburn, 2002).

Simple prototypes, such as those presented on paper, are a well-established tool in UCD (Gould et al., 1997) and are also used in some agile methods. Nevertheless, Constantine and Lockwood, 2002 (p.5), is skeptical. They argue that paper prototypes are not a complete substitute for usability tests of working software. However, they maintain that paper prototypes are highly-valuable tools for design and evaluation throughout the design phase, especially in the early stages. User reactions to paper prototypes are constructive when evaluating different design solutions (Hudson, 2003; p. 11, Kane, 2003; Nielsen, 1993; Gould et al., 1997). The greatest benefit of paper prototypes is their intrinsic simplicity – it is possible to explore and evaluate different design solutions rapidly, without turning to expensive usability labs. With highly-complicated models and prototypes, however, time restrictions prevent building more than only a few, and the design space is thus limited.

12.5.7 Process Customization

Although agile processes value individuals and interactions over processes and tools, processes still have an important role to play; however, this role must be adaptive and actively support the work of skilled individuals and communication on all levels. The idea behind the *Agile Manifesto* is that there is no single process that fits all purposes; consequently, there is no unified agile process. Each software development process must be selected, adapted and customized to suit each project. One agile principle indicates that the team should reflect and fine-tune its behavior at regular intervals, if needed. This attitude works well with the UCD principle of process customization.

In UCD, a tailored, user-centered process is a component that is essential to achieving usability. Agile developers do not deny the value of a prescribed software development process, yet rely to a greater extent on talented developers and good management in order to make a difference. In practice, this could be misinterpreted as a 'license to hack', leaving out anything that could be regarded as a method or process.

Another issue is the heavy reliance on talented people instead of processes. As Constantine and Lockwood, 2002, writes: *"There are only so many Kent Becks in the world to lead the team."* This makes the need for premium programmers, managers and designers a critical issue. Finding all these skillful and experienced individuals is another challenge altogether.

12.6   DISCUSSION

12.6.1   Is Agile Development User-Centered?

To summarize the arguments presented above, there are a number of qualities inherent to agile project culture that can provide a solid foundation for a user-centered attitude: a focus on people, communication, customer collaboration, adaptive processes and customer/user needs. The question is whether this is enough to label agile development as user-centered design.

The *Agile Manifesto* does not cover all the key principles of UCD. Consequently, the answer is no – agile development processes do not fully qualify as user-centered design. The main reason is not that agile values work explicitly against UCD; instead, it is because they do not reflect the necessary focus on users and usability. Furthermore, some of the agile processes' prioritized areas of interest can prevent a user-centered attitude: a focus on programming and programmers, automated tests, very short iterations and fast increments, and executable software as a measure. Other problem areas are the confusion between users and customers, unsatisfactory techniques for modeling users and tasks (*i.e.*, user stories and use cases), the fear of early design, as well as insufficient activities for interaction design.

However, there is no contradiction between agile approaches and UCD; in fact, there are several basic values that the two approaches share, as presented above. It should therefore be possible to integrate the basic values and principles of agile development with UCD. So far, there is no predominant reason why agile processes could not be customized or adapted to UCD, or vice-versa.

It may also be fully possible to integrate specific agile methods and techniques with UCD, at least to a certain level. The diversity of the various agile methods and techniques makes it impossible to make any blanket recommendations, however. For example, SCRUM, is actually more of a project management model; whereas XP concerns both project management and detailed techniques for coding. The former category might be easier to integrate with UCD because it covers the different aspects of a process. However, each method/technique must be carefully examined in order to determine if it can be integrated with usability methods, and what the consequences will be.

12.6.2   Is User-Centered Design Agile?

> *The pace of technology change brings with it some new challenges. Although behavioral science provides us with many tools and theoretical frameworks for observing behavior, they are generally tuned for use in a fairly stable environment and not for providing design advice in a rapidly changing one.*

(Karat and Karat, 2003, p.539)

An ongoing debate is whether UCD can occasionally become too unwieldy and resource consuming. As a reaction, lighter methods, such as Discount Usability Engineering (Nielsen, 1993), have emerged. Also, usability professionals have been criticized for focusing on "studies" instead of generating designs and products (Siegel and Dray, 2003). Hence, UCD can benefit from becoming more agile. For example, Karat and Karat, 2003, argue for a shift towards design methods that work better in rapidly-changing technological environments.

12.7   TOWARDS A MODEL FOR BRIDGING AGILE AND UCD

The key point at issue is how to bridge the gap between agile software development and user-centered design. Several viable strategies can be envisioned, depending on the aim of the integration. Should the goal be to improve an agile process so it becomes more user-centered, or should the goal be to define a complete new *agile-user-centered* process? A number of related objectives are also conceivable.

Another aspect of integration is the kind of integration to discuss. There are at least two possible levels. On a concrete level, topics to discuss might include how to integrate specific processes, for example XP and Contextual Design. On a more abstract level, the focus would shift to how to best integrate the basic values and principles of agile and UCD respectively. We have chosen the abstract level for this chapter, and complemented it with selected examples from concrete methods. We believe that any discussion of how to bridge this gap must start at this abstract level so it may serve as a foundation for more concrete attempts.

We have outlined an abstract-level model for bridging the gap between agile software development and user-centered design. This model is described from three different integration perspectives, all of which are briefly discussed below. The model's third approach is the preferred method and is hence discussed in greater detail.

In the first approach, UCD methods are integrated, along with basic values, in an agile development framework (Figure 12.1). The level of integration can range from incorporating only a few UCD techniques to coordinating a more complete set of methods and techniques with agile methods. Regardless of the level of integration, however, the agile values still constitute the fundamental framework. The underlying principles of agile development permeate the developing organization, and UCD methods will to some degree become more agile.

An advantage of this approach is that organizations that are familiar with agile development in general or that use a specific agile process can deliver more usable systems without abandoning their established methods.

The disadvantage is that the usability work can act like cake-frosting – by adding it on top of an agile process, we might believe that all usability problems have been

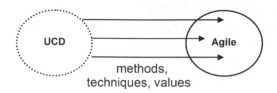

Figure 12.1   UCD methods integrated in agile development

managed. As discussed above, however, user-centered design is more than *doing a little design here and a little testing there*. Furthermore, the entire project must be committed to the importance of usability. Another disadvantage is that some UCD methods are simply too cumbersome for easy integration in agile development. It must be possible to adapt the selected methods to an agile environment.

Some examples of how to integrate UCD in an agile development framework are discussed by Hudson, 2003, and Kane, 2003. Hudson suggests that an XP project require the following basic UCD techniques as a starting point in order to produce more usable systems:

- Context of use

- Personas

- Modifying user stories to include the context of use

- Conceptual models

- Paper prototypes for design and early evaluation

- Usability testing

- Involving usability specialists

Kane, 2003, discusses how to incorporate discount usability engineering techniques (Nielsen, 1993) with agile development, as well as with the agile process, SCRUM, (see for an example Highsmith, 2002). The rationale for attempting to blend them is that both disciplines share the same underlying values of advocating simple and low-cost techniques. Kane, 2003, suggests a few representative "discount" techniques that can improve specific gaps in agile development:

- *Scenarios* for eliciting user feedback implemented in simple paper prototypes

- *Simplified thinking aloud*: an interview technique where users verbalize their actions while testing a user interface

- *Heuristic evaluation*: usability experts evaluate a user interface (a simple prototype or a working system) from a set of usability guidelines

- *Card sorting*: a technique that explores the users' conceptual models for the future system. Features or concepts of the system are written on index cards, then sorted and grouped by the users

In the second approach of the integration model, agile methods and techniques as well as basic values are all integrated in a user-centered design framework (Figure 12.2). This approach is similar to the first one, only the roles of the two disciplines have been reversed. Although the integration can be carried out to a greater or lesser degree, user-centered values remain the fundamental framework. Agile methods must be more or less adapted to suit user-centered processes. Some of these methods, such as pair programming, can be easily integrated in UCD. Others, such as refactoring, need a more careful incorporation.

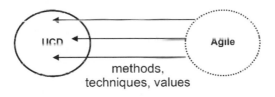

Figure 12.2   Agile methods integrated in UCD

The question is how much more agile does the resulting UCD process become once the agile methods and techniques have been integrated. If the primary goal is to have a design process that is both truly user-centered and more light-weight and adaptive, it can most likely be achieved through this integration. If agility is an equally important goal, however, another approach may be considered.

Constantine and Lockwood, 2002, describes an attempt at integration that is comparable to this approach, in which a simplified variant of a UCD-like process called *usage-centered design* and agile methods are outlined. In the resulting process, a minimal set of usage-centered activities is used in association with agile methods. However, usage-centered design places emphasis on modeling, which is not shared by agile approaches. The integrated process still focuses on models, but uses simplified models based on index cards. XP's user stories are used here, but in a different manner. Users' tasks are modeled through index cards.

12.7.1   A Balanced Integration Between Agile Development and UCD

The problems related to the first two integration approaches suggest the integration and coordination of a more complete set of user-centered methods and agile methods. However, this is no easy task because the integration must strike a balance between the two perspectives in order to maintain their core values.

The disciplines of UCD and agile development do not target precisely the same issues in systems development. Agile values and practices are more concerned with project management and organizational issues, as well as making coding more efficient. UCD, on the other hand, has a closer focus on design methods and user involvement. This distinction is, in fact, advantageous when it comes to integrating UCD and agile development, and results in a balanced cross-pollination between the two disciplines (Figure 12.3). By combining UCD and agile development, both basic values and methods/techniques can be better adapted to suit and complement one another.

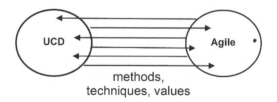

methods,
techniques, values

Figure 12.3   Balanced integration: cross-pollination between agile development and UCD

This type of cross-pollination integration can occur at different levels. On a small scale, values and methods from one perspective can complement or fill gaps in the other perspective. Usability testing, for example, can complement acceptance tests. Agile values regarding people and face-to-face communication can be utilized to improve communication between users and developers, as well as between developers and usability designers.

On a larger scale, the integration can result in new hybrid methods, or even complete hybrid processes, which are both agile and user-centered. Such methods and processes should be based on a foundation that integrates the basic values of each discipline, as well as process-specific activities. An example of this sort of integration is discussed by Armitage, 2004. He describes how he, along with colleagues, developed a hybrid iterative design method, integrating iterative techniques from both XP and UCD. Design work occurred both on a detailed low level in short iterations (typical XP) and on higher levels to facilitate an overall design (typical usability design).

A hybrid process can be created more or less 'from the ground up'. From the ground up means that specific processes do not serve as a basic foundation; instead, existing methods and techniques from the diverse field of agile development and UCD are selected and integrated into a new process. The resulting process should be consistent with the values and principles of agile development and UCD. Another way is to start with two specific processes – fusing an existing agile process with a UCD process. This approach has both strengths and weaknesses. On the positive side is the fact that the processes may be both well-tried and familiar to the developers. However, a process fusion involves a greater degree of coordination than does the cross-pollination approach. There is also a greater risk of encountering detailed activities that do not fit with each other or even that are incompatible. In addition, the approach may be more labor-intensive and complex than simply creating a new process from scratch.

Some concrete suggestions on how to achieve a more balanced integration of agile development and UCD are listed below.

- The prime objective is delivering *working* and *usable* software. Usability activities are important, but too much time devoted to endless user studies or prototyping is not going to benefit the users in the end. There must be a balance between actually releasing products and improving the usability of the system one step further. A system is not usable unless it is both released and put to use. Releasing increments of the real system is beneficial because the developers can learn from actual usage.

- There is often a need to prioritize the system's features in order to deliver on-schedule. It is the users who should ultimately decide which features they need; however, the usability designers should assist them with their decision so the system retains a high degree of usability.

- The individuals involved in the development process are important — both developers and users alike. How the development team and work practices are organized must be taken into consideration. Ultimately, people are more important than processes.

- Actively involve users (not just customers) in all phases of development. Users should be co-located with the developers for at least some parts of the development process. At the very least, the developers should visit the users workplace in order to grasp the details of the users' context.

- Development projects require skilled usability designers. They should be empowered to make decisions about matters that affect the system's usability.

- Improve team communication by working in pairs. In addition to pair programming, pairing users with usability designers and/or usability designers with programmers will contribute to boosting communication.

- Usability validation is needed at different stages of the development cycle. Usability tests cannot be carried out at the same frequency as the automatic functional tests, for example. However, if users are ready at hand, simple low-scale usability tests can be performed frequently. By using lo-fi prototypes, it is possible to conduct simple usability tests early on and frequently. These basic usability tests must nonetheless be complemented with more thorough usability acceptance tests in which more complete parts of the system are validated.

- Evolutionary development is essential for several reasons. Many aspects that influence a system under development are complex or tacit, and therefore difficult to specify in advance. A process must allow for changes in requirements. However, the agile approach and UCD implement iterative and incremental development differently, as described above. Armitage's (Armitage, 2004) hybrid method, also described earlier, represents a potentially-successful solution.

- The process should include suitable methods to determine and specify usability goals that can direct the course of the iterative development. Users are generally unable to specify all the details of their needs on their own; however, techniques such as user stories and use cases are not sufficient to capture usability requirements. For these reasons, usability designers are required to complete a full analysis together with users and transform the information into usability goals and design criteria.

- An evolutionary approach must be combined with early and coordinated usability design activities, such as user and task analysis, personas, scenarios, conceptual models and paper prototypes, as well as the iterative design method suggested by Armitage, 2004.

- Relatively simple models such as paper prototypes and lo-fi. mock-ups should be used as part of development. These models can be utilized, for example, as basic methods to create and test design solutions in rapid iterations. It is more effective to develop and test simple prototypes than released increments of the system; as such, some of the increments can be effectively replaced by prototypes. The added value of paper prototypes is their simplicity – through them, it is feasible to explore and evaluate different design solutions quickly, without resorting to expensive usability labs.

12.7.2   Conclusion

Deciding which is the better approach for integrating agile development and UCD depends on a number of factors, such as the developing and user organizations, the tradition of processes in use and the personnel's level of skill. Ultimately, the integration approach should be selected based on the different prerequisites and the process should be tailored to the specific project.

This being said, in our opinion, the integration approach with the likeliest chances for success is balanced integration (3). We opine that the other approaches (1 and 2) can be risky because they could be implemented by simply adding new features on top of an existing tradition. In such a case, there is no coordination of the methods with each other, nor with the basic values and the process. Methods that are plugged into an existing process may not work with the basic values that already exist or may require so much adaptation that they become too undermined to be beneficial. The coordination of methods, people, basic values and process is more likely to succeed with the cross-pollination approach.

12.7.3   Future Work

Future work should fall into two main areas:

The first is to continue with the present work on a more detailed level by studying specific agile and UCD processes, *i.e.*, how they relate to each other and to what degree they support the agile and UCD values.

The second is to study the various integration approaches currently in practice and evaluate the integration work, as well as the resulting development project. The results can be used to help design new development processes that bridge agile development and user-centered design.

13   RIPPLE: AN EVENT DRIVEN DESIGN REPRESENTATION FRAMEWORK FOR INTEGRATING USABILITY AND SOFTWARE ENGINEERING LIFE CYCLES

Pardha S. Pyla,

Manuel A. Pérez-Quiñones, James D. Arthur, and H. Rex Hartson

Department of Computer Science, Virginia Polytechnic Institute and State University,
660 McBryde Hall, Blacksburg, VA 24061, USA
{ppyla, perez, arthur, hartson}@cs.vt.edu

Abstract

Ripple is a database-centered, event-triggered, shared design representation frame-work that provides a development infrastructure within which the usability engineering and software engineering life cycles co-exist in cooperative and complementary roles. Ripple identifies connections and dependencies within each life cycle and between the two life cycles and provides a framework to represent artefacts generated at each stage of the two development life cycles. Our approach to integrating these two development life cycles does not merge them into a single life cycle; rather it coordinates each life cycle's activities, timing, scope, and goals using a shared design representation and management for the two life cycles. Ripple incorporates tech-

A. Seffah (eds.), Human-Centered Software Engineering – Integrating Usability
in the Development Process, 245–265.

niques to accommodate communication about design insights and change. In response to design changes by either the interface or software side, Ripple sends possibly cascading messages (ripples) to inform developers on both sides, asking them to satisfy associated constraints (dependencies, relationships) affecting related other parts of the overall design. We describe the motivation, barriers, rationale, arguments, and implementation plan for the need, specification, and potential contributions of such an integrated design representation framework. We provide a high level description of this design representation framework and conclude with the usefulness and potential shortcomings of this approach.

13.1   INTRODUCTION

13.1.1   Parts and Processes of Interactive Software Systems

Interactive software systems have both functional and user interface parts. Although the separation of code into two clearly identifiable modules is not always possible, the two parts exist conceptually and each must be designed on its own terms.

The user-interface part, which often accounts for half or more of the total lines of code (Myers and Rosson, 1992), begins as an interaction design, which is ultimately implemented in user interface software. Interaction design requires specialized usability engineering (UE) knowledge, training, and experience in topics such as human psychology, cognition, visual perception, specialized design guidelines, task analysis, etc. The ultimate goal of UE is to create systems with measurably high usability, i.e., systems that are easy to learn, easy to use, and satisfying to their users. A practical objective is also to provide interaction design specifications that can be used to build the interactive component of a system by software engineers. In this chapter we define the UE role as that of the developer who has responsibility for building such specifications. (We use the term developer to refer to someone who has the skills to participate in all stages of a software development life cycle and not just a software coding or implementation expert).

The functional part of a software system, sometimes called the functional core, is manifest as the non-user-interface software. The design and development of this functional core requires specialized software engineering (SE) knowledge, training, and experience in topics such as algorithms, data structures, software architectures, calling structures, database management, etc. The goal of SE is to create efficient and reliable software systems containing the specified functionality, as well as integrating and implementing the interactive portion of the system. We define the SE role as that of the developer who has the responsibility for this goal.

To achieve the UE and SE goals for an interactive system, i.e., to create an efficient and reliable system with required functionality and high usability, effective development processes are required for both the UE (Figure 13.1) and SE life cycles (Figure 13.2). The UE development life cycle is an iteration of activities for requirement analysis (e.g., needs, task, work flow, user class analysis), interaction design (e.g., usage scenarios, screen designs), prototype development, and evaluation thereby producing a user interface interaction design specification. The SE development life cycle consists primarily of concept definition and requirements engineering, design (preliminary and detailed design), design review, implementation, and integration & testing, I&T).

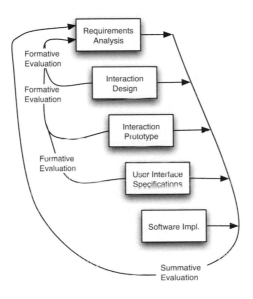

Figure 13.1 Usability engineering life cycle

13.1.2 The Problem: Coordinating the Development of the Two Life Cycles

Given the facts that each of these development life cycles is now reasonably mature and well established, both have the same high level goal of producing software that the user wants and needs, and that the two must function together to create a single system, one might expect well-defined connections for collaboration and communication between the two development processes. However, the two disciplines are still considered as separate entities and are applied independently with little coordination during product development. For example, it is not uncommon to find usability engineers being brought into the development process after the SE implementation stage. They are asked to test and/or 'fix' the usability of an already-implemented system, and then, of course, many changes proposed by the usability engineers that require significant modifications must be ignored due to budget and time constraints. Those few changes that actually do get included require a significant investment in terms of time and effort because they must be retrofitted.

The lack of coordination between the usability and software engineers often leads to conflicts, gaps, design and requirements mismatches, miscommunication, "spaghetti" code due to unanticipated changes, brittle software, and other serious problems during development. The result is a system falling short in both functionality and usability,

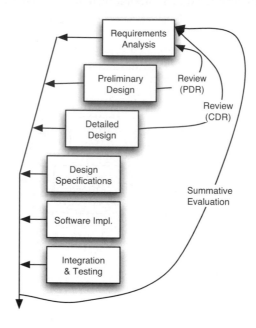

Figure 13.2   Software engineering life cycle

and in some cases a completely failed project. In particular, for the projects containing a significant interaction component, there is a need for:

■   communication between the UE and SE roles, each of which uses different development activities, techniques, and vocabularies;

■   coordination of independent development activities (usability and software engineers coordinating while mostly working separately on role-specific activities);

■   identification and understanding of constraints and dependencies between the SE and UE processes;

■   synchronization of dependent development activities (timely readiness and timeliness of making use of respective work products); and the

■   provision on each side for anticipating and reacting to change on the other side.

Unfortunately, the significance of UE and the importance of the bulleted items above are not described or prescribed in most of the software development standards that exist today. For example, the 31-page IEEE-830 standard (IEEE, 1998) on recommended practices for software requirements specification (SRS) contains only about

10 lines relating to user interfaces (Section 5.2.1.2), and states that user interface specifications should be a part of the SRS. This part of the standard takes an ad hoc stab at a few user interface issues (e.g. required screen formats, page and window layouts, screen content, availability of programmable function keys, etc.) which seem arbitrarily chosen from the enormous possibilities not mentioned. More importantly, it says nothing about the UE life cycle process for creating the interaction design, which is a main part of the user interface software specification. It is misguided (and worse, misguiding) to expect the user interface specifications to be available that early in the requirements process without having followed a proper UE design life cycle. We believe that this document should have a reference to another standard for user interface software requirements.

Another source of confusion with the IEEE-830 standard is that the items mentioned in this document such as required screen formats, page and window layouts, and screen content are design specifications for usability engineers (the standard includes nothing about how to design them for usability). For the UE role, 'requirements' are mostly stated in terms of usability attributes such as learnability, subjective satisfaction, ease of use, etc. Even these usability specifications are subject to calibration in later stages of the UE development process.

However, we do not disagree with the intent behind the idea that user interface requirement specifications for user interface software are properly a part of the SRS. But in reality it is not possible to generate requirements specifications for user interface software without going though an iterative process of interaction design and evaluation, but standards such as the above described IEEE-830 (on SRS) and IEEE/EIA-12207.1 (on software life cycle processes-life cycle data Software Productivity Consortium, 1997) do not acknowledge the kind of life cycle process that is needed to develop a high usability interaction design. Neither do they acknowledge the myriad relations and dependencies between the activities and work products of the SE life cycle with that of UE and vice versa.

13.1.3   Objective

The objective of our work has been to produce a design representation infrastructure that:

- integrates the two life cycles under one common framework;

- retains the two development processes as separately identifiable processes, each with its own life cycle structure, development activities, and techniques; and

- is built upon a database-centered, event-triggered and constraint-based framework, that provides a common 'overall design representation and management' approach, shared by the SE and UE roles and activities.

The common 'design representation and management' is the key to the coordination of interface and functional core development activities, and to the communication among the UE and SE roles. The constraint-based event triggers are important in recognizing an event with an associated dependency or constraint and sending a message to remind the developers to enforce a constraint. The common 'design representation' identifies and addresses the effects of change and also incorporates techniques to record design reminders. This allows the two life cycle roles to

- design for change by keeping the design flexible,

- analyze the implications of change in either of the processes,

- take necessary corrective action to address change,

- mitigate the changes that could be imposed on each life cycle, and to

- record design insights and reminders for future development activities.

13.2   BACKGROUND

13.2.1   Operating hypothesis

A strong hypothesis for our work is to maintain UE and SE as separate, but coordinated, life cycle development processes. It is not our goal to merge either development process into the other, but to establish a development infrastructure in which both can coexist and function in parallel. UE and SE processes each require special knowledge and skills. Given the differences in activities and focus, it is not realistic or desirable to expect the two roles to 'work together'. A combined life cycle process is unlikely to give balanced attention to both parts. Trying to combine, for example, the UE life cycle into the SE life cycle, as done in (Ferre, 2003), creates a risk (and a high likelihood) of deciding conflicts in favor of software development needs and constraints, and against those of usability. The two roles must however communicate, coordinate, and synchronize as they work on essentially two different parts of a larger design, parts that must come together for implementation of a single system.

13.2.2   Similarities Between Life Cycles

At a high level, UE and SE share the same objectives:

- seeking to understand the client's, customer's, and users' wants and needs;

- translating these needs into system requirements;

- designing a system to satisfy these requirements; and

- testing to help ensure their realization in the final product.

13.2.3   Differences Between Life Cycles

The objectives of the SE and UE are achieved by the two developer roles using different development processes and techniques. At a high level, the two life cycles differ in the requirements and design phases but converge into one at the implementation stage (Figure 13.3). This is a natural expectation because ultimately software developers implement the user interface specifications. At each stage, the two life cycles have many differences in their activities, techniques, timelines, iterativeness, scope, roles, procedures, and focus. Several of the salient differences are identified next.

Different Levels of Iteration and Evaluation.   Developers of interaction designs often iterate early and frequently with design scenarios, screen sketches, paper prototypes, and low-fidelity, roughly-coded software prototypes before much, if any, software is committed to the user interface. Often this frequent and early iteration is done on a small scale and scope, and primarily as a means to evaluate a part of an interaction design in the context of a small number of user tasks. Usability engineers evaluate interaction designs in a number of ways, including early design walk-throughs, focus groups, usability inspections, and lab-based usability testing. The primary goal is to find usability problems or flaws in the interaction design.

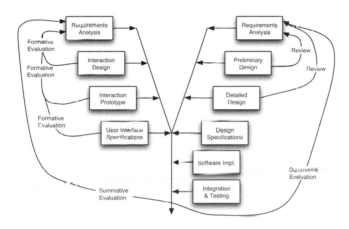

Figure 13.3   Current practices: Process without communication/coordination

Software engineers identify the problem, decompose and represent the problem in the form of requirements (requirements analysis block in Figure 13.2), transform the requirements into design specifications (preliminary and detailed design blocks in Figure 13.2), and then implement those design specifications. In the early days of software engineering, these activities were often performed using the sequential waterfall model (Royce, 1970). Later, these basic activities were incorporated into more iterative processes such as the spiral model (Boehm, 1988) (which has a risk analysis and an evaluation activity at the end of each stage). Even though the more recent SE development life cycles are evolving towards the UE style by anticipating and accommodating changes at each iteration, they still stress iteration on a larger scale and scope. Moreover, testing and validation, which ensures integration accuracy and conformance to system specifications, are performed more towards the end of the development process and can include software for both the functional core and the user interface.

Differences in Terminology. Even though certain terms in both life cycles sound similar they often mean different things. For example:

- In UE, 'testing' is a part of design, and is diagnostic in nature and is used to find and fix problems in the interaction design (identified as formative evaluation in Figure 13.1). In SE 'testing' is an independent stage where the objective is to check the implementation of the system and to validate its conformance to specifications. Analysis and verification of the design specifications performed in SE is often called 'review' (identified in Figure 13.2). When the specifications pass the review stage, they become a binding document between the client and the development team.

- A (use case) scenario in SE (in object oriented design paradigm) is used to "identify a thread of usage for the system to be constructed (and) provide a description of how the system will be used" (Pressman, 2005b). Whereas in UE, a design usage scenario is "a narrative or story that describes the activities of one or more persons, including information about goals, expectations, actions, and reactions (of persons)" (Rosson and Carroll, 2002a).

- The SE group refers to the term 'develop' to mean creating software code, whereas the usability engineers use 'develop' to mean iterate, refine, and improve usability to create an interaction design.

Overall, the software engineers concentrate on the system whereas the usability engineers concentrate on users. Such fundamental difference in focus is one more reason why it is difficult to merge these two life cycles.

Differences in Requirements Representation. Most requirement specifications documented by software engineers use plain English language and are generally very detailed. These specifications are written specifically to drive the SE development process. On the other hand, usability engineers specify interactive component issues such as feedback, screen layout, colors, etc. using artefacts like prototypes, design scenarios, and screen sketches. These artefacts are not detailed enough to derive software design, instead they require additional refinement and reformulation before implementation. Therefore, they cannot be used to directly drive the software development process.

13.3 CURRENT PRACTICES

In spite of the extensive research and maturity levels achieved in the UE and SE life cycle areas, there has been a marked deficiency of understanding between the corresponding developer roles. In general, the two teams do not understand the other's goals and needs and do not have an appreciation for the other's area of expertise (see Chapter 15 by Battle for more on a practical view of the relationship between the two sides of this issue). One apparent reason for this situation is the way computer science courses are typically offered in colleges: SE courses often omit any references to user interface development techniques (Douglas et al., 2002), and UE courses do not discuss the SE implications of usability patterns (Pyla et al., 2004).

Some software life cycles in practice today are documentation intensive and static in nature. The ponderous weight of voluminous static documentation does not allow effective mechanisms to predict or counter the effects of change, especially changes that occur very rapidly in early stages of a life cycle. It can be argued that configuration management processes (Joeris, 1997) that exist in SE are an exception to this. Configuration management tools provide mechanisms and procedures to track changes in the work artefacts generated in a software development life cycle. However, these tools and techniques were mostly developed for SE life cycles; whereas, our work brings some of these principles to the UE side and between the two sides and also incorporates change prediction.

On the other side of the spectrum, many project managers use intensively hands-on-project-management principles wherein a project leader walks around managing and communicating with the various developers in a direct "hands-on" manner taking individual responsibility to make sure all the details are addressed. This approach is based on the potential effectiveness of an informal and low-documentation approach to software development and the fact that a skilled human manager can keep track of what needs to be done better than an automated system. However, this approach does not scale up well as projects get more complex because one person cannot keep track of all the little details and insights about a very large project as it progresses. While intensively hands-on project management can work for some SE life cycles, they are not as suitable for a rapidly evolving and changing life cycle like that of UE, and are even less likely to be effective in communicating all the details of rapid changes between the SE and UE teams.

The general principles and tools of project management (Reifer, 2002) are useful and are well studied in the SE literature. We are aware of their existence and acknowledge their usefulness. However, these tools and principles are mostly about high level issues such as schedules and timelines. Our contribution is more about improving the communication, collaboration, and synchronization of the SE and UE life cycles and thereby increasing the awareness of the specific needs, details and insights for the overall design process. In the process we are hoping to bring some of the advantages of SE life cycle project management to the UE side.

13.3.1   Lack of Coordination of Development Activities

When translated into development activities, this lack of understanding between the two developer roles, combined with an urgency to get their own work done, often leads to working without collaboration (as shown in Figure 13.3), when they could be more efficient and effective communicating and coordinating with one another. For example, both SE and UE roles include field visits to learn about client, customer, and user needs, but they often do this without coordination. Software engineers elicit functional requirements (Pressman, 2005b), and determine the physical properties and operational environments of the system (Lewis, 1992), etc. Usability engineers visit clients and users to determine, often through "ethnographic studies" (Blomberg, 1995), how users work and what computer-based support they need for that work. They seek task information, inputs for usage scenarios, and user class definitions. Why not coordinate this early systems analysis effort? Much value can be derived from cooperative system analysis and requirements gathering. Such joint activities help in team building, communication, and in each life cycle role recognizing the value, and problems, of the other, in addition to early agreement on goals and requirements. Instead, each development group reports its results in documentation not usually seen by people in the other life cycle. Each uses those results to drive only their part of the system design and finally merge at the implementation stage (Figure 13.3), where it is much too late to discover the differences, inconsistencies, and incompatibilities between the two parts of the overall design. Moreover, this lack of coordinated activities presents a disjointed appearance of the development team to the client. It is likely to cause confusion on the clients: "why are we being asked similar questions by two different groups from the same development team?"

Another significant shortcoming of the practice shown in Figure 13.3 is the fact that the independently generated user interface specifications on the UE side and functional design specifications on the SE side are submitted to the development team at implementation stage. However, because these specifications were developed without coordination and communication, when they are now considered together in detail, developers typically discover that the two design parts do not fit with one another because of large differences and incompatibilities.

13.3.2   Lack of Synchronization of Development Schedules

In current practices, the life cycle roles must synchronize the work products eventually for the implementation and testing phases. However, waiting until one absolutely must synchronize obviously creates problems. Therefore, it is better to have many synchronization points, earlier and throughout the development life cycle. These timely synchronization points would allow earlier, more frequent, and less costly 'calibration' to keep both design parts on track for a more harmonious final synchronization with fewer harmful surprises.

However, as shown in Figure 13.3, the more each team works without communication and collaboration, the less likely they will be able to schedule their development activities to arrive simultaneously at common checkpoints.

13.3.3   Lack of Communication Among Different Life Cycle Roles

Although the two life cycle roles can successfully do much of their development independently and in parallel, a successful project demands that the two roles communicate so that each knows generally what the other is doing and how that might affect its own activities and work products. Each group needs to know how the other group's design is progressing, what development activity they are currently performing, what features are being focused on, what insights and concerns they have for the project, and so on. Especially during the early requirements and design activities, each group needs to be 'light on its feet' and able to respond to events and activities occurring in the counterpart life cycle. However, current practices (Figure 13.3) do not permit that necessary communication to take place because the two life cycles operate independently; that is, there is no structured development framework to facilitate communication between these two life cycles.

One might argue that the communication process need not be more formal than it is right now and that the usability and software engineering practitioners should be on the same analysis team. Indeed, in their day-to-day life, the two developers are technically on the same analysis team. But our real world experience has shown that this is not enough to foster the necessary communication (especially about features and changes) because each role still focuses almost completely on their own problems and their own designs. For example, the SE role in general is not concerned about UE role's interaction design and vice versa. So the communication focus is not on being formal, but on being complete. Based on our real world experience, day-to-day communication processes have proven to be inadequate and often result in nasty surprises that are revealed only at the end when serious communication finally does occur. This is often too late in the overall process.

13.3.4   Lack of Constraint Mapping and Dependency Checks

Because each part of an interactive system must operate with the other, many system requirements have both SE and UE components. If SE component or feature is first to be captured, it should trigger (or be mapped to) a reminder that a UE counterpart is needed, and vice versa. When the two roles gather requirements separately and without communication, it is easy to capture requirements that are conflicting, incompatible or one-sided. Even if there is some ad-hoc form of communication between the two groups, it is inevitable that some parts of the requirements or design will be forgotten or will "fall through the cracks."

As an example, software engineers perform a detailed functional analysis from the requirements of the system to be built. Usability engineers perform a hierarchical task analysis, with usage scenarios to guide design for each task, based on their requirements. Documentation of these requirements and designs is maintained separately and not necessarily shared. However, each view of the requirements and design has elements that reflect counterpart elements in the other view. For example, each task in the task analysis can imply the need for corresponding functions in the SE specifications. Similarly, each function in the software design can reflect the need for access to this functionality through one or more user tasks in the user interface. When tasks are missing in the user interface or functions are missing in the software, the respective sets of documentation are inconsistent - a detriment to success of the project.

Constraints, dependencies, and relationships exist not only among activities and work products that cross over between the two life cycles but also within each of the life cycles. For example, on the UE side, a key task identified in task analysis should be considered and matched later for a design scenario and a benchmark task. To our knowledge, there are no life cycle frameworks that help in addressing such internal and external constraints, dependencies, and relationships among life cycle activities.

In general, design choices made in one life cycle constrain the design options in the other. In our consulting experience we often encountered situations where the user interfaces to software systems were designed from a functional point of view and the code was factored to minimize duplication on the backend core. The resulting systems had user interfaces that did not have proper interaction cues to help the user in a smooth task transition. Instead, a task oriented approach would have supported users with screen transitions specific to each task; even though this would have resulted in a possibly "less efficient" composition for the backend. Another case in our consulting experience was about integrating a group of individually designed web-based systems through a single portal. Each of these systems was designed for separate tasks and functionalities. These systems were integrated on the basis of functionality and not on the way the tasks would flow in the new system. The users of this new system had to go through awkward screen transitions when their tasks referenced functions from the different existing systems.

The intricacies and dependencies between user interface requirements and functional core have begun to appear in the literature. For example, in (Bass and John, 2001b), user interface requirements and styles, such as support for undo, are mapped to particular software architectures required for the implementation of such features (see Chapter 6 by Adams, Bass, and John).

Because of the constraints on one another, independent application of the two life cycles (Figure 13.3) is likely to fail. Hence, an integrated design representation framework that facilitates communication and coordination between these two life cycles is essential.

13.3.5   Lack of Provision for Change

In the development of interactive systems, each phase and each iteration has a potential for change. In fact, at least the early part of the UE process is intended to change the design iteratively. This change can manifest itself during the requirements phase (growing and evolving understanding of the emerging system by developers and users), design stage (evaluation identifies that the interaction metaphor was not easily understood by users), etc. Such changes often affect both life cycles because of the various dependencies that exist between and within the two processes. Therefore, change can conceptually be visualized as a design perturbation that has a *ripple* effect on all stages in which previous work has been done. For example, during the usability evaluation, the usability engineer may recognize the need for a new task to be supported by the system. This new task requires updating the previously generated hierarchical task analysis document to reflect the new addition (along with the rationale). This change to the HTA generates the need to change the functional decomposition (by adding new functions to the functional core to support this task on the user interface) on the SE side. These new functions, in turn, mandate a change to the design, schedules, and in some cases even the architecture of the entire system. Thus, one of the most important requirements for system development is to identify the possible implications and effects of each kind of change and to account for them in the design accordingly. Another important requirement is to try to mitigate the impact of change by communicating about changes as early as possible, and by directing that communication directly to the development activities most affected. The more the two developer roles work without a common structure (Figure 13.3) the greater the possibility that inevitable changes in each part will introduce incompatibilities, revealed as "surprises" when they finally do communicate.

13.3.6   Lack of Provision for Accommodating Design and Development Insights

Some dependencies between life cycle parts represent a kind of 'feed-forward', giving insight to later life cycle activities. For example, during the early design stages in the UE life cycle, the usage scenarios provide insights as to how the layout and design of the user interface might look like. In other words, for development phases that are connected to one another (in this case, the initial screen design is dependent on or connected to the usage scenarios), there is a possibility that the designers can forecast or derive insights from a particular design activity. Therefore, as and when the developer encounters such premonitions or potential effects on later stages (on the screen design in this example), there is a need to document them when the process is still in the initial stages (usage scenario phase). This way, when the developer reaches the initial screen design stage, the previously documented insights are readily available to aid the screen design activity. To our knowledge, none of the current approaches to the development of systems with interactive components provide this capability.

13.4   RIPPLE: A DESIGN REPRESENTATION FRAMEWORK

Ripple, a work-in-progress research effort, is a design representation framework that draws concepts from graph theory (relations), analogies from physics (perturbations and ripples), and of course, content from SE and UE. Ripple provides mechanisms for the two development roles to communicate, collaborate, and synchronize with one another, while allowing each life cycle role to function independently. Ripple provides each developer role with activity awareness, information about changes and insights from the developer's own life cycle and from the other development life cycle. It uses a common design representation, which includes an aggregation of the work artefacts from each development life cycle, and the semantics of various constraints, dependencies and relationships between and within the two life cycles. Ripple addresses changes and design perturbations using messages that can be passed along (ripples) among developer roles. Ripple can be implemented within a database-centered tool using database triggers to recognize events associated with constraints and dependencies and to respond by sending various types of messages to the appropriate developers.

In this section we provide a high level description of Ripple, our design representation framework. Ripple embraces:

- the *definition* of the stages and associated activities and work products from each life cycle in the integrated development effort;

- the *definition* of dependencies, constraints, relationships;

- the triggers and messages for *enforcement* of constraints and dependencies between and within the two development life cycles; and

■   the *implementation* of a constraint-based, database-centered tool that works within this framework to support the concepts in the above bullets.

13.4.1   Constraint-based Database-centered Framework

Ripple is a constraint-based framework that supports the complementary existence of the SE and UE development roles. A constraint is a "relation that must be maintained" (Borning and Duisberg, 1986). Such relations are generally enforced by "delegating to the constraints solver the task to satisfy them automatically" (Kwaiter et al., 1998). In other words, a constraint-based system is one that automatically updates a predefined set of relations and dependencies between different entities when a change occurs in one or more of such entities. Constraint-based systems were traditionally used to specify declaratively the relative layout of interface objects according to pre-specified rules (Szekely and Myers, 1988). Some of the other important applications for constraint-based systems include:

■   specification of relations (constraints) among the user interface objects that should be maintained upon resizing a given UI window (Mugridge et al., 1996; Chok and Marriott, 1995),

■   visual representation of simulation algorithms (Ege, 1988),

■   automatic updating of (to make consistent) multiple views representing the same data when the objects in one of the views is changed (Borning and Duisberg, 1986), and

■   triggering of events based on changes made to objects in a dataset (Bharat and Hudson, 1995).

It is this last application of constraint-based systems that we focus on. Conceptually, this framework represents the various products of the shared design process in a single database with each of the SE and UE roles having two separate views to this single dataset. When any life cycle role changes or updates the database through their corresponding view, the system automatically triggers update messages or design reminders to all related or connected phases of the integrated development process. Such reminders or updates are propagated in our framework using *messages*.

13.4.2   Constraints and Dependencies Among Related Activities

When a new insight is gained into the system being development, or when something changes in either of the two life cycles, or when the developer roles needs to communicate with one another, the system triggers a message of a particular type to the related and connected phases of the design representation framework. Also, it should be noted that, constraints and relationships exist among activities and work products within each of the life cycles as well as those that cross over between the two life cycles. An example of such a relationship on the UE side is when a key task is identified in task analysis, that task should be flagged for consideration for a design scenario and a benchmark task later in the life cycle.

13.4.3   Messages and Triggering Agents

Messages are the communication and synchronization agents in Ripple. They convey the ripple effects of change, design insights, notes, and observations made during a particular development activity on future design stages. The five types of messages are discussed below:

For Your Information Message.   This type of message informs the software engineers and usability engineers about the completion of a particular activity or phase in the life cycle and shows the link where the relevant products of this development stage are located. The developers in the other life cycle or developers at a different stage of the project (within the same life cycle) can use this link to view the product (artefacts). This message is generally used when the type of communication is purely informational and no corresponding action is necessarily required. For example, when the usability engineers complete the initial screen layouts or the derivation of the conceptual metaphor for the interaction design, they can send this type of message to the software engineers to peruse. Another example for this type of a message is when the usability engineer informs the software engineer about the completion of the screen design so that the user interface can be implemented by the functional core developers pending the summative evaluation.

Synchronize Activity Message.   This type of message informs about the need for a joint activity by both the SE and UE roles. In other words, this message addresses the synchronization need for activities that require a combined presence of the two developer roles. For example, when the usability engineers plan an evaluation session, they can send this type of message to the software engineers to request them to be present (to help argue the case for required changes in the user interface when the SE role sees the users having problems). Similarly, early systems analysis and ethnographic study activities that require joint presence can be arranged using this kind of message (to help identify the broader constraints of the project and get the overall context).

Consistency Check Message.   This type of message is used to enforce the consistency of data objects in the database. This message informs the developers of the need to perform a consistency check on the two development roles' products. For example, when the software and the usability engineers complete the hierarchical task analysis and the functional decomposition, respectively, there is a need for a consistency check to see that every task in the HTA has a function or set of functions in the SE specifications, and vice-versa. In the object oriented development paradigm, this type of message can be initiated after the use case specifications phase in the SE life cycle or the usage scenario descriptions in the UE life cycle. Since these two stages of development concentrate on two aspects of the same issue: interaction between the system and user, there is a need to ensure that they are consistent. Another important example for the need for consistency is after the usability specifications phase in the UE life cycle and functional requirements in the SE life cycle. A consistency check message is required here to initiate an analysis that ensures that these specifications are supportable by the functional core (and to discuss alternatives if not supportable or negotiate for middle ground). This type of a message is used to enforce such mandatory consistency checks.

Change Request Message.   This type of message is used to inform the two developer roles of changes made in one part of the design and the potential effects of that change in that and other parts of the design. This is perhaps the most useful message in the development of interactive systems because of the potential for constant and frequent changes in the products during the development life cycles. As an example, this message can be used when a new task is identified by the UE role, and that new addition should be communicated to other development activities within the UE role and to the SE role. Upon the receipt of the message by the SE role, efforts can be made to incorporate the necessary functions in the functional specifications to support the corresponding task. These updates in the functional specifications, in turn, can trigger changes in various dependent stages' products in the integrated life cycle.

Response to a Change Request Message.   A response to a change request message is sent by developers to acknowledge a change request message. Because the control of decisions to make changes or not ultimately resides with the developer roles, one possible response to change could be 'change request considered fully, but declined' with an explanation or note, for the record, saying why the request was declined.

Change-in-response-to-change Message.   The need for this kind of message is to avoid endless loops of messages due to cycles in the graph of relations. Suppose a relation 'R' exists from function A to B ($A \xrightarrow{R} B$). For example, if A is task analysis in UE and B is functional decomposition in SE, then R is a relation meaning that changes in task analysis (A) require related changes to be considered in functional decomposition (B). The relation R is expressed as a message that is sent whenever a change occurs in A, informing the developer role in charge of B to consider changing B accordingly. These dependency relations are often symmetric (i.e. changes in functional decomposition also require consideration of changes if task analysis), so that a development process could have both $A \xrightarrow{R} B$ and $B \xrightarrow{R} A$ among its dependencies. This could lead to endless loops; a change in A triggers a change in B, which in turn triggers a change in A, and so on. To break these cycles we introduce a new message type called the 'change-in-response-to-change' message. A change made in B due to a change request message from A would return a change-in-response-to-change message that would not require further changes in A.

Design Reminders.   Design reminders are a type of message used to record design reminders for future development stages. This type of message could be used as a reminder to handle something later (such as a feature that has been temporarily stubbed in the current activity, say, in the prototype stage), where there is no time presently to consider it. For example, while developing a calendar management system the developers may "hard wire" the alarm feature to go off 10 minutes before each appointment, but want a reminder to fix the design later by allowing the user to set the lead time for the alarm.

Framework generated messages are formalized in terms of the life cycle activities of both the development processes and the communication/dependency relationships identified. The database implementation of our framework will automatically generate the consistency and change messages.

In addition to messages automatically generated by Ripple due to pre-defined constraints, messages can be sent by developers for design reminders and 'for your information' purposes. For example, the developers can specify when they would like to send a "for your information" message to the other groups. Developers can send a "for your information" message to the other developer role to let them know work is being done on a certain part of the design, even though the current state of work is not ready for sharing yet. On the other hand, if they come across new insights or new additions to the project, they can send a change request message.

13.4.4   The Ripple Framework

Consider the following schematic (Figure 13.4) in which the two development processes are shown, simplified as three stages in the life cycles: 1, 2, and 3 for UE stages and A, B, and C for SE stages. The messages from each phase are labeled using the $<$development stage ID$>_{<messagecounter>}$. The different types of communication or dependency relations are marked using different line widths and styles.

In the example shown in Figure 13.4, the UE cycle triggers three messages in stage one: $M1_1$, $M1_2$, and $M1_3$. Similarly, SE cycle triggers MA_1 and MA_2 and so on.

A developer using Ripple to work on a particular life cycle stage, will have a list of waiting messages from other phases in the SE and UE cycles. These waiting lists are shown on the far right and left sides of the figure as 'message queues' at each phase. These messages can be reminders from previous stages or constraints or change effects from other stages. Depending on the type of message, the developer responds accordingly.

When developers make changes to existing documents in the design repository, those changes, in turn, trigger ripples of new messages. The history of ripple messages can support traceability of changes in the overall framework, and includes a rationale for the change and details of who initiated the change and when.

Ripple uses a 'score card' approach to list the status of each phase of the development life cycle, showing which stages are bottlenecks and which stages need the most attention.

13.5   CONTRIBUTIONS

13.5.1   Activity Awareness and Life Cycle Independence

Using Ripple (Figure 13.5), each developer role has significant insights into their own and the other's life cycle status, activities, the iteration of activities, the timeline, techniques employed or yet to be employed, the artefacts generated or yet to be generated, and the mappings between the two life cycles if present. The view of each role shows

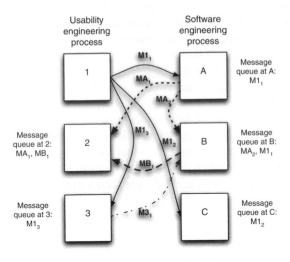

Figure 13.4   Message passing and accumulation in the integrated process framework

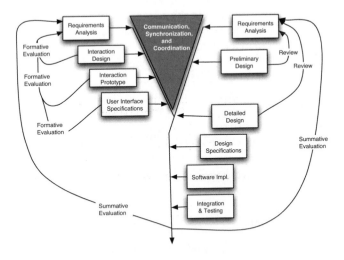

Figure 13.5   Ripple: Framework with communication/coordination

only those activities that are relevant to that role. Each role views the shared design representation through its own filters (Figure 13.6). For example, the software engineers see only the software implications that result from the previously mentioned iterativeness in UE, but not the techniques used or the procedure followed. Similarly, if software engineers need iteration to try out different algorithms for functionality, it would not affect the usability life cycle. Therefore, the process of iteration is shielded from the other role, only functionality changes are viewable through the UE filter. Each role can also contribute to its own part of the life cycle; Ripple allows each role to see a single set of design results, but through its own filter. Ripple emphasizes the placement of these connections and communication more on product design and less on development activities. This type of 'filter' acts as a layer of insulation, between the two processes, i.e. Ripple helps isolate the parts of the development processes for one role that are not a concern for the other role. This insulation needs to be concrete enough to serve the purposes, but not over specified so as to restrict the software design that will implement the user interface functionality. This prevents debates and needless concerns emanating from the use of specialized techniques. Because Ripple does not merge, but coordinates, the two development processes, life cycle roles from one process need not know the language, terminology, and techniques of the other, and therefore can function pseudo-independently.

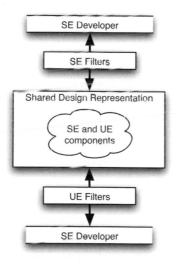

Figure 13.6   Shared design representation

13.5.2   User Interface and Functional Core Communication Layer

Ripple advocates the need for the two life cycle roles to specify a common communication layer between the user interface and the functional core parts. This layer is similar to the specification of the communication between the model and the other two parts (view and controller) in the 'model view controller' (MVC) architecture (Krasner and Pope, 1988). This communication layer describes the semantics and the constraints of each life cycle's parts. For example, the usability engineer can specify that an undo operation should be supported at a particular part of the user interface, and that in the event of an undo operation being invoked by the user, a predetermined set of actions must be performed by the functional core. This type of communication layer specification will be recorded by our design representation framework, and allows the software engineers to proceed with the design by choosing a software architecture that supports the undo operation (Bass and John, 2001b). How the undo operation is shown on the user interface does not affect the SE activities. This type of early specification of a common communication layer by the two life cycles minimizes the possibility of change on the two life cycle activities. However, this common communication layer specification can be difficult to specify and might change with every iteration. These changes should be made and take into account the implications that such a change will have on the already completed activities, and/or the ones planned for the future.

13.5.3   Coordination of Life Cycle Activities

Ripple coordinates schedules and specifies the various activities that have commonalities within the two life cycle processes. For such activities, Ripple indicates where and when those activities should be performed, who the involved stakeholders are, and communicates this information to the two groups. For example, if the schedule says it is time for usability engineers to visit the clients/users for ethnographic analysis, Ripple automatically alerts the software engineers and prompts them to consider joining the usability team and to coordinate the SE's user related activities such as requirements analysis, etc.

13.5.4   Communication Between Development Roles

Another important contribution of Ripple is the facilitation of communication between the two roles. Communication between the two roles takes place at different levels during the development life cycle. The three main levels in any development effort are: requirements analysis, architecture analysis, and design analysis. Each of these stages results in a set of different artefacts based on the life cycle. Ripple has the functionality to communicate (using messages) these requirements between the two life cycles. For example, at the end of UE task analysis the usability group enters the task specifications into the design representation framework and the SE group can view these specifications to guide their functional decomposition activities. At the end of such an activity, the SE group enters their functional specifications into Ripple for the usability people to cross check. This communication also helps in minimizing the effects of change and the costs to fix these changes. By communicating the documents at the end of each stage, the potential for identifying errors or incompatibilities early in the process increases compared to waiting till the usability specifications stage. This early detection of mismatches is important because the cost to fix an error in the requirements that is detected in the requirements stage itself is typically four times less than fixing it in the integration phase and 100 times less than fixing it in the maintenance stage (Boehm, 1981).

13.5.5   Constraints, Dependencies and Provision for Change

Ripple incorporates automatic mapping features, which will map the SE and UE part of the overall design based on their dependencies on each other. Recall the example of the many-to-many mapping between the tasks on the user interface side, the functions on the functional side, and how Ripple will automatically alert the software group about the missing function(s) and vice versa. So, when the software engineer tries to view the latest task addition, a description that clearly specifies what the task does and what the function should do to make that task possible, is provided. This way the developers can check the dependencies at regular time intervals to see that all the tasks have functions and vice versa. It also helps ensure that there are no 'dangling' tasks or functions that turn up as surprises when the two roles finally do get together.

13.6   POTENTIAL DOWNSIDES OF RIPPLE

Ripple has the following downsides due to the various overheads and additional tasks that arise because of the coordination of the two life cycles:

- Increase in the overall software development life cycle;

- Additional effort required by the roles in each life cycle for document creation and entry into the design representation framework;

- Additional effort required for coordination of various activities and schedules;

- Need for stricter verification process than conventional processes to enforce the various synchronization checkpoints during the development effort; and

- Resource overhead to carry out all the above mentioned drawbacks.

13.7   CURRENT STATUS

Ripple is a work-in-progress. We have currently identified many different dependencies and constraints within the UE life cycle. We will do a similar mapping on the SE life cycle and then on an integrated framework. We are currently working toward representing the products of a development effort in a database system. We have yet to implement the triggers and constraints. We also intend to test the framework using a project in simulated real life settings. We plan to do this by offering the SE and UE courses in an academic semester and having half the teams use the current practices and the other half use our framework.

Acknowledgements

The authors would like to thank the reviewers and editors for their insightful comments and feedback. This feedback helped us address some of the issues we overlooked in our early versions of this chapter.

V UCD Knowledge and UI design Patterns

14 INTEGRATING USER-CENTERED DESIGN KNOWLEDGE WITH SCENARIOS

Steven R. Haynes, John M. Carroll, Mary Beth Rosson

School of Information Sciences and Technology,
The Pennsylvania State University

Abstract

This chapter explores issues related to integration, management, and use of multi-disciplinary, user-centered system design knowledge. A pressing need exists for theory, techniques, and tools for management of the knowledge emergent in complex system development efforts. Challenges to effective system design knowledge management are many, and span the range of engineering, psychological, and social sciences. We need repositories and other points of exchange for system design knowledge, and conceptual catalysts to support value-added integration of the results from multi-disciplinary, user-centered design research and practice. This chapter outlines a research program for design knowledge management based on the use of *scenarios* as anchors for design rationale, and on the importance of interaction activity design as a means to make this knowledge accessible. We describe an example of how the approach is being applied and report on our on-going projects in the area.

14.1 INTRODUCTION

An increasingly large proportion of society's intellectual activity is directed at the design of software-intensive systems. On a typical implementation project, software developers, domain subject matter experts, and prospective system users combine forces

269

A. Seffah (eds.), Human-Centered Software Engineering – Integrating Usability
in the Development Process, 269–286.
© 2005 *Springer. Printed in the Netherlands.*

to determine requirements and create system designs to reflect their stance towards work or other activity in a target domain. In the process they bring to the surface, albeit too briefly, a wealth of domain, task, user, and technology knowledge, and carefully consider how this knowledge should be reified in software data structures, algorithms, objects, interfaces (both system and human-computer), and supporting material such as documentation, training, and help facilities.

The artefacts that emerge from most system development projects are, however, an incomplete representation of the knowledge applied to their creation. Much of the complete design space, the software engineering, human-computer interaction, domain knowledge, and contextual detail including the full range of use scenarios, design questions, solution alternatives, and a variety of design constraints, is lost to future developers, and even to the developers who first generated the knowledge. More effective capture and management of user-centered system design knowledge and more fully realizing its value are the focus of this chapter.

The value embedded in design is more than metaphorical, information technologies now account for 3.3% of gross domestic product in the United States, a doubling since 1991, with software systems now providing over half this contribution (Mandel, 2002). What the GDP statistic does not measure however is the value of the knowledge and experience generated in the design and production of these technologies, though researchers and practitioners increasingly recognize the importance of more effectively capturing and exploiting the lessons learned from information technology research and development activities (Baskerville and Pries-Heje, 1999; Kautz and Thaysen, 2001). Of particular importance is the especially ephemeral knowledge emergent when designers and users work in concert to envision how a new technology, such as an information system, will support and improve performance of complex activities *in context*.

Accumulated principles of design may be especially important in software systems where the forces that guide and constrain design are not apparent to the end user. These principles emerge from and are applied in the interaction of designers with their tools and materials. The causal chain represented in this interaction leads to the form the artefact finally takes, but is invisible to those who use it. Casaday (Casaday, 1996) argues that to effectively evaluate systems, something must be "offered up", made visible in order to evoke meaningful feedback. By making apparent the rationale underlying the structure and behavior of the tools they employ, system users are empowered to provide meaningful feedback on the design and to guide the design's evolution to better fit their work context.

14.2   WHAT'S IN DESIGN?

Many say we are living in the age of the knowledge economy (Webber, 1993), suggesting that knowledge is a good that can be traded and that value in this economy is a function of the quantity, quality, and utility of the knowledge that is exchanged between traders in a market. Implicit in this view is that knowledge is something that can be identified, measured, and transferred, but this view may be deeply problematic for a number of reasons. Measuring or even estimating the value of knowledge is notoriously difficult (Armour, 2004; Glazer, 1998; Stewart et al., 2000). Different market goods can have either or both high value in exchange (e.g., diamonds) or high value in use (e.g., water), with the latter perspective suggesting that the value of knowledge is highly dependent on how the knowledge is used in context. The implication of these views is that regardless of which perspective is taken, knowledge that is never exchanged or that is never used is essentially valueless. While knowledge management is acknowledged as an important strategy for firms to capitalize on the intellectual assets they possess, clear conceptions on the nature of knowledge, and solution strategies for proving IT support for knowledge management all remain relatively under specified (Hahn and Subramani, 2000).

Attempts to develop a useful definition for the concept knowledge are legion yet little consensus exists as to its exact formulation. One approach to conceptualizing knowledge is as part of a hierarchy that also includes data, information, and, sometimes, wisdom (Ackoff, 1989). These four concepts are considered to exist in a pyramid extending with increasing utility and value from data, to information, to knowledge and on through to wisdom. Data are the elemental symbols in the system and have no meaning on their own, for example, the points on a graph. Information is data coupled in an attribute-value form that gives meaning to the embedded data, the points on a graph combined with axes, labels, and a legend. Understanding what the graph means and how to use it in some effective activity is knowledge. WISDOM obtains when this knowledge is considered in the light of experience with using graphs, and the successes and failures that resulted from applying their knowledge in different scenarios and contexts.

The graph-building example suggests that knowledge (and wisdom) result from additive functions performed on data and information. As symbols are combined with others to form attribute-values and then with meaning and experience they become more useful and presumably more valuable. Moreover, the addition is heterogeneous in that the knowledge combined emerges from consideration of design criteria from a range of topic areas including the mathematics underlying the graph form, the cognitive ergonomics underlying how best to represent the graph data, and the domain context supplying the graph with significance relative to an activity such as planning or evaluation.

14.2.1 System Design Knowledge is Inscribed

Complex information technologies and especially computer-based software applications embed significant value over and above that which is apparent in the artefact. Several theoretical positions of technology design and use suggest that designers and developers *inscribe* knowledge into artefacts, knowledge that extends far beyond the engineering know-how required to build them (Bowker and Leigh-Star, 1994; Hutchins, 1995a; Latour and Woolgar, 1986). This inscribed knowledge consists of patterns of human activity that can be predicted as stable within a domain, along with the intent of the designers and design initiators and the constraints imposed by a myriad of sources from standards bodies to development tool vendors to the demeanor of a design team at the time of a particular design decision.

Conceptualizations such as Actor-Network Theory (Akrich, 1992; Latour, 1991) suggest that technologies and systems are actors in knowledge networks of humans and non-humans and that non-humans are inscribed by their designers with motives, aspirations, and prejudices, among other attributes, that represent an intention or prediction related to how they will be used in context. Through these inscriptions designers essentially delegate responsibility for ensuring that scenarios of use are flexibly supported in different contexts. In Latour's view, these inscriptions for action can be weaker or stronger depending on the domain and the desired balance of explicit protocol support versus flexible interpretation by individual users (human actors). For example, the strength of the inscriptions in a system to operate a weapons system are likely to be greater than those for one supporting computer-mediated communication because of the need for accuracy and safety in the former versus flexible support for human social processes in the latter.

In a similar vein, distributed cognition (DCog) is a perspective on work practice that attempts to account for the interplay between the cognitive capacities of individual actors, their tools and other artefacts, and the active environment in which tools are used (Hutchins, 1995a; Hutchins, 1995b). Distributed cognition considers the primary level of analysis to be systems that are made up of people, technology, and these other artefacts. The DCog perspective posits that the "representational states" of different nodes in the system, and the inter-nodal communicative activities (dialogue, gesture, digital and analog information transfer) that cause these states to be transformed, are the nexus of knowledge and intelligent information processing (Rogers and Ellis, 1994).

Hutchins (Hutchins, 1995b) provides perhaps the most complete explication of the role of inscribed knowledge. In his study of the aircraft landing task, he describes how determination of appropriate landing speeds for different aircraft configurations is precomputed and represented in the aircraft cockpit as a book of tables. Pilots combine the knowledge inscribed in these tables along with readings from appropriate gauges, for example, speed and landing weight, in a simple look-up task which replaces what would otherwise be time-consuming, cognitively demanding, and knowledge intensive sequence of steps. The landing speed tables combine knowledge of aircraft structure and behavior, axioms of aeronautics, and data on the effects of environmental factors (e.g., wind) into an accessible and easy to use knowledge base. Tools may therefore be conceived of as embodying a theory of how different factors mediate the activities performed as humans interact with them.

Information technologies have been described as representing "frozen organizational discourse" (Bowker and Leigh-Star, 1994), a stance towards activity in some domain, which embodies current thinking about the best way to work in the domain. Of course not all of this knowledge is explicit in these inscriptions and software-based information systems, with their lack of physical structure and other cues to help understand their design, are even more difficult to comprehend *prima facie* with respect to the design space from which they emerged. This embedded knowledge receives little attention from its owners. Among the reasons for this are its embeddedness and its invisibility, and, importantly, a relative lack of success stories from use that can be evoked to highlight the benefits derived from extracting and exploiting this knowledge.

14.2.2   System Design Knowledge is Invisible

A major barrier to understanding and effective use of software-intensive systems is the invisibility of the underlying structure of these systems relative to the functions that they perform. Users and other stakeholders of a system do not necessarily understand the process by which these abstract systems are derived from the concrete use contexts they do understand and that make up the domain in which the system is intended for use. Scenarios of use (Carroll, 1995; Carroll, 2000; Carroll and Rosson, 1992) act as a starting point for system design, but as analysis, design, and construction progresses the design that evolves to realize these requirements is molded and distorted by a diverse array of factors including the material constraints of hardware and software performance, the psychological constraints of cognition, organizational constraints of time and other resources, and social constraints imposed by standards bodies and accepted professional best practice. This disjunction, Norman (Norman and Draper, 1986) has called it the "gulf of understanding", that exists between the system's (really, the designer's) understanding of the use context and the understanding by users and other stakeholders of how the system fits this context is one of the key challenges to design knowledge management.

Clancey (Clancey, 1983) developed a conceptual framework to help understand the nature of the knowledge inscribed into systems, in particular into knowledge-based systems. This framework consist of three categories of knowledge: *strategic, structural,* and *support.* Strategic knowledge consists of the methods and high-level problem-solving approaches underlying the behavioral aspects of the system. This behavioral dimension consists of high-level flows, data transformations, aspects, methods, and algorithms that represent the heuristic knowledge embedded in software engineering designs. A good user-interface design exposes some of this strategy in the way that it represents navigation through a task, for example, but the abstraction and indirection inherent in even the best designs means that though exposed, domain strategies are often opaque to system users.

Structural knowledge refers to information embedded in the static design underlying the foundation of a system. In Clancey's examples these are the rule hierarchies and orderings in a production system but conceptually the idea applies just as well to the design of an object-oriented analysis model, or to the entity-relationship structure of a database schema. Extracting the rationale implicit in a system's structural design is crucial to understanding the mental model underlying a design (Wenger, 1987). Structural knowledge acts as the bridge between the abstract, generic problem solving and representational entities identified at the *strategic* level, and the domain-specific engineering hypotheses, objectives, and rules in a particular application.

This engineering knowledge inscribed into system structure may be especially important for supporting conceptual understanding of a system. In an empirical study of structural knowledge, for example, Lamberti and Wallace (Lamberti and Wallace, 1990) examined the relationship between the level of task uncertainty, the proficiency of the user (expert or novice), and the nature of the explanation content provided to system users. They found that access to this structural knowledge supported both experts and novices as they attempted to form mental linkages and relationships between the elements of a given problem domain as represented in the system design.

By *support* knowledge, Clancey was referring to the low-level, detailed information that was used to relate a design element to an underlying causal process in the world, the facts that justify the existence of the given design element. Support knowledge is used to connect strategic and structural properties in a design to observed phenomena and empirically supported generalizations in the problem domain. Support knowledge is further sub-divided into four types of justifications: identification, causal mechanism, world fact, and domain fact. Identification knowledge is used to classify an entity or event, to show that an entity or event is an instance of a given concept or has properties that relate it to a concept. Causal mechanism knowledge refers to facts and arguments that may be linked together to demonstrate the mechanistic structure of a domain or sub-domain. These causal links may be well understood or may be only suggested by empirical evidence in the domain. World fact knowledge is characterized as "common sense" knowledge about the world. Included in this category is what Clancey calls "social patterns of behavior". His example describes an army recruit, whose living conditions in close proximity to others puts him at increased risk of a given disease (the example domain is diagnosis of infectious disease). The final category of knowledge used in the justification of a rule is domain facts, which are well-established heuristics that help with problem solving in a particular domain, for example, to have been administered adequately, a drug must be detectable in the body at a certain concentration.

Clancey described the missing link between the high-level strategies and the domain-specific facts as *focusing principles*. These focusing principles, which he felt could take the form of an argument or a justification, were thought to be crucial in attempting to teach novices in a domain since they connected ambiguous, high-level, problem-solving strategies with the facts of a single system use scenario. He argued that an important aid to making these links was the causal chain behind the phenomenon to be explained, how it describes the knowledge roles that particular pieces of information play in system comprehension, and how certain these pieces of information are combined to help make sense of system entity or an event. The existence of underlying causal forces, and our ability to connect explanatory facts to these forces, are key components in the process of understanding the knowledge embedded in a design of interest.

14.2.3   Evoking and Integrating with Design Rationale

A number of challenges attenuate efforts to more effectively manage design knowledge from systems development projects. Software systems are inherently complex, and the source or rationale for this complexity is largely invisible to all but those with intimate knowledge of how different factors interacted to realize a design (Brooks, 1987). Devanbu and colleagues (Devanbu et al., 1991) argue that especially on larger projects, the interaction between complexity and invisibility combined with inevitable personnel turnover eventually results in a critical dissipation of the knowledge a development team may initially possess. As a system evolves through enhancements and repairs, the knowledge underlying the original architectural model further dissipates from its original, assumedly coherent and known design basis. In the use context, the problem's scope is multiplied as project stakeholders such as users, managers, and system support staff attempt, in the system maintenance and use contexts, to understand how the design relates to the task domain. Because the system architectural model is essentially invisible, efforts to establish or re-establish the level of comprehension once possessed by the original architects are faced with potentially intractable problems of knowledge reconstruction (Brooks, 1987).

Much of the knowledge surfaced in the software-intensive systems design process, for example, in design meetings, in conversation and e-mail, and by designers and developers working independently, is not captured for use and later reuse. Information captured about the decisions made in systems design typically consists of only the course-of-action decided, not the rich knowledge content emerging from the individual and group deliberations that led to the decision. This body of information has been described as a *design space* (MacLean et al., 1996) and the tools and techniques developed to help capture, represent, and use this information are part of an approach to design known as *design rationale* (Moran and Carroll, 1996). A design space represents an organization's stance or posture towards some problem domain. As a design team 'moves' through a design space they surface a wealth of knowledge to resolve emerging design questions. Capturing the full breadth and depth of a design space and effectively using and reusing this knowledge promises a number of benefits, but realizing these benefits poses significant scientific and engineering challenges.

Design rationales represent a base of knowledge about the domain and tasks for which the artefact is intended, its purpose; the physical, natural, psychological, organizational, social, and other constraints that were seen by the design team as most important to design option selection; and about the pragmatic, bounded-rationality of the design process itself. Though design rationale formalisms and tools often embed prescriptive or normative guidelines for how the design process should proceed, their importance to the knowledge management goal is that they show what did happen, regardless of whether decisions were appropriate or correct. Later reflection on a complete design space may allow for these evaluations and judgments, but their power in the knowledge management context is that they are available to be reflected upon.

Designs always include structure, the assemblies of sub-systems, components, and raw materials that interact to deliver behaviors or capabilities (Jeffries et al., 1981; Leveson, 2000). The precise form of the behaviors and structure that emerge from a design effort are a result of decisions, and other cognitive and social processes, carried out in the course of trying to provide the highest quality solution, or most satisficing resolution (Arias et al., 2000) that meets the intention underlying the design effort. Design moves necessarily involve retrieving, generating, and organizing data and information into operationalized problem solving knowledge. A significant proportion of the effort invested in a systems design effort is dedicated to co-construction of this design knowledge as team members and project stakeholders seek to maintain a common understanding of the evolving design (Curtis et al., 1988).

Fischer (Fischer, 1999) has argued that design rationale and related approaches can support closer integration of system producers and consumers and, ideally, evolve consumers (users and other stakeholders) into system producers. This closer integration of producers and consumers may also result in more complete rationale capture, to include the consumers' domain-oriented input to the design deliberations. Fischer's work incorporates a social model where producers and consumers of the IS product work together closely towards system evolution, creating in essence a representation of the principles underlying a community of practice. The critical knowledge needed to understand a system relative to its application domain is often concentrated in the minds of one or two exceptional system architects (Curtis et al., 1988), and more general studies of organizational competence suggest a significant trend towards the control by expert knowledge workers of the critical information assets of the organizations that they serve (Albert and Bradley, 1997). To surface and leverage these knowledge assets more broadly across the span of stakeholders, including system users, organizations require well-defined approaches and facilitating tools to capture both system knowledge and knowledge of the domains of user activity supported by these technologies.

14.3   AN INTEGRATIVE EXAMPLE

An example helps to illustrate the range of different knowledge brought to bear in development of a complex system and how it is inscribed in the process of design. Since spring of 2002, the first author has been working with the United States Marine Corps (USMC) on the analysis, design, and development of a cognitive aid to support decision making in the domain of defensive anti-terrorism (AT) resource allocation (Haynes et al., 2005). The basic requirement is to provide Marine and Navy officers and civilian engineers with a decision model and software system for allocating constrained funds to the most important and deserving AT mitigation projects. The projects span the range of those defensive building construction and augmentation mitigations that can help to lessen the effects of car and truck bomb and other attacks on service facilities. Mitigations can include window coatings and other glazing enhancements, various wall hardening techniques, vehicle stand-off barriers, fences, and so on. The basic decision model includes three central activities: prioritizing facilities, for example, a headquarters building versus an airfield versus base family housing; determination of mitigation project utility, deriving a value to represent the protective benefit of different mitigations relative to their cost; and identifying the set of projects to be selected based priority and utility subject to the AT budget constraint.

The project has involved marshaling an array of knowledge and incorporating it into the system design. First and foremost is ensuring the usability of the system realized to support the requirement. From early in the project is became clear that one of the key trade-offs would be resolving the tension between providing the most accurate results from the allocation process, and building a system for a user population with diverse backgrounds and different training and ease-of-use requirements. Resource allocation models become more complex and laborious to use as they are engineered to be more accurate. Parameter data requirements especially become more demanding, which necessitates both more data entry by the user and more integration with source systems to provide this information. The latter issue introduces its own set of design trade-offs and knowledge requirements. More data entry decreases usability and user satisfaction, especially when the data exists in other systems, but building interfaces between systems is costly and time consuming, increases complexity, and weakens system reliability.

Design and development of the system has involved interacting with about 100 different people – including Marine commanders, anti-terrorism officers, military police, Navy civil engineers, civilian engineers and facilities planners, among others – to determine requirements and then to assess increasingly more complete designs and prototypes. At each of these reviews additional knowledge was collected, interpreted, translated into design (including design of training and help facilities), and then inscribed into the system. We regularly give demonstrations of the system and we are using it as a test-bed apparatus for research into the usability and performance support requirements for cognitive aids to AT decision making. In these contexts we are regularly asked *why* a particular feature exists, *why* it has been implemented a certain way, and *why* it has the particular user interface characteristics that it does. At this point, two years into the project, these questions are often difficult to answer with real fidelity, even by core members of the design team.

The system has been implemented as a set of discrete web services each of which implements either a component of the decision model, a significant user interface function such as sensitivity analysis, or a necessary administrative feature. The rationale behind using the web services approach for development included our desire to ensure that each major unit of functionality could be reused or re-purposed in related domains. For example, prioritization of alternatives is an element of many decision problems and we hope to use the web service developed for AT in other projects. To effectively reuse or re-purpose the service requires knowledge of how it works and why it works the way that it does. Future users of the service may also want to know which other approaches to prioritization we considered, and why we chose the one (actually, two) that we did. As it stands now this knowledge exists but is distributed in elements of the system itself, in the help and training system content, in design documentation, in notes from field research, in digital recordings of design reviews and cognitive walkthroughs, and in the minds of different members of the design team. This situation is not uncharacteristic of the complex systems design process but is problematic nonetheless and is emblematic of the issues addressed throughout this chapter and is the target of the research agenda discussed in the section that follows.

14.4   A DESIGN KNOWLEDGE RESEARCH AGENDA

This discussion so far suggests that system design knowledge is characterized by its multi-disciplinary nature, by its embeddedness, and by its invisibility in the artefacts where it is inscribed. Design rationale is one potential approach to evoking and integrating this knowledge, but significant challenges confront both researchers and practitioners who attempt to apply its methods. Our work in this area is focused on developing software tools and content to support large-scale studies of design knowledge ecologies. We are particularly interested in identifying and understanding the causal and mediating factors that lead from a design's inception to the artefact in its context of use, its design rationale. The number, range, and intractability of many of these factors presents a substantial challenge to researchers in systems design. Our belief is that the development of a system design knowledge management infrastructure, and evolving communities of practice around its use, will lead to and facilitate more integrative studies to inform and extend current theory.

14.4.1   Nurturing Design Knowledge Communities

Knowledge only exists, can only be measured, and only has value to the extent that it is used (Glazer, 1998). Knowledge has been described as existing only in the interaction between individuals and social systems and evolving only as it is translated between its tacit and explicit forms (Nonaka, 1994). Providing support for collaborative communities of interest and practice is a critical dimension of next generation design knowledge management systems and design knowledge management research (Poltrock et al., 2003). A necessary step in development of the multi-disciplinary design knowledge management field is fostering recognition and appreciation for the value of design knowledge. We need communities of interested, practicing design knowledge management researchers to make progress on the difficult problems inherent in multi-disciplinary, socio-technical design.

Glazer (Glazer, 1998) argues that unlike many commodities, knowledge creation is a "self-regenerative" process. New knowledge creates demand and opportunities for added value in use as well as for the creation of additional new knowledge. Critical mass has been elsewhere identified as one of the key factors in the use of collaborative technologies within communities of interest and practice (Grudin, 1988). One of the goals of the design repository project discussed in the next section is to lay the foundation for development of a critical mass of systems design knowledge that can achieve self-sustaining growth through use.

Promoting recognition and appreciation of design knowledge value is a prerequisite to growth of interested communities. Making design knowledge readily amenable to transportation, translation, and reuse requires a motivated investment of time, energy, and other resources (von Hippel, 1998). Nowhere may this be more true than in the knowledge maintenance and evolution strategies employed to ensure that captured design is cultivated for less effortful and more productive use. Though maintenance remains a critical problem in software knowledge management (Selfridge et al., 1992), field research indicates that even somewhat out-of-date design content can still be useful to developers, especially for higher level, more abstract types of design information that are more likely to generalize across projects and domains (Lethbridge et al., 2003).

Participatory design suggests design teams, prospective users, and other stakeholders can actively engage in co-development of artefacts for use. Practical constraints, however, often impede attempts to operationalize this concept. End users almost always have more work than will allow them to become system designers (Carroll and Rosson, 1987), and they typically do not have the expertise to make their participation in design efficient (Clancey, 1983). What is needed are tools to support informed participation (Arias et al., 2000) that is at once effective and efficient. Providing incentives is another means to motivate potential contributors to codify and submit their knowledge to a repository, but this approach has proven problematic when, for example, experts contribute volume but the value of their contributions is minimal in terms of its utility in reuse (Hahn and Subramani, 2000).

One perspective on the transferability of knowledge from one individual or community of practice to another is that some knowledge is inherently expensive, and "sticky" to transfer (von Hippel, 1998). Central to the challenge of creating transportable, reusable knowledge is overcoming this local embeddedness through reflection on what is general and what is particular to a situation and context. It may be however that this local reflection is best evoked at the point of use rather than as a process of analysis and reification practiced during knowledge capture. Knowledge may in fact be more useful with all of its local details accessible to potential re-users. One challenge is to provide access to a critical mass of design knowledge where a designer is likely to find useful components within an environment that facilitates ease of navigation, retrieval, and comprehension.

14.4.2 Building Design Knowledge Repositories

Information systems design and development research still lacks a critical mass of design knowledge accessible and useable as a large-scale, distributed case base for interactive software system designs. The idea of software repositories is not at all new. However, to-date no large-scale software design repository has been created and evaluated longitudinally in multiple contexts using a theory-driven, principled approach to the technical, psychological, and social phenomena that appear to bear most heavily as factors in the success or failure of such projects. The complexity of most significant design efforts involving interactive software systems is such that no one person can be expected to maintain a comprehensive knowledge base representative of what is in the design (Curtis et al., 1988). Technology support is therefore needed to provide for distributed, collaborative design2 knowledge capture and use.

Central to the research agenda we propose is developing, populating, and studying the use of a design repository, a case base, for system design knowledge management. The objective driving this facet of the research agenda is creation of a system *design* resource equivalent in utility to popular source code repositories such as *SourceForge* and *FreshMeat*. These repositories are enjoying enormous success. SourceForge for example currently hosts almost 80,000 projects and has over 800,000 registered users, yet to-date no equivalent base of system designs exists. Among the foci of the proposed project are three parallel efforts. The first is to construct a set of web applications and a supporting data store derived from our own existing designs and code and to provide interactive services identified as essential to design knowledge capture, management, and use. The second is analysis and capture of the design space for a set of identified seed projects including some of our ongoing projects in community computing, anti-terrorism resource allocation, and, self-referentially, the design repository itself. These first two efforts enable the third, which is studying design knowledge use and usability with different representational schemata and access tools. We hope to achieve a state of productive use in which work and results from each of the three parallel efforts informs work on the other two in an iterative cycle of design-build-evaluate-report.

Knowledge capture is among the most significant challenges confronting this task. A central problem with design knowledge capture interventions is preserving the fluidity of the design process while at the same time capturing design-relevant deliberations wherever or whenever they occur. Design knowledge capture strategies should enable capturing all the valuable knowledge that is reified, however briefly, in design deliberations, whenever and wherever such discussions occur. This requires development of usable, pervasive capture strategies and tools. Design capture technologies should be easy to use with minimal training, they should be mobile, relatively inexpensive, and integrated with existing tools and representations. Crucially, they should provide user services that justify and provide incentives for use.

Tools and techniques for capturing information generated during the different phases of the systems development lifecycle must integrate as unobtrusively as possible into the day-to-day activities of the team responsible for the system (Moran and Carroll, 1996). Increasingly, this integration is seen as best accomplished through integration with other software tools used routinely by design team members and components of the design capture core should themselves be tightly integrated and easy to learn. Challenges associated with this integration are becoming more acute as system development methods move away from the more formal and towards the 'agile'.

Tacit knowledge (Polanyi, 1958) has long been recognized as the gadfly of knowledge acquisition, management, and reuse. Early on in artificial intelligence research it emerged that even with the most careful methods applied to the knowledge elicitation task, experts in complex domains experienced considerable difficulty articulating the full range of skilled thought that was brought to bear for problem solving (Clancey, 1983). Knowledge management has been described as consisting of two essential challenges: resolving and balancing questions related to its location, in databases and documents, or in people's heads and their social networks; and deciding upon an appropriate degree of structure and formality, the extent to which the knowledge is not only explicit but codified for representation, storage, and retrieval (Hahn and Subramani, 2000). These are among the target criteria considered central to our own repository development efforts.

The approach we are taking to designing the repository is one of service-based computing, in particular, the use of discrete web services to implement the essential services required for a design knowledge capture and management repository (critical aspects of design interaction are discussed in the next section). The service approach overcomes some of the problems that have plagued researchers building software tools for research infrastructure including development continuity and succession planning as student developers move through a graduate program and especially the inevitable research focus shifts that occur and which can make monolithic applications obsolete overnight. By decomposing the design repository solution space into discrete web services, we hope to build units of functionality that are fundamental to the design task but that can be recomposed into aggregate applications to conform to higher-level task and functional models in response to empirical findings from studying repository use.

A web service-based architecture supports access to design services by prescribing a browser as the only requirement for global access. This degree of accessibility is essential to facilitate the kind of multi-disciplinary usage that we hope to promote. An illustration of the architecture we are developing appears in the UML component diagram below and its different elements are described in the sections that follow.

The *scenarios of use* component captures the intent underlying a design effort. Design intent is implicitly defined as developing a design specification and corresponding artefacts so that scenarios of use are supported in a manner that minimizes the negative tension expressed in the design rationale subject to domain and contextual constraints.

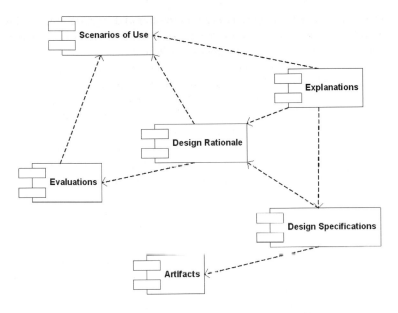

Figure 14.1   A design repository component architecture

This is a user and use-centric perspective, in which design proceeds in response to a set of human requirements expressed as concrete, envisioned examples of the technology in action. This component will provide services to capture and maintain scenarios, as well as to publish them for use by both repository users and other repository services.

The *design rationale component* is the engine at the core of the repository architecture. It uses information from the scenarios component as the grist for design deliberations. This component also uses the evaluation component in cases of design reuse, re-design, and design evolution to help assess prior deliberations with respect to performance and perceptions of the resulting artefacts in scenarios of use. Design rationale is a complex component providing a range of services for capturing design moves relative to stated requirements (scenarios) as well as publishing information to serve as the input to design specifications and explanations of the resulting artefacts.

The *design specifications component* is an integration component that manages the flow of design decisions from the rationale component to and from standard system modeling environments such as Rationale Rose and other computer-aided software engineering (CASE) tools. A key objective underlying the architecture is to make the knowledge embedded in scenarios and design rationale available from within both standard modeling environments and through application performance and learning support tools such as online documentation, help, and explanation facilities.

The *artefact component*, like the design specifications component provides a bridge from the knowledge contained in other repository components and the targets of this knowledge, the built technology.

The *explanation component* exists as an interpreter of design rationale and scenario information. This component is responsible for providing views into these bases of knowledge that are tractable for users inquiring from different perspectives.

Finally, the *evaluation component* is responsible for managing and integrating information generated from studies of repository-based systems back into the knowledge base of scenarios and design rationale. This is a unique dimension of our work supporting both design knowledge evolution and acting as a knowledge base in its own right by supporting grounded reflection on the design rationale and the way in which designers responded to the design intent as expressed in identified scenarios.

Martin and Sommerville (Martin and Somerville, 2004) describe their efforts to develop a repository of enthnographically-informed patterns of cooperative interaction. Their work draws heavily from socio-technical perspectives on systems development and from Christopher Alexander's design patterns approach (Alexander et al., 1977), which they are using to inform development of a web-annotatable pattern library for researchers and practitioners. This work is very similar to ours in its intent, but their pattern-focused approach does not include explicit linking between designed artefacts and the scenarios of use (requirements) that initiate the design intent. Nor does it focus on the rationale produced from translating requirements into artefact specifications, and links between the rationale and the specifications and artefacts themselves. We believe these are among the more important aspects of design knowledge management and use and they weigh heavily both in the schemas we are developing to represent design knowledge and the interactions we envision for users of the repository.

14.4.3   Designing Design Interactions

Relatively little research has examined the usability and other factors that impact the efficacy of different software engineering environments and representations (Agarwal et al., 1999). This is a critical gap in the extant research and one directly targeted by this aspect of the design knowledge management research program we are undertaking. In the late 1980s and early 1990s significant efforts were undertaken to understand how programmers used languages and tools and created documentation (see (Shneiderman and Carroll, 1988)). However, this stream of research has not continued at the same pace to account for the different languages and especially the range of sophisticated computer-aided software engineering systems and application frameworks commonly used by today's designers and developers.

Schön (Schön, 1983) describes design as a sort of "reflective conversation with materials" where designers engage in a cycle of trial, assessment, re-trial, and reflection. Tools to support interactive design of systems where materials are almost infinitely malleable and constraints range from those of computability to those introduced by the social, organizational, and psychological aspects of interactive system interventions themselves require careful design and especially identification of those issues apparently common across different scenarios of use. Design support tools should provide a certain freedom of movement to preserve the nuanced fluidity of the design process, while at the same time acting to help guide designers towards a satisfactory resolution in the design solution space.

Design activity consists of moves through a design space motivated by some intention or purpose and resulting the specification of behaviors and structure all subject to the myriad of constraints that emerge from both the domain and from the materials that are used to implement the design. Complex, interactive software systems, like almost all technology, are designed in response to an identified requirement, an intention to support humanity at work (or at play) (Pitt, 2000). Complex, interactive software system design is characterized by a set of processes found to be common across different domains but to differ somewhat in their application by designers with different backgrounds and skill levels (Jeffries et al., 1981). The most prevalent of these common processes are decomposition, evaluation of alternatives, and retrieval of applicable solutions or partial solutions resulting from prior design efforts.

Creative proposal and then evaluation are the pillars of design activity. Creative proposal is the instantiation of design solution elements in response to a perceived design question. Evaluation is the act of considering whether the proposed solution is appropriate to the challenge or question that has been raised. Evaluation also helps identify incrementally more appropriate solutions from the deficiencies identified in prior evaluations. Both creative proposal and evaluation are typically better when the designer is able to bring to bear the full range of criteria and constraints that might impact a proposal. This ability to actively manage large numbers of information elements is of course one of the strengths of computer-based systems and one where a design interaction environment might conceivably add cognitive value to the demanding task faced by the designer. The challenge is to provide access to large amounts of information where, when, and how the designer needs it (Fischer et al., 1993).

As an activity, design drives information needs that result in individual and collaborative information seeking and information assessment (Poltrock et al., 2003). Complex interactive systems design is characterized by the very broad range of knowledge required to understand an entire architecture at any degree of completeness (Curtis et al., 1988). Design may also be viewed as a cycle of trials, breakdowns, interpretation, and reflection (Fischer et al., 1993). All these conceptions point to the need for studies to help understand and design technology support for one of the most basic yet most complex of human activities.

Among the questions driving research into interactive design environments are those that ask whether and how to support these different design 'moves'. Design interactions occur at the cognitive level, when a single designer uses a support tool to work through a design problem, and at the distributed-cognitive or social level where groups of designers interact both with the materials of the evolving design and with prospective users and other project stakeholders. These two dimensions present very different challenges for tool design and both are important to ensure that the work of individuals is appropriately supported within their social network.

Design critiquing systems consist of a rule base for analyzing an evolving design, a signaling mechanism to inform the designer when a design representation deviates from the normative model in the rule base, and an advice-giving system for helping the designer to recover from the error or breakdown and to continue with design resolution (Sumner et al., 1997). More active design environments such those that include critics, are enticing but themselves introduce a number of difficult issues, such as the need for accurate task and user modeling required to ensure that interventions are appropriately timed with the appropriate content (Fischer et al., 1993). Design of environments for interacting with design knowledge must avoid embedding too strict a process model for an activity that is characterized as much by serendipity and opportunism as it is by any single characterization. A key challenge therefore is providing a set of useful but loosely coupled service that support design cognition in its variety of forms with aids designed specifically to enhance creativity, evaluation, reflection, and learning.

To be useful and therefore to have value, design knowledge generated in an interactive environment must be retrievable, comprehensible, and then mappable to appropriate, analogous problem domains and solution spaces. Designing interaction support for these activities involves studying designers and design information retrieval and use, and developing new human-computer interaction models to account for the complexity, pervasiveness, and uniqueness of design as human activity. We are interested, for example, in how to design scenario taxonomies so that scenarios and related rationales informing a current design challenge can be easily retrieved and applied. One of the strengths of design rationale is that it provides rich, context-specific details of how a design solution emerged from consideration of prospective scenarios. The amount of information collected as scenarios and design rationale from a complex development project can be large, however, and among our other core interests is how different information design and architecture strategies can be integrated with modern approaches to information retrieval to facilitate exploration and reuse of these prior design cases.

14.5   RELATED WORK

Our work in this area is largely derivative of the design rationale movement of the 1980s and 1990s. See Moran and Carroll's collection (Moran and Carroll, 1996) and more recent work such as Sutcliffe's *domain theory* (Sutcliffe, 2002) for more on the design rationale research program. The domain theory is an approach to reusing design knowledge that relies on an interleaved set of models including object system models that describe transaction-oriented problems (see Chapter 5 of this volume) and generic tasks that describe human activity in the domain. Each of these model types is elaborated with generic requirements that describe when a given model is potentially appropriate.

One key differentiator of our approach involves the level of formalization we apply to knowledge taxonomy and representation. While we acknowledge that more structured representations of stored knowledge enable a broader range of computational services, we feel that the demands and overhead of design knowledge capture still offset the advantages gained from more highly structured data capture. It is hard to ask designers and design teams to consider classification and categorization issues for every potentially useful element of knowledge they uncover in their work. Our approach to design knowledge management is somewhat less rigorous than that described in the domain theory. We use *claims* as an adaptive unit of design knowledge capture, analysis and reuse. Though claims are relatively unstructured, designers can choose to apply more or less fine-grained claims taxonomies to suit their needs, or they can choose to incrementally formalize and refactor their design knowledge as opportunities arise for reuse.

The BORE (Building an Organizational Repository of Experiences) project (Henniger, 2003) is one of the most mature research software knowledge repositories. BORE is a repository toolset that extends the *experience factory* concept (Basili and Rombach, 1988) to include rule-based support for software development process engineering, and organizational learning. Unlike the approach we have described here, BORE focuses on the engineering *process* knowledge accumulated from development activities. Though knowledge of development best practices and lessons learned is critically important, especially given the so-called 'software crisis', we are more concerned here with the design knowledge linking domain concepts to the system design moves made in response. This knowledge, expressed as claims and anchored to scenarios, may fill an important knowledge gap between the relative abstraction of a design pattern and the raft of particular solutions available to today's designer/developer.

Significant effort has been invested in development of forms and methods to ease and ensure the reuse of design. The design patterns movement (Gamma et al., 1995) has probably enjoyed the most success and though certainly software patterns are being written and disseminated, in spite of these efforts to foster large-scale reuse of software designs, this appears to still rarely occur in practice (Ockerman and Mitchell, 1999; Prieto-Diaz, 1993). The lure of *generic* design knowledge that can be pulled off the shelf and applied to a myriad of situations and problems is great and has given rise to substantial works in theory and practice In addition to the design patterns work see also (Jackson, 2001; Sutcliffe, 2002).

14.6 CONCLUSION

In the course of a systems development or software implementation project, individuals and organizations bring to the surface knowledge regarding the domain in which the system is intended for use, about the individual's and organization's stance towards the domain, and, ideally, innovative approaches to addressing specific problems emergent within the domain. Software-intensive, interactive systems embed inscribed knowledge about their domain, about their users, about tasks, about software engineering, about human-computer interaction, about the social dimensions of computing, about standards and regulations; the list goes on. But, this design knowledge is complex, and at the same time both evolving and entropic. Consideration of the knowledge vested in a complex system design increases the value of the design and artefact to an extent only insomuch as the knowledge can be extracted or evoked from the artefact for subsequent re-use and application.

We have proposed the use of scenarios and design rationale as an orienting framework of concepts, techniques, and tools for addressing the design knowledge management challenge. Research on design rationale has been less active since its peak of research activity in the early and mid 1990s. One reason for the lack of current interest may be that a number of studies pointed to (or resurfaced) some difficult problems with the usability and especially with the *reusability* of design rationales (Shum, 1996; Shum and Hammond, 1994). However, these studies were relatively small-scale and did not attempt to integrate modern information retrieval and other user-interface technology into the experimental design.

There is a recognized dearth of industrial strength experiences of design rationale in use within real organizations. One of the few exceptions is (Conklin and Burgess-Yakemovic, 1996), where design rationale techniques were applied longitudinally on an actual design project. They found that the use of design rationales improved design meetings by providing an agenda and capturing results of previous meetings, and assisted in the processes of training and acclimating new team members to a project. They also found the results accumulated were effective for communicating the status of different issues in the evolving design. We need more ecologically valid field studies of design knowledge management in the field both to better understand the cost-benefit profile of these efforts and to identify criteria for advanced technology designs.

This lack of empirical support, or convincing disprovals, in design rationale studies is not unique. In general, studies of designers at work are scarce and there are few replications of results that have been obtained from prior research. Still, this situation has left the design rationale program appearing as a set of unfulfilled promises. The promises are potentially rich however, and are deserving of larger-scale empirical studies.

Though significant work has addressed the form and content of reusable units of design knowledge, for example, as design patterns, less success has been achieved in attempts to ease capture and access to large bases of design knowledge. Larger organizations tend to be better at producing design documentation, but even these have a poor understanding of how to maintain and use this resource to gain the value embedded within it. Fostering recognition of and commitment to programs of intervention in this milieu requires 'bootstrapping' cases to act as proof-of-concept examples of the value lost through inattention to design knowledge management.

Studies of the systems development process in large organizations suggest that as often as not this process is characterized by no small degree of chaos and *ad hocery*, rather than the rational, methodical process descriptions commonly attributed to software engineering. The interplay between people and technology, and between design and use, results in a complex web of knowledge describing human activity within a problem domain. Technologies are both a source of knowledge (e.g., as scientific instruments), and repositories for knowledge and experience (e.g., as cognitive aids), but so much of the knowledge they evoke in development and in use is invisible to those who might benefit from access and reuse.

Approaching design knowledge management requires that we understand a network of factors within which people, technologies, and other artefacts interact to understand, structure, and design solutions to important problems in complex domains. Any single study finding or single technology development effort is unlikely to resolve the critical issues attending design knowledge management; we need infrastructure and programs to facilitate coordinated streams of research in this important domain.

15 PATTERNS OF INTEGRATION: BRINGING USER CENTERED DESIGN INTO THE SOFTWARE DEVELOPMENT LIFECYCLE

Lisa Battle

Lockheed Martin

Abstract

Faced with a need to integrate user-centered methods into existing software development lifecycles, many practitioners lack clear direction and continue to negotiate the scope of their involvement on a project-by-project basis. There are best practices that can be adopted, however. This chapter distills the experiences of many practitioners into a collection of process patterns that describe an evolutionary path towards full integration.

15.1 INTRODUCTION

Despite the increasing recognition of the value of usability and user-centered design in the software industry (Butler, 1996; Trenner and Bawa, 1998) integrating user-centered methods into existing software development lifecycles remains a significant challenge. As discussed in Chapter 2, some organizations claim to be committed to usability but seem to be at a loss as to how to achieve it. The challenge may arise from the fact that the software engineering community already has techniques and tools for

A. Seffah (eds.), Human-Centered Software Engineering – Integrating Usability
in the Development Process, 287–308.

managing the whole development lifecycle, and it is unclear where to integrate user-centered methods (Antunes et al., 2001). Differences in terminology and language may impede communication, since practitioners of usability and human-computer interaction (HCI) typically come from non-engineering disciplines (Ferre, 2003). Or, the techniques of user-centered design (UCD) may appear subjective or disorganized when viewed by developers and analysts who are not familiar with the process (Quesenbery, 2000). There is evidence in Chapter 4 that communication between engineers and HCI professionals remains limited at best.

At the same time, the software industry remains frustrated with the problem of requirements. It has long been recognized that requirements analysis is the most error-prone part of the development process, and errors in requirements not detected at an early stage can lead to expensive system failures (Hofmann and Lehner, 2001; Boehm, 1981). In the 1990s, the field of requirements engineering (RE) gained much more prominence as a discipline, as evidenced by the emergence of several new conferences and journals dedicated to the subject (Nuseibeh and Easterbrook, 2000). RE researchers have proposed a variety of methods for improving requirements elicitation and the communication between users and analysts (Valenti et al., 1998). It has been suggested that these methods would benefit from integration with complementary human-computer interaction approaches (Sutcliffe, 1995).

15.1.1   Representing Practitioner Experiences as Patterns

The question of how to integrate UCD into mainstream software development processes has been discussed by groups of UCD practitioners and software engineers in several recent conferences and workshops (Gulliksen et al., 2003a; Seffah and Forbrig, 2001; Kreitzberg and Quesenbery, 1999; Seffah and Engelberg, 1999). *IEEE Software* magazine published a special issue on usability engineering in January 2001, suggesting an interest in cross-fertilization. Several case studies have also been published from a practitioner perspective on the experience of introducing UCD into organizations (Wheeler et al., 2003; Anderson et al., 2001; Carlshamre and Rantzer, 2000). However, UCD/HCI practitioners in many organizations continue to negotiate their role and the scope of their involvement on a project-by-project basis. The need for clearer direction to guide practitioners towards strategies for integration prompted our workshop at the Usability Professionals' Association (UPA) Conference (Battle et al., 2003). In the workshop, UCD practitioners discussed their experiences and shared examples of how UCD was integrated into their organizations' software development lifecycles.

This chapter is based on the ideas generated during that workshop, a written survey of usability practitioners conducted at the same conference, feedback received from local UPA chapters in response to presentations of this material, and lessons learned from the author's experience. The information is distilled into process patterns that describe best practices for integrating user-centered design with the software development lifecycle. Process patterns are derived from the idea of design patterns originally introduced in architecture by Alexander et al., 1977, and adapted more recently for user interface and software design. Process patterns draw on combined experiences to describe a proven, successful approach or series of actions (Coplien, 1995; Ambler, 1998). Although patterns are widely accepted by both UCD and software engineering communities (see Ambler's process patterns at http://www.ambysoft.com/processPatternsPage.html, for example), the author has not found any previous work describing the integration of UCD and software engineering in terms of process patterns.

15.1.2   Can Integration be Described in a Generic Way?

Several challenges arise when trying to describe the integration of user-centered methods in a generic way. Many decisions are influenced by the context in which the methods are being integrated, including the lifecycle model, the organizational culture, and the position of the UCD practitioner.

Different lifecycle models. The type of lifecycle model, such as waterfall or iterative, may suggest different opportunities for integration of UCD. Chapters 14 and 15 in this book provide more detail on integrating UCD with two popular lifecycle models: Agile development and the Rational Unified Process (RUP). Although it could certainly be argued that there is no such thing as a "generic" software development lifecycle, the illustrations in this chapter attempt to represent generic phases by labeling them "Early," "Middle," and "Late," along with examples of actual phase names that are used in specific lifecycles. This approach is based on a compromise made during the UPA workshop, when it became clear that the differences in terminology from one lifecycle to another were so significant that any attempt to label the phases would risk miscommunication. In the future, it may be useful to introduce variations of these process patterns to reflect customization for different lifecycle models.

Different organizational cultures. The organizational culture may vary in terms of its openness to new approaches, who the decision makers are, the formality and/or maturity of the existing process, and level of management support for UCD in the organization. For example, in some organizations, a marketing department may be the most powerful decision maker with regard to new products; in other organizations, the culture may be that the developers know best. Some organizations follow a formally documented lifecycle, while others do not. Although some of these differences are discussed in the patterns, it may be valuable in the future to refine the patterns for specific organizational contexts.

Different perspectives. In the UPA workshop and survey, it quickly became clear that an internal usability group and an external consultant have different experiences when bringing user-centered design into an organization. This led to the creation of two different patterns describing how practitioners can get a "foot in the door" for user-centered design.

15.1.3   Overview of the Process Patterns

The four patterns described in this chapter, outlined in Table 15.1, represent an evolutionary process, from the first introduction of user-centered design to a full integration of methods.

Table 15.1   Overview of patterns

Pattern	Area of Focus in a "Generic" Lifecycle		
	Early	Middle	Late
Foot in the door (for internal usability group)	x		
Foot in the door (for external consultants)			x
UCD focus on early definition and design	x		
UCD in every phase	x	x	x

Although this chapter approaches the topic of integration from the UCD practitioner's perspective, it is hoped that the ideas contained in it will be of value to developers, requirements analysts, and project managers as well.

15.2   PATTERN A: FOOT IN THE DOOR (FOR INTERNAL USABILITY GROUP)

Integrating UCD into a software development lifecycle does not happen all at once. The idea typically has to be introduced and piloted on a small scale. For an internal usability group, introducing UCD into an existing process becomes an exercise in organizational change. This pattern describes how an internal usability group gets a "foot in the door" to demonstrate the value of UCD as a first step towards integrating the methods.

15.2.1   Initial Context

In the beginning, the organization has an existing process or lifecycle that does not involve user-centered design. There is little or no awareness of user-centered methods.

15.2.2   Problem

The challenge is to introduce user-centered design practices into an organization and its existing software development lifecycle. From the perspective of the software development group, which may have no awareness of UCD/HCI, the introduction of this new profession may be confusing or threatening. From the perspective of management, a new method needs to prove its value before it can be widely introduced into the organization.

15.2.3   Solution

For an internal usability group, the key to getting a foot in the door is to find targeted opportunities to influence an early lifecycle phase (the name of this phase, of course, varies from one organization to another). As indicated in Figure 15.1, the UCD practitioner focuses on creating or enhancing a key deliverable in a way that incorporates a user-centered perspective.

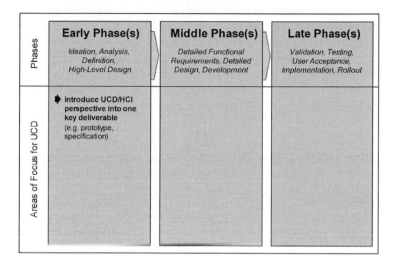

Figure 15.1   Foot in the door (for internal usability groups)

The deliverable to focus on is typically a low-fidelity prototype, a requirements document, or a specification document. The UCD practitioner should choose the deliverable that is most appropriate given the existing lifecycle and organizational context, and contribute to it from a UCD perspective. For example, if the UCD practitioner notices that a specification document is typically handed off from a user representative to the development team with little or no communication, the UCD practitioner might initiate a collaborative review of this document, introducing a usability perspective while at the same time starting a dialogue between the user representatives and developers. If the project team has not used low-fidelity prototypes before, the UCD practitioner can create them as input to the specification document, drawing upon any information available about the users and tasks, as well as standard principles of HCI. The resulting specification document will likely be much more complete.

Best Practices for UCD Practitioners.   The UCD practitioner who is working to apply this pattern is encouraged to follow these best practices.

Evaluate the organization and understand what it needs.

- Analyzing the organizational environment and conducting an informal gap analysis can identify some of the weaknesses in the existing process where UCD might help.

- If the organization has a formally documented lifecycle, become familiar with the phases in the lifecycle and the deliverables produced in each phase.

- If the organization has more informal methods, start building relationships with people and understanding their roles in the process.

Stop "telling people that their baby is ugly." If the organization conducts end-of-the-line usability testing, but does not incorporate UCD/HCI methods in the early design phase, the usability input is probably ignored because it comes too late. Usability specialists in such an organization are constantly in the position of giving bad news immediately before a product is released, and they realize that this is not productive. They will need to overcome the organization's perception of usability as a research discipline. A practitioner working in this context should:

- Seek training in user-centered analysis and design techniques

- Consider involving an outside consultant (at least temporarily) as a catalyst for change. Some internal employees have found that it is easier to convince decision-makers by bringing in an outside expert.

- Get out of a role that focuses primarily on reviewing a finished product. If possible, start turning away requests for this type of testing, and explain to project teams why end-of-line usability testing alone is not effective.

Be opportunistic. At the beginning, seek any opportunity to get involved in an early design phase activity. Look for ways to help people:

- When a project team is low on resources, the UCD practitioner can offer to share the workload.

- When the project team finds itself arguing about the same issue over and over, the UCD practitioner can point out that there is a method of resolving the dispute, and offer to lead or facilitate the process of collecting user input, testing design alternatives, etc.

- When the project team receives negative feedback from a customer, the UCD practitioner can offer to investigate the problem and recommend a solution.

Show real value on a small scale first. Starting small can be less disruptive and easier for the organization to accept.

- Identify a small pilot project as an opportunity to try the new process. This should not be a mission-critical project, and it should not be under too much deadline pressure.

- Do not try to apply too many UCD activities in the first few projects. While it is important to do enough to demonstrate the benefit, it does not pay to overwhelm the project team.

Get people talking to each other. It is surprising how often the lack of communication is a barrier to success on project teams.

- Facilitate working sessions. The UCD/HCI practitioner is often more comfortable than technical staff in facilitating conversations within a project team, between stakeholders, or between users and developers.

■ Facilitate meetings involving users. This may be considered an unpleasant task, and your colleagues may be relieved that someone else is willing to do it.

■ Invite people from different groups to the same meeting. If you do nothing more than fostering communication between groups, you may still be seen as adding tremendous value. This can also be a first step towards multidisciplinary teamwork.

Partner with advocates of quality or customer focus.

■ Look for other groups within the organization that are also interested in improving existing processes. These might include quality assurance specialists, process improvement specialists, or new high-level managers who are interested in improving products or making their mark on the organization.

■ Start to build strategic partnerships with these groups, engage them in dialogue, and explain how you can help them achieve their goals by applying user-centered methods.

■ Take advantage of new quality initiatives or executive mandates. For example, in one organization, a new executive challenged project teams to aim for "demonstrably superior" products. UCD methods were able to help those teams achieve the goal and articulate how the products they produced were superior to the competition. In another organization, a new executive promoted the idea of a customer-centered organization, which paved the way for UCD as a standard part of requirements gathering.

Common Challenges.

Organizational change is difficult. General resistance to change is an initial challenge for any new process, and introducing user-centered design to an organization is no exception. Experts in organizational change recommend seeking advocates both at the high level and at the grass-roots level (Senge, 1999). Some UCD practitioners begin by making presentations to high-level managers about the potential value of UCD to the bottom line. This approach should target especially those high-level managers who would likely benefit from the results of UCD. A high-level champion for usability can help to establish organizational commitment, provide resources, and create opportunities for process change. However, some UCD practitioners start by educating and gathering support at a grassroots level, recognizing that new way of working cannot be sustained without buy-in from individual developers, analysts, and project managers. Ultimately, support at all levels of the organization is needed.

Adopting a UCD process all at once is too difficult for most organizations. UCD practitioners who try to do too much at once may end up alienating others in the organization (Vutpakdi, 2004). Prioritize UCD activities, keeping in mind how they will fit into the corporate culture. Suggest small steps that developers, marketers, and others can take immediately to become more user-focused. Adopt the organization's own language/terminology if possible rather than forcing new terms and work practices.

Phase in the implementation of UCD, recognizing that large-scale change does not occur rapidly.

There is a lack of support for involving users in product design. Sometimes UCD practitioners find that they cannot get access to users for input because the organization does not see the value of user involvement. One strategy for dealing with this situation is to keep asking detailed questions about the users' tasks and context that the organization cannot answer without user involvement. Another option is to spend time interviewing the people who have the most direct contact with users, which may include the technicians who configure software at the client site, service representatives, or help desk personnel. When starting to introduce new methods, it is sometimes necessary to do the best you can with whatever information you have, keeping in mind that the short-term goal is to get a foot in the door.

Existing timelines do not allow for any new steps. When there is no time to add UCD activities to an existing schedule, practitioners can still participate, for example by contributing to a work product that is already in the lifecycle. If any meetings with users are already scheduled—for example, marketing focus groups or customer site implementation visits—try to get invited. If time has already been allotted to the activity, having one more person attend will not affect the deadline.

UCD practitioners may become discouraged. When they feel that their work is far from the ideal user-centered design process, UCD practitioners may be frustrated. The key is to be patient, share ideas and experiences with other practitioners, and remind each other that even small accomplishments are worthwhile. Each project where UCD adds value provides more leverage to incorporate user-centered activities earlier in the next project.

15.2.4 Resulting Context

As a result of performing the process pattern, UCD has been shown to add value to some deliverables, and positive feedback has been received from some colleagues or project team members. There is now potential to progress to the next level: UCD focus on early definition and design.

15.3 PATTERN B: FOOT IN THE DOOR (FOR EXTERNAL CONSULTANTS)

The experience for an external consultant trying to introduce UCD is different than the experience for an internal usability group. The end-of-line testing role that can become a trap for internal usability groups is in fact the most common starting point for an external consultant. This pattern describes how an external consultant gets a foot in the door to begin applying UCD.

15.3.1 Initial Context

A software development organization that does not follow user-centered methods suspects that it has a usability problem, possibly as a result of negative feedback from customers on an existing product. This organization makes an initial contact with a UCD/HCI consultant.

15.3.2   Problem

The challenge is to sell user-centered design services to a client organization that is not normally interested in usability, and to make a big impact while keeping costs low.

15.3.3   Solution

For external consultants, the key to getting a foot in the door is to communicate with the client in business terms and show results quickly. Because the client may be in a "firefighting" mode, the external consultant must focus on fixing the immediate problem and helping the client to achieve quick "wins," while at the same time beginning to present a longer-term vision.

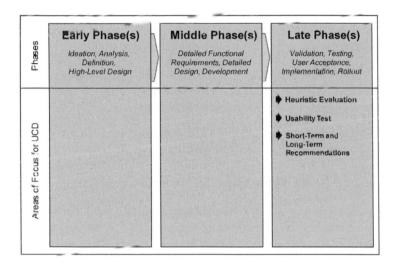

Figure 15.2   Foot in the door (for external consultants)

Figure 15.2 shows that an external consultant typically starts by evaluating the existing product, identifying issues to be addressed, and making recommendations for improvement. Sometimes the consulting service includes facilitating a usability test. This solution is quite different from the internal usability group's strategy of focusing on adding value to an early design deliverable. The external consultant's ability to influence an existing product is aided by the fact that the client already recognizes the need for some type of improvement. The UCD/HCI consultant typically has his/her own model of the UCD process. However, due to the nature of the consultation and the typical time pressures, the question of how best to integrate the consultant's model of UCD with the client organization's existing processes may not arise at all at this stage.

Best Practices for UCD Practitioners.   The UCD practitioner who is working to apply this pattern is encouraged to follow these best practices.

Position your involvement in business terms.

- Evaluate the organization's business goals and discuss the usability issues from the perspective of what motivates the company, whether this is the need to comply with regulations and standards, competitiveness with other products on the market, customer loyalty, or return on investment.

- Avoid UCD jargon, which may seem confusing or overly academic to executives who are focused on business issues (Dodd, 2003).

- Target decision-makers at the highest possible level in the organization. External consultants often have the opportunity to come into an organization at a higher level than is typically possible for an internal usability group. This may provide opportunities to talk with decision makers about strategic issues.

Conduct an expert evaluation. The external consultant may begin by conducting an expert review of the existing product and identifying issues.

- Find out as much as possible about the real users and their tasks as input to this evaluation. Walkthroughs based on typical user tasks are more valuable than walkthroughs based on standard heuristics alone.

- Conduct competitive evaluations, which compare the existing product with similar products, to produce valuable insights.

Conduct usability tests and use video clips to demonstrate issues.

- Encourage usability testing with real users as soon as possible. The voice of the customer can be powerful in making a business case.

- Videotape the tests and create a presentation of highlights. Video clips of real users having problems are highly persuasive.

- Comparative usability tests showing users trying similar tasks with two competing products can also be persuasive.

Provide a vision that will lead into the next phase.

- Short-term recommendations give the client a tangible solution to the usability problem, proving the value of UCD involvement (and your value as a consultant).

- Follow up with longer-term recommendations and help the client to articulate a vision for the product that achieves business goals while meeting user needs. Getting a foot in the door can often lead to an opportunity to work with the client on the design of the next generation product.

Common Challenges.

Funding is limited. The external consultant typically has to work within the constraints of a tight budget, a short time frame, or both, at least for the initial engagement. This increases the pressure to show the maximum value with minimum effort.

The existing process is fundamentally flawed. While internal usability groups normally feel a need to fit into the existing process, an external consultant may be more free to work outside of the existing process. If appropriate, the consultant may consider advising the client that the existing process is broken and suggesting changes to the process.

15.3.4   Resulting Context

As a result of performing the process pattern, the consultant's evaluation has led to short-term fixes and a longer-term vision for the product. There is now potential to progress to the next level: UCD focus on early definition and design.

15.4   PATTERN C: UCD FOCUS ON EARLY DEFINITION AND DESIGN

UCD practitioners agree that they need to be involved as early as possible in a project in order to analyze the real needs and influence the design of a usable solution. This pattern describes how UCD is integrated with an early lifecycle phase.

15.4.1   Initial Context

The organization has recognized the benefit that a user-centered perspective has added in past projects, whether in early design phase deliverables (outcome of pattern A) or in recommendations for improvement (outcome of pattern B). UCD involvement is now more formally requested at the beginning of projects. There is some management support for UCD, at least at the project manager level if not at higher levels in the organization.

15.4.2   Problem

The challenge is to integrate standard user-centered analysis and design activities as early as possible in the project, while being sensitive to existing processes and roles.

15.4.3   Solution

The UCD practitioner chooses methods that fit in well with the organization and produce outcomes that are seen as valuable. Figure 15.3 shows how typical UCD activities such as identifying user and business goals, analyzing user needs, iterative prototyping, and the creation of a user interface (UI) specification, are integrated with early phases of the lifecycle.

The key is to coordinate UCD activities with other requirements engineering activities that happen during the early phase. UCD activities such as user/task analysis

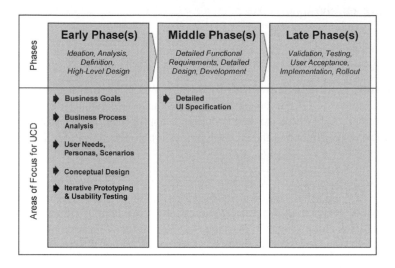

Figure 15.3   UCD focus on early definition and design

and iterative design can be central to eliciting the right requirements. The UCD practitioner should work as closely as possible with other team members throughout these activities to promote multidisciplinary collaboration and ensure that the outcomes of the UCD activities feed into downstream deliverables.

Best Practices for UCD Practitioners.   The UCD practitioner who is working to apply this pattern is encouraged to follow these best practices.

Focus on eliciting and clarifying user and business requirements.

- Gather as much information as possible about the users, tasks, and context, following best practices of UCD. For example, apply contextual inquiry methods to interview or observe users, and apply low-fidelity paper prototyping methods to test proposed designs as early as possible with real users.

- If direct access to users is not possible, gather information from others in the organization who do have direct frequent contact with them, such as trainers, technicians who go to customer sites to implement new systems or fix problems, help desk personnel, etc.

- Learn about the organization's requirements engineering function (in different organizations, requirements may be defined by marketing groups, internal customer groups, technical groups, or some combination of these). If it does not exist, UCD practitioners may need to fill that role. If it does exist, UCD practitioners need to coordinate with it.

- Learn about the types of requirements defined in your organization and the language used in describing them (for an example of types of requirements, (see

Wiegers, 1999), so that you can take an active role in translating your analysis findings into requirements.

Focus on the next release, not the current one. Some UCD practitioners find that they never have the time to conduct user analysis because they are always working on an immediate deadline.

- Focusing on the next release while the current one is still in development creates a little bit of breathing room in the schedule, and it gets you involved at the beginning of a next generation product.

- If necessary, ask for a small pilot project in which you can focus on a future release and demonstrate the benefits of a more complete user-centered analysis and design.

Communicate the vision and the design. UCD practitioners have an important role in communicating the design to the project team, stakeholders, and developers. Building a shared understanding of the vision among the team and stakeholders improves the project's chances of success (Beyer and Holtzblatt, 1998).

- Present highlights of the analysis to decision makers. By describing real needs and showing how the resulting design meets those needs, you can also demonstrate to decision-makers how UCD activities are improving the overall quality of the products.

- Communicate the design clearly to developers. This is essential to ensure that the design is built as intended.

- Evaluate how well the UCD deliverables are working as communication tools, and iterate them to ensure that they are communicating as well as possible.

Create detailed user interface specifications. Although detailed documentation can be tedious to produce, doing so is in the best interests of both the UCD practitioners and the project team:

- Requirements analysts can use these specifications as input to their detailed functional requirements.

- Developers can refer to them throughout the development process.

- People in the quality assurance and testing roles can use them as the basis for creating test plans.

Create UCD deliverables to feed into other project deliverables. There is a risk that valuable requirements information gathered during a UCD analysis will be lost as it is reinterpreted into functional specifications and code (Coble et al., 1997; Butler, 1996). To reduce this risk:

- Coordinate work products between UCD practitioners and other team members who use other styles of deliverables, such as those based on UML. For example, if the UCD practitioners describe the user's work in scenarios, and the requirements analysts create use cases, discuss the relationship between these deliverables and decide how scenarios can provide input to use cases (Degler et al., 2003). If the UCD practitioners create low-fidelity prototypes, ensure that those prototypes are documented in a way that directly feeds into the creation of the specifications or functional requirements needed by other members of the project team. Coordinating effort can reduce everyone's workload, prevent misunderstandings, and preserve the information collected during analysis.

- Find out how your deliverables are being used by the people in downstream processes. Then, improve the your deliverables iteratively to ensure that they provide the information and the level of detail that those people need.

- Ensure that UCD deliverables are built into the project plan. If your project manager creates a "release schedule" that defines all major activities and deliverables, make sure that UCD activities and deliverables are included. In some organizations, such a plan may be created a full year prior to a major software release.

Work collaboratively with multidisciplinary teams. UCD is inherently multidisciplinary and encourages the involvement of people with different specialties because doing so results in better products. For example, meeting with developers to walk through preliminary prototypes provides early insights into technical constraints and opportunities.

- Expose people from across the organization to user-centered perspectives and encourage the whole project team to take ownership of the outcomes of the UCD process.

- Making decisions throughout the project in a team setting, rather than handing over a complete design at the end. This allows everyone to participate and reduces the chance of arbitrary changes later.

- If the involvement of UCD resources may not continue into the development phase, it is a good strategy to involve a developer in all UCD activities, so that later he or she can explain the design rationale to other developers.

Common Challenges.

A role for UCD on the project team may overlap with (or change) the roles of other team members. Chapter 5 addresses some of the overlaps in roles and skills between software engineering and UCD/HCI. Creating a new role for the UCD group may cause other people's roles to change, and in some cases it may threaten their traditional "ownership" of certain decisions.

- Try to come to an agreement on the roles that different people will play in the new process.

- Make it clear that people from various disciplines play a critical role in analysis and design activities.

- Be sensitive to people's feelings. Some developers who consider the UI to be an opportunity for their creativity may feel frustrated if UCD practitioners appear to be taking it over, and they should be included in collaborative design and prototyping activities. Other developers who are not interested in the UI will be pleased to devote more of their time to back-end processes.

- Be sensitive to the additional pressure that some developers may feel when asked to work from detailed UI specifications. If this is new to them, it introduces the possibility that they may fail to meet the requirements and need to justify any changes. To minimize the risk that developers will feel "trapped" by UI designs, UCD practitioners should be prepared to respond quickly and work collaboratively unforeseen implementation issues arise during development.

The relationship between requirements and design may be confusing. While requirements definition is typically thought of as an analysis process, it actually encompasses design activities as well, and includes the design of the user interface (Paech and Kohler, 2003). Requirements emerge through design activities (Carroll et al., 1997), and elicitation of requirements using artefacts or prototypes can be extremely effective (Sutcliffe, 1995; Wiegers, 1999). If there are requirements analysts in your organization, work collaboratively with them on analysis and design activities that will lead to both high-level requirements and UI design. Involving analysts in paper prototyping and iterative testing sessions can encourage them to understand prototyping as one valuable method of gathering and clarifying user requirements.

The organization may not understand what the UCD group does. Some communication methods include publishing articles in the company newsletter, offering "lunch and learn" training sessions, publishing an Intranet site for the UCD group, and providing a basic orientation to UCD for project teams.

The design may change during development. Some UCD practitioners have reported that developers assume that the final product has to look similar to the UI specification but not exactly like it. In this situation, it is best for project managers to communicate clearly that UI specifications are not suggestions but requirements. Even without this misunderstanding, it is common for changes to be introduced during development. If the organization does not have a change control process, the first step is to introduce one. If it does have change control, ensure that UCD practitioners participate in decisions about handling changes.

Release dates are determined as soon as the project/function is identified. Unrealistic dates can be a challenge for all members of a project team. In organizations where this happens often, there may be a need to develop a more realistic planning process, enlisting the support of various groups in the organization who share an interest in this. Some organizations have tried a phased approach to sizing/scoping projects, in which the initial time estimate is a ballpark figure, and checkpoints are built into the process to refine the estimate as more details become known. It is also useful to introduce an

"Evaluate" phase at the end of the project lifecycle to gather metrics and use them to improve estimating for future projects.

The UCD group may not have the resources to support all projects. The UCD group cannot afford to become a bottleneck. Even with the addition of more resources to the UCD group, many organizations will find that there are not enough resources to dedicate UCD specialists to each project. This leads to a need to prioritize involvement and focus resources on projects where UCD can have the greatest impact (Battle, 2004).

The organization may perceive that UCD slows down the lifecycle. This perception, whether or not it has any basis in reality, can become a significant obstacle. It makes sense for UCD practitioners to anticipate it and to address it with several different strategies simultaneously. These strategies may include:

1. Cost-justify the process to management. Discuss return on investment and look at the whole range of costs, including the costs of training, returned products, or help desk support. Demonstrate the difference in quality between projects that involve user input and those that do not.

2. Use executive champions to foster a culture that places more value on the customer. This shift in focus may motivate technical groups to spend more time with the customers understanding their needs.

3. Conduct UCD activities in conjunction with other existing activities, and show management how this results in adding value without adding calendar time. For example, UCD activities can be incorporated into typical walkthroughs, customer meetings, and requirements gathering activities.

4. Ensure that the outcomes of user-centered design activities are merged into "downstream" deliverables, so that they are not seen as "extra" but as input to existing documents. For example, work closely with requirements analysts to ensure that UCD deliverables feed into the functional requirements document, and work closely with quality assurance specialists to ensure that UCD deliverables feed into test plans.

5. Ask people in the downstream processes how UCD deliverables can be improved to save time—and ask them to tell management when they do see a time savings. For example, quality assurance specialists may report that they save time when they receive more complete UI specifications, or when they receive them earlier in the process.

6. As early as possible in the project, separate the parts of the system that directly affect the user experience from those parts that are invisible to the user. Then, you can work on the parts that do affect the user, while others work on the back end processes. However, remember that keeping concurrent activities coordinated requires some "touch points" built into the process.

7. Become part of the project team and stay with them throughout the lifecycle. Some UCD practitioners report that when they are perceived as team members,

the time spent on their activities draws less attention than if they are perceived as outside consultants stepping into the project briefly to pass judgment or add requirements.

8. Work towards integrating user-centered methods into all phases of the lifecycle and building infrastructure to make user-centered activities more efficient (see pattern D).

15.4.4   Resulting Context

As a result of performing the process pattern, many projects in the organization incorporate user-centered analysis and design activities during an early lifecycle phase. There is now a potential to progress to the next level: UCD in Every Phase.

15.5   PATTERN D: UCD IN EVERY PHASE

UCD practitioners seem to have a shared vision or goal of introducing UCD into every phase of the lifecycle. This goal surfaced in the UPA 2003 workshop, when it was noted that most UCD practitioners talked about their work as if UCD was included in, or *should be* included in, each phase of the lifecycle. This was confirmed in discussing the workshop results with groups of practitioners at UPA chapter meetings. Although this degree of integration must be phased in gradually, it is not unrealistic— many organizations already conduct UCD activities in multiple phases throughout the lifecycle. This pattern consolidates those experiences to describe how an organization might apply UCD in every phase.

15.5.1   Initial Context

The organization typically incorporates user-centered design in an early phase of the lifecycle (outcome of pattern C). There is support for UCD among mid-level and upper management.

15.5.2   Problem

The challenge is to become a more customer-focused organization, streamline development, and improve strategic decision-making by incorporating UCD into all phases of the lifecycle.

15.5.3   Solution

The key is to create a continuous, interconnected flow of communication and feedback mechanisms throughout the lifecycle, from initial product concept to post-implementation. Figure 15.4 shows how UCD involvement starts even earlier, influencing vision and strategic planning. It also continues after the early phase, taking on a role in change management during development and participating in ongoing reviews to ensure that the design is implemented as specified. After the product is released, UCD activities include a post-release evaluation, user surveys, longitudinal studies with actual users of the product, and analysis of usage or management information (MI) data.

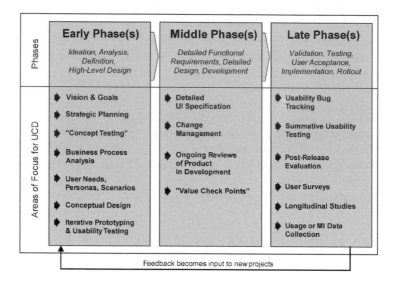

Figure 15.4   UCD in every phase

Information about the users, tasks, and context collected during analysis and design activities, as well as feedback from a variety of sources, are provided to executives as input to visioning and strategic planning for future releases and new products. As a result, the organization is able to make more informed business decisions.

Best Practices for UCD Practitioners.   The UCD practitioner who is working to apply this pattern is encouraged to follow these best practices.

Stay with the project team throughout development. It can be all too easy for a UCD practitioner to get pulled into another project immediately after handing over a design or specification. When this happens, it introduces the risk that the design will change in development, as described in the previous pattern. Responsibilities for the UCD practitioner during development include:

- Participate actively in change management. At the level of formal process, the organization should implement change management procedures in which the UCD practitioner is included as a member of the change control board. This helps to ensure that any necessary changes can be discussed and decisions made that balance the usability requirements with technical feasibility.

- Encourage team members to ask for clarification when needed, extending the collaborative working relationships beyond the early phase. The UCD practitioner says, in essence, "If you're not sure which way it should be done, call me. I'll help you figure it out and document the decision."

- Review the product during development. Some organizations implement what they call "value checkpoints" during the development phase, in which UCD practitioners who were involved in the design are asked to review the code to make sure it meets the requirements and specifications. UCD practitioners should make time to participate in review meetings like these during development, even if their time is limited.

Keep the specifications updated. In addition to creating a detailed specification, the UCD practitioner should take the responsibility for maintaining it throughout the lifecycle. Because of the level of detail involved in most specifications, this can require a significant investment of time. However, making this the routine responsibility of the UCD practitioner provides a valuable service to the project team and again reduces the risk of changes being introduced in the development phase due to miscommunication of requirements.

Use the tools of the software development team.

- If the team uses an automated tool to track requirements and ensure traceability, learn to use it, and become an owner (or at least a reviewer) of the requirements that are identified through UCD activities such as user analysis, prototyping, and UI specification.

- Learn to use the bug-tracking system to log usability problems. This at least puts the issues on the list and increases the communication between the UCD practitioner and the development team.

- Try to document issues and resolutions in a central location for everyone's future reference. Avoid too much reliance on email for addressing issues, because people may be inadvertently left out of the thread, and answers may be harder to find later.

Create an infrastructure that enables UCD activities to be done more efficiently. As the UCD process matures in the organization, there are opportunities to improve efficiency and reuse. Some examples include:

- Create and use templates for UCD deliverables.

- Create style guides and standards for user interface design.

- Create a library of personas and scenarios that have been produced through UCD activities on past projects, which can be reused in future generations of similar products.

- Initiate a "design partner program," or a panel of users who are signed up in advance to participate in usability tests and give feedback on short notice. This can facilitate quick iterative testing.

- Implement Web-based questionnaires, and standard questionnaire templates, to facilitate quick collection of feedback from end users.

Evaluate user feedback on an ongoing basis. An organization with a mature UCD practice seeks opportunities to collect user feedback not just through usability testing, but through multiple channels and over the long term. This is typically done through a combination of usage tracking, management information (MI) data, help desk reports, surveys, customer meetings, and longitudinal studies. The UCD practitioner can be instrumental in helping the organization design these feedback collection mechanisms, analyzing and interpreting the feedback, and determining how to use it as input to the design of new projects.

Influence strategic decisions and long-range project planning. The information collected in analysis and through feedback mechanisms can be valuable to high-level decision makers when considering new products or new releases. If the organization's initial product concepts or business goals are sketchy and incomplete, UCD practitioners may be able to assist in shaping and "concept testing" new ideas, using standard UCD methods. Information about the users and goals helps to define a broad vision for the future, not just for the current project.

Influence architecture decisions. The usability of a product may be compromised because of architectural constraints (see Chapter 6 for more information on usability and architecture). Traditionally, system architects and other technical leaders have had few tools or examples of ways that usability can be embedded in system design at the architecture level (Comstock and Duane, 1996). This is beginning to change as usability researchers are drawing connections between specific aspects of usability, such as the ability to "undo," and software architecture (Bass and John, 2001a). UCD practitioners can collect examples of usability needs that have not been met and initiate dialogues with the people responsible for designing architectures to seek longer-term solutions.

Encourage people from different roles to take more responsibility for user experience. Sharing the responsibility reduces the risk that only a small percentage of projects will have a usability focus due to resource constraints. To encourage this sharing, UCD practitioners should:

- Avoid dogmatism, which can alienate others. UCD practitioners must recognize that usability is just one of several perspectives, and is not always the most important development priority.

- Provide educational opportunities for people from other disciplines. When usability becomes the responsibility of other members of the project team, developers must at least understand the importance of usability and acquire basic HCI skills (Seffah, 2003).

- Ensure that the standard software development process and infrastructure used by all project teams incorporates a usability perspective. When standard processes are documented or when templates are created for deliverables, try to insert a UCD perspective. For example, a description of the analysis activities in the lifecycle can be augmented with a description of user profiling.

Common Challenges.

Projects do not necessarily follow the documented processes. Even when there is a documented lifecycle, there is frequently a gap between the documented lifecycle and the steps that are actually followed in a given project. There is also a natural variation between projects in terms of the steps followed and the degree of importance given to usability. In a written survey of attendees at the UPA 2003 conference, about 25% of those who said that their organization integrated UCD into multiple phases of the project lifecycle also wrote in the margins comments like "but not on every project" and "less than half of the time." Especially in organizations that are trying to achieve Capability Maturity Model (CMM) certification, teams are required to follow repeatable processes; however, in reality projects do cut corners in response to various pressures. Addressing these discrepancies in practices becomes a challenge not just for the UCD practitioner, but for project management in general.

The lifecycle does not support iteration. Iteration is a key principle of user-centered design (Butler, 1996). If the software development lifecycle itself does not support iterative refinement, it is difficult to integrate it with an essentially iterative UCD process. One researcher suggests that the existing development process must be based on iterative refinement as a prerequisite to introducing usability techniques and activities (Ferre, 2003). At least, UCD practitioners must realize that project managers and developers alike are uncomfortable with an unknown number of iterations, and become better at estimating, scheduling, and managing iterative activities. For example, project schedules can include placeholders for several iterations of early design concepts. The creation of a more mature UCD infrastructure as described above may also help make an iterative process quicker and more predictable. For example, an organization that has a standard process in place for collecting quick feedback from users through web questionnaires may be able to iterate a design more rapidly.

The optimal structure of the UCD group needs to be defined. As UCD is practiced more widely in the organization, the question arises whether UCD practitioners should be centralized or dispersed throughout the organization. There are advantages to the UCD practitioners themselves in being a centralized group, where members act as consultants to project teams, but maintain their identity as a group and are able to work collaboratively with one another. However there are also advantages to being co-located with the project teams and seen as team members who stay with the projects throughout the lifecycle. A matrix organization has the potential to allow the best of both options, but it is not always implemented successfully in practice.

15.5.4   Resulting Context

As a result of performing the process pattern, the organization has become more user-focused and the quality of its products continues to improve through better communication and feedback mechanisms throughout the lifecycle. Strategic decisions about product concepts and architecture are based on real data about users, tasks and context, collected over time from a variety of reliable sources.

15.6 CONCLUSION

This chapter has described a set of process patterns that synthesize the experience of many UCD practitioners in integrating user-centered methods with existing software development lifecycles. The evolutionary nature of these process patterns is important, because in reality user-centered methods cannot be assimilated all at once. Each step towards integration brings its own rewards and challenges.

More research and case studies are needed in several areas. First, best practices for integrating UCD deliverables with other project deliverables should be explored and documented. Second, approaches to integrating UCD activities with different lifecycle models (such as iterative, incremental, waterfall) should be further refined. Third, more research is needed to determine the best way to teach usability/HCI skills and perspectives to other professional groups such as developers, analysts, and user representatives. Finally, practitioners of UCD and RE should encourage sharing techniques and working more collaboratively towards our common goals of better understanding and meeting the needs of the business and the end users.

Acknowledgements

I would like to thank my colleagues, Brenda D'Angelo and Darrell Taylor, who co-facilitated the UPA 2003 workshop with me. I am grateful for the thoughtful discussion of the people who participated in that workshop: Valerie Arneson, Larry Constantine, Chris Jasek, Dave Kellmeyer, Kristina McBlain, Joi Roberts, and David Travis. I appreciate the opportunities provided by the Montreal Chapter and the Washington, DC Chapter of UPA to speak on this subject at local chapter meetings and the valuable feedback that I received from their members. Finally, I would like to thank Ahmed Seffah and Jan Gulliksen for their support and encouragement.

16 UI DESIGN PATTERNS: BRIDGING USE CASES AND UI DESIGN

John M. Artim

Expert Support, Inc.
201 San Antonio Circle, Suite 102
Mountain View, California 94040-1234 USA

Abstract

This chapter describes a formal and recursive UI design pattern description supporting UI design work subsequent to use-case-based specification. The multipart representation described in this chapter balances the need to define task elements supported by the pattern, the design elements comprising the pattern's prototypical solution, as well as the elements needed to map from the pattern to a specific domain of use.

16.1 INTRODUCTION

The pattern language work of the architect, Christopher Alexander (1977), has had profound effect on the way in which object-oriented technologists think about and express expertise in object-oriented design. Object technologists have put a great deal of effort into building up libraries of design patterns. The focus of these cataloging efforts ranges from domain-specific patterns in telecommunication, to analysis patterns, to patterns capturing accepted norms of computer language idiom, to extending the repertoire of proven design elements.

At the same time, HCI practitioners have explored the use of patterns in expressing user interface (UI) designs that have demonstrated utility and usability. Jennifer

A. Seffah (eds.), Human-Centered Software Engineering – Integrating Usability
in the Development Process, 309–329.

Tidwell has been working on a catalog of UI patterns since 1998 (Tidwell, 2004). Tidwell's patterns form a language of UI design. That is, her pattern catalog describes proven design elements in broad use by human-computer interaction (HCI) professionals.

Erik Nilsson (Nilsson, 2002) extends this notion of UI pattern through formal descriptions. Nilsson formalizes the description of a UI pattern with a UML class model of the presentation elements defining each UI pattern. Nilsson defined the optimum level of abstraction for these UI patterns as cross-platform—that is, at a level that abstracts cross-platform design differences.

The real contribution in Nilsson's paper is in the discussion of mapping of a pattern onto concrete design solutions and in the recursive nature of a UI pattern language. For Nilsson, pattern mapping from abstract design pattern to concrete solution entails identifying the concrete use of low-level pattern features corresponding to low-level presentation mechanisms. For example, Nilsson in describing the mapping for the tree-view (composite) pattern would focus on presentation mechanisms such as choice of icon in representing each component or the meaning of a single- or double-click on a component.

Recognizing the complexity of real-world design solutions Nilsson also notes the importance of a mechanism for recursively coupling UI patterns. Coupling supports recombination of patterns into the complex compositional presentation hierarchy that corresponds to a real-world domain task. Nilsson does not, however, describe a mechanism to support pattern coupling.

On the face of it, these two threads of effort—UI patterns on the one hand and patterns of object-based design on the other—converge in the sense that both emphasize abstract models of the components used to build solutions for a particular domain. For the UI practitioner these patterns focus on presentation elements. The object-technologist's patterns describe how to construct well-designed code implementing applications on the computer.

Alexander, in his keynote address (Alexander, 1996) to the OOPSLA96 conference, suggested the possibility of a deeper connection. In this address he described his sense of building architecture pattern language as a vast composition of design elements. Each level of design supports some aspect of human living and working. At the level of finest detail there are work spaces supporting specific task domains the user of the architected space needs or wants to engage in.

As I listened to this keynote address I was struck by the similarities between Alexander's sense of unfolding spaces and the HCI professional's sense of unfolding task description. Each task in a task composition will ultimately be matched with the space in which the task can be completed. The HCI sense of space often involves windows within a WIMP interface or some sort of dedicated interface—that is, physical control panel or surface. These surfaces of interest to the HCI professional are in fact lower-level design elements in the composition envisioned by Alexander.

While Nilsson focuses on recursive composition—that is, recursive coupling—of UI design patterns he fails to address the composition of primary importance to both the building architect and the human-computer interface designer—the hierarchy of tasks of interest to the end-user.

Fabio Patterno (Paternò, 2000) in his work on concur task trees describes a notation for modeling user tasks and task patterns. Daniel Sinnig (Sinnig et al., 2005) describes a taxonomy of UI design patterns divided into presentation, task, and dialog patterns. These approaches emphasize the importance of task patterns in moving from descriptions of user work—typically in the form of use cases or other task models—to user interface design. What is missing is a unified approach to UI design patterns that is task-based in its pattern-selection criteria but which covers the gamut of UI design patterns as elaborated by Sinnig.

The remainder of this chapter discusses a formal pattern representation that addresses the nature of the coupling between UI design patterns. This coupling complements techniques using a use-case-based task decomposition and the concrete domain entities manipulated by these tasks. This formal approach to UI design pattern modeling has implications for use case modeling, UI design, UI implementation, and the teaching of HCI techniques.

This formal UI pattern model includes:

- A description of the task characteristics defining the context of use where the pattern is correctly applied. This abstract description defines the kind of problem space addressed by the pattern.

  The characteristics determine which pattern applies to a particular use case— that is, to a particular user task.

- An object model defining the problem space representation or representation elements provided by the pattern.

  This model describes the common user interface elements defined by the pattern—that is to say it describes the chunk of UI design prescribed by the pattern. This corresponds to the kind of pattern element models proposed by Nilsson.

- A composable metamodel of the required and optional domain mappings needed to apply the pattern to a domain of use.

  This metamodel itemizes the elements needed to map the abstract problem space representation described by a design pattern to the elements of a user's domain. The mapping describes the chunk of presentation needed to support a corresponding chunk of user tasks.

  These domain mappings combined with the object model of the elements of the pattern form the specification of user interface framework support for the design pattern including the complete property mapping required to support graphical construction environments.

This approach is based on a model-based understanding of human-computer interaction and software engineering methods as previously described by Artim, 2001. A model-based understanding of these methods need not require formal modeling in practice but does require a formal understanding of the underpinnings of the methods.

The formal descriptions of UI design patterns proposed here bridge the gap between use case scenarios used in software functional specification and the analysis of these use cases to derive a usable user interface design. This bridge step uses the common task characteristics to analyze use case scenario text to identify the appropriate UI design pattern—that is, problem space representation—that supports the problem space described within the scenario text. The final link is the description of mapping elements bridging between the elements of the domain described in the scenario text and the elements of the UI design pattern.

16.2   TREE—AN EXAMPLE OF A UI PATTERN

Tree is a good UI design pattern to illustrate the current approach. *Tree* is also known as *Hierarchical Set* Tidwell's catalog (Tidwell, 2004). Current graphical operating system interfaces, including those for the Apple®, Microsoft®, and X Window platforms, provide a file browser which features a tree widget to aid in visualizing the file hierarchy.

In the pattern approach described here, a tree pattern is described and defined in a number of ways.

First of all, a tree is operationally defined as:

> *The tree design pattern is used to browse and manipulate a whole-part structure. The whole-part structure is often complex in its associations and large in its extent.*

> *Alternately, a tree design pattern is used to browse and manipulate a subset of a domain network. The domain network subset must be composed of associations forming a tree topology. In this alternative case a set of domain associations are behaving as though they are whole-part relationships. That is, these associations are being used to define the composition of some root entity.*

This operational definition provides a coherent overview of the primary and important alternative uses of the pattern. Though operational definitions are useful in gaining an initial understanding of a pattern, a more systematic breakdown of pattern usage is needed. In the current approach this systematic breakdown of correct pattern usage is provided through a list of the user task characteristics supported by the pattern. These characteristics describe the kinds of user tasks to which the pattern is well-suited.

For the tree pattern this list includes:

- The task space is a whole-part structure from a domain network rooted on a single entity. In this structure each node in the network decomposes into child nodes by traversing one step in the whole-part hierarchy. Each step consists of one or more whole-part associations. If more than one whole-part association forms one step in the hierarchy, the child nodes reached by traversing each of these sibling whole-part associations are of equivalent meaning with respect to the task space.

  Or the task is a domain network rooted on a single entity. From the root entity instance the network is traversed in steps. Each step consists of one or more associations collectively forming a single one-to-many expression. Each of these traversal steps has domain significance. Each step may be defined by multiple one-to-many expressions but where multiple expressions are defined they must be of equivalent meaning with respect to the task space.

- Task completion involves search through successive steps in the hierarchy.
  Or task completion involves exploration through successive steps in the hierarchy.
  Or task completion involves comparison of two or more paths through the hierarchy.

- Each step of the hierarchy represents a domain categorization. The user knows the meaning and use of the categories at all—or at least most—levels within the hierarchy and arrives at a task solution by traversing the hierarchy through one or more paths.

- **C** Traversing each step—that is expanding a node—typically results in at most seven to ten child nodes.

  > Nodes that expand to greater than ten or so child nodes impose greater cognitive load on the user. This load is typically large enough that categorization of the children of that node should be treated as a secondary task demanding a share of the attention that could otherwise be devoted to the primary task.

The preceding text describes four characteristics of the tree pattern.

The first paragraph of the first characteristic describes the use of tree to visualize a whole-part structure. The second paragraph is a continuation providing an equivalent alternative to the first paragraph. It allows use of the tree pattern when visualizing domain associations other than whole-part associations.

The second characteristic describes what sorts of tasks the user does that involve the whole part structure. This characteristic is defined in three equivalent bullet points—that is, each of these three types of task equivalently describe what the user might be doing when needing to visualize a whole-part hierarchy.

The third characteristic defines what it means, in terms of a user domain, to traverse a level in the hierarchy.

Finally, the point labeled with a **C** denotes a potential constraint on the use of this pattern. A particular user task might violate this constraint and still, in principal at least, appropriately use the tree pattern. Constraints indicate when the designer might experience difficulty in appropriately using a pattern—that is, when usability problems might result even from the correct application of the pattern.

Potential uses of this pattern appear everywhere since whole-part structures pervade our conceptual world. To illustrate use of the tree pattern let's look at an example from biology. Classification of organisms is a critical part of biological theory. Taxonomy is the systematic classification of organisms into a whole-part structure or hierarchy. For the zoologist, this classification scheme includes seven major levels: Kingdom, Phylum, Class, Order, Family, Genus, and Species. As you explore this whole-part structure there are more entries as you descend each level of the structure. Each level categorizes the species in question into an increasingly more specific and therefore smaller category. Figure 16.1 illustrates the tree pattern by showing a few invertebrate species and the taxonomic classification for them. Each leaf node in this tree represents a species in the taxonomy.

One species shown in Figure 16.1 is *Luidia alternata*[1] . To determine how *L. alternata* fits into higher-level taxonomic categories read down the tree from the root down to the leaf node of interest. For *L. alternata*, this reads: Kingdom *Animalia*, Phyla *Echinodermata*, Class *Asteroidia*, Order *Platyasterida*, Family *Luidiidae*, Genus *Luidia*, Species *alternata*.

Taxonomists have built into their domain terminology an interesting feature. Taxonomic names are all based on Latin's rules of construction. Taxonomists take this one step further and have created stylized suffixes for each level in the taxonomy. For example, Family names typically end in the *ae* suffix. In addition to the icons representing each of the taxonomic levels, the professional taxonomist has the names themselves as an aid indicating taxonomic level.

It is not essential to understand biological taxonomy to see that this domain features a large whole-part classification scheme and that this whole-part structure can be well-represented by a tree display.

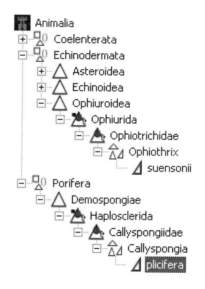

Figure 16.1   A chunk of UI based on the tree pattern

16.2.1   Tree Metamodel

A tree is a root node that contains other nodes. Each node represents an instance of an entity in the user's domain—in Figure 16.3 each node represents a biologists'

---

[1]Taxonomists identify species by their genus and species only—each genus and species combination is unique across all other taxonomic categories. Subsequent references to one genus on one page are abbreviated by the first letter of the genus name when such an abbreviation is unambiguous.

taxonomy category. Each node is presented as a glyph that indicates to the user the type of domain entity the node represents. The node is also presented using a text label whose value uniquely identifies the node. The composition of one node within other nodes is the only relationship depicted in a tree— Figure 16.1 shows the composition of taxonomic groups.

An object-model description of a tree pattern is shown in Figure 16.2. This diagram includes:

- A *Tree* starts with a root *Tree Node*

- *Tree Nodes*, including the root, can contain other *Tree Nodes*

- Each *Tree Node* contains a *Tree Node Creation Map* describing how to derive the next level of *Tree* using an entry, a *Tree Node Creation Mapping*, for each type of domain entity that can be contained in this level of the whole-part hierarchy. Each *Tree Node Creation Mapping* consists of the following:

    - A glyph to represent the domain entity type
    - A description of how to trace through the domain from the last node's entity to the collection of entities composing the current branch
    - Another map representing part levels in the hierarchy below the current level

In order to apply the tree pattern to the biologists' taxonomy domain we need a domain model of taxonomy concepts.

16.2.2   Simplified Taxonomy Domain Model

The taxonomy domain is illustrated in Figure 16.3. This figure includes the units of taxonomy—*Phylum*, for example—shown as classes in a UML class diagram and the whole-part relationships among the taxa shown as UML whole-part—that is, aggregation—relationships.

16.2.3   Domain Metamodel

The elements in Figure 16.3 represent the concepts that make up a task domain—in this case the domain of biological taxonomy. To successfully apply any UI pattern, the UI practitioner must map the UI pattern onto a specific task domain. The domain metamodel shown in Figure 16.4 defines the generalized model of concepts used by the UI pattern approach described in this chapter to map a pattern onto a task domain's concepts.

Figure 16.4 describes a straightforward concept model where an *Entity* represents a domain concept, an *Attribute* represents a characteristic of an Entity, and different kinds of relationship—such as *Whole-Part Relationship*—represent the ways in which concepts are defined in terms of other concepts. This approach to concept modeling is described elsewhere by Artim (Artim, 2001).

To understand this example, think of a whole-part relationship as a kind of composition where the whole composition is defined by the kinds of parts that make it up.

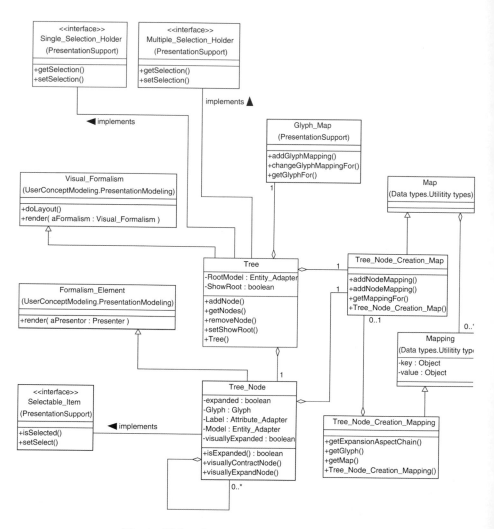

Figure 16.2 Object model for the tree pattern

For example, a car can be defined as being composed of a body, two or more doors, a number of windows, four wheels, steering and speed control for the driver, and some sort of engine. In this case the car is the whole and the body, doors, windows, and what not are the parts.

Figure 16.5 applies this domain metamodel to the mapping of a chunk of the taxonomy domain model onto the taxonomy tree presentation shown in Figure 16.1. For brevity, only a portion of the taxonomy tree is depicted in this diagram. Two versions of the diagram are shown. In each version, the entities and relationships of the taxonomy domain are shown down the left-hand side of this diagram. The right-hand side of each version shows the parts of the taxonomy tree display: this abbreviated diagram includes the *Kingdom Node* representing the root node of the tree, the *Kingdom Expansion Node* representing the presentation ability to expand a node into its children[2], and the *Phylum Node* representing child nodes of the root node.

The left-hand version of the diagram depicts the domain concepts of *Kingdom* and *Phylum* as UML classes (boxes) and the whole-part relationship between them as a UML composition relationship (the link with a diamond at its origin). In this version the mapping from the *Kingdom Node Expansion* is drawn pointing to the whole-part relationship. This representation of a link pointing to another link is not supported notation in UML.

The second version of the diagram depicts the whole-part relationship between *Kingdom* and *Phylum* as a class to which the *Kingdom Node Expansion* can be directly linked. First note that the diagram makes explicit the domain's whole part relationships—such as *Kingdom to Phylum WholePart rel*—as first-class objects. From this class diagram you can immediately see the benefits and the liabilities of representing relationships as objects. The mapping from UI pattern—*Kingdom Node Expansion* for example—to domain—*Kingdom to Phylum WholePart Rel* in this case—is explicit. While this does help emphasize that the whole-part relationships are themselves concepts it also makes the diagram larger and somewhat unwieldy. This diagram represents only two out of seven taxonomic concepts and one out of six whole-part relationships yet the diagram is already large. Also, using the same notation for a domain entity and for relationships among entities makes this representation much harder to understand. While the right-hand diagram version shown in Figure 16.5 strictly adheres to UML notation standards I believe the left-hand version provides a clearer sense of the mapping of a chunk of presentation onto a chunk of domain.

The other problem with the representation in Figure 16.5 is that in use, UI patterns are nested into elaborate compositions supporting real-world tasks. Figure 16.5 shows the tree pattern as its component display elements: *Kingdom Node*, *Kingdom Node Expansion*, and *Phylum Node*. Though nested UI patterns can be shown as a nesting of their display elements this kind of diagram gives no indication of which compositions are valid and which are not. It is not that there is any inherent difficulty in representing compositions of patterns in this way—there simply is not any indication of correctness nor completeness.

The class diagrams in this section help illuminate the problem of mapping UI patterns to user domains. But, because the class diagram representation of the mapping is both unwieldy and lacks support for validation, other compositional tools are required.

---

[2]This is shown as a plus-minus control in Windows® or an upward or sideways pointing arrow on the Macintosh®.

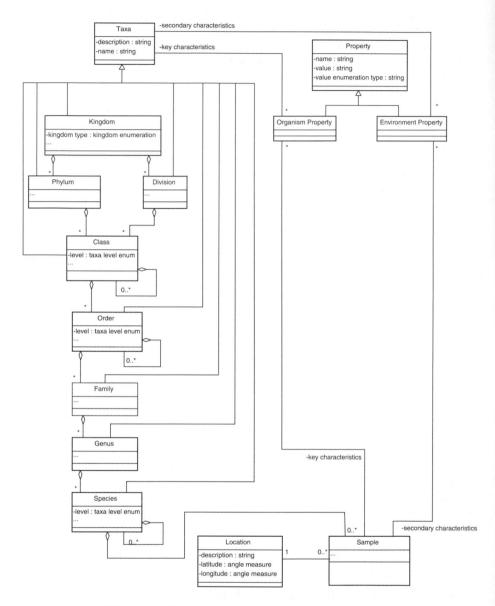

Figure 16.3   A UML class diagram of the biologist's taxonomy domain

16.2.4   Mapping Presentation to the User's Domain with XML

What is needed to create a compact, verifiable representation of a UI pattern to user domain mapping is a simple declarative representation of the structure. XML (Extensible Markup Language) provides a straightforward and extensible mechanism for building declarative representations.

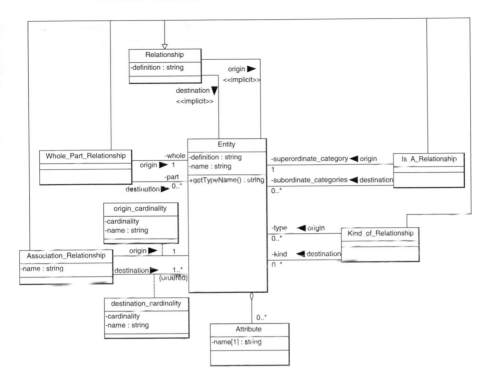

Figure 16.4   Domain metamodel class diagram

There are two parts to XLM structures: a meta-description of document content—the Document Type Definition (DTD)—and valid XML documents based on a meta-description.

Typically, an XML document is thought of as specified by one DTD. In practice, DTDs can be nested one within another to create a document meta-description. In the present approach to composable UI patterns, each pattern is described by a DTD. These pattern DTDs define two aspects of each pattern:

1. Connection points between the pattern and a user domain

2. Connection points between patterns

Figure 16.6 shows the DTD describing the tree UI pattern. This DTD defines:

- The icons (glyphs) mapping to each domain entity type (lines 3 and 4)

- The chain of aspects to follow to get a label for each node (lines 7 and 8)
  The chain of aspects are directions for tracing a path through the domain from an Entity to be represented as a tree node to the attributes of that entity that specify the tree node's label.

- The definition of a *Root* as an *Entity* and a mapping describing the *Aspects* of the domain that define the expansion of each level of the tree (line 9, 10)

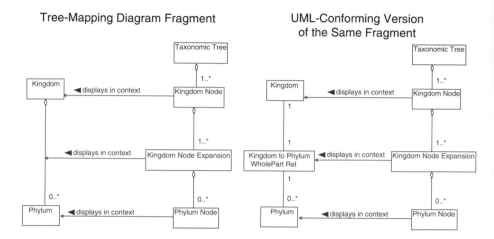

Figure 16.5   The mapping of a tree pattern onto the Taxonomy domain

This mechanism provides a nested description of the domain expansion that defines the nodes of the tree as well as the attributes used for labels for each node. This corresponds to the nested sequence of destinations of the *Display in Context* links off of each *node expansion*—for example in Figure 16.5, the whole-part relationship pointed to by the link from the *Kingdom Node Expansion* is the first aspect in the *Taxonomy Tree's* description.

- The mechanism for describing the preceding nested mapping description (line 12 to 15)

- Lines 3 to 8 and 16 to 23 are reusable mechanisms used throughout the pattern set

This DTD provides a relatively compact and complete specification of a UI Pattern. The next test is to see how reasonable it is to build representations of pattern to domain mappings using XML based on a pattern's DTD.

Figure 16.7 is a partial listing of the XML description of the chunk of user interface shown in Figure 16.1 (the taxonomy tree UI). The XML shown describes the domain mapping for the first two levels in the hierarchy: *Kingdom* and *Phylum*. The XML to describe icon mapping, the selection mechanism, and the remainder of the tree decomposition is omitted. The entire description is 127 lines long.

This representation is not too cumbersome. Each level in the hierarchy is described by nine XML elements:

- A *DisplayMapping* element and a *DisplayMapEntry* (lines 10 and 11, for example) form the mapping for one level in the hierarchy

- The *EntityType* that applies to the *DisplayMapEntry* which is provided in case there are multiple entity types supported at one level in the whole-part hierarchy (line 12, for example)

```
1.)     <!ELEMENT Tree (IconMapping?, SelectionHolder?, Root)>
2.)     <!ATTLIST Tree ID CDATA #REQUIRED >
3.)     <!ELEMENT IconMapping (IconMapEntry+)>
4.)     <!ELEMENT IconMapEntry (EntityType, IconType)>
5.)     <!ATTLIST EntityType TypeName CDATA #REQUIRED>
6.)     <!ATTLIST IconType TypeName CDATA #REQUIRED>
7.)     <!ELEMENT LabelMapping (LabelMapEntry+)>
8.)     <!ELEMENT LabelMapEntry (EntityType, Aspect+)>
9.)     <!ELEMENT Root (PresentationParent | Entity,
10.)                            DisplayMapping+)>
11.)    <!ATTLIST PresentationParent ID CDATA #REQUIRED >
12.)    <!ELEMENT DisplayMapping (DisplayMapEntry+,
13.)                            DisplayMapping?) >
14.)    <!ELEMENT DisplayMapEntry (EntityType, Aspect+,
15.)                            LabelMapping)>
16.)    <!ATTLIST Aspect AspectName CDATA #REQUIRED>
17.)    <!ELEMENT SelectionHolder (SingleSelectionHolder |
18.)                            MultipleSelectionHolder)>
19.)    <!ATTLIST SelectionHolder ID CDATA #REQUIRED>
20.)    <!ELEMENT SingleSelectionHolder (Entity)>
21.)    <!ELEMENT MultipleSelectionHolder (Entity+)>
22.)    <!ELEMENT Entity (EntityType)>
23.)    <!ATTLIST Entity ID CDATA #REQUIRED >
```

Figure 16.6   Fragment 1. DTD content describing the tree UI pattern

- The *Aspect* that describes how to retrieve the entities for the level in the hierarchy described by the *DisplayMapEntry* (line 13, for example)

- The *LabelMapping, LabelEntry, EntityType,* and *Aspect* that describe how to derive the label for nodes representing the entities retrieved for the DisplayMapEntry (lines 14 to 19, for example)

This representation is adequately compact, at least for the purpose of experimenting with composition of UI patterns. The next section of this chapter discusses a more complete example use of patterns and pattern composition.

16.3   COMPOSED UI DESIGN PATTERNS IN USE

This section focuses on the use of UI design patterns in software design and construction. In particular, the section focuses on the use of UI design patterns in conjunction with use case descriptions of functional requirements.

16.3.1   Extending the Taxonomy Example

The example discussed in the remainder of the chapter describes a zoology student learning taxonomic concepts. The UML use case diagram shown in Figure 16.8 lists the tasks that make up this user task domain.

The overall task is *Explore Zoological Taxonomy*. This task includes *Browse Taxonomic Relationships* and *Browse Individual Taxon*—that is, browse an individual family, species, or the like.

```
1).    <Tree ID="TaxonomyTree">
2).        <SelectionHolder ID="SelectedTaxa">
3).            <SingleSelectionHolder>
4).                <Entity ID="">
5).                    <EntityType TypeName=""/>
6).                </Entity>
7).            </SingleSelectionHolder>
8).        </SelectionHolder>
9).        <Root>
10).            <DisplayMapping>
11).                <DisplayMapEntry>
12).                    <EntityType TypeName="Kingdom"/>
13).                    <Aspect AspectName="Whole-Part"/>
14).                    <LabelMapping>
15).                        <LabelMapEntry>
16).                            <EntityType TypeName="Kingdom"/>
17).                            <Aspect AspectName="Name"/>
18).                        </LabelMapEntry>
19).                    </LabelMapping>
20).                </DisplayMapEntry>
21).                <DisplayMapping>
22).                    <DisplayMapEntry>
23).                        <EntityType TypeName="Phylum"/>
24).                        <Aspect AspectName="Whole-Part"/>
25).                        <LabelMapping>
26).                            <LabelMapEntry>
27).                                <EntityType TypeName="Phylum"/>
28).                                <Aspect AspectName="Name"/>
29).                            </LabelMapEntry>
30).                        </LabelMapping>
31).                    </DisplayMapEntry>
32).                        . . .
33).                </DisplayMapping>
34).            </DisplayMapping>
35).        </Root>
36).    </Tree>
```

Figure 16.7   Fragment 2. A fragment of the 127 lines of XML specifying the Figure 16.1 UI

The selection of a UI pattern to provide presentation support for a particular user task focuses on scenario text for the use case describing that user task. Scenario text describes, in episodic form, the procedural content of a task. We start our analysis with the normal success scenario for the highest-level task—*Explore Taxonomy* in this example. This scenario includes the following steps:

1. Browse the relationships among zoological taxonomic categories. This step is described in detail in the *Browse Taxonomic Relationships* use case. This step culminates in selection of one taxon in the taxonomic hierarchy.

2. Browse the specifics of the individual taxonomic category selected in the previous step. This step is described in detail in the *Browse Taxon Definition* use case.

3. Repeat the preceding steps in a free-form exploration of zoological taxonomic concepts.

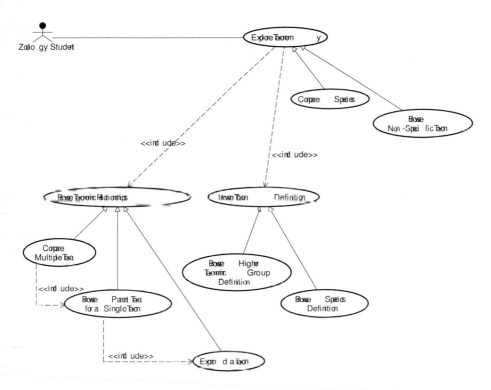

Figure 16.8   A use case diagram for taxonomy learning tasks

Even this short scenario tells us three things about the presentation needed to support this use case. First, there will be two main parts to this presentation: one to support the *Browse Taxonomic Relationships* use case and one to support the *Browse Individual Taxon* use case. Second, the presentation supporting the *Browse Individual Taxa* use case presents the details of the taxonomic category selected in the presentation for the *Browse Taxonomic Relationships* use case. Third, the overall presentation comprised of the *Browse Taxonomic Relationships* presentation and the *Browse Individual Taxon* presentation must support ad hoc exploration—that is, the user will be repeatedly performing first one and then the other of these two use cases.

The main success scenario for *Browse Taxonomic Relationships* includes the following steps:

1. The user completes one of the specialized versions of this use case.

This scenario text indicates that the generic use case, *Browse Taxonomic Relationships*, has no concrete scenario associated with it. The scenarios for the specific use cases derived from *Browse Taxonomic Relationships* describe how this task is accomplished.

The scenario for the *Expand a Taxon* use case includes the following steps:

1. The user chooses one of the currently displayed taxa.

2. The user expands this taxon to display its sub-taxa.

The main scenario for the *Browse Parent Taxa for a Single Taxon* use case includes the following steps:

1. The user expands a taxon of interest. This step is described in the *Expand a Taxon* use case.

2. The user chooses one of the sub-taxa newly displayed by the previous step and expands this taxon. This step is described in the *Expand a Taxon* use case. This step is repeated, as needed.

3. The user, finding the taxon of interest, can now follow the chain of expanded taxa from the leaf taxon up through progressively more general taxa until they reach the phylum for the taxon of interest and then, ultimately, the kingdom *Animalia*.

The main scenario for the *Compare Multiple Taxa* use case includes these steps:

1. The user selects and browses the first taxon of interest. This step is described in the *Browse Parent Taxa for a Single Taxon* use case.

2. The user selects and browses subsequent taxa of interest at the same taxonomic level as the taxon selected in the previous step. This step is described in the *Browse Parent Taxa for a Single Taxon* use case. This step is repeated, as needed.

3. The user compares the selected taxa. The user may be interested in common branches in the taxonomic tree or simply in comparing the expansion of taxonomic categorization for two or more organisms.

To illustrate this scenario in a more extended context, consider the user-interface mock-up in Figure 16.9. This mock-up is typical of what might be seen in a storyboard illustrating the content of this set of use cases.

Figure 16.9 shows the state of the UI after the user has expanded first the branch leading to *Callyspongia plicifera* (the vase-shaped Caribbean sponge pictured in the mock-up). Upon reading the image caption the user expands the taxonomic path leading to *Oreaster reticulatus*, the brittle star whose arms are seen protruding from the vase-shaped sponge. The user compares the two co-occurring species by alternately selecting one species in the tree widget in the left-hand portion of the UI then selecting the other species. This change in selection changes the content of the right-hand portion of this UI to reflect the details of first one and then the other species.

By analyzing the Browse Taxonomic Relationships use case and its specific use cases the UI designer would see a strong match with task characteristics described for the tree pattern.

The right-hand portion of the UI mock-up is described in the *Browse Taxon Definition* use case. Consider the main scenario which includes the following steps:

1. The user reads the name of the taxon.

2. The user reads a description of where the taxon is found. This includes a description of habitat and of the geographic range of the taxon.

3. The user reads a physical description of the taxon including its static structure and dynamic behavior.

4. The user compares the physical description from the preceding step with an image—either photographic or diagrammatic—of the taxon.

The *Browse Taxon Definition* use case is specialized in the *Browse Species Definition* use case whose main scenario steps include:

1. The user reads the latin binomial designation for the species—that is, the full species name. This includes the genus name and species name.

2. The user reads a description of where the species is found. This includes a description of the species habitat and the geographic range throughout which the species is found.

3. The user reads a physical description of the species including the salient features distinguishing this species from other, visually similar organisms and this species dynamic behavior including differences in behavior from other, visually similar species.

4. The user compares the physical description from the preceding step with a set of images of the species including one or more photographs representative of the range of its appearance and one or more diagrams of its salient physical features.

Analyzing this and the remainder of the use cases and scenarios results in the list of patterns shown in Table 16.1, "Descriptions of the tasks from Figure 16.9 and matching UI Patterns."

This set of composed patterns ultimately leads to an XML description approximately 170 lines long describing the UI mock-up shown in Figure 16.9.

16.4   PATTERN DESCRIPTIONS IN PRACTICE

The UI design pattern description outlined in this chapter is used differently and has a different affect depending on the role of the stakeholder considered. In this section these differences among key stakeholders are explored.

Table 16.1   Descriptions of the tasks from Figure 16.9 and matching UI Patterns

Task Names	Task Step	Supporting Patterns
Explore Taxonomy		• Composition of Patterns: patterns for *Browse Taxonomic Relationships* and *Browse Taxon Definition* compose to form overall presentation • Selection Dependence: *Browse Taxon Definition* presentation based on selected taxon in *Browse Taxonomic Relationships* presentation
Browse Taxonomic Relationships, Compare Multiple Taxa, Browse Parent Taxa for a Single Taxon, Expand a Taxon		• Tree
Browse Species Definition	Read taxon name	• Grouping Box • Static Label • Text Box
	Read where found	• Group Box • Static Label • Text Box or Text Area
	Read physical description	• Grouping Box • Static Label • Text Area
	See appearance	• Graphic Area • Grouping Box • Static Label • Text Box

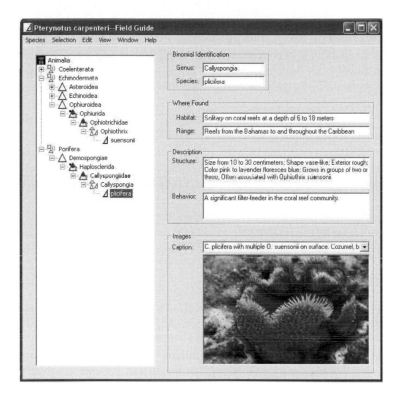

Figure 16.9   A complete UI design, a taxonomy Field Guide Explorer

16.4.1   Use Case Author

For the use case author, the task characteristics listed for each pattern guide the construction of scenario text. The task characteristics are worded to avoid polluting analysis with design decisions—including decisions regarding the design of the user interface.

As the use case author gains experience in UI design patterns they come to recognize these patterns in the tasks they document. As a consequence, the task descriptions are cleaner and better reflect the user's requirements for optimal problem space representations.

Too often in current software requirements practice the use case author goes beyond requirements and on to specifying UI design. A UI design pattern catalog structured as described in this chapter provides the use case author with increased sensitivity to the distinction between presentation requirements and UI design.

16.4.2   User Interface Designer

The user interface designer's interest in the pattern descriptions primarily focuses on the task characteristics that define proper use of each pattern. The UI designer uses these characteristics to choose the appropriate pattern to support each user task. If the patterns are documented in a catalog or UI style guide that also provides examples of use of each pattern the designer might use these examples to verify pattern choices.

The UI designer is also concerned, either explicitly or implicitly, with the pattern to domain mapping for each pattern. The UI designer must completely map how each UI design pattern used in the final design onto the portion of the user's domain that is to be displayed.

Use of the components of a pattern description may shift in more futuristic situations as when, for example, a tool such as described by Sinnig (Sinnig et al., 2005), is used to construct a user interface out of parameterized component patterns. In this envisioned situation the designer, after selecting patterns based on the task characteristics described in use case scenario text, might use a diagram editor to create the mapping links between each pattern's elements and the concepts of the user's domain.

A pattern catalog structured as described in this chapter provides the UI designers with an awareness of the relationship among the presentation elements in their design and between these presentation elements and the user tasks the elements must serve.

16.4.3   UI Architect

Even in project contexts making use of today's tools UI architects use many aspects of the pattern descriptions outlined in this chapter. When discussing difficult design decisions with peer architects the object model or XML parameterized descriptions of patterns help to formalize problems and highlight sources of conflict in design. When selecting class libraries or other implementation support for user interface the architect can use these same object models or XML descriptions as feature checklists to compare implementation alternatives. And, should the architect need to merge implementation services from multiple sources these formal descriptions can serve as a blueprint for how to approach design of the merged software.

16.4.4   UI Services Designer

Whether implementing a conventional class library, or a framework of user interface services, or a construction environment as described by Sinnig (Sinnig et al., 2005), the designer of UI services requires the level of requirements details provided by the formal pattern descriptions outlined in this chapter—especially the level of detail found in the mapping DTDs.

16.5   FUTURE WORK

The author is compiling a pattern catalog listing common UI design patterns covering:

- Visual formalisms—such as Tree, Form, and Table

- Formalism elements—such as Text Box, Static Label, and Group Box

- Mechanisms—such as Single and Multiple Selection

- Architectural Elements—such as Window and Desktop

- Task patterns—such as Task Order Guidance and Mandatory Task Order

This pattern catalog will be published in open-source format at http:www. primaryview.org. It is the author's intention to include information on use of the pattern entries in authoring UI style guides.

The application of a catalog of pattern descriptions in the design of UI frameworks and UI-enabling tools such as described by Sinnig (Sinnig et al., 2005) are obvious and would provide a more complete validation of the formal content of the pattern descriptions.

16.6   CONCLUSIONS

When formalizing descriptions of UI design patterns object models provide compact and useful descriptions of a pattern's metamodel. This chapter extends this static model of UI design patterns by examining pattern composition. Patterns and pattern composition can be documented and verified through the use of DTD descriptions of the mapping elements each pattern requires to describe its mapping to a user task domain. Descriptions of specific domain instantiations of a UI design pattern are compactly and usably expressed in a by the XML markup instantiating the DTDs defining the pattern. This explicit mapping from user tasks to design elements places the focus of UI design patterns squarely back on the user.

17 UI DESIGN PATTERNS: FROM THEORY TO PRACTICE

Janet Wesson and Lester Cowley

Nelson Mandela Metropolitan University, South Africa

Abstract

In this chapter, we discuss how user interface (UI) design patterns can assist in bridging the gap between requirements and design in software development, and the research challenges posed by their use. Completed and ongoing research done by the authors and co-workers on UI pattern use in transaction processing and E-commerce system development and evaluation is used to illustrate the discussion.

17.1 INTRODUCTION

Software design patterns have proved useful at the coding level in object-orientated software engineering (SE). There is some empirical evidence that the quality of software produced using patterns is better than that of equivalent software produced through conventional means (Schmidt and Cleeland, 2000). A number of large enterprises have successfully made use of software design patterns. Many developers know about patterns and a number of books have been published on the subject. UI design patterns, however, have yet to prove themselves in the way that software design patterns have and there is little empirical evidence that the quality of interfaces produced using UI design patterns is better than that of equivalent interfaces produced through conventional UI design methods (e.g. using guidelines). Thus studies of the

*A. Seffah (eds.), Human-Centered Software Engineering – Integrating Usability
in the Development Process, 331–351.*

process of using UI patterns and pattern languages (PLs) and the quality of the arte-facts (patterns and designs) used and produced are necessary.

Studying the process of using UI patterns in more detail is necessary for three reasons. Firstly, it would clarify how useful UI patterns really are. Secondly, knowing how designers and developers actually use patterns would enable one to formalise UI pattern use within the software development process, train software engineers in the use of patterns and manage the process (Wesson, 2001). Thirdly, once the use of patterns is properly understood, usable tool support for them can be developed.

We present a study by Kok and Wesson of the use of UI design patterns in the development of transaction processing (TP) systems that has yielded interesting information on the process of using UI patterns from a developer's perspective (Section 17.3). This study revealed that existing pattern collections provide patterns suitable for lower-level UI design but not for higher level design. New high-level TP patterns were identified deductively by constructing a generalised task model from a number of extant systems and comparing this model with a normative task model for TP.

The UI pattern study also presents evidence that suggests that if developers use good-quality UI patterns, the usability of the systems they develop might be better. The quality of the TP PL was evaluated as good using Fincher's properties (Fincher, 1999) and the usability of the UIs produced was measured as good by means of usability testing. These results provide empirical evidence that UI patterns are useful tools for supporting the design process.

Pattern quality is difficult to measure (Wesson and Cowley, 2003). Lea (Lea, 1994) and Fincher (Fincher, 2000) have proposed different pattern property lists that can be used to evaluate patterns statically. The surface (static) features of a pattern, however, do not fully reveal its dynamic quality in use. It seems reasonable to assume, therefore, that a competent designer or developer using good-quality UI patterns, as described in the case study in Section 17.3, will produce UIs of good usability. The usability of these systems can be measured quite easily using standard techniques.

In this chapter, a study by Cowley and Wesson which is currently in the data analysis stage, is described (Section 17.4). This study aims to understand the process of pattern-based design and to determine the attitudes of a sample of designers and developers to using UI patterns in the design and development of E-commerce web sites.

The next section discusses how UI patterns should be identified.

17.2   PATTERN IDENTIFICATION

Pattern identification is the process of discovering new patterns. Apart from new patterns, the process may reveal relationships (connections) between these patterns and between them and pre-existing patterns. It may be possible to describe the type of each relationship (subordinate, supra-ordinate, etc.) (Salingaros, 2000). The new patterns and relationships may extend and modify existing pattern languages, and reveal new ones.

Although over 200 UI patterns exist in several pattern collections (for example, see Tidwell, 1998a; Alexander, 1979; Duyne et al., 2002, the need for pattern identification has not fallen away. UI design is still developing, the pattern collections are tentative and evolving and there are application domains which have not been studied yet. It is quite likely that there are numbers of UI patterns as yet unidentified (the DOME case study presented in Section 17.3 describes several new TP patterns which were recently identified). Thus it is important for pattern researchers and users to understand the pattern identification process.

UI pattern identification may be done in one of two ways: finding patterns by studying existing practice and knowledge (Section 17.2.1); or generating them through the UI design (UID) lifecycle (Section 17.2.2).

17.2.1 Pattern Identification Through Induction

Finding patterns by studying existing practice and knowledge is the most common means of pattern identification and has yielded most of the UI patterns currently in collections. This process is called *pattern mining* (Appleton, 2000). Pattern mining is an inductive process; by identifying and studying sufficient examples of good practice, patterns are identified through generalisation

Pattern mining may be done by studying the static form and dynamic behaviour of a number of good quality systems to find good designs, and by learning from the accumulated design and development experience of designers and developers of good quality systems.

Mining patterns is very difficult and time-consuming. Alexander (Alexander et al., 1977) gives a three step process to follow in order to identify a pattern, which Griffiths and Pemberton (Griffiths and Pemberton, 2000) have elaborated for the identification of UI patterns:

- Identify the *subject* of the pattern, by finding usable and useful examples of an interface artefact in existing systems.

- Identify the *problem* that the pattern resolves, and the set of conflicting *forces* that shape a *solution* to the problem.

- Identify *invariance*, by examining the interface artefact exemplified in a number of existing systems to see how successful solutions balance the forces and unsuccessful solutions fail to do this.

The evolving, tentative pattern (or protopattern) needs to be captured in a standard format and this activity is called *pattern writing*. Vlissides (Vlissides, 1995) suggests seven habits that pattern writers should cultivate in order to successfully mine patterns. Meszaros and Doble (Meszaros and Doble, 2000) present a pattern language for pattern writing. This pattern language models a software design pattern format that may be unsuitable for UI patterns and the language contains internal inconsistencies. Nevertheless it can be a useful aid for pattern writers.

At least three instances of a successful design solution should exist onto which a pattern can be mapped (Appleton, 2000). This so-called "*Rule of Three*" is a rule of thumb to help ensure that the pattern identified is a recurring phenomenon and not just an isolated case.

Learning from the design and development experience of designers and developers can be done in a number of ways. Rising, discussing software design pattern identification in businesses, presents several of these drawn from her experiences at AG Communication Systems (Rising, 2001):

- Interviewing expert designers and developers;

- Borrowing between businesses in the same domain that can share information;

- Teaching pattern writing classes;

- Pattern mining in workshops;

- Mining personal experience;

- Mining in meetings; and

- Mining in training classes.

It would be preferable if the people identifying patterns were not the designers and developers of the systems yielding the patterns, to make pattern mining more objective. However, this may not be practical or possible in practice and introspection has been very valuable in contributing patterns to the existing UI pattern collections.

17.2.2   Pattern Identification Through Deduction

At this stage in the evolution of UI design and UI patterns, it may be difficult to find sufficient (or any) examples of good practice in a particular application domain. Thus it may be necessary to identify patterns deductively, instead of inductively. The work done by Richter at Siemens AG in identifying B2B patterns using the UID lifecycle (Richter, 2003) is an example of how this can be done, although it must be noted that the Siemens group became aware that van Welie (van Welie and Traetteberg, 2001) had begun to publish similar patterns on his website at a later stage of their project.

The Siemens group identified patterns by means of the following process: applications of interest to the company were identified. Through participatory design, requirements were gathered, and UIs were designed, evaluated and redesigned. The redesigned UIs were described as patterns, using a modified Alexandrian format. The set of patterns obtained included *Product Finder, Product Catalogue, Configuration, Product Comparison* and *Listed Results*.

Patterns obtained deductively following Richter's method should be regarded as more tentative than those obtained though studying existing practice and knowledge for two main reasons. Firstly, such patterns may be grounded in single cases and secondly, the people identifying the patterns were probably closely involved in designing the UIs from which the patterns came (reducing objectivity).

In Kok and Wesson's DOME case study discussed in Section 17.3 below, a method for identifying UI patterns, which differs from Richter's, is described. In this study, TP patterns were identified deductively by constructing a generalised task model from a number of extant systems and comparing it with a normative TP task model. This revealed a number of new TP patterns (Section 17.3.1). Since Kok and Wesson's method considers several extant systems, patterns identified through this method are likely to have a higher degree of invariance than those identified through Richter's method.

We note that the experiences documented below are the type of useful design knowledge that Haynes et al. make a strong case for in Chapter 14 ("Integrating Multi-Disciplinary Design Knowledge"). Even if structured methodologies that integrate UI design pattern use into software engineering are in place, it is possible that appropriate patterns are not known and must be discovered through the process of creating a system.

17.3   PATTERN USE: THE DOME CASE STUDY

The recent study by Kok and Wesson resulted in the development of a pattern language for TP systems (Kok, 2004; Kok and Wesson, 2002). This research was motivated by a finding that UI design knowledge gained by experienced software developers was not being transferred to new, inexperienced developers within companies developing TP systems. The hypothesis was that a TP pattern language could be constructed to contain UI design knowledge to support the development of the UI for a TP system. A further hypothesis was that the usability of the UIs produced using this PL would be good.

The DOME system was developed by Kok for the Nuclear Energy Corporation of South Africa (NECSA) in 2003 to manage the exposure of employees to occupational hazards. This section will discuss the development of the TP PL, the application of this PL to produce the UI for the DOME system and the usability evaluation of the resulting system.

17.3.1   The TP Pattern Language

A TP system provides tools and techniques to automate transactions found in common application domains such as communications or manufacturing. A TP system in its simplest form can be represented as comprising the following tasks: View data, Add data, Change data and Delete data (Kok, 2004). Currently available pattern collections such as those from Tidwell (Tidwell, 1998a) and van Welie and Trætteberg (van Welie and Traetteberg, 2001) focus more on general aspects of UI design or on specific application domains such as the World Wide Web (Duyne et al., 2002). No other PL focuses specifically on TP or the development of UIs for TP systems.

A two-level structure was used to organize the patterns in the TP PL. This simple structure allowed a clear separation between patterns relating to TP and patterns relating to general UI design. A diagram illustrating the architecture of the TP PL is given in Figure 17.1 below.

The first level corresponds closely to the posture and experience levels as proposed by van Welie and van de Veer (van Welie and van de Veer, 2003) and comprises patterns relating specifically to TP. The second level corresponds to the task and action level patterns as proposed by van Welie and van de Veer and consists of patterns relating to more general UI design.

Different methods were used to develop the patterns in the TP PL. The UI patterns were sourced from existing pattern collections including Tidwell (Tidwell, 1998a; Tid-

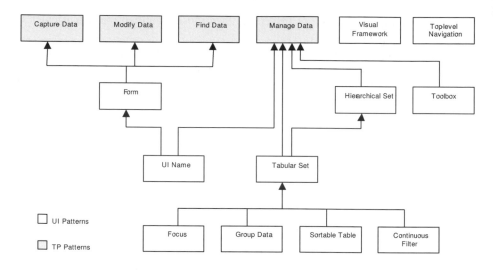

Figure 17.1   Architecture of TP PL (Kok, 2004)

well, 2004) and van Welie and Trætteberg (van Welie and Traetteberg, 2001). These patterns were re-formatted and rewritten in a tabular style using a similar format to that used by van Welie and Trætteberg (for example, see Figure 17.2 and Figure 17.3). The patterns used and the original authors are the following: *Form, Hierarchical Set, Sortable Table, Tabular Set, Toolbox, Top-level Navigation* and *Visual Framework* (Tidwell, 1998a); and *Continuous Filter* and *Focus* (van Welie and Traetteberg, 2001).

Two new, additional UI patterns were also developed: *Group Data* and *UI Name*. These additional patterns were identified by analysing existing systems such as Microsoft Outlook and Microsoft Word. The *Group Data* pattern supports the grouping of related data to facilitate dynamic reordering on a specific column. The *UI Name* supports the identification of each UI with a unique name or current status.

The UI patterns in the TP PL in Figure 17.1 form the foundation of the TP PL and serve as building blocks for the TP patterns. The *Capture Data, Modify Data* and *Find Data* patterns are derived from the *Form* pattern which in turn uses the *UI Name* pattern. The *Manage Data* pattern uses the *UI Name, Tabular Set* and *Hierarchical Set* patterns. The *Tabular Set* pattern is comprised of the *Continuous Filter, Focus, Group Data* and *Sortable Table* patterns. The *Top-level Navigation* and *Visual Framework* patterns can be used independently of the other patterns for the design of the TP system as a whole.

The TP patterns were identified deductively by constructing a generalised task model from four existing TP systems (Section 17.2.2). This analysis revealed that all four of the related systems had a requirement for managing data. This data management included the display of information in a clear and concise manner, while providing the user with the facility to perform other operations such as capturing, changing and deleting data. This process of viewing, capturing, changing and deleting data was repeated in other areas of the different systems.

The TP patterns identified using the above process were *Manage Data, View Data, Capture Data* and *Modify Data* (Figure 17.1). The key usability principles inherent in the design solution of these patterns are efficiency and error prevention since fast, error-free data entry is an inherent requirement of all TP systems. The *Manage Data* pattern is illustrated in Figures 17.2 and 17.3 below.

Property	Description
Name	Manage Data
Author	Dirk Kok
Problem	The user needs to perform a set of tasks on a dataset. These tasks include adding data, modifying data, viewing data and deleting data.
Usability Principle	Efficiency, Consistency
Context	Most TP systems require that users manage various sets of data. These datasets can range from small data lists to large sets of hierarchical data.
Forces	Data needs to be displayed in a presentable and understandable way. Users must be able to locate the proper data effectively. Users must be able to perform their tasks with ease and minimum effort.
Solution	This pattern makes use of a large variety of micro UI patterns. In its simplest form it makes use of a *UI Name* pattern with a *Toolbox* pattern below and then a *Tabular Set* pattern, which takes up the rest of the screen space. The *UI Name* pattern describes the data being managed using this pattern. The *Toolbox* pattern contains all the functionality that can be performed on the data. The *Tabular Set* pattern is used to present the data. The *Tabular Set* pattern also relies on the *Current Focus* pattern to convey the current data selection to the user. Variations on this simple form can include the use of the *Group Data, Sort Data* and *Continuous Filter* patterns. This pattern can also be used to represent hierarchical data relationships by reusing it in conjunction with the *Hierarchical Set* pattern.
Rationale	This pattern makes use of various UI patterns to provide the user with a centralised data management platform. It serves as an effective tool for presenting data and allowing the user to interact with the data.

Figure 17.2   Manage Data Pattern (Part 1) (Kok, 2004)

All of the example TP systems also require users to work with large sets of data; browsing through long lists in order to locate specific records. The *Find Data* pattern was thus identified to support the task of locating records efficiently according to specific criteria (Figures 17.4).

Property	Description
Examples	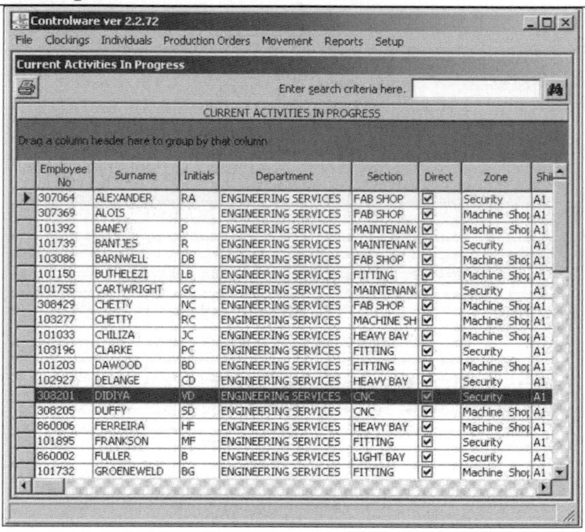
Known Uses	Microsoft Windows Explorer

Figure 17.3   Manage Data Pattern (Part 2) (Kok, 2004)

17.3.2   Task Analysis

The task analysis for the DOME system was performed by analysing an extant legacy system and conducting user interviews. The two main tasks identified were the following:

- **Maintain system information:** This includes building and workplace structure, possible stressors (hazardous forces), tests to be conducted per stressor, types of radiation, hazardous chemicals, and testing and examination methods.

- **Maintain employee occupational exposure information:** This represents the main goal of the system. Information kept here includes employee information, employees per workplace, exposure of employees to stressors, and testing information.

The workplace, stressor and testing information must be recorded for each of the employees in the system. Historical data has to be kept for 30 years, which implies that a large volume of data must be stored and displayed for each employee. Users should therefore be able to work with current data and request historical data on demand.

The results of medical examinations and routine testing need to be captured for each employee. Health and safety regulations require NECSA to routinely monitor the exposure of each employee to occupational hazards. This monitoring is performed on a daily basis and captured per test and per employee. The system must also provide functionality to schedule testing and medical examinations per employee in order to

Property	Description
Name	Find Data
Author	Dirk Kok
Problem	The user needs to find a record in a set of records.
Usability Principle	Efficiency
Context	The user needs to locate a record in a dataset in order to perform a task on this data.
Forces	The user effort must be minimised. The search mechanism must be transparent to the user. The search results must be visible to the user.
Solution	Provide the user with a floating UI that is always on top. This UI should allow the user to enter the search criteria. The search results can be displayed by placing the focus on the found record. Allow the user to cycle between the correct results. Inform the user if no matching records were found.
Rationale	The floating UI that is always on top does not interfere with the user's workspace. The search results are presented with the data and the user doesn't have to go to another "place" to view the results.
Examples	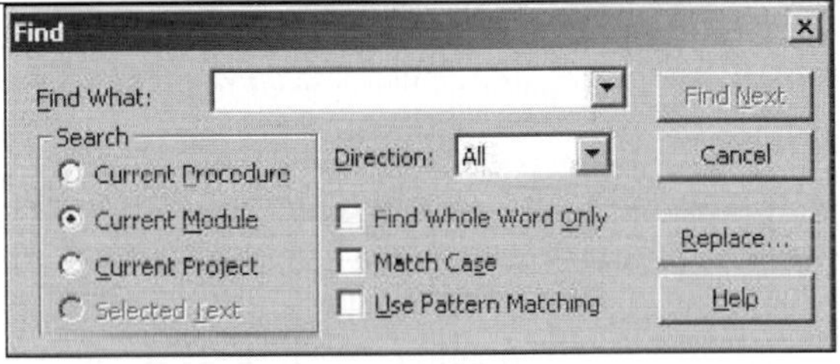 Microsoft Visual Basic 6 Find screen
Known Uses	Microsoft Visual Basic

Figure 17.4 Find Data Pattern (Kok, 2004)

ensure that the correct employees are tested at the correct time, thereby improving the organization's adherence to health and safety regulations.

17.3.3 Pattern Selection

The UI design of the DOME system was derived from the task analysis and user constraints discussed in the previous section. Appropriate pattern selections were made from the TP PL in Figure 17.1 by matching the system tasks to the relevant patterns. These patterns were then used as a basis for the development of the various UIs in order to meet the system requirements.

The two main tasks identified in Section 17.3.2 were subsequently expanded to include the following five tasks: Maintain chemical information; Maintain building structure information; Maintain employee occupational exposure information; Maintain employee testing information; and Capture employee testing information.

The following discussion is given to illustrate how the different patterns in the TP PL were selected to be used for the design of the UIs to support the above tasks:

- **Maintain chemical information:** The user tasks involved here include viewing the current chemicals in the system, adding new chemical records, modifying existing chemical records and deleting obsolete chemical records. Based on these tasks, the *Manage Data* pattern was selected as the main UI component (Figure 17.2 and 17.3). This pattern provides a workspace from which the operations of viewing data, adding data, modifying data and deleting data can be performed. The *Capture Data* pattern was then used to provide users with a workspace from which to capture new chemicals into the system. The *Modify Data* pattern was also used to facilitate changes to the hazardous chemical records. This standardized pattern-based approach to design allowed the design of UIs that behave in the same way regardless of the underlying data.

- **Maintain building structure information:** The task involved here includes managing the hierarchical relationship between buildings and workplaces which is typical of many master-detail relationships. The user must be able to manage data for the buildings and their related workplaces. The *Manage Data* pattern was used again to represent this hierarchical relationship with the *Capture Data* and *Modify Data* patterns being used to maintain building and workplace information.

- **Maintain employee occupational exposure information:** This task had the most complex user constraints and requirements since the user needs to be able to manage employee information, employee workplace information and employee stressor information. Each of these subtasks was solved, however, by re-using the *Manage Data* pattern in a nested fashion. The additional tasks of adding, changing and deleting data were solved by using the *Capture Data* and *Modify Data* patterns for each of the data sets represented. The user is provided with filter capabilities in terms of the *Continuous Filter* pattern and specific views are provided to meet the requirement of providing historical data.

- **Maintain employee testing information:** This task requires the user to manage the testing information for employees. The user needs to view currently scheduled tests, schedule new tests, change testing information and delete incorrect test results. This task was accomplished by using the *Manage Data* pattern as discussed above together with the *Capture Data* and *Modify Data* patterns.

- **Capture employee testing information:** This task represents one of the most frequently used tasks in the system as test details are captured on a daily basis. The nature of the task requires the user to capture a sheet of information for a group of employees. The *Capture Data* pattern could therefore not be used as it is more suited to capturing a single record at a time. The same layout as the paper-based form was therefore used to reduce the amount of user input required.

17.3.4   UI Design

The UI design was completed using the pattern selections as described in the previous section. The DOME system was developed using the Microsoft Visual Basic 6 programming environment. The main application workspace was based on the *Visual Framework* and *Top-level Navigation* patterns. The following section will discuss the development of some of the UIs in order to illustrate how the TP patterns were used to support the design process.

The **Maintain Chemical Information UI** represents the simplest of the data management tasks in the DOME system. The workspace is based on the *Manage Data* pattern and is illustrated in Figure 17.5 below. The toolbar, which is based on the *Toolbox* pattern, contains the main user tasks, i.e. add, edit, delete and print records. The data is presented using a grid with an arrow and navy coloured bar indicating the current record as described in the *Tabular Set* and *Current Record* patterns. In order to add new records, the user selects the New task from the toolbar and is presented with the **Add New Chemical UI** (Figure 17.6). This workspace is based on the *Capture Data* pattern. A similar workspace is provided for editing existing chemical information, based on the *Modify Data* pattern.

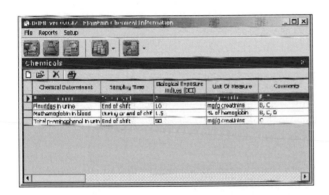

Figure 17.5   Maintain chemical information UI (Kok, 2004)

The **Maintain Building Structure UI** represents the master-detail relationship between buildings and the workplaces that belong to each building (Figure 17.7). This UI is also based on the *Manage Data* pattern; the master-detail relationship being represented by two nested *Manage Data* patterns. The top area contains the building information and the bottom area contains the workplaces for the currently selected building. As a different building is selected; the information for the related workplaces is displayed.

The **Maintain Employee Occupation Exposure UI** is designed similarly to the **Maintain Building Structure UI**, using three nested *Manage Data* patterns to represent the hierarchical relationships between employees, workplaces and the stressors to which these employees are exposed in these workplaces.

The **Maintain Employee Testing UI** is also designed similarly to the **Maintain Building Structure UI**, using two nested *Manage Data* patterns to represent the re-

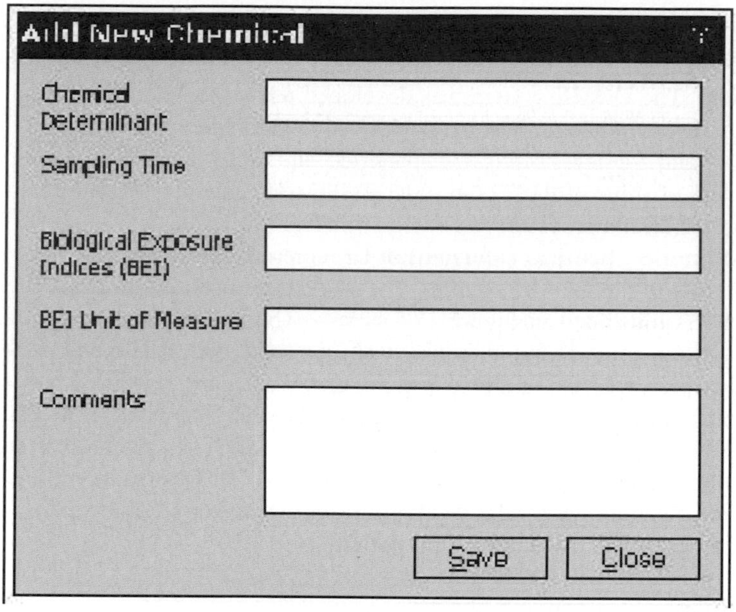

Figure 17.6   Add new chemical UI (Wentling et al., 2000)

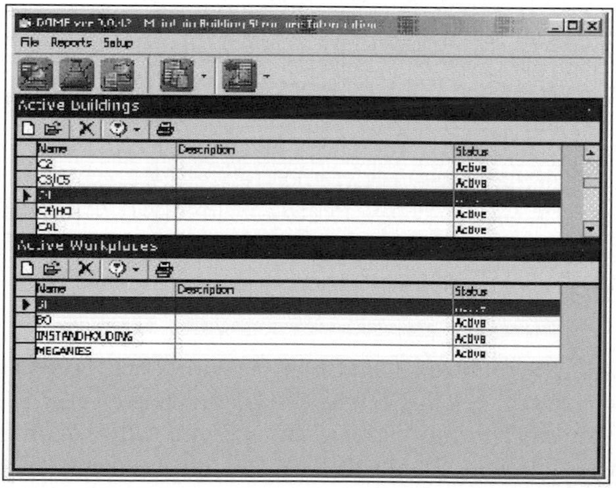

Figure 17.7   Maintain building structure UI (Griffiths and Pemberton, 2000)

lationships between employees and the tests scheduled for these employees. This UI also provides extended data grouping and filtering using the *Group Data* and *Continuous Filter* patterns. The data grouping feature allows the user to sort the list of employees by any of the employee attributes, e.g. surname, to facilitate easy retrieval. The data filtering feature allows the user to filter the list of employees according to user-specified criteria, e.g. complete or partial surname, to facilitate locating specific records efficiently in a large dataset.

Most of the UIs for the DOME system could be designed using the TP PL. The only exception to this was the **Capture Employee Test Results UI** which was designed so that the test results could be captured in the same order as the paper-based form. The pattern-based design approach had several benefits including reduced development time and consistency which also resulted in improved learnability.

17.3.5 Evaluation

The usability of the UIs produced using the TP PL was assessed by means of a heuristic evaluation and a user questionnaire. The heuristic evaluation was conducted using Nielsen's ten usability heuristics (Nielsen, 1994) and involving three evaluators. The only usability problems identified were in the areas of user control and freedom, flexibility and efficiency of use and aesthetic and minimalist design. The usability problems identified were the following (Kok, 2004):

- **User control and freedom:** The evaluators felt that they could not change the UIs sufficiently to suit their needs.

- **Flexibility and efficiency of use:** The evaluators felt that some of the system tasks were implemented too rigidly since events seldom occur in a fixed order.

- **Aesthetic and minimalist design:** The evaluators thought that the Maintain Employee Occupation Exposure UI was too cluttered (Section 17.3.4). A suggestion was made to split the hierarchical information into two separate UIs, which was implemented.

The NECSA employees were also asked to complete a modified version of the Questionnaire for User-Interaction Satisfaction (QUIS) (Norman, 1995). Several questions were asked in each section and the users were asked to rate their satisfaction with the user interface using a 5-point Likert scale, with 1=Very poor and 5–Excellent. The results obtained for this questionnaire are contained in Table 17.4 below.

Table 17.4 QUIS results

No.	Section	Mean	Std. Dev.
3	Overall User Reactions	4.24	0.82
4	Terminology and System Information	4.38	0.70
5	Learning	4.19	0.86
6	System Capabilities	4.47	0.59
7	Screen Design	4.15	0.88

All of the sections received mean responses above 4.0 (Table 17.4). We can thus deduce that the users were generally satisfied with the overall system design, the ease of learning, the system capabilities and the UI design.

The only significant problems identified in the questionnaire were the ease of capturing and changing data on the grid with respect to the **Capture Employee Test Results UI** (Section 17.3.4). This UI was not designed according to the *Capture Data* and *Modify Data* patterns as discussed previously. The initial idea was to capture the results in the order in which they appeared in the reports. In practice, however, the results never came back in this order. This problem was solved by redesigning this UI using the original TP patterns for capturing and modifying data.

From the above discussion, we can conclude that the general usability of the UIs produced using the TP PL was good. Some minor changes had to be made, but these were in order to make the final UI design closer to the original pattern specifications. This evaluation also revealed, however, that existing methods for evaluating patterns are not well defined. It should also be noted that the same person was responsible for the development of the TP PL as well as the DOME system. The usefulness of these patterns could therefore not be measured objectively (Section 17.2.1). This problem is explored in more detail in the next section.

17.4 PATTERN EVALUATION

As noted in Chapter 3 by Seffah *et al.* ("HCI, Usability and Software Engineering Integration"), although UI patterns and pattern languages are potentially useful for UI design and integration in the software engineering lifecycle, they have various unresolved problems. The existing pattern collections are works in progress and the quality of the patterns and pattern languages contained within them is largely unknown. The patterns may be flawed in their content or their format may be deficient. The pattern languages may be lacking (as is the case with pattern catalogues), fragmentary or inconsistent. Empirical evidence about pattern use, either as a design aid or an evaluation tool, is limited (Wesson and Cowley, 2003). As an evaluation tool, there is some evidence that guidelines may be easier and more effective to use than patterns. More research is needed to empirically validate and refine current pattern collections. Several research questions are unanswered, most notably how to evaluate patterns in their static form and dynamically in use.

In order to gather more empirical evidence about pattern use, the NMMU UI Design Patterns Evaluation Project is currently underway. The aim of this project is to understand how usable UI patterns are and how to measure this (*pattern evaluation*). Three aspects of patterns that can be evaluated are:

- The extent to which the solution embodied in a pattern (its content) is a good solution.

- The extent to which different pattern formats are a good means of capturing design knowledge for the intended users (designers, developers and end users involved in participatory design).

- The extent to which a pattern collection (in the form of a catalogue or pattern language) is usable by its intended users.

As part of the Project, a study was recently conducted which focused on the attitudes of designers and developers to using UI patterns in UI design, their design activities and the artefacts produced. The results are currently being analysed. The following aspects of the pilot study are discussed: advantages of pattern use, research questions, research design and preliminary results.

17.4.1   Advantages of UI Pattern Use

The advantages of UI pattern use as described in the literature are useful for grounding the research questions of the study. Griffiths and Pemberton state the advantages of UI patterns by comparing them to guidelines (Griffiths and Pemberton, 2000):

- Patterns record useful meta-information for design that guidelines with their imperative structure do not.

- Pattern use emphasises the process of developing and using guidelines, rather than the product produced.

- Pattern languages, being structured, allow large amorphous collections of guidelines to be navigated with confidence.

- Patterns, due to their form and development process, are engaging to their users.

- Pattern language use could possibly promote participatory design (involving users as participants).

According to Dearden et al. (Dearden et al., 2002), UI pattern language use exhibits three classical Alexandrian outcomes:

- It empowers users to participate in UI design.

- It supports generative design.

- It produces life-enhancing outcomes for the designers and users.

Experimental work done by Dearden et al. on the use of pattern languages in participatory design provides evidence that supports this.

van Welie and van der Veer (van Welie and van de Veer, 2003) suggest two functions of pattern languages for designers:

- Pattern languages make the mental models of pattern-writers visible and accessible to others.

- Pattern languages can function as shared design languages between designers.

Although van Welie and van der Veer do not state this explicitly, pattern language sharing can take place directly (synchronously) between designers or indirectly (asynchronously) via languages in analogue or digital repositories (UI pattern collections).

Tidwell (Tidwell, 1998a) lists the advantages of pattern use in more detail than encountered in other sources. According to her, pattern use can:

- Help individual designers build better interfaces.

- Give designers a shared design language.

- Help designers achieve the *"Quality without a Name"* (QWAN) in artefacts.

- Diversify design solutions.

- Draw on design knowledge in related fields.

- Preserve design knowledge that otherwise might become lost over time.

17.4.2   Research Questions

The research questions focus on designers and developers' attitudes towards UI pattern use, and are grounded in the three aspects of patterns listed in Section 17.4, the literature discussed in Section 17.4.1, and several ways that UI patterns could be employed in the software lifecycle. In iterative development/prototyping, the following are possible modes of pattern use:

- Heuristic evaluation of the usability of existing systems (either existing systems or as part of an iterative design process).

- Support for the redesign of existing systems to correct potential usability problems.

- Support for the design of user interfaces from specifications (initial prototype).

These modes of use correspond to those highlighted in the process patterns in Chapter 10 by Battle ("Patterns of Integration"). Heuristic evaluation of the usability of existing systems (either existing systems or as part of an iterative design process) and support for the redesign of existing systems to correct potential usability problems is described in the Foot in the Door (for External Consultants), UCD Focus on Early Definition and UCD in Every Phase patterns. Support for the design of user interfaces from specifications (initial prototype) is described in the Foot in the Door (for Internal Usability Groups) pattern.

The research questions are divided into a primary research question and fifteen secondary questions based on the primary question. The secondary questions focus on the mode of pattern use as listed above, their format, content, organisation, ease of learning and ability to function as a design language. The questions that deal with the mode of pattern use are expressed in terms of the three standard components of usability (*efficiency, effectiveness and user satisfaction*), measured for a particular user group in a specific context of use. The research questions are presented in tabular form in Table 17.6 below.

17.4.3   Research Design

A group of 33 postgraduate (Masters and Honours level) students registered for the 2004 E-Commerce module at the former University of Port Elizabeth, now incorporated within NMMU, were recruited for the study. These students had some experience of design and development from a software engineering perspective, as well as HCI,

Table 17.6   Research questions

No.	Research Question
1.	**Primary Research Question:**
	To what extent do developers consider UI patterns to be useful during the development process?
2.	**Secondary Research Questions:**
	To what extent do developers consider UI patterns to be:
2.1	An efficient evaluation aid (enabling rapid identification of potential usability problems in existing designs)?
2.2	An effective evaluation aid (enabling identification of a significant number of potential usability problems in existing designs)?
2.3	Satisfying to use as an evaluation aid?
2.4	An efficient redesign aid (enabling rapid correction of potential usability problems in existing designs)?
2.5	An effective redesign aid (enabling successful correction of potential usability problems in existing designs)?
2.6	Satisfying to use as a redesign aid?
2.7	An efficient design aid (enabling rapid generation of designs)?
2.8	An effective design aid (embodying and producing good designs)?
2.9	Satisfying to use as a design aid?
2.10	Expressed in a useful format (their parts and how these are arranged)?
2.11	Useful in terms of their content (the information embodied in the parts)?
2.12	Useful when linked together into a pattern language (organisation)?
2.13	Easy to become familiar with when first encountered?
2.14	A personal design language to use when designing UIs?
2.15	A means of sharing design knowledge between designers?

as a result of their academic education and training, at a novice to intermediate level. Consequently, they did not inhabit the balkanised work spaces common in software production environments described by Seffah *et al.* in Chapter 3. The group was divided into an experimental and a control group. The experimental group were required to perform design tasks using UI design patterns, whereas the control group were required to perform the same tasks using design guidelines. The objective of this was to obtain a comparison of the usability and capabilities of UI design patterns compared to a generally accepted design aid like guidelines.

Stratified sampling was employed to split the group into two equivalent groups, based on two attributes, namely postgraduate degree registered for and average mark obtained for third year Computer Science modules. It was important to ensure that the mark distribution for each degree type was the same or nearly the same in the two groups in order to remove any performance bias.

The UI design patterns selected for use in this study by the experimental group were van Welie's Amsterdam Pattern Collection (van Welie and Traetteberg, 2001) and van

Duyne *et al*'s Design of Sites Pattern Browser (Duyne et al., 2002). The design guidelines selected for use by the control group were Barnard's E-commerce guidelines (Barnard and Wesson, 2003), which are based on those proposed by Nielsen *et al* (Nielsen et al., 2001). Permission was obtained from the owners of these resources to use them for the study.

The study involved the capture of quantitative and qualitative data. The subjects' biographical and background information and existing perceptions of pattern use were captured by means of a Pre-Questionnaire. A Project Diary was used to record individual experiences during the pilot study. A Post-Questionnaire was used to capture feedback on the use of the UI design patterns and guidelines after the pilot study.

The pilot study comprised three assignments which were done individually within the two groups over a period of six weeks. The goal of Assignment 1 was to perform a heuristic evaluation of the Porcupine Ceramics web site (http://www.porcupine.co.za/), to produce a heuristic evaluation report and to evaluate the content of the design aids used in the heuristic evaluation. The goal of Assignment 2 was to redesign the Porcupine Ceramics web site and to evaluate the content of the design aids used in the redesign. The artefacts to be produced were a site (or navigation) map, a collection of wireframes that described the web pages and a report that analysed the usefulness of the content of the design aids used. The goal of Assignment 3 was to design a new E-commerce web site using the design aids, and to evaluate the form of the design aids used in the design. The artefacts to be produced were a site (or navigation) map, a collection of wireframes and a report that analysed the usefulness of the design aids used and the Project Diary.

17.4.4   Preliminary Results

Preliminary results were obtained for the Post-Questionnaire and are summarised in Table 17.8. The questions in the Post-Questionnaire were divided into five categories: Evaluation, Redesign, New design, Format & Content and General. The subjects were asked to rate their experiences with using the respective design aids in these five categories using a 5-point Likert scale, with 1 indicating Strongly Disagree, and 5 indicating Strongly Agree. Several questions were asked in each of these categories, relating to the research questiosn in Table 17.6, expressend as hypotheses. Descriptive statistics were calculated for each of the questions including means and standard deviations.

With regard to the use of guidelines as compared with patterns as an evaluation tool, the mean ratings obtained from the guideline users were all higher than the pattern users (Table 17.8). The mean ratings obtained from the pattern users were, however, above 3.5 for efficiency (3.6) and effectiveness (3.5) but lower for user satisfaction (3.1). We can thus provisionally accept hypotheses 2.1 and 2.2 and deduce that developers consider patterns to be an efficient and effective evaluation aid (Table 17.6).

With regard to the use of guidelines as compared with patterns as a means of redesigning an existing system, the mean ratings for both groups were very similar for efficiency, effectiveness and satisfaction. The mean ratings for satisfaction (3.3), however, were lower than those for efficiency and effectiveness. We can thus provisionally

Table 17.8   Results of post-questionnaire

Category	Property	Hypothesis	Guideline Users			Pattern Users			
			N	Mean	Std Dev	N	Mean	Std Dev	Result
Redesign	Efficiency	2.4	20	3.6	0.8	31	3.6	0.9	A
	Effectiveness	2.5	20	3.7	0.7	31	3.6	0.9	A
	Satisfaction	2.6	20	3.3	0.8	31	3.3	1.2	N
New Design	Efficiency	2.7	40	3.3	0.8	60	3.5	1.1	A
	Effectiveness	2.8	40	3.7	0.8	29	3.8	0.8	A
	Satisfaction	2.9	40	3.3	0.9	30	3.6	1.1	A
Format/Content	Form	2.10	21	3.4	1.2	34	3.4	1.1	A
	Content	2.11	20	3.3	1.3	34	3.5	1.0	A
	Organisation	2.12	10	4.3	0.7	33	3.5	1.0	A
General	Learnability	2.13	33	3.4	1.0	48	3.4	1.0	N
	Personal Lang.	2.14	11	3.5	0.7	16	3.7	0.9	A
	Shared Lang.	2.15	8	3.1	1.0	15	3.1	1.1	N
	Future use		11	4.1	0.7	16	4.1	1.1	A

accept hypotheses 2.4 and 2.5 and deduce that developers consider patterns to be an efficient and effective redesign aid (Table 17.6).

With regard to the use of guidelines as compared with patterns as a means of designing a new system, the mean ratings for both groups were very similar for effectiveness only. The mean rating obtained from the pattern users for efficiency (3.5) was higher than that obtained for the guideline users (3.3). Similarly, the mean rating obtained from the pattern users for satisfaction (3.6) was higher than that obtained from the guideline users (3.3). We can thus provisionally accept hypotheses 2.7, 2.8 and 2.9 and deduce that developers consider patterns to be an efficient, effective and satisfying design aid for designing new systems (Table 17.6).

With regard to the format and content of the guidelines as compared with the patterns, the mean ratings for both groups were very similar. The mean rating obtained from the guideline users for the organisation and structure of the guidelines (4.3) was significantly higher than that obtained from the pattern users (3.5). The mean ratings obtained from the pattern users for this category were, however, all above 3.5. We can thus provisionally accept hypotheses 2.10, 2.11 and 2.12 and deduce that developers consider the format, content and organisation of the pattern collections used to be generally useful (Table 17.6).

With regard to the ease of learning of guidelines as compared with patterns, the mean rating for both groups was the same (3.4). Similar ratings were also obtained for both groups in terms of personal usage, sharing of knowledge and future usage. For this category, only the mean ratings obtained from the pattern users for personal usage (3.7) and future usage (4.1) were above 3.5. We can thus provisionally accept hypothesis 2.14 and deduce that developers consider patterns to be a personal design language that can be used when designing UIs (Table 17.6). Both groups indicated strongly that they would consider using guidelines and patterns respectively in the future (4.1).

Further qualitative analysis still needs to be performed to analyse the general comments provided by the subjects in the Post-Questionnaire, the reports and the project diary in order to understand the participants' mental models and processes. The quality of the design artefacts produced also needs to be evaluated to determine if there were any significant differences in quality between the designs produced by the two groups.

The study did not span the entire software engineering lifecycle from requirements to delivery of a production system. The UI design patterns were used "as is" from the collections, according to a heuristic specified by the researchers. We note the possibilities of a formal UI pattern model, like that described by Artim in Chapter 15 ("UI Design Patterns: Bridging Use Cases and UI Design") in making UI design pattern use more structured and productive of standardized high-quality outcomes.

17.5   FURTHER RESEARCH

Over the last five years, interest in UI patterns has shifted from determining what patterns are to studying how usable and useful they are in practice.

Further research needs to be done to clarify the following issues:

- Continuing empirical evaluation of the usability of UI patterns in the UI design process (for heuristic evaluation, redesign and design from specifications);

- Development of heuristic evaluation techniques for UI patterns based on format, content and properties;

- The effect of format on the usability of UI patterns and pattern languages by designers and developers;

- The effect of content on the usability of UI patterns and pattern languages by designers and developers;

- The quality of the content of the patterns and pattern languages contained within the existing UI pattern collections;

- The usability of the existing UI pattern collections (print and online format) as reference tools;

- Integration techniques for pattern-based design in the Software Engineering lifecycle; and

- Requirements for Software Engineering tool support for UI patterns.

17.6 CONCLUSIONS

Pattern-based UI design has the potential to bridge the gap between high-level requirements and UI design. Unlike software design patterns which are used by developers to build the internals of a system, UI design patterns provide a shared language between designers and users, which is closer to Alexander's vision for architectural design patterns (Section 17.1). UI design patterns could be used effectively by software engineers once they are grounded in theory and empirical research (Section 17.2 and 17.3).

Design patterns offer many opportunities for UI design but existing pattern collections are flawed and empirical evidence of pattern use is limited (Section 17.4). More research is needed to empirically validate and refine current pattern collections. Several research questions also remain to be answered, most notably how to evaluate patterns (Section 17.5).

The pattern evaluation study conducted in South Africa in 2004 has shown that designers and developers generally consider patterns to be a useful tool for evaluating existing systems, redesigning existing systems and designing new systems (Section 17.4.4). Patterns can thus play an important role in the software development lifecycle and assist with bridging the gap between software engineering and user interface design.

Acknowledgements

The authors wish to acknowledge the contributions of Dirk Kok with respect to the DOME case study and Martijn van Welie in the planning of the pattern evaluation study.

REFERENCES

Abrahamsson, P., Warsta, J., Siponen, M., and Ronkainen, J. (2003). New directions on agile methods: A comparative analysis. In *Proceedings of the 25th International Conference on Software Engineering*, pages 244–254, Portland, Oregon, USA.

Abran, A., Moore, J. W., Bourque, P., Dupuis, R., and Tripp, L. L. (2004). *SWEBOK: Guide to the Software Engineering Body of Knowledge*. IEEE.

Ackoff, R. L. (1989). From data to wisdom. *Journal of Applied Systems Analysis*, 16:3–9.

ACM (1992). *ACM SIGCHI curricula for human-computer interaction*. ACM Press.

Agarwal, R., De, P., and Sinha, A. P. (1999). Comprehending object and process models: An empirical study. *IEEE Transactions on Software Engineering*, pages 541–556.

Agile Alliance (2001). Manifesto for agile software development. Technical report, Agile Alliance. http://www.agilealliance.org.

Akrich, M. (1992). The de-scription of technical objects. In Bijker, W. E. and Law, J., editors, *Shaping Technology/Building Society: Studies in Sociotechnical Change*, pages 205–224. Cambridge, MA: MIT Press.

Albert, S. and Bradley, K. (1997). *Managing Knowledge: Experts, Agencies and Organizations*. Cambridge, UK: Cambridge University Press.

Alexander, C. (1979). *A Timeless Way of Building*. New York: Oxford University Press.

Alexander, C. (1996). Keynote address at the OOPSLA96 conference held in san jose, california, usa.

Alexander, C., Ishikawa, S., Silverstein, M., Jacobson, M., Fiksdahl-King, I., and Angel, S. (1977). *A Pattern Language*. New York: Oxford University Press.

Ambler, S. (1998). *Process Patterns*. Cambridge University Press.

Ambler, S. (2002). *Agile Modeling: Effective Practices for EXtreme Programming and the Unified Process*. New York: J. Wiley.

Anderson, J., Fleek, F., Garrity, K., and Drake, F. (2001). Integrating usability techniques into software development. *IEEE Software*, 18(1):46–53.

Anderson, J. R. and Lebiere, C. (1998). *Representing Cognitive Activity in Complex Tasks*. Lawrence Erlbaum Associates, Mahwah NJ.

ANSI/INCITS (2001). *ANSI/INCITS-354: Common Industry Format for Usability Test Reports*. NCITS 354-2001.

Antunes, H., Seffah, A., Radhakrishnan, T., and Pestina, S. (2001). Unifying user-centered and use-case driven requirements engineering lifecycle. In (Gulliksen and Boivie, 2001). Summary of the INTERACT'00-workshop. Also available as technical report from the department of information technology, Uppsala university, Report number 2001-026. (http://www.it.uu.se/research/reports/2001-026/2001-026.pdf).

Apple Computer, I. (1987). *Human Interface Guidelines: The Apple Desktop Interface*. Addison-Wesley Publishing, Reading, MA. OCLC 17424669.

Appleton, B. (2000). Patterns and software: Essential concepts and terminology [online]. Technical report, http://www.enteract.com/~bradapp/doc/patterns/patterns-intro.html.

Arias, E., Eden, H., Fischer, G., Gorman, A., and Scharff, E. (2000). Transcending the individual human mind — creating shared understanding through collaborative design. *ACM Transactions on Computer-Human Interaction*, 7:84–113.

Armitage, J. (2004). Are agile methods good for design? *Interactions*, 11(1):14–23.

Armour, P. G. (2004). Beware of counting LOC. *Communications of the ACM*, 47:21–24.

Arrow, H., McGrath, J. E., and Berdahl, J. L. (2000). *Small groups as complex systems: Formation, coordination, development and adaptation*. Sage Publications, Thousand Oaks CA.

Artim, J. and van Harmelen, M. (1998). Incorporating work, process and task analysis into commercial and industrial object-oriented systems development. In *Proceedings of ACM CHI 98 Conference on Human Factors in Computing Systems (Summary)*, volume 2 of *Workshops*, page 198.

Artim, J., van Harmelen, M., Butler, K. A., Gulliksen, J., Henderson, A., Kovacevic, S., Lu, S., Overmyer, S., Reaux, R., Roberts, D., Tarby, J.-C., and Linden, K. V. (1998). Incorporating work, process and task analysis into commercial and industrial object-oriented systems development. *SIGCHI Bull.*, 30(4):33–36.

Artim, J. M. (2001). *Entity, task, and presenter classification in user interface architecture: an approach to organizing HCI practice*, pages 115–158. Addison-Wesley Longman Publishing Co., Inc.

Bannon, L. (1991). From human factors to human actors. In Greenbaum, J. M. and Kyng, M., editors, *Design at work: Cooperative Design of Computer Systems*, page 34. Hillsdale, N.J.: L. Erlbaum Associates.

Barnard, L. and Wesson, J. L. (2003). Usability issues for e-commerce in South Africa: an empirical investigation. In *SAICSIT '03: Proceedings of the 2003 annual research conference of the South African institute of computer scientists and information technologists on Enablement through technology*, pages 258–267. South African Institute for Computer Scientists and Information Technologists.

Barnard, P. J. and May, J. (1999). Representing cognitive activity in complex tasks. *Human-Computer Interaction*, 14(1-2):93–158.

Barnard, P. J., May, J., Duke, D., and Duce, D. (2000). Systems, interactions and macrotheory. *ACM Transactions on Computer-Human Interaction*, 7(2):222–262.

Basili, V. R. and Rombach, H. D. (1988). The TAME project: Towards improvement-oriented software environments. *IEEE Transactions on Software Engineering*, 14:758–773.

Basili, V. R., Shull, F., and Lanubile, F. (1999). Building knowledge through families of experiments. *IEEE Transactions on Software Engineering*.

Baskerville, R. and Pries-Heje, J. (1999). Knowledge capability and maturity in software management. *The Data Base for Advances in Information Systems*, 30:26–43.

Bass, L., Clements, P., and Kazman, R. (1998). *Software Architecture in Practice*. Reading, Massachusetts: Addison-Wesley, 1 edition.

Bass, L., Clements, P., and Kazman, R. (2003). *Software Architecture in Practice*. Reading, Massachusetts: Addison-Wesley., 2 edition.

Bass, L. and John, B. E. (2001a). Achieving usability through software architecture. In *ICSE '01: Proceedings of the 23rd International Conference on Software Engineering*, page 684. IEEE Computer Society.

Bass, L. and John, B. E. (2001b). Supporting usability through software architecture. *Computer*, 34(10):113–115.

Bass, L. and John, B. E. (2003). Linking usability to software architecture patterns through general scenarios. *Journal of Systems and Software*, 66(3):187–197.

Bass, L., John, B. E., Juristo, N., and Sanchez-Segura, M.-I. (2004). Usability and software architecture. In *Tutorial materials presented at the 26th International Conference on Software Engineering, ICSE 2004*, Edinburgh, Scotland.

Battle, L. (2004). When your group can't do it all: Investing UCD resources wisely. In *Usability Professionals' Association 13th Annual Conference*.

Battle, L., D'Angelo, B., and Taylor, D. (2003). Integrating user centered design into the software development lifecycle. In *Usability Professionals' Association 12th Annual Conference*.

Beck, K. (2000). *Extreme Programming Explained: Embracing Change*. Boston, Massachusetts, USA: Addison-Wesley.

Beck, K., Cockburn, A., Jeffries, R., and Highsmith, J. (2001). Agile manifesto. Technical report, The Agile Alliance.

Bellotti, V., Buckingham, S. S., MacLean, A., and Hammond, N. (1995). Multidisciplinary modelling in HCI design: Theory and practice. In Katz, I. R., Mack, R., Marks, L., Rosson, M. B., and Nielsen, J., editors, *Human Factors in Computing Systems: CHI 95 Conference Proceedings*, pages 146–153. New York: ACM Press.

Benyon, D. and Macaulay, C. (2002). Scenarios and the HCI-SE design problem. *Interacting with Computers*, 14(4):397–405.

Bevan, N. (1999). Quality in use: Meeting user needs for quality. *The Journal of Systems and Software*, 49(1):89–96.

Bevan, N. and Claridge, N. (2002). *Guide to Specifying and Evaluating Usability as Part of a Contract, Version1.0. PRUE project*. London, Serco Usability Services: 47.

Beyer, H. and Holtzblatt, K. (1998). *Contextual Design: Defining Customer-Centered Systems*. San Francisco, CA: Morgan Kaufmann.

Bharat, K. A. and Hudson, S. E. (1995). Supporting distributed, concurrent, one-way constraints in user interface applications. In *UIST '95: Proceedings of the 8th annual ACM symposium on User interface and software technology*, pages 121–132. ACM Press.

Bias, R. G. (1994). The pluralistic usability walkthrough: coordinated empathies. In *Usability Inspection Methods*, pages 63–76. John Wiley & Sons, Inc.

Birk, A., Dingsøyr, T., and Stålhane (2002). Postmortem: Never leave a project without it. *IEEE Software*, 19(3):43–45.

BIUSEM (1995). Final report biusem. benefits of integrating usability and software engineering methods. Technical report, BIUSEM Consortium.

Blackmon, M. H., Kitajima, M., , and Polson, P. G. (2003). Repairing usability problems identified by the cognitive walkthrough for the web. In *CHI 2003 Conference Proceedings: Conference on Human Factors in Computing Systems*, pages 497–504.

Blomberg, J. L. (1995). Ethnography: Aligning field studies of work and system design. In Monk, A. F. and Gilbert, N., editors, *Perspectives on HCI: Diverse approaches*, pages 175–198. London: Academic Press.

Bly, S. (1997). Field work: is it product work? *Interactions*, 4(1):25–30.

Bödker, S. (1998). Understanding representation in design. *Human-Computer Interaction*, 13(2):107–125.

Boehm, B. (1981). *Software Engineering Economics*. Englewood Cliffs, N.J.: Prentice-Hall.

Boehm, B. (1988). A spiral model of software development and enhancement. *Computer*, 21(5):61–72.

Boehm, B. (1991). Software risk management: Principles and practice. *IEEE Software*, 8(1):32–41.

Boehm, B. (2002). Get ready for agile methods, with care. *Computer*, 35(1):64–69.

Boehm, B., Bose, P., Horowitz., E., and Lee, M. J. (1994). Software requirements as negotiated win conditions. In *Proceedings: Requirements Engineering '94*, pages 74–83.

Boehm, B. and Turner, R. (2003). Observations on balancing discipline and agility. In *Agile Development Conference*, Salt Lake City, Utah, USA. http://agiledevelopmentconference.com/2003/files/P4Paper.pdf.

Boivie, I., Åborg, C. Persson, J., and Löfberg, M. (2003). Why usability gets lost, or usability in in-house software development. *Interacting with Computers*, 15(4):623–639.

Booch, G., Rumbaugh, J., and Jacobson, I. (1999). *The Unified Modeling Language user guide*. Reading MASS.: Addison-Wesley.

Borning, A. and Duisberg, R. (1986). Constraint-based tools for building user interfaces. *ACM Trans. Graph.*, 5(4):345–374.

Bosch, J. and Juristo, N. (2003). Designing software architectures for usability. In *Tutorial materials presented at the 25th International Conference on Software Engineering, ICSE 2003*, Portland, Oregon.

Bosser, T. and Melchior, E.-M. (1992). The SANE toolkit for cognitive modelling and user-centred design. In Galer, M., Harker, S., and Ziegler, J., editors, *Methods and Tools in User-Centred Design for Information Technology*, number 4 in 1 – Supporting the Design Process from Conception to Use, pages 93–125. North-Holland, Elsevier Science Publishers, Amsterdam.

Bowker, G. and Leigh-Star, S. (1994). Knowledge and infrastructure in international information management: Problems of classification and coding. In Bud-Frierman, L., editor, *Information Acumen: The understanding and use of knowledge in modern business*. London: Routledge.

Brooks, F. P. (1987). No silver bullet: Essence and accidents of software engineering. *IEEE Computer*, 20:10–19.

Buschmann, F., Meunier, R., Rohnert, H., Sommerlad, P., and Stal, M. (1996). *Pattern-Oriented Software Architecture: A System of Patterns.*, volume 1. John Wiley & Sons.

Butler, K. A. (1996). Usability engineering turns 10. *Interactions*, 3(1):58–75.

Buur, J. and Bödker, S. (2000). From usability lab to "design collaboratorium": re-framing usability practice. In *DIS '00: Proceedings of the conference on Designing interactive systems*, pages 297–307. ACM Press

Calde, S., Goodwin, K., and Reimann, R. (2002) SHS Orcas: The first integrated information system for long-term healthcare facility management. In *CHI '02: Case studies of the CHI2002/AIGA Experience Design Forum*, Minneapolis, Minnesota. New York, NY: ACM Press.

Card, S. K., Moran, T. P., and Newell, A. (1983). *The Psychology of Human-Computer Interaction*. Lawrence Erlbaum, Hillsdale.

Carlshamre, P. and Rantzer, M. (2000). Dissemination of usability: The failure of a success story. *Interactions*, 8(1):31–41.

Carroll, J. M., editor (1995). *Scenario-based design: Envisioning work and technology in system development*, New York: Wiley.

Carroll, J. M. (1997). Scenario-based design. In Helander, M,, Landauer, T. K., and Prabhu, P. V., editors, *Handbook of Human-Computer Interaction. Second Edition*, pages 383–406. Amsterdam; New York: Elsevier, 2 edition.

Carroll, J. M. (2000). *Making use: Scenario-based design of human-computer interactions*. Cambridge MA: MIT Press.

Carroll, J. M. (2003). *HCI Models, Theories, and Frameworks: Toward a Multidisciplinary Science*. San Francisco: Morgan Kaufmann.

Carroll, J. M. and Rosson, M. B. (1987). Paradox of the active user. In Carroll, J. M., editor, *Interfacing Thought: Cognitive Aspects of Human-Computer Interaction*, pages 80–111. Cambridge, MA: MIT Press.

Carroll, J. M. and Rosson, M. B. (1992). Getting around the task-artifact cycle: how to make claims and design by scenario. *ACM Transactions on Information Systems*, 10(2):181–212.

Carroll, J. M., Rosson, M. B., Chin, G., and Koenemann, J. (1997). Requirements development: stages of opportunity for collaborative needs discovery. In *DIS '97: Proceedings of the Conference on Designing Interactive Systems*, pages 55–64. ACM Press.

Carter, J. A. (1990). Juggling concern for completeness and consistency with concerns for flexibility and adaptability using most. In *Proceedings of the 34th Annual Meeting of the Human Factors Society*, pages 341–345.

Carter, J. A. (1991). *Combining task analysis with software engineering in a methodology for designing interactive systems*, pages 209–234. Academic Press Professional, Inc.

Carter, J. A. (1997). Putting usability first in the design of web sites. In Lobodzinski, S. and Tomek, I., editors, *WebNet, Proceedings of WebNet 97 - World Conference on the WWW, Internet & Intranet, Toronto, Canada, November 1-5, 1997*, pages 142–148. AACE.

Carter, J. A. (2002a). *Developing E-commerce Systems*. Upper Saddle River, N.J.: Prentice Hall.

Carter, J. A. (2002b). A framework for the development of multimedia systems for use in engineering education. *Computers and Education*, 39(2):111–128.

Casaday, G. (1996). Rationale in practice: Templates for capturing and applying design experience. In Moran, T. and Carroll, J. M., editors, *Design Rationale: Concepts, Techniques, and Use*, pages 361–372. Mahwah, NJ: Lawrence Erlbaum.

Castro, J. and Kolp, M. (2002). Towards requirements-driven information systems engineering: the tropos project. *Information Systems*.

Chok, S. S. and Marriott, K. (1995). Automatic construction of user interfaces from constraint multiset grammars. In *VL '95: Proceedings of the 11th International IEEE Symposium on Visual Languages*, pages 242–249. IEEE Computer Society.

Clancey, W. J. (1983). The epistemology of a rule-based expert system - a framework for explanation. *Artificial Intelligence*, 20:215–251.

Clegg, C., Axtell, C., Damodaran, L., Farbey, B., Hull, R., Lloyd-Jones, R., Nicholls, J., Sell, R., and Tomlinson, C. (1997). Information technology: a study of performance and the role of human and organizational factors. *Ergonomics*, 40(9):851–871.

Coble, J. M., Karat, J., and Kahn, M. G. (1997). Maintaining a focus on user requirements throughout the development of clinical workstation software. In *CHI '97: Proceedings of the SIGCHI Conference on Human Factors in Computing Systems*, pages 170–177. ACM Press.

Cockburn, A. (1997). Structuring use cases with goals. *Object-Oriented Programming*, Sept-Oct.

Cockburn, A. (1998). Basic use case template (tr 96.03a, version 2). Technical report, http://alistair.cockburn.us/usecases/uctempla.htm (Personal Web Site of Alistair Cockburn).

Cockburn, A. (2001). *Writing Effective Use Cases*. Boston: Addison-Wesley.

Cockburn, A. (2002). *Agile Software Development*. Boston, MA: Addison-Wesley.

Comstock, E. M. and Duane, W. M. (1996). Embed user values in system architecture: The declaration of system usability. In *CHI '96: Proceedings of the SIGCHI conference on Human factors in computing systems*, pages 420–427. ACM Press.

Conallen, J. (2003). *Building Web Applications with UML*. Boston: Addison-Wesley.

Conklin, E. J. and Burgess-Yakemovic, K. C. (1996). A process-oriented approach to design rationale. In Moran, T. and J. M. Carroll, E., editors, *Design Rationale: Concepts, Techniques and Use*, pages 393–427. Mahwah, NJ: Lawrence Erlbaum.

Constantine, L. L. (1995). Essential modeling: use cases for user interfaces. *Interactions*, 2(2):34–46.

Constantine, L. L. (2002). Process agility and software usability: towards lightweight usage-centered design. In *Information Age*. http://www.foruse.com/articles/agiledesign.pdf.

Constantine, L. L. and Lockwood, L. A. D. (1999). *Software for Use: A Practical Guide to the Models and Methods of Usage-Centered Design*. Addison-Wesley, Reading, Massachusetts.

Constantine, L. L. and Lockwood, L. A. D. (2001). Structure and style in use cases for user interface design. In van Harmelen, M., editor, *Object Modeling and User Interface Design*, pages 245–279. Boston: Addison-Wesley.

Constantine, L. L. and Lockwood, L. A. D. (2002). User-centered engineering for web applications. *IEEE Software*, 19(2):42–50.

Cooper, A. (1999). *The Inmates Are Running the Asylum: Why High Tech Products Drive Us Crazy and How To Restore The Sanity*. Sams, Indianapolis, IN.

Cooper, A. and Reimann, R. (2000). *About Face 2.0: The Essentials of User Interface Design*. John Wiley and Sons.

Coplien, J. O. (1995). *A generative development-process pattern language*, pages 183–237. ACM Press/Addison-Wesley Publishing Co.

Costabile, M. F. (2001). Usability in the software life cycle. In Chang, S. K., editor, *Handbook of Software Engineering and Knowledge Engineering*, pages 179–192. World Scientific Publishing, Singapore.

Coutaz, J. (1987). PAC: an implementation model for dialog design. In *Proceedings Interact'87*, pages 431–436.

Covey, S. R. (1994). *Daily Reflections for Highly Effective People: Living The 7 Habits Of Highly Successful People Every Day*. Fireside.

Curtis, B., Krasner, H., and Iscoc, N. (1988). A field study of the software design process for large systems. *Communications of the ACM*, 31:1268–1287.

da Silva, P. P. and Paton, N. W. (2001). A UML-based design environment for interactive applications. In *UIDIS '01: Proceedings of the Second International Workshop on User Interfaces to Data Intensive Systems (UIDIS'01)*, page 60. IEEE Computer Society.

Dayton, T., Kramer, J., McFarland, A., and Heidelberg, M. (1996). Participatory GUI design from task models. In *Proceedings of ACM CHI 96 Conference on Human Factors in Computing Systems*, volume 2 of *Tutorial 25*, pages 375–376.

Dearden, A., Finaly, J., Allgar, E., and McManus, B. (2002). Using pattern languages in participatory design. In *Proceedings of Participatory Design Conference (PDC) 2002*.

Degler, D., Battle, L., and Taylor, D. (2003). Sharing the vision = designs that get built. In *Usability Professionals' Association 12th Annual Conference*.

DeMarco, T. and Lister, T. (1999). *Peopleware, Productive Projects and Teams*. Dorset House, 2nd edition.

Derniame, J. C., Kaba, B. A., and Wastell, D. (1999). *Software Process: Principles, Methodology and Technology*. Berlin; New York: Springer.

Devanbu, P., Brachman, R. J., Selfridge, P. G., and Ballard, B. W. (1991). LaSSIE: A knowledge-based software information system. *Communications of the ACM*, 34:34–49.

Dewan, P. (1996). Multiuser architectures. In *Proceedings of the IFIP TC2/WG2.7 Working Conference on Engineering for Human-Computer Interaction*, pages 247–270. Chapman & Hall, Ltd.

Dix, A., Findlay, J., Abowd, G., and Beale, R. (1998). *Human Computer Interaction, (2nd ed.)*. Prentice Hall: New York.

Dodd, J. (2003). Speaking their language: Placing usability on the board room table.

Donahue, G. M. (2001). Usability and the bottom line. *IEEE Software*, 18(1):31–37.

Douglas, S., Tremaine, M., Leventhal, L., Wills, C. E., and Manaris, B. (2002). Incorporating human-computer interaction into the undergraduate computer science curriculum. In *SIGCSE '02: Proceedings of the 33rd SIGCSE technical symposium on Computer science education*, pages 211–212. ACM Press.

Dourish, P. (1999). Software infrastructures. In Beaudouin-Lafon, editor, *Computer Supported Cooperative Work*. JohnWiley & Sons Ltd.

DSDM (1995). *DSDM Consortium: Dynamic Systems Development Method*. Tesseract Publishers: Farnham Surrey.

Dumas, J. S. and Redish, J. (1999). *A Practical Guide to Usability Testing. Revised Edition*. Norwood, N.J.: Ablex Pub. Corp.

Duyne, D. K. V., Landay, J., and Hong, J. I. (2002). *The Design of Sites: Patterns, Principles, and Processes for Crafting a Customer-Centered Web Experience*. Addison-Wesley Longman Publishing Co., Inc.

Earthy, J. (1999). Human centred processes, their maturity and their improvement. In *IFIP TC.13 International Conference on Human-Computer Interaction (INTER-ACT'99)*, volume 2, pages 117–118.

Earthy, J., Sherwood-Jones, B., and Bevan, N. (2001). The improvement of human-centred processes – facing the challenge and reaping the benefit of ISO 13407. *International Journal of Human-Computer Studies*, 55(4):553–585.

Eason, K. D., Harker, S. D. P., and Olphert, C. W. (1996). Representing socio-technical systems options in the development of new forms of work organisation. *European Journal of Work and Organisational Psychology*, 5(3):399–420.

Ege, R. K. (1988). Constraint-based user interfaces for simulations. In *WSC '88: Proceedings of the 20th conference on Winter simulation*, pages 263–271. ACM Press.

Engelberg, D. (2001). Workshop summary: integrating human factors analysis methods with use cases. In Branaghan, R., editor, *Proceedings of UPA 99, Design for People: Essays on Usability*.

EPSRC (2002). *Report on International Review of Computer Science*. EPSRC.

Erickson, T. (2000). Lingua francas for design: sacred places and pattern languages. In *Proceedings of DIS'00: Designing Interactive Systems: Processes, Practices, Methods, & Techniques*, Pattern Languages, pages 357–368.

Evans, G. (2002). Why are use cases so painful? [online: http://www.evanetics.com/articles/Modeling/UCPainful.htm]. Technical report, Evanetics.

Fayad, M. E. and Johnson, R. E. (2000). *Domain-specific application frameworks: Frameworks experience by industry*. New York: Wiley.

Fenton, N. E. and Neil, M. (1999). Software metrics: success, failures and new directions. *J. Syst. Softw.*, 47(2-3):149–157.

Ferre, X. (2003). Integration of usability techniques into the software development process. In *Proceedings of the Workshop on Bridging the Gaps Between Software Engineering and Human-Computer Interaction at International Conference on Software Engineering (ICSE '03)*.

Ferre, X., Juristo, N., and M., M. A. (2002a). STATUS project. deliverable d.5.1. selection of the software process and the usability techniques for consideration. Technical report, Software Architecture that supports Usability (STATUS).

Ferre, X., Juristo, N., and M., M. A. (2002b). STATUS project. deliverable d.5.2. specification of the software process with integrated usability techniques. Technical report, Software Architecture that supports Usability (STATUS).

Fincher, S. (1999). Analysis of design: an exploration of patterns and pattern languages for pedagogy. *Journal of Computers in Mathematics and Science Teaching: Special Issue CS-ED Research*, 18(3):331–348.

Fincher, S. (2000). Capture of practice: Is it obvious? In *Proceedings of BCS HCI Group/IFIP WG13.2 Workshop on HCI Patterns*.

Finney, K., Fenton, N. E., and Fedorec, I. (1999). The effects of structure on the comprehensibility of formal specifications. *IEEE Software*, 146(4):193–202.

Fischer, G. (1999). Domain-oriented design environments: supporting individual and social creativity. In Gero, J. and Maher, M. L., editors, *Computational Models of Creative Design IV, Key Centre of Design Computing and Cognition*, pages 83–111, Sydney, Australia.

Fischer, G., Nakakoji, K., Ostwald, J., Stahl, G., and Sumner, T. (1993). Embedding computer-based critics in the contexts of design, human factors in computing systems. In *presented at INTERCHI'93 Conference Proceedings*, Amsterdam, Netherlands.

Folmer, E. and Bosch, J. (2004). Architecting for usability. *Journal of systems and software*, 70(1):61–78.

Folmer, E., van Gurp, J., and Bosch, J. (2003). Investigating the relationship between software architecture and usability. In *Software Process - Improvement & Practice: Special Issue on Bridging the Process and Practice Gaps between Software Engineering and Human Computer Interaction*.

Forbrig, P. (1999). Task- and object-oriented development of interactive systems – how many models are necessary? In Duke, D. J. and Puerta, A., editors, *Design, Specification and Verification of Interactive Systems '99*, Eurographics, pages 225–237, Wien. Springer-Verlag. Proceedings of the Eurographics Workshop in Braga, Portugal, June 2 – 4, 1999.

Fowler, M. (2002). The agile manifesto: Where it came from and where it might go. Technical report, http://martinfowler.com/articles/agileStory.html.

Fowler, M. (2003a). The new methodology. Technical report, http://www.martinfowler.com/articles/newMethodology.html.

Fowler, M. (2003b). *UML Distilled: A Brief Guide to the Standard Object Modeling Language*. Reading, Massachusetts: Addison-Wesley, 3 edition.

Fowler, M. and Scott, K. (1997). UML distilled: applying the standard object modeling language. In Fowler, M., editor, *UML Distilled*. Addison Wesley Longman Inc., Reading, MA.

Fuggetta, A. (2000). Software process: A roadmap. In *ICSE '00: Proceedings of the Conference on The Future of Software Engineering*, pages 25–34. ACM Press.

Gamma, E., Helm, R., Johnson, R., and Vlissides, J. (1995). *Design Patterns: Elements of Reusable Object-Oriented Software*. Addison Wesley Professional Computing Series. Addison Wesley. http://www.aw.com.

Glass, R. A. (1995). A structure-based critique on contemporary computing research. *Journal of Systems and Software*, 28:3–7.

Glass, R. L. (2003). *Facts and Fallacies of Software Engineering*. Boston, MA: Addison-Wesley.

Glazer, R. (1998). Measuring the knower: towards a theory of knowledge equity. *California Management Review*, 40(175-194).

Golden, E., John, B. E., and Bass, L. (2005). The value of a usability-supporting architectural pattern in software architecture design: A controlled experiment. In *Proceedings of the Intrenational Conference on Software Engineering, ICSE 2005*, St. Louis, Missouri.

Good, M., Spine, T. M., Whiteside, J., and George, P. (1986). User-derived impact analysis as a tool for usability engineering. In *CHI '86: Proceedings of the SIGCHI conference on Human factors in computing systems*, pages 241–246. ACM Press.

Göransson, B. (2004). *User-Centred Systems Design: Designing Usable Interactive Systems in Practice*. Phd thesis, Uppsala, Sweden: Acta Universitatis Upsaliensis. Comprehensive Summaries of Uppsala Dissertations from the Faculty of Science and Technology, ISSN 1104-232X; 981.

Göransson, B. and Gulliksen, J. (2003). The usability design process — integrating user-centred systems design in the software development process. *Software Process: Improvement and Practice*, 8(2):63–65.

Göransson, B. and Sandbäck, T. (1999). Usability designers improve the user-centred design process. In *Proceedings for INTERACT'99*, Edinburgh, UK.

Gould, J. D., Boies, S. J., and Ukelson, J. (1997). How to design usable systems. In Helander, M., Landauer, T. K., and Prabhu, P., editors, *Handbook of Human-Computer Interaction*. Amsterdam: Elsevier Science B.V.

Gram, C. and Cockton, G. (1996). *Design Principles for Interactive Systems*. Chapman and Hall, London, England.

Gray, W. D., John, B. E., and Atwood, M. E. (1993). Project ernestine: A validation of GOMS for prediction and explanation of real-world task performance. *Human-Computer Interaction*, 8(3):237–209.

Greenbaum, J. and Kyng, M. (1991). *Design at Work: Cooperative Design of Computer Systems*. Hillsdale, NJ, Lawrence Erlbaum Associates.

Greenspan, S. J., Mylopoulos, J., and Borgida, A. (1982). Capturing more world knowledge in the requirements specification. In *Proceedings of the 6th International Conference on Software Engineering*, pages 225–235. IEEE Computer Society Press.

Griffiths, R. N. and Pemberton, L. (2000). Don't write guidelines write patterns! [online]. Technical report, http://www.it.bton.ac.uk/staff/lp22/guidelinesdraft.html.

Grudin, J. (1988). Why CSCW applications fail: Problems in the design and evaluation of organizational interfaces. In *presented at Proceedings of CSCW'88*.

Guindon, R. (1987). A model of cognitive processes in software design: An analysis of breakdowns in early design activities by individuals. Technical Report MCC Technical Report STP-283-87, Microelectronics and Computer Technology Corporation, Austin TX.

Gulliksen, J. and Boivie, I. (2001). Usability throughout the entire software development lifecycle. *SIGCHI Bulletin*, 33(3). Summary of the INTERACT'00-workshop. Also available as technical report from the department of information technology, Uppsala university, Report number 2001-026. (http://www.it.uu.se/research/reports/2001-026/2001-026.pdf).

Gulliksen, J., Forbrig, P., Seffah, A., van Welie, M., and Borchers, J. (2003a). The role of patterns. In *2nd Workshop on Software and Usability Cross-Pollination, INTERACT 2003' Conference*.

Gulliksen, J. and Göransson, B. (2001). Reengineering the systems development process for user centered design. In Hirose, M., editor, *Proceedings of INTERACT 2001*. IOS Press.

Gulliksen, J., Göransson, B., Boivie, I., Blomkvist, S., Persson, J., and Cajander, Å. (2003b). Key principles for user-centred systems design. *Behaviour and Information Technology*, 22(6):397–409. reproduced with permission in this book (chap. 2).

Gulliksen, J., Lantz, A., and Boivie, I. (1998). User-centered design in practice – problems and possibilities. *SIGCHI Bulletin*, 31(2):25–35. Summary of the PDC'98 workshop on User Orientation in Practice - Problems and Possibilities. Also available with all accepted contributions as technical report TRITA-NA-D9813, CID-40. (www.nada.kth.se/cid/pdf/cid_40.pdf).

Gulliksen, J., Lantz, A., and Boivie, I. (2001). How to make user centred design usable. *SIGCHI Bulletin*, 33(3). Summary of the INTERACT'00-workshop on How to make user centred design usable. Also available with all accepted contributions as technical report TRITA-NA-D0006, CID-72. (http://cid.nada.kth.se/pdf/cid_72.pdf).

Hackos, J. T. and Redish, J. (1998). *User and Task Analysis for Interface Design*. New York: Wiley.

Hahn, J. and Subramani, M. R. (2000). A framework of knowledge management systems: Issues and challenges for theory and practice. In *Proceedings of the Twenty-first International Conference on Information Systems*, pages 302–312, Brisbane, Australia.

Hall, A. and Chapman, R. (2002). Correctness by construction: Developing a commercial secure system. *IEEE Software*, 19(1):18–25.

Harning, M. B. and Vanderdonckt, J. (2003). Closing the gaps: Software engineering and human-computer interaction. In *Workshop at the Ninth IFIP TC13 International Conference on Human-Computer Interaction (IN-*

TERACT 2003). [online: http://www.interact2003.org/workshops/ws9-description.html.

Harris, J. and Henderson, A. (1999). A better mythodology for system design. In Williams, M. G., Altom, M. W., Ehrlich, K., and Newman, W., editors, *CHI 1999 Conference on Human Factors in Computing Systems Proceedings.* ACM Press.

Haynes, S. R., Kannampallil, T. G., Larson, L. L., and Garg, N. (2005). Optimizing anti-terrorism resource allocation. *Journal of the American Society for Information Science and Technology,* 56:299–309.

Hefley, W. E., Buie, E. A., Lynch, G. F., Muller, M. J., Hoecker, D. G., Carter, J. A., and Roth, J. T. (1994). Integrating human factors with software engineering practices. In *Proceedings of the 1994 Annual Meeting of the Human Factors and Ergonomics Society,* pages 315–319. Carnegie Mellon University.

Henniger, S. (2003). Tool support for experience-based software development methodologies. *Advances In Computers,* 59:29–82.

Henninger, S. (2000). A methodology and tools for applying context-specific usability guidelines to interface design. *Interacting With Computers,* 12(3):225–243.

Highsmith, J. (2002). *Agile Software Development Ecosystems.* Boston, Massachusetts, USA: Pearson Education.

Highsmith, J. and Cockburn, A. (2001). Agile software development: The business of innovation. *Computer,* 34(9):120–122.

Hix, D. and Hartson, H. R. (1993). *Developing User Interfaces: Ensuring Usability Through Product and Process.* John Wiley & Sons, New York, New York. OCLC QA 76.9 U83 H59.

Hoare, C. A. R. (1969). An axiomatic basis of computer programming. *Communications of the ACM,* 12:576–580.

Hofmann, H. F. and Lehner, F. (2001). Requirements engineering as a success factor in software projects. *IEEE Software.,* 18(4):58–66.

Hudson, W. (2001). Toward unified models in user-centered and object-oriented design. In van Harmelen, M., editor, *Object Modeling and User Interface Design: Designing Interactive Systems.* Addison-Wesley: Boston.

Hudson, W. (2003). Adopting user-centered design within an agile process: A conversation. *Cutter IT Journal,* 16(10). http://www.syntagm.co.uk/design/articles/ucd-xp03.pdf.

Hutchins, E. (1995a). *Cognition in the wild.* Cambridge, Mass.: MIT Press.

Hutchins, E. (1995b). How a cockpit remembers its speeds. *Cognitive Science,* 19:265–288.

Hynninen, T., Liukkonen-Olmiala, T., and Kinnunen, T. (1999). No pain, no gain, applying user-centered design in product concept development. In Brewster, S., Cawsey, A., and Cockton, G., editors, *Proceedings of the Seventh IFIP Conference on Human-Computer Interaction, INTERACT'99,* volume 2, pages 201–205. IOS Press.

IEEE (1990). *IEEE Std 610.12-1990. IEEE Standard Glossary of Software Engineering Terminology.* IEEE, New York NY.

IEEE (1998). *IEEE 830: Recommended Practice for Software Requirements Specifications.* IEEE.

Imaz, M. and Benyon, D. (1999). How stories capture interactions. In In Sasse, M. A. and Johnson, C., editors, *Proceedings of the Seventh IFIP Conference on Human-Computer Interaction, INTERACT'99*, pages 321–328. IOS Press.

ISO (1998). *ISO/IEC Technical Report 15504-2: Information technology – Software process assessment*. ISO.

ISO (2002). *ISO Technical Specification 16982: Ergonomics of human-system interaction – Usability methods supporting human centered design*. ISO.

ISO (2003). *ISO 14915-3: Software ergonomics for multimedia user interfaces – Media selection and combination*. ISO.

ISO/IEC (1998). *ISO/IEC 9241-11: Ergonomic requirements for office work with visual display terminals (VDT)s - Part 11 Guidance on usability*. ISO/IEC 9241-11: 1998 (E).

ISO/IEC (1999). *ISO/IEC 13407: Human-Centred Design Processes for Interactive Systems*. ISO/IEC 13407: 1999 (E).

ISO/IEC (2000a). *ISO/IEC 18529: Human-centred Lifecycle Process Descriptions*. ISO/IEC TR 18529: 2000 (E).

ISO/IEC (2000b). *ISO/IEC 9126: Information Technology, Software Product Evaluation, Quality, Characteristics and Guidelines for their Use*. ISO/IEC 926: 2000.

ISO/IEC (2002). *International Standard: Information Technology. Software Life Cycle Processes. Amendment 1. ISO/IEC Standard 12207:1995/Amd.1:2002*. ISO, Geneva, Switzerland.

ISO/IEC (2003). *ISO/IEC 18152: A specification for the process assessment of human-system issues*. ISO/PAS 18152: 2003.

Jackson, M. (2001). *Problem Frames: Analysing and Structuring Software Development Problems*. Reading, MA: Addison-Wesley.

Jacobson, I. (1992). *Object-oriented software engineering: A use case driven approach*. Reading, MA.: Addison-Wesley.

Jacobson, I. (1995). The use-case construct in object-oriented software engineering. In *Scenario-based design: envisioning work and technology in system development*, pages 309–336. John Wiley & Sons, Inc.

Jacobson, I., Booch, G., and Rumbaugh, J. (1999). *The Unified Software Development Process*. Addison Wesley Longman Inc., Reading, Mass., U.S.A.

Jambon, F., Girard, P., and Ait-Ameur, Y. (2001). Interactive system safety and usability enforced with the development process. In *EHCI '01: Proceedings of the 8th IFIP International Conference on Engineering for Human-Computer Interaction*, pages 39–56. Springer-Verlag.

Jarke, M. (1999). Scenarios for modeling. *Communications of the ACM*, 42(1):47–48.

Jeffries, R. (1997). The role of task analysis in the design of software. In Helander, M., Landauer, T. K., and Prabhu, P., editors, *Handbook of Human-Computer Interaction*, pages 347–359. Amsterdam: Elsevier, 2 edition.

Jeffries, R., Turner, A. T., Polson, P. G., and Atwood, M. E. (1981). The processes involved in designing software. In Anderson, J. R., editor, *Cognitive Skills and Their Acquisition*, pages 255–283. Hillsdale, NJ: Lawrence Erlbaum.

Joeris, G. (1997). Change management needs integrated process and configuration management. In *ESEC '97/FSE-5: Proceedings of the 6th European conference held jointly with the 5th ACM SIGSOFT international symposium on Foundations of software engineering*, pages 125–141. Springer-Verlag New York, Inc.

John, B. E., Bass, L., Juristo, N., and Sanchez-Segura, M.-I. (2004a). Avoiding "we can't change THAT!": Software architecture and usability. In *Tutorial materials presented at CHI 2004*, Vienna, Austria.

John, B. E., Bass, L., Kazman, R., and Chen, E. (2004b). Identifying gaps between hci, software engineering, and design, and boundary objects to bridge them. In *CHI '04: CHI '04 extended abstracts on Human factors in computing systems*, pages 1723–1724, New York, NY, USA. ACM Press.

John, B. E., Bass, L., Sanchez-Segura, M.-I., and Adams, R. J. (2004c). Bringing usability concerns to the design of software architecture. In *Proceedings of The 9th IFIP Working Conference on Engineering for Human-Computer Interaction and the 11th International Workshop on Design, Specification and Verification of Interactive Systems*, Hamburg, Germany.

John, B. E. and Kieras, R. E. (1995). The GOMS family of user interface analysis techniques: Comparison and contrast. *ACM Transactions on Computer-Human Interaction*, 3:320–351.

Johnson, P. (1989). Supporting system design by analyzing current task knowledge. In Diaper, D., editor, *Task Analysis for Human-Computer Interaction*. UK: E. Horwood Press.

Jokela, T. (2004a). Evaluating the user-centredness of development organisations: Conclusions and implications from empirical usability capability maturity assessments. *Interacting with Computers*, 16(6):1095–1132.

Jokela, T. (2004b). The KESSU usability design process model. Technical report, Oulu University. Version 2.1.

Jokela, T. and Abrahamsson, P. (2004). Usability assessment of an extreme programming project: close co-operation with the customer does not equal to good usability. *Lecture Notes in Computing Science*, 3009(2004):393–407.

Jokela, T. and Pirkola, J. (1999). Using quantitative usability goals in the design of a user interface for cellular phones. *INTERACT'99*.

Jones, C. B. (1986). *Systematic software development using VDM*. London: Prentice Hall.

Juristo, N., Lopez, M., Moreno, A. M., and Sanchez-Segura, M.-I. (2003). Improving software usability through architectural patterns. In *Proceedings of the ICSE 2003 Workshop Bridging the Gaps Between Software Engineering and Human-Computer Interaction*, pages 12–19, Portland, Oregon, USA.

Kaindl, H. (1995). An integration of scenarios with their purposes in task modeling. In Olson, G. M. and Schuon, S., editors, *Proceedings of the Symposium on Designing Interactive Systems: Processes, Practices, Methods and Techniques*, pages 227–236, New York. ACM Press.

Kane, D. (2003). Finding a place for discount usability engineering in agile development: throwing down the gauntlet. In *Proceedings of the Agile Development Conference*, pages 40–46.

Kapor, M. (1990). Software design manifesto. In Winograd, T., editor, *Bringing Design To Software*. Addison-Wesley.

Karat, J. (1997). Evolving the scope of user-centered design. *Commun. ACM*, 40(7):33–38.

Karat, J., Atwood, M. E., Dray, S. M., Rantzer, M., and Wixon, D. R. (1996). User centered design: quality or quackery? In *CHI '96: Conference companion on Human factors in computing systems*, pages 161–162. ACM Press.

Karat, J. and Karat, C. M. (2003). The evolution of user-centered focus in the human-computer interaction field. *IBM Systems Journal*, 42(4):532–541.

Kautz, K. H. and Thaysen, K. (2001). Knowledge, learning and IT support in a small software company. *Journal of Knowledge Management*, 5:349–357.

Kawalek, P. and Wastell, D. G. (1996). Organizational design for software development: A cybernetic perspective. In *EWSPT '96: Proceedings of the 5th European Workshop on Software Process Technology*, pages 258–270. Springer-Verlag.

Kazman, R., Bass, L., and Bosch, J. (2003). Workshop overviews: Bridging the gaps between software engineering and human-computer interaction. In *Proceedings of the 25th international conference on Software engineering*. IEEE Computers Society.

Kazman, R., Klein, M., and Clements, P. (2000). ATAM: Method for architecture evaluation. Technical report, Software Engineering Institute, Carnegie Mellon University, Pittsburgh, PA. Technical Report No. CMU/SEI-2000-TR-004.

Keller, G. and Teufel, T. (1998). *SAP/R3 process oriented implementation*. Reading, MA: Addison Wesley-Longman.

Kieras, D. E. and Meyer, D. E. (1997). An overview of the EPIC architecture for cognition and performance with application to human-computer interaction. *Human-Computer Interaction*, 12(4):391–438.

Kirwan, B. and Ainsworth, I. K. (1993). *A guide to task analysis*. London ; Washington, DC: Taylor & Francis.

Kok, D. (2004). An investigation into a HCI pattern language for transaction processing systems. Technical report, Department of Computer Science & Information Systems. University of Port Elizabeth.

Kok, D. and Wesson, J. L. (2002). Designing transaction processing systems: a patterns approach. In *SAICSIT '02: Proceedings of the 2002 annual research conference of the South African institute of computer scientists and information technologists on Enablement through technology*, pages 257–257. South African Institute for Computer Scientists and Information Technologists.

Krasner, G. E. and Pope, S. T. (1988). A cookbook for using the model-view controller user interface paradigm in Smalltalk-80. *Journal of Object Oriented Program*, 1(3):26–49.

Kreitzberg, C. and Quesenbery, W. (1999). Crossing the chasm: A methodology framework for promoting usability in the software development community. In *Usability Professionals' Association 8th Annual Conference*.

Kroll, P. and Kruchten, P. (2003). *The Rational Unified Process Made Easy: A Practitioner's Guide to the RUP*. Boston, MA: Addison-Wesley.

Kruchten, P. (1998). *The Rational Unified Process - An Introduction*. Addison Wesley Longman Inc., Reading, Mass., USA.

Kruchten, P. (1999). Use-case storyboards in the rational unified process. In *Proceedings of the Workshop on Object-Oriented Technology*, pages 249–250. Springer-Verlag.

Kühn, T. S. (1962). *The Structure of Scientific Revolutions*. University of Chicago Press, Chicago , IL , USA.

Kujala, S. (2003). User involvement: a review of the benefits and challenges. *Behaviour & Information Technology*, 22(1):1–16.

Kujala, S., Kauppinen, M., Nakari, P., and Rekola, S. (2003). Field studies in practice: Making it happen. In *Proceedings of INTERACT 2003*, pages 359–366.

Kujala, S., Kauppinen, M., and Rekola, S. (2001a). Bridging the gap between user needs and user requirements. In Avouris, N. and Fakotakis, N., editors, *Advances in Human-Computer Interaction I, (Proceedings of the Panhellenic Conference with International Participation in Human-Computer Interaction, PC-HCI 2001)*, pages 45–50. Typorama Publications.

Kujala, S., Kauppinen, M., and Rekola, S. (2001b). Introducing user needs gathering to product development: Increasing innovation and customer satisfaction. In *Proceedings of Interact 2001 Conference*, pages 856–861. IOS Press.

Kujala, S. and Mäntylä, M. (2000a). How effective are user studies? In *Proceedings of HCI'2000 Conference*, pages 61–71.

Kujala, S. and Mäntylä, M. (2000b). Studying users for developing usable and useful products. In *Proceedings of the 1st Nordic Conference on Computer-Human Interaction*, pages 1–11.

Kwaiter, G., Gaildrat, V., and Caubet, R. (1998). Modelling with constraints: A bibliographical survey. In *IV '98: Proceedings of the International Conference on Information Visualisation*, pages 211–220. IEEE Computer Society.

Kyng, M. (1995). Making representations work. *Comm. of the ACM*, 38(9):46–55.

Lamberti, D. M. and Wallace, W. A. (1990). Intelligent interface design: An empirical assessment of knowledge presentation in expert systems. *MIS Quarterly*, 14:279–311.

Landauer, T. K. (1995). *The Trouble with Computers*. MIT Press.

Larman, C. (2002). *UML and Patterns: An Introduction to Object-Oriented Analysis and Design and the Unified Process*. Upper Saddle River, NJ: Prentice Hall PTR, 2 edition.

Larman, C. (2004). *Agile and Iterative Development: A Manager's Guide*. Boston, MA: Addison-Wesley.

Latour, B. (1991). Technology is society made durable. In *A Sociology of Monsters. Essays on Power, Technology and Domination*, pages 103–131. London: Routledge.

Latour, B. and Woolgar, S. (1986). *Laboratory life: The construction of scientific facts (reprint edition)*. Princeton, NJ: Princeton University Press.

Lea, D. (1994). Christopher alexander: an introduction for object-oriented designers. *SIGSOFT Softw. Eng. Notes*, 19(1):39–46.

Lethbridge, T., Singer, J., and Forward, A. (2003). How software engineers use documentation: The state of the practice. *IEEE Software*, 20:35–39.

Leveson, N. G. (2000). Intent specifications: An approach to building human-centered specifications. *IEEE Trans. Software Eng.*, 26:15–35.

Lewis, C. and Wharton, C. (1997). Cognitive walkthroughs. In Helander, M., Landauer, T. K., and Prabhu, P. V., editors, *Handbook of Human-Computer Interaction*, chapter 30, pages 717–732. Elsevier, Amsterdam, 2 edition.

Lewis, R. O. (1992). *Independent verification and validation: A life cycle engineering process for quality software*. New York: Wiley.

Lilly, S. (2000). How to avoid use-case pitfalls. Technical report, Software Development Magazine.

Lim, K. Y. and Long, J. (1994). *The MUSE Method for Usability Engineering*. Cambridge; New York: Cambridge University Press.

Lindvall, M., Basili, V., Boehm, B., Costa, P., Dangle, K., Shull, F., Tesoriero, R., Williams, L., and Zelkowitz, M. V. (2002). Empirical findings in agile methods. In *Proceedings of XP/Agile Universe 2002 Conference*, Chicago, Illinois, USA.

Long, J. and Dowell, J. (1989). Conceptions of the discipline of HCI: Craft, applied science, and engineering. In *Proceedings of the HCI'89 Conference on People and Computers V*, Conference Theme Invited Keynote Paper, pages 9–32.

MacLean, A., Young, R. M., Bellott, V. M. E., and Moran, T. (1996). Questions, options, and criteria: Elements of design space analysis. In Moran, T. P. and Carroll, J. M., editors, *Design Rationale: Concepts, Techniques and Use*, pages 21–51. Mahwah, NJ: Lawrence Erlbaum.

Maguire, M. (1998). RESPECT user-centred requirements handbook. version 3.3. Technical report, HUSAT Research Institute (now the Ergonomics and Saftety Research Institute, ESRI), Loughborough University, UK.

Maguire, M. (2001a). Context of use within usability activities. *Int. J. Hum.-Comput. Stud.*, 55(4):453–483.

Maguire, M. (2001b). Methods to support human-centred design. *Int. J. Hum.-Comput. Stud.*, 55(4):587–634.

Makarainen, M., Tiitola, J., and Konkka, K. (2001). How cultural needs affect user interface design.

Malan, R. and Bredemeyer, D. (1999). Functional requirements and use cases. Technical report, Bredemeyer Consulting.

Mandel, M. J. (2002). Tech's weakness is only relative: Its share was much lower in '91. In *Business Week*, page 30.

Markopoulos, P. and Marijnissen, P. (2001). UML as a representation for interaction design. In *Proceedings of OZCHI 2000*, pages 240–249.

Martin, D. and Somerville, I. (2004). Patterns of cooperative interaction: Linking ethnomethodology to design. *ACM Transactions on Computer-Human Interaction*, 11:59–89.

Mathiassen, L. and Munk-Madsen, A. (1986). Formalizations in systems development. *Behaviour and Information Technology*, 5(2):145–155.

Mayhew, D. J. (1999). *The Usability Engineering Lifecycle: A Practitioner's Guide to User Interface Design*. Morgan Kaufmann Publishers Inc., San Francisco, CA.

McCoy, T. (2002). Usability, who cares?: An analysis of indifference towards usability within the IT industry. In *Proceedings of the IFIP 17th World Computer Congress - TC13 Stream on Usability*, pages 283–294. Kluwer, B.V.

McGraw, K. L. and Harbison, K. (1997). *User-centered requirements: The scenario-based engineering process*. Lawrence Erbaum Associates, NJ.

Meszaros, G. and Doble, J. (2000). A pattern language for pattern writing [online]. Technical report, `http://hillside.net/patterns/writing/patternwritingpaper.htm`.

Metzker, E. (2003). An experimental process metrics support environment and a cross-organizational study on its acceptance by practitioners. In *METRICS '03: Proceedings of the 9th International Symposium on Software Metrics*, page 135. IEEE Computer Society.

Metzker, E. and Offergeld, M. (2001). An interdisciplinary approach for successfully integrating human-centered design methods into development processes practiced by industrial software development organizations. In *EHCI '01: Proceedings of the 8th IFIP International Conference on Engineering for Human-Computer Interaction*, pages 19–34. Springer-Verlag.

Microsoft Corporation (1995). *The windows interface guidelines for software design*. Microsoft Press, Redmond, WA.

Milner, R. (1989). *Communication and concurrency*. Hemel Hempstead: Prentice-Hall.

Mitchell, A. A. and Chi, M. T. H. (1984). Measuring knowledge within a domain. In P., N., editor, *The Representation of Cognitive Structures*. Toronto: Ontario Institute for Studies in Education.

Monk, A., Wright, P., Haber, J., and Davenport, L. (1993). *Improving your Human-Computer Interface: A Practical Technique*. London: Prentice Hall.

Moran, T. P. and Carroll, J. M. (1996). *Design Rationale: Concepts, Techniques, and Use*. Mahwah, N.J.: L. Erlbaum Associates.

Mori, G., Paternò, F., and Santoro, C. (2002). CTTE: support for developing and analyzing task models for interactive system design. *IEEE Trans. Softw. Eng.*, 28(8):797–813.

Mugridge, W. B., Hosking, J. G., and Grundy, J. (1996). Towards a constructor kit for visual notations. In *OZCHI '96: Proceedings of the 6th Australian Conference on Computer-Human Interaction (OZCHI '96)*, pages 169–176. IEEE Computer Society.

Myers, B. A. and Rosson, M. B. (1992). Survey on user interface programming. In *CHI '92: Proceedings of the SIGCHI conference on Human factors in computing systems*, pages 195–202. ACM Press.

Mylopoulos, J., Chung, L., and Yu, E. (1999). From object-oriented to goal-oriented requirements analysis. *Commun. ACM*, 42(1):31–37.

Nardi, B. (1993). *A small matter of programming*. Cambridge MA: MIT Press.

Newman, W. and Lamming, M. (1995). *Interactive System Design*. Wokingham, England: Addison-Wesley Publishing.

Nielsen, J. (1993). *Usability Engineering*. Boston, MA: Academic Press Inc.

Nielsen, J. (1994). Top 10 heuristics for usability [online]. Technical report, `http://www.useit.com/papers/heuristic/heuristic_list.html`.

Nielsen, J. (1995). Scenarios in discount usability engineering. In Carroll, J. R., editor, *Scenario-based design: envisioning work and technology in system development*, pages 59–83. John Wiley & Sons, Inc.

Nielsen, J. and Mack, R. L. (1994). *Usability Inspection Methods*. New York: Wiley.

Nielsen, J., Molich, R., Snyder, C., and Farrell, S. (2001). E-commerce user experience: High-level strategy. Technical report, Nielsen Norman Group.

Nilsson, E. G. (2002). Combining compound conceptual user interface components with modelling patterns — a promising direction for model-based cross-platform user interface development. In *DSV-IS '02: Proceedings of the 9th International Workshop on Interactive Systems. Design, Specification, and Verification*, pages 104–117. Springer-Verlag.

NIST (2004). Proposed industry format for usability requirements. Technical report, NIST.

Nonaka, I. (1994). A dynamic theory of organizational knowledge creation. *Organization Science*, 5:14–37.

Norman, D. A. (1988). *The psychology of everyday things*. New York: Basic Books.

Norman, D. A. (1990). *The Design of Everyday Things*. Doubleday.

Norman, D. A. (2004). *Emotional Design: Why We Love (or Hate) Everyday Things*. New York: Basic Books.

Norman, D. A. and Draper, S. W. (1986). *User Centered System Design: New Perspectives on Human-Computer Interaction*. Lawrence Erlbaum Associates, Hillsdale, NJ.

Norman, K. (1995). QUIS: The questionnaire for user interaction satisfaction [online]. Technical report, http://www.cs.umd.edu/hcil/quis/.

Nunes, N. J. (2001). *Object Modeling for User-Centered Development and User Interface Design: The Wisdom Approach*. PhD thesis, Universidade da Madeira, Portugal.

Nunes, N. J. and e Cunha, J. F. (2000). Towards a UML profile for interaction design: the wisdom approach. In Evans, A., Kent, S., and Selic, B., editors, *UML 2000 - The Unified Modeling Language. Advancing the Standard. Third International Conference, York, UK, October 2000, Proceedings*, volume 1939 of *LNCS*, pages 101–116. Springer.

Nuseibeh, B. and Easterbrook, S. (2000). Requirements engineering: A roadmap. In *Proceedings of the Conference on The Future of Software Engineering*, pages 35–46.

Ockerman, J. J. and Mitchell, C. M. (1999). Case-based design browser to support software reuse: theoretical structure and empirical evaluation. *International Journal of Human-Computer Studies*, 51:865–893.

OMG (2003). OMG unified modeling language specification, version 1.5. Technical report, Object Management Group, Inc.

Paech, B. and Kohler, K. (2003). Usability engineering integrated with requirements engineering. In *Workshop at the conference "Bridging the Gaps Between Software Engineering and Human-Computer Interaction", IEEE International Conference on Software Engineering*.

Paternò, F. (2000). Model-based design of interactive applications. *Intelligence*, 11(4):26–38.

Paternò, F. (2001). Towards a UML for interactive systems. In *EHCI '01: Proceedings of the 8th IFIP International Conference on Engineering for Human-Computer Interaction*, pages 7–18. Springer-Verlag.

Patton, J. (2002). Hitting the target: adding interaction design to agile software development. In *OOPSLA '02: OOPSLA 2002 Practitioners Reports*, pages 1–ff. ACM Press.

Paulk, M. C., Curtis, B., Chrissis, M. B., and Weber, C. V. (1993). Capability maturity model, version 1.1. *IEEE Software.*, 10(4):18–27.

Persson, J. (2003). *Basic values in software development and organizational change.* Licentiate thesis 2003-002, Uppsala, Sweden: Uppsala University.

Pitt, J. C. (2000). *Thinking About Technology: Foundations of the Philosophy of Technology.* New York: Seven Bridges.

Plowman, R., Rogers, Y., and Ramage, M. (1995). What are workplace studies for? In *Proceedings of the Fourth European Conference on Computer-Supported Cooperative Work*, pages 309–324. Kluwer.

Polanyi, M. (1958). *Personal Knowledge: Towards a Post-Critical Philosophy.* University of Chicago Press.

Polanyi, M. (1966). *The tacit dimension.* Garden City, N.Y., Doubleday.

Poltrock, S., Grudin, J., Dumais, S., Fidel, R., Bruce, H., and Pejtersen, A. M. (2003). Information seeking and sharing in design teams. In *presented at Proceedings of Group'03*, Sanibel Island, FL.

Poltrock, S. E. and Grudin, J. (1994). Organizational obstacles to interface design and development: Two participant observer studies. *ACM Transactions on Computer-Human Interaction*, 1(1):52–80.

Poppendieck (2002). Wicked problems. *Software Development Magazine.*

Potts, C. (1999). ScenIC: A strategy for inquiry-driven requirements determination. In *Proceedings: 4th IEEE International Symposium on Requirements Engineering*, pages 58–65. IEEE Computer Society Press.

Potts, C., Takahashi, K., and Anton, A. I. (1994). Inquiry-based requirements analysis. *IEEE Software*, 11(2):21–32.

Prakash, A., Shim, H. S., and Lee, J. H. (1999). Issues and tradeoffs in CSCW systems. *IEEE Transactions on Data and Knowledge Engineering*, 11(1):213–227.

Preece, J., Rogers, Y., Sharp, H., Benyon, D., Holland, S., and Carey, T. (1994). *Human-Computer Interaction.* Addison Wesley, Harlow, England.

Pressman, R. S. (2005a). *Software Engineering: A Practitioner's Approach.* McGraw-Hill, 6 edition.

Pressman, R. S. (2005b). *Software Engineering: A Practitioner's Approach.* McGraw-Hill, 5 edition.

Prieto-Diaz, R. (1993). Status report: Software reusability. *IEEE Software*, 10:61–66.

Pyla, P. S., Pérez-Quiñones, M. A., Arthur, J. D., and Hartson, H. R. (2004). What we should teach, but don't: Proposal for a cross pollinated HCI-SE curriculum. In *Proceedings of the Frontiers in Education (FIE 2004) Conference.*

Quesenbery, W. (2000). Crossing the chasm: Promoting usability in the software development community. *UPA Common Ground*, 10(1).

Radle, K. and Young, S. (2001). Partnering usability with development: How three organizations succeeded. *IEEE Software*, 18(1):38–45.

Rational (2002). What's new in rational development accelerators? version 2002. Technical report, Rational Software Corporation.

Rational Software Corporation (1999). *UML: Unified Modelling Language method.* http://www.rational.com.

Redish, J. and Wixon, J. (2003). Task analysis. In Jacko, J. A. and Sears, A., editors, *The human-computer interaction handbook: fundamentals, evolving technologies, and emerging applications*, pages 922–940. Mahwah, N.J.: Lawrence Erlbaum Associates.

Reifer, D. J. (2002). *Software Management*. Los Alamitos, CA: IEEE Computer Society Press, 6 edition.

Rengell, B. and Horst, M. (2001). An industrial case study on distributed prioritisation in market driven requirements engineering for packaged software. *Requirements Engineering*, 6(1):51–62.

Richter, A. (2003). Generating user interface design patterns from web-based e-business applications. In *Proceedings of IFIP INTERACT '03 Workshop on Software & Usability Cross-Pollination: The Role of Usability Patterns*.

Rising, L. (2001). Patterns mining [online]. Technical report, http://www.agcs.com/supportv2/techpapers/patterns/papers/mining.htm.

Roberts, D., Berry, D., Isensee, S., and Mullaly, J. (1998). *Designing for the User with OVID: Bridging the Gap Between Software Engineering and User Interface Design*. Macmillan Technical Publishing.

Robertson, J. (2001). Information design using card sorting. Technical report, Step Two Designs Pty Ltd.

Robertson, J. and Robertson, S (1999). *Mastering the Requirements Process*. Addison Wesley, Harlow.

Rogers, Y. and Ellis, J. (1994). Distributed cognition: an alternative framework for analyzing and explaining collaborative working. *Journal of Information Technology*, 9:119–128.

Rolland, C., Ben Achour, C., Cauvet, C., Ralyt, R., Sutcliffe, A. G., Maiden, N. A. M., Jarke, M., Haumer, P., Pohl, K., Dubois, E., and Heymans, H. (1998). Proposal for a scenario classification framework. *Requirements Engineering Journal*, 3(1):23–47.

Rosenbaum, S., Rohn, J. A., and Humburg, J. (2000). A toolkit for strategic usability: results from workshops, panels and surveys. In Turner, T., Szwillius, G., Czerwinski, M., and Paternò, F., editors, *CHI 2000 Conference on Human Factors in Computing Systems Proceedings*. ACM Press.

Rosson, M. B. (1999). Integrating development of task and object models. *Commun. ACM*, 42(1):49–56.

Rosson, M. B. and Carroll, J. M. (2002a). *Usability Engineering: Scenario-based Development of Human-Computer Interaction*. San Fancisco: Academic Press.

Rosson, M. B. and Carroll, J. M. (2002b). *Usability Engineering: Scenario-Based Development of Human-Computer Interactions*. Morgan Kauffmann, San Francisco, CA.

Royce, W. W. (1970). Managing the development of large scale software systems. In *Proceedings of the IEEE WESCON*, pages 1–9.

Rubinstein, R., Hersh, H. M., and Ledgard, H. F. (1984). *The Human Factor: Designing Computer Systems for People*. Maynard, MA: Digital Press.

Rumbaugh, J. (1994). Getting started - using use cases to capture requirements. *Journal of Object-Oriented Programming*, 7(5):8–23.

Sachs, P. (1995). Transforming work: collaboration, learning, and design. *Communications of the ACM*, 38(9):36–44.

Salingaros, N. A. (2000). The structure of pattern languages. *Architectural Research Quarterly*, 4:149–161.

Scapin, D. and Pierret-Goldbreich, C. (1990). Toward a method for task description: MAD. In *Proceedings of Work and Display Units 89*. Elsevier Science Publishers B.V. North Holland.

Schmidt, D. C. and Cleeland, C. (2000). Applying a pattern language to develop extensible orb middleware. In Rising, L., editor, *Design patterns in communications software*, pages 393–438. Cambridge University Press.

Schön, D. A. (1983). *The Reflective Practicioner: How Professionals Think in Action*. New York: Basic Books.

Seffah, A. (2003). Learning the ropes: human-centered design skills and patterns for software engineers' education. *Interactions*, 10(5):36–45.

Seffah, A. and Andreevskaia, A. (2003). Empowering software engineers in human-centered design. In *ICSE '03: Proceedings of the 25th International Conference on Software Engineering*, pages 653–658. IEEE Computer Society.

Seffah, A., Djouab, R., and Antunes, H. (2001). Comparing and reconciling usability-centered and use case-driven requirements engineering processes. In *AUIC '01: Proceedings of the 2nd Australasian conference on User interface*, pages 132–139. IEEE Computer Society.

Seffah, A. and Engelberg, D. (1999). Integrating human factors analysis techniques with use cases and OO methods. In *Usability Professionals' Association 8th Annual Conference*.

Seffah, A. and Forbrig, P. (2001). Software and usability engineering cross-pollination: A roadmap for integrating usability in software engineering. In *Workshop at Interact 2001*.

Seffah, A. and Hayne, C. (1999). Integrating human factors into use cases and object-oriented methods. *Lecture Notes in Computer Science*, 1743:240–250.

Seffah, A. and Metzker, E. (2004). The obstacles and myths of usability and software engineering. *Commun. ACM*, 47(12):71–76.

Selfridge, P. G., Terveen, L. G., and Long, M. D. (1992). Managing design knowledge to provide assistance to large-scale software development. In *presented at Proceedings of KBSE 1992*, McLean, VA.

Senge, P. M. (1999). *The Dance of Change*. Currency/Doubleday, New York.

Shaw, M. (1990). Prospects for an engineering discipline of software. *IEEE Software*, 7(6):15–24.

Shaw, M. (1991). Heterogenous design idioms for software architecture. In *Proceeding of the Sixth International Workshop on Software Specification and Design*, Software Engineering Notes, pages 158–165, Como, Italy. IEEE Computer Society.

Shneiderman, B. (1998). *Designing the User Interface*. Reading, MA: Addison-Wesley, 3 edition.

Shneiderman, B. and Carroll, J. M. (1988). Ecological studies of professional programmers (introduction to the special section). *Communications of the ACM*, 31:1256–1258.

Shum, S. B. (1996). Analyzing the usability of a design rationale notation. In Moran, T. P. and Carroll, J. M., editors, *Design Rationale: Concepts, Techniques, and Use*, pages 185–215. Hillsdale, NJ: Lawrence Erlbaum Associates.

Shum, S. B. and Hammond, N. (1994). Argumentation-based design rationale: What use at what cost? *International Journal of Human-Computer Studies*, 40:603–652.

Siegel, D. and Dray, S. M. (2003). Living on the edges: user-centred design and the dynamics of specialization in organizations. *Interactions*, 10(5):18–27.

Sinnig, D., Ashraf, G., Reichart, D., Forbrig, P., and Seffah, A. (2005). Patterns in model-based engineering.

Smith, A. and Dunckley, L. (1998). Using the LUCID method to optimize the acceptability of shared interfaces. *Interacting with Computers*, 9(3):335–345.

Smith, S. L. and Mosier, J. N. (1986-08). Guidelines for designing user interface software. Technical Report ESD-TR-86-278, The MITRE Corporation, Bedford, MA 01730. Electronic Systems Division Available as DOS software as NaviText SAM from Northern Lights Software Corp., Westford, MA 01886.

Software Productivity Consortium (1997) *ISO/IEC 12207: Software life Cycle Processes–life Cycle Data*. Software Productivity Consortium.

Sommerville, I. (2002). *Software Engineering*. Addison Wesley: London.

Sommerville, I. and Sawyer, P. (1997). *Requirements Engineering: A Good Practice Guide*. Wiley.

Standish Group (1995). The CHAOS report. Technical report, Standish Group. http://www.scs.carleton.ca/~beau/PM/Standish-Report. html.

Stewart, K. A., Baskerville, R., Storey, V. C., Senn, J. A., Raven, A., and Long, C. (2000). Confronting the assumptions underlying the management of knowledge: an agenda for understanding and investigating knowledge management. *The Data Base for Advances in Information Systems*, 31:41–53.

Sumner, T., Bonnardel, B., and Harstad, B. (1997). The cognitive ergonomics of knowledge-based design support systems. In *presented at Proceedings of the Conference on Human Factors in Computing Systems (CHI'97)*, Atlanta, GA.

Sun Microsystems, I. and Javasoft (1999). *Java Look & Feel Design Guidelines*. Addison-Wesley Longman Publishing Co., Inc.

Sun Microsystems Inc. (2003). Model-view controller. Java blueprints. Technical report, Sun Microsystems Inc. Retrieved September 18th, 2003 from http://java.sun.com/blueprints/patterns/MVC-detailed.html.

Sutcliffe, A. G. (1995). Requirements rationales: integrating approaches to requirement analysis. In *DIS '95: Proceedings of the conference on Designing interactive systems*, pages 33–42. ACM Press.

Sutcliffe, A. G. (2000). On the effective use and reuse of HCI knowledge. *ACM Transactions on Computer-Human Interaction*, 7(2):197–221.

Sutcliffe, A. G. (2002). *The Domain Theory: Patterns for Knowledge and Software Reuse*. Lawrence Erlbaum.

Sutcliffe, A. G. (2003). *Multimedia and Virtual Reality: Designing Multisensory User Interfaces*. Mahwah NJ: Lawrence Erlbaum Associates.

Sutcliffe, A. G. and Carroll, J. M. (1999). Designing claims for reuse in interactive systems design. *International Journal of Human-Computer Studies*, 50(3):213–241.

Szekely, P. and Myers, B. (1988). A user interface toolkit based on graphical objects and constraints. In *OOPSLA '88: Conference proceedings on Object-oriented programming systems, languages and applications*, pages 36–45. ACM Press.

Thimbleby, H. (1990). *User interface design*. Reading MA: ACM / Addison Wesley.

Thomas, C. and Bevan, N. (1996). Usability context analysis: A practical guide. version 4.04. teddington. Technical report, National Physical Laboratory.

Tidwell, J. (1998a). Common ground: A pattern language for human-computer interface design [online]. Technical report, `http://www.mit.edu/~jtidwell/common_ground.html`.

Tidwell, J. (1998b). Interaction design patterns. In *PLOP'98 Conference on Pattern Languages of Programming*.

Tidwell, J. (2004). UI patterns and techniques [online]. Technical report, `http://time-tripper.com/uipatterns/index.php`.

Tollinger, I., McCurdy, M., Vera, A., and Tollinger, P. (2004). Collaborative knowledge management supporting mars mission scientists. In *Proceedings of the ACM Conference on Computer Supported Cooperative Work, CSCW 2004*, Chicago.

Trenner, L. and Bawa, J. (1998). *The politics of usability: a practical guide to designing usable systems in industry*. Springer-Verlag: London, New York.

UsabilityNet (2003). Stakeholder meeting. Technical report, UsabilityNet.

Valenti, S., Panti, M., and Cucchiarelli, A. (1998). Overcoming communication obstacles in user-analyst interaction for functional requirements elicitation. *SIGSOFT Software Engineering Notes*, 23(1):50–55.

van Harmelen, M., Artim, J., Butler, K. A., Henderson, A., Roberts, D., Rosson, M. B., Tarby, J.-C., and Wilson, S. (1997). Object models in user interface design: A CHI 97 workshop. *ACM SIGCHI Bulletin*, 29(4):55–62.

van Harmelen, M. and Wilson, S. (1997). *Object Modeling and User Interface Design: Designing Interactive Systems*. Object-Oriented Series. Addison-Wesley, Reading, Massachusetts.

van Lamsweerde, A. (2000). Requirements engineering in the year 00: A research perspective. In *Proceedings: 22nd International Conference on Software Engineering*, pages 5–19. New York: ACM Press.

van Lamsweerde, A. (2003). Goal-oriented requirements engineering: from system objectives to uml models to precise software specifications. In *ICSE '03: Proceed-*

ings of the 25th International Conference on Software Engineering, pages 744–745. IEEE Computer Society.

van Lamsweerde, A. and Letier, E. (2000). Handling obstacles in goal-oriented requirements engineering. *IEEE Transactions on Software Engineering*, 26(10):978–1005.

van Welie, M. and Traetteberg, H. (2001). The Amsterdam collection of patterns in user interface design [online]. Technical report, http://www.cs.vu.nl/~martijn/patterns/index.html.

van Welie, M. and van de Veer, G. (2003). Pattern languages in interaction design: Structure and organisation. In *Proceedings of IFIP INTERACT '03. Zurich, Switzerland: IOS Press*.

Vanderdonckt, J. (1999). Development milestones towards a tool for working with guidelines. *Interacting with Computers*, 12(2):81–118.

Vicente, K. J. (2000). HCI in the global knowledge-based economy: Designing to support worker adaptation. *ACM Transactions on Computer-Human Interaction*, 7(2):263–280.

Vlissides, J. (1995). Seven habits of successful pattern writers [online]. Technical report, http://hillside.net/patterns/papers/7habits.html.

von Hippel, E. (1998). Economics of product development by users: The impact of "sticky" local information. *Management Science*, 44:629–644.

Vredenburg, K. (2003). Building ease of use into the IBM user experience. *IBM Syst. J.*, 42(4):517–531.

Vredenburg, K., Mao, J.-Y., Smith, P. W., and Carey, T. (2002). A survey of user-centered design in practice. In *Proceedings of CHI'2002 Conference on Human Factors in Computing Systems Proceedings*, pages 471–478, Amsterdam.

Vutpakdi, R. (2004). Too much usability? In *Usability Professionals' Association 13th Annual Conference*.

Webber, A. M. (1993). What's so new about the new economy? *Harvard Business Review*, pages 4–11.

Wenger, E. (1987). *Artificial Intelligence and Tutoring Systems*. Los Altos, CA: Morgan Kaufmann.

Wentling, T. L., Waight, C., Gallaher, J., La Fleur, J., Wang, C., and Kanfer, A. (2000). E-learning — a review of literature [online]. Technical report, Knowledge and Learning Systems Group, NCSA, University of Illinois at Urbana-champaign.

Wesson, J. L. (2001). The role of HCI design patterns in software development. *Journal of Research and Practice in Information Technology*, 33(1).

Wesson, J. L. and Cowley, L. (2003). Designing with patterns: Possibilities and pitfalls. In *Proceedings of IFIP INTERACT'03 Workshop on Software & Usability Cross-Pollination: The Role of Usability Patterns*.

Wharton, C., Reiman, J., Lewis, C., and Polson, P. (1994). The cognitive walkthrough method: A practitioners guide. In Nielsen, J. and Mack, R. L., editors, *Usability Inspection Methods*, pages 105–140. New York: Wiley.

Wheeler, S., D'Angelo, B., and Battle, L. (2003). Nurturing change: Introducing user-centered design to a large software development organization. In Dickelman, G., editor, *EPSS Revisited: A Lifecycle for Developing Performance-centered Systems*. International Society for Performance Improvement.

Whiteside, J., Bennett, J., and Holtzblatt, K. (1988). Usability engineering: Our experience and evolution. In Helander, M., editor, *Handbook of Human Computer Interaction*. Amsterdam: North-Holland.

Wiegers, K. E. (1999). *Software Requirements*. Microsoft Press.

Wilson, S., Bekker, M., Johnson, H., and Johnson, P. (1996). Cost and benefits of user involvement in design: Practitioners' views. In Sasse, A., Cunningham, J., and Winder, R., editors, *People and Computers*, pages 221–240. Springer Verlag, London.

Wilson, S., Bekker, M., Johnson, H., and Johnson, P. (1997). Helping and hindering user involvement - a tale of everyday design;. In Ware, C. and Dixon, D., editors, *Proceedings of ACM CHI'97*.

Wirfs-Brock, R. and Mckean, A. (2003). *Object Design: Roles, Responsibilities, and Collaborations*. Addison Wesley.

Wixon, D. R., Holtzblatt, K., and Knox, S. (1990). Contextual design: An emergent view of system design. In *Proceedings of CHI'90, Conference of Human Factors in Computing Systems, ACM*, pages 329–336.

Wixon, D. R., Jones, S., Tse, L., and Casaday, G. (1994). Inspections and design reviews: Framework, history, and reflection. In Nielsen, J. and Mack, R. L., editors, *Usability Inspection Methods*, pages 77–104. New York: Wiley.

Wixon, D. R., Ramey, J., Holtzblatt, K., Beyer, H., Hackos, J. T., Rosenbaum, S., Page, C., Laakso, S. A., and Laakso, K.-P. (2002). Usability in practice: Field methods evolution and revolution. In *CHI '02: CHI '02 extended abstracts on Human factors in computing systems*, pages 880–884. ACM Press.

Wixon, D. R. and Wilson, C. (1997). The usability engineering framework for product design and evaluation. In Helander, M., Landauer, T. K., and Prabhu, P. V., editors, *Handbook of Human-Computer Interaction*, pages 653–688. Amsterdam; New York: Elsevier, 2 edition.

Wood, L. E. (1996). The ethnographic interview in user-centered work/task analysis. In Wixon, D. and Ramey, J., editors, *Field Methods Casebook for Software Design*, pages 35–56. John Wiley & Sons, Inc.

Wood, L. E. (1997). Semi-structured interviewing for user-centered design. *Interactions*, 4(2):48–61.

Yin, R. K. (1994). *Case Study Research: Design and Methods*. Thousand Oaks, CA: SAGE Publications, 2 edition.

Zelkowitz, M. V. and Wallace, D. (1998). Experimental models for validating computer technology. *IEEE Computer*.

AUTHORS INDEX

379

SUBJECT INDEX